CHANNELS TO CHILDREN:

Early Childhood Activity Guide for Holidays and Seasons

Carol Beckman
Roberta Simmons
Nancy Thomas

Illustrated by Debbie Reisbeck

ISBN 0-9616396-0-1

ACKNOWLEDGEMENTS AND COPYRIGHTS

The fingerplays, poems, and songs used in *CHANNELS TO CHILDREN: EARLY CHILDHOOD ACTIVITY GUIDE FOR HOLIDAYS AND SEASONS* have either been written by the authors or have come from their collection of early childhood education materials. A diligent effort has been made to trace the ownership of all material included and to make full acknowledgement of its use. If any errors have occurred, they will be corrected in future editions upon notification of the publisher. For permission to use material in this book, grateful acknowledgement is made to the following publishers and authors. The acknowledgement includes title of each selection followed by page and item number where it can be located in this book.

PUBLISHERS

Belwin Mills Publishing Corp. "Johnny Appleseed's Song," words by Francis Frost, Copyright by Belwin Mills Publishing Corp., Melville, New York, 11747. All rights reserved. Used by permission. "Johnny Appleseed's Song" (p.49 #2).

Harper and Row, Publishers, Inc., from *A POCKETFUL OF RHYMES* by Marie Louise Allen, Text Copyright © 1957 by Marie Allen Howarth. By permission of Harper and Row, Publishers, Inc. "The Mitten Song" (p.86 #6).

Hayes School Publishing Company, Inc., from *FINGER FUN* By Marguerite Gode, Copyright 1963. "Jack Frost" (p.5 #9), "Red Apple" (p.5 #6), "Xmas Brownie" (p.59 #12), "Our Christmas Tree" (p.60 #19).

Henry Z. Walck, Inc. Division of David McKay, Inc., from *A SMALL CHILD'S BOOK OF VERSE* by Pelagie Doanne, Copyright 1948. Also printed in Youth's Companion. "Easter Duck" by Elsie Parrish (p.114 #21).

Instructor Publications, Inc., from *FINGER AND ACTION RHYMES*. Used with permission of the publisher, The Instructor Publications, Inc., Dansville, New York, 14437. "Jack-o'-lantern" (p.21 #7), "Christmas Bells" (p.63 #7), "Be My Valentine" (p.96 #14).

Northern Music Company, "MAGIC PENNY" by MALVINA REYNOLDS © Copyright 1955, 1958 by Northern Music Co., 445 Park Avenue, New York, N.Y. 10022, USED BY PERMISSION ALL RIGHTS RESERVED. (p.106 #6).

Pitman Learning, Inc., From *CREATIVE MOVEMENT FOR THE DEVELOPING CHILD*, Revised Edition, by Clare Cherry. Copyright © 1971 by Clare Cherry. Reprinted by permission of Pitman Learning Inc., Belmont, CA 94002. "Popcorn Game"(p.49 #4), "Clouds are Floating" (p.139 #1), "Skipping Songs" (p.50 #10).

Richards Institute of Music Education and Research, from *EXPERIENCE GAMES THROUGH MUSIC FOR THE VERY VERY YOUNG, FOR THE VERY YOUNG* by Sister Fleurette Sweeney S.C.H. and Margaret Wharram, Copyright 1973. "Hickety Tickety Bumble Bee" (p.15 #4), "Mary Finds a Friend" (p.100 #8).

Robert B. Luce, Inc., from *LETS DO FINGERPLAYS* by Marion F. Grayson, © 1962-1966. By permission of R.B. Luce, Company. "Make a Valentine" (p.95 #1).

The Standard Publishing Company, Fingerplays are from *FINGER PLAYS AND HOW TO USE THEM*, © 1952. The Standard Publishing Company, Cincinnati, Ohio. Division of Standex International Corporation. Reprinted by permission. "Our Turkey" by Thea Cannon (p.39 #18), "A Christmas Tree Story" by Thea Cannon, adapted (p.81 #4), "Swimming" by Thea Cannon, adapted (p.169 #9), "The Squirrel" by Louise M. Oglevee (p.6 #21), "Spring Has Come" by Lillien E. Landman (p.153 #3).

T.S. Denison and Company, Inc., from *FINGERPLAY APPROACH TO DRAMATIZATION* by Mary Jackson Ellis, Copyright 1960. "Taking a Walk" (p.6 #15), "Christmas Bells" (p.59 #13), "Five Little Snowman" (p.78 #14).

T.S. Denison and Company, Inc., from *FINGER PLAYTIME* by Mary Jackson Ellis and Frances Lyons, Copyright 1960. "Snow" (p.78 #8), "Jack-o'-lantern" (p.21 #6), "My Rabbit" (p.113 #13), "Raindrops" (p.126 #6).

T.S. Denison and Company, Inc., from *FINGERPLAYS THAT MOTIVATE* by Don Peek, Copyright 1975. "The Witch" (p.21 #10), "Mr. Duck and Mr. Turkey" (p.39 #17).

Webster/McGraw-Hill Publishing Company. Reprinted from *RHYMES FOR FINGERS AND FLANNELBOARDS* by L.B. Scott and J.J. Thompson, Copyright 1960, with permission of Webster/McGraw-Hill. "Five Little Pilgrims" (p.39 #19), "The Angel On My Christmas Tree" (p.58 #2).

The Willis Music Company, found in *SONGS FOR THE NURSERY SCHOOL* by Laura Pendleton MacCarteney, The Willis Music Company, Cincinnati, Ohio. "Zum, Zum, Zum" (p.161 #6).

AUTHORS

Marjorie Barrows, "Three Little Witches" (p.32 #2) from *READ—ALOUD POEMS* published by Rand McNally and Company, Copyright 1957, 1966.

Lois Holt, "Jack-o'-lantern" (p.20 #4) Copyright by inheritance from Aunt: Mabel E. Clark, confirm Bobbs Merrill Publishing Company.

Dixie Willson, "Mr. Rabbit" (p.113 #15) by permission of Dana W. Briggs.

This book
belongs to
<u>Karen Dwelly</u>

Published by:
CHANNELS TO CHILDREN
P.O. Box 25834
Colorado Springs, Colorado
80936

*To our families whose love, patience, and support
have made this book possible.*

TABLE OF CONTENTS

INTRODUCTION

Channels to Children: Early Childhood Activity Guide for Holidays and Seasons is composed of activities for young children under six years of age. However, many of the ideas can be used with older children. It includes instructive projects for groups of children, but many can be adapted for use with the individual child.

Important goals when working with young children are to develop in each child a positive self-image and to foster joy of learning. The activities presented are designed to expand the child's understanding, increase manipulative skills, and unleash creative potential. However, these activities provide only a medium for achieving these goals. To develop a healthy child, many factors must be considered. The following are some suggestions.
1. Provide an atmosphere conducive to each child's self-expression.
2. Use positive reinforcement and immediate feedback.
3. Provide potential success experiences that develop each child's self-confidence.
4. Remember that the process is more important than the end product.
5. Do not compare children or their work.
6. Place activities at children's level.
7. Plan activities in advance but be flexible in their implementation. For added interest, indoor activities can be experienced outside.
8. Give opportunity to use materials freely in a creative environment. This does not mean children are to function without direction. Establish broad guidelines that are consistent.
9. Allow children to help prepare and clean up activities.
10. Teach proper care and use of materials, equipment, books, and toys.
11. Encourage but do not force participation by children.
12. Teach with enthusiasm. It can make the difference in a child's attitude towards learning.

Each chapter is designed to foster social, emotional, physical, and intellectual development. The first ten chapters include the sections described below. Many separate projects are included in each section. Choose activities that correspond with the attention span, developmental stage, and interests of the children in the group. Be creative and adapt activities to the group's particular needs or for use in other themes.

CONCEPTS TO BE TAUGHT are facts that will be presented to the children through projects, activities, fingerplays, and stories.
1. Good teaching is a result of careful planning and foresight.
2. Children learn by doing. Choose activities from each section so that concepts will be reinforced through repetition as well as variety. When more than one sense is stimulated, learning is improved.

ART ACTIVITIES include projects which develop imagination, individuality, and aesthetic appreciation. Art is a good release for emotions. It also develops eye-hand coordination as well as large and small muscles.
1. Eliminate patterning of any kind. Let each child express himself in a creative way.
2. Allow each child to do his own artwork. Do not make additions or complete artwork for child.
3. Lend support, show interest, and give praise. Rather than ask, "What is it?" say, "That's interesting. Tell me about it."
4. Periodically allow each child to select artwork to display so all young artists are positively reinforced.
5. Use proper equipment. Brushes, crayons, pencils, and papers should be large because small muscles are not completely developed.

6. Although not mentioned in each chapter, make EASEL PAINTING (see page 2) and PLAY DOUGH (see page 84) available often.
7. Use of recyclable items is encouraged. Examples are computer paper, baby food jars, and egg cartons.

COOKING ACTIVITIES include foods from the Basic Four Food Groups that are low in salt, sugars, and fats. Because food habits develop during early years, introduce children to a balanced diet of nutritious foods. Recipes are simple so children can prepare food.
1. Some ingredients for recipes are available and might be less expensive at health food stores. Examples are carob and sesame seeds.
2. Use large bowls to prevent spilling. Assemble necessary utensils on tray. Place tray so it is readily available.
3. Use safety precautions. Adult should cut fruits and vegetables in half. Place flat side on cutting board so pieces will not roll when cut by children. Use knives that are semisharp and that have serrated edges. Use hand egg beaters and hand grinders. Maintain strict supervision around heat or hot water.
4. Keep group small so every child can participate. A child who has helped in the preparation of a new food will be more likely to taste it.
5. For snacks and meals serve a variety of foods from the Basic Four Food Groups which are: milk and milk products; fruits and vegetables; bread and cereal which include pasta and rice; and protein which includes meat, fish, poultry, eggs, and legumes.
6. Nutritious snacks are necessary because a child's capacity for food is limited. He cannot eat enough food to supply energy until the next meal.
7. Serve small portions. A guideline is one level tablespoon per year of the child's age.
8. Provide a pleasant atmosphere for a positive eating experience.
9. Introduce one new food at a time. Encourage a child to taste it. If he doesn't like the new food, try it another day, perhaps prepared differently.

FINGERPLAYS are simple poems children recite while performing appropriate actions.
1. Select a few fingerplays from each chapter that best teach the concepts to be learned.
2. Use simple fingerplays for younger, less mature children. Use more complex verses for older children or as a group shows readiness.
3. Recite verse and perform actions slowly.
4. Teach through repetition. Periodically, send parents a copy of the fingerplays so verses can be used at home.
5. Use for transition between activities or to quiet children.

LANGUAGE DEVELOPMENT includes discussions, word games, flannel board stories, suggested books, and experiences to increase communication skills.
1. Listen to what children say. Talk to a child at his own level because eye contact is very important.
2. Select books that have simple plots, attractive illustrations, and accurate information.
3. When reading a book or telling a flannel board story to a group, consider visibility so all children can see the pictures.
4. Provide a quiet area with proper lighting for children to read books.
5. To make flannel board, cover piece of cardboard with felt or flannel. Flannel board pieces can be pictures cut from magazines, old story books, or coloring books. Attach rolled masking tape or small square of felt to back of each piece. Flannel board pictures can also be cut from felt or interfacing fabric.

6. Rehearse story and organize felt pieces in advance so placement of pieces will not distract from the story.
7. Allow time for individual children to use the flannel board creatively.
8. The use of a recorder to tape children's voices can enhance listening skills and aid in speech development.

GAMES AND SOCIAL ACTIVITIES have instructions and suggestions for organizing group activities.
1. Keep games simple. Demonstrate while giving instructions. Participate in games.
2. Play in small groups to eliminate long waits between turns.
3. Games that involve continuous participation by everyone are best.
4. Emphasize playing the game. Winning should not be stressed because losers can develop negative self-images.
5. A "group project" is an activity in which all members cooperate to complete a finished product. These projects are usually too difficult or complicated for a child to do alone.
6. Make SAND PLAY (see pages 84 and 174) and WATERPLAY (see page 132) available often.

CREATIVE DRAMATICS AND MOVEMENT implements use of puppets, prop boxes, blocks, dramatic play area, dramatics, and movement. It encourages free expression and group interaction.
1. When dramatizing verse, the group uses simple movements and actions with few or no props.
2. Provide stimulus and allow each child to explore his own movement.
3. Use props and equipment in dramatic play area to facilitate role play and re-creation of life experiences.
4. Allow ample space and time for block building. Arrange blocks on easily accessible shelves according to shape and size.

PHYSICAL DEVELOPMENT includes games and exercises which increase physical skills and coordination.
1. Provide adequate space for size of group.
2. Large muscle activities and outdoor play should be included in the daily routine.
3. Indoor physical activity is necessary on days when inclement weather prevents children from going outside.

MATH includes games, activities, and materials that provide a foundation for understanding mathematical concepts.
1. Incorporate math into daily routine and other activities. For example, count the number of children when attendance is taken.
2. Use concrete objects to teach abstract concepts. For example, provide flannel board with felt shapes and numbers for individual children to use.
3. For number or game cards, use small squares of matt board which are often given away by stores that frame pictures.
4. Math includes counting, identification of shapes, one-to-one concepts, concepts of quantity, terminology, measurements, sorting, and comparisons.

SCIENCE has experiments and observations to increase awareness of the world.
1. Concepts that are simple and ordinary to adults are sources of wonder and discovery for children.
2. To insure a balanced science program, provide a variety of simple experiences in biology (plants and animals), earth sciences (soil, air, and water), astronomy (sun, moon, and stars), chemistry, and physics (heat, light, magnetism, and sound).

3. Explain cause-effect relationships. Things that happen in experiments are real, not fantasy. They happen for a reason.
4. Encourage children to think and increase observation skills by asking questions. For example, "What do you see, feel, hear, or smell?"
5. Work in small groups to allow each child the opportunity to discover.
6. Use simplified concepts, define words, and supply accurate information.
7. Display related books and objects for observation and manipulation.
8. Inspire each child to respect all living things.

MUSIC includes simple songs. Familiar tunes will be given with songs.
1. Enjoying music is more important than singing in tune.
2. Use rhythm instruments and encourage creative movement.
3. Teach songs through repetition.
4. Incorporate music spontaneously into different activities.
5. Enhance musical experiences by using records for learning songs, setting moods, or for leading activities.
6. Use a flannel board to illustrate sequence of items mentioned in the song. For example, while singing "Jack and Jill," place a picture of a boy, girl, hill, and pail on flannel board at appropriate times. Items can be used to demonstrate activity in song. Seeing the sequence of events helps children learn the song.
7. Place one item from several familiar songs on flannel board. Select a child to choose a symbol or item from the flannel board to introduce the next song to sing. This adds variety to song selection.
   Variation: Make several seasonal symbols for flannel board. For example, in autumn use leaves. Write name of song on each leaf. Child chooses a leaf.

FIELD TRIPS:
1. Children should feel secure in the group before taking a field trip. The first field trip can be a short walk.
2. Plan excursions carefully. Make reservations and visit location in advance. Tell children generally what will happen. Clearly define limits.
3. Provide sufficient adult supervision. A field trip should include at least two adults. One adult can solve a problem with an individual child while the other supervises the group. When walking, one adult leads the group and one follows so all children are between these two adults.
4. Written parental permission must be given before field trips are taken. Notify parents prior to each trip (include specific needs and plans).
5. Take a list of the children, emergency medical information for each child, and a first aid kit.
6. To each child tape a name tag with telephone number to be called if child is lost.
7. Snacks and drinks may be necessary on long field trips. Make certain restroom facilities are available for these excursions.
8. For a total learning experience, incorporate related activities with field trip. For example, bake before visiting bakery.
9. When appropriate, help children express appreciation by sending thank you notes. This can include pictures of field trip drawn by children or messages children have dictated to adult about the trip.

AUTUMN

AUTUMN, the season between summer and winter, has characteristics of both of these seasons. In the Northern Hemisphere autumn begins in September, marked by hot days and cool nights. By the end of fall, it becomes colder and frosts at night. Pre-winter storms may occur. With this change in weather, activities of people and animals change in preparation for the winter months ahead.

As the weather turns colder, plants also prepare for a dormant period. The sap stops flowing through the trees and stays in the roots. Each leaf's food supply is then depleted, causing the green color to fade and the colors of the other materials in the leaves to appear. The red, yellow, orange, and brown leaves then fall. Autumn is also called fall because of these falling leaves, which is the most outstanding characteristic of the season.

CONCEPTS TO BE TAUGHT

1. Autumn is the season between summer and winter.
2. Another word for autumn is fall, because this is the time leaves change color and fall from trees.
3. Fall is a time for harvesting fruits and vegetables, preserving foods, and saving seeds.
4. Fall activities include beginning school, playing football, hunting, and pre-paring for winter.
5. Animals prepare for the colder months ahead: some birds migrate south to warmer places; squirrels collect and store nuts; animals fatten and grow heav-ier coats.

ART ACTIVITIES

1. AUTUMN TREE: Draw, cut, or tear a tree trunk from brown paper. Glue to piece of construction paper. Dip sponges that have been cut into small squares in red, yellow, and green paint. Dabble on paper to form leaves. Spring clothes-pins can be attached to sponges for easier handling.
    Variations:
    A. Tear small pieces of yellow and orange variegated tissue paper (or tear scraps of construction paper). Paste onto tree for leaves.
    B. Cut 1" squares of variegated tissue paper. Place center of square over eraser of pencil. Hold tissue paper onto pencil. Dip end into glue. Place tissue paper on tree. Remove pencil.
    C. Paper punch holes in yellow, orange, and brown paper. Place glue around trunk. Sprinkle punched holes onto glue.

1

2. LEAF SPATTER PAINT: Use lid from box that is approximately 9" x 12" x 2". Cut rectangle from top of lid leaving 1 1/2" border. Invert lid. Place wire screen over opening. Tape screen to border with strapping tape. Arrange leaves on paper. Place lid over arrangement. Dip toothbrush into thin paint and brush across screen. When dry, remove leaves.

3. WATERCOLOR LEAF: Cut a leaf from yellow construction paper. Paint leaf with watercolors. Leaves can be hung from the ceiling as a mobile.

4. FALL FINGER PAINTING: Mix red and yellow paint on paper. Presto! Orange appears. Encourage finger painting in the following ways: circles; zigzags like lightning, mountains, or fire; wiggly lines like a worm, fish, or snake; arcs like waves; and continuous circles or loops.
   Variation: Use different parts of the hand (palm, side, or fingernail).
   Note: Finger paint can be made by adding soap flakes to liquid tempera and shaking. Increase amount of soap flakes to thicken paint.

5. EASEL PAINTING: Fill baby food jars with tempera paint. Provide a variety of fall colors. Set jars on shelf of easel. Place one large brush in each paint jar. Mount large paper on easel. Spring clothespins can be used to hold paper. Allow ample time for painting.
   Variation: For paper, use large brown sack cut to fit easel.

6. LEAF BOOKMARK: Use leaves that are real or cut from paper. Arrange leaves on clear self-adhesive plastic. Place another piece of plastic over leaves. Cut into narrow strips or around leaves for a bookmark.
   Variation: Cut around leaves, leaving a border of plastic. Punch hole near edge. String yarn through hole. Hang from ceiling to create mobile.

7. NATURE COLLAGE: Arrange and glue leaves, grasses, seeds, and flowers on construction paper. Flowers and leaves may need to be flattened before gluing. To flatten, press in a book between layers of paper toweling.
   Variation: Arrange on a piece of waxed paper and cover with another sheet of waxed paper. Adult covers with paper or fabric and presses with warm iron. Tape arrangement to cardboard frame and hang in window.

8. LEAF RUBBINGS: Arrange leaves in a design. Place lightweight paper over design. Rub back and forth with side of peeled crayon.
   Variation: Instead of leaves use grass, twigs, plants, or bark.

9. LEAF CREATURES AND PEOPLE: Glue real or paper leaf on paper. Create a person or animal using leaf for body. To make head, tail, limbs, or wings, use twigs, crayons, or felt-tipped pens.

10. BLOCK PRINTING WITH HARVESTED FRUITS AND VEGETABLES: Use foods with natural juices. Examples are beets, pomegranates, or tomatoes. Cut each into a size convenient for child to grasp. Stamp food onto paper towel, newsprint, or other absorbent paper.
    Variation: Dip fruits or vegetables which do not have enough natural juices into paint and then stamp on paper.
    A. Use a cross-section of cabbage. It makes an interesting design!
    B. Use a potato cut in half. Make a pattern by cutting a design approximately 1/8" in depth into the flat surface of the potato with a knife. Remove background by cutting to the design from the outer edge of the potato. Leave top half of potato for child to hold.

11. SCHOOL BACK PACK: To make straps, cut two 1 1/2" strips from the top of a medium-sized brown sack. Decorate sack with felt-tipped pens or crayons. Staple strap to flat side of sack along opposite sides at top, middle, and bottom.
Note: Draw on computer paper with crayons for "school" papers. Place papers in back pack.

12. FOOTBALL COLLAGE: Cut pictures of football players and related scenes from old sports magazines. Examples are stadium, fans, field, and football. Glue onto a large piece of paper that is the shape of a football.

13. FOLDED BIRD:
    A. Color diamond-shaped piece of paper. Fold paper in half.
    B. Fold each side the reverse direction.
    C. Adult places staple close to center fold.

14. SQUIRREL: Cut 3/4" x 8" strip of brown paper. For base, form strip into a circle and staple. Cut a 6 1/2" x 3" oval from brown paper for tail. Fringe edge of oval. Staple tail to base. For body, use large plastic egg (hosiery container). Cover egg with thin coat of liquid starch. Place large end of egg in base. Cover egg with pieces of brown variegated tissue paper. When completely covered, paint with liquid starch. When dry, add facial features with felt-tipped pens or small pieces of paper.
Variation: Instead of liquid starch, use thin glue.

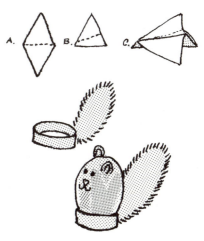

15. COFFEE GROUNDS BEAR: Save coffee grounds. Dry. Place in jar with holes in lid. Cut large brown circle for bear's face and two smaller ones for ears. Glue together to form head. Paint with thin coat of glue. Shake coffee grounds onto head. Facial features can be small pieces of construction paper, old buttons, scraps of material, or pop bottle lids.

COOKING ACTIVITIES

1. APPLE BANANA FROSTY: 1 Yellow Delicious apple, diced   1/4 cup milk
                          1 peeled, sliced banana   3 ice cubes
Blend all of the above ingredients in a blender. Serve.

2. APPLESAUCE: 3 cored, sliced apples
                2 cups water
Place water and apples in electric skillet. Boil until soft. Mash in a rotary food press or food mill with metal paddle.
Variation: Peel apples. Boil until soft. Blend in blender.

3. *CHAROSES*: 6 medium apples   1/2 cup chopped nuts
                1/2 cup raisins   1/4 cup white grape juice
                1/2 teaspoon cinnamon
Chop the peeled or unpeeled apples. Add the remaining ingredients. Mix well.

4. DRIED APPLES: Peel, core, and cut apples into slices or rings 1/8" thick. Place in salt water solution (2 tablespoons salt per 1 gallon water) for several minutes. Place in 180° oven for 3 to 4 hours until dry. Turn apples occasionally.
Variation: Dry vegetables for use in soups or other cooked recipes.

5. FRUIT LEATHER: Preheat oven to 400°. Pour applesauce onto greased shallow pan. Spread to 1/8" thickness. Place pan in oven and lower temperature to 180°. Cook for approximately 3 hours until leather can be peeled from pan. Cut with scissors to serve.
Variation: Use puree of peaches, bananas, apricots, or a combination of any two of these fruits. This is a good use for overripe fruit.

6. BEAN SALAD: 1 can green beans, drained   1 can kidney beans, drained
                1 can waxed beans, drained   1/3 cup bottled Italian dressing
Combine vegetables. Marinate in Italian dressing. Serve chilled.

7. FOOTBALL CRACKER: Shell one pound of peanuts. Chop till fine in blender. Add 1 to 2 tablespoons cooking oil. Add salt to taste. Spread peanut butter on oval crackers. Use thin pretzel sticks for lace.

8. FOOTBALL SALAD: On lettuce leaf, form goal post with three carrot sticks. Use HARD-COOKED EGG (see page 110). Cut egg in half lengthwise. In center of goal post, place half egg with flat side on lettuce. Make football lace with strips of pimento or olive.

FINGERPLAYS

1. Pretty leaves are falling down:
     (flutter fingers)
   Green, orange, yellow, and brown.
     (point to colors)
   Here comes one colored red.
   It landed on my head! (tap head)

2. "Come autumn leaves," said the wind
     one day. (motion to come)
   "Fly into the sky with me and play.
     (lift hand upward)
   We can dance and twirl (twirl)
   Until the days grow cold; (shiver)
   Then into a corner you will curl."
     (curl into ball)

3. Autumn leaves float quietly down
     (flutter fingers and whisper)
   And form a carpet on the ground.
     (move hands just above floor)
   But when those leaves are stepped
     upon, (pretend to step on leaves)
   Listen and they will make a
     crackling sound. (place hand
     behind ear)

4. Leaves are falling to the ground.
     (flutter fingers)
   Some are orange, others brown.
   Flowers disappear from sight.
   Birds fly south in patterned
     flight. (pretend to fly)
   Fall is here. Warm weather is
     gone.
   Soon the snow will cover the lawn.
     (shiver)

5. Five autumn leaves hanging from a
     tree: (hold up five fingers)
   The first one said, "Very soon
     we'll be free."
   The second one said, "I'm falling
     to the ground."
   The third one said, "I'll sail to
     town."
   The fourth one said, "Let's not
     wait."
   The fifth one said, "Fall sure is
     great." (hold up respective fin-
     gers)

6. A little red apple (form circle
      with hands)
   Hung high in a tree. (reach up)
   I looked up at it, (look up)
   And it looked down at me.
   "Come down, please," I called.
   And what do you suppose?
   That little red apple (form circle
      with hands)
   Dropped right on my nose! (point
      to nose)
                    Marguerite Gode

7. Way up high in the apple tree
      (hands above head)
   Two little apples smiled at me.
      (form apples with each hand still
      raised)
   I shook that tree as hard as I
      could, (shaking motion)
   Down came the apples. (drop hands)
   Ummmmmmmmmmm. Were they good!
      (rub stomach)
                    Traditional

8. A squiggly little worm into my
      apple bit. (wiggle index finger)
   He chomped and chomped until the
      core he hit. (place index finger
      in center of fist)
   I asked him why he did it,
   And though it sounds absurd, (shrug
      shoulders)
   He said, "I love apples." (rub
      stomach)
   Now that is what I heard.

9. Who comes creeping in the night
      (pretend to creep)
   When the moon is clear and bright?
      (make circle with fingers)
   Who paints tree leaves red and gold
      (pretend to paint)
   When the autumn day turns cold?
      (shiver)
   Up the hill and down he goes, (move
      hand up and down)
   In and out the brown corn rows,
      (move hand in and out)
   Making music crackling sweet
   With his frosty little feet.
      (point to feet)
   Jack Frost!
                    Marguerite Gode

10. Where do we go to color and sing,
    To paint, to play, to go outside
       and swing, (swing arms)
    To listen to stories and have so
       much fun? (spread arms wide)
    Why it's here at preschool. Come!
    It's begun! (motion to come)

11. Five preschool children in a row.
       (five fingers)
    The first one is wearing a bright
       red bow. (raise respective fin-
       gers)
    The second one's hands are in his
       lap.
    The third one has a new blue cap.
    The fourth one says, "It's a nice
       day."
    The fifth one met a friend on the
       way.
    Who is that friend so new?
    Is that friend you? (point to
       friend)

12. Our school is a friendly place.
    Each child wears a happy face.
       (fingers to corners of mouth)
    There are books, toys, and lots of
       space. (spread arms out)
    We sometimes play games or have a
       race. (move two fingers)
    We make new friends at school.
    We share with them because that's
       the rule! (shake index finger)

13. Two little houses all closed up
       tight. (make fists)
    Open up the windows and let in the
       light. (open fist)
    Ten little finger people tall and
       straight, (ten fingers)
    Ready for school at half past
       eight. (walk with fingers)
                    Author Unknown

14. I rake and rake the leaves into a
       great big heap. (pretend to
       rake)
    Then into the leaves I take a great
       big leap. (jump and squat)
    I cover myself with the leaves and
       hide from you.
    Then I jump up and say, "PEEK-A-
       BOO!" (jump)

15. Taking a walk is so much fun.
We don't hurry; we don't run.
(move finger sideways)
We watch for birds; we watch for
bees. (point to eye)
We look for all the falling leaves.
(flutter fingers)
Mary Jackson Ellis

16. Let's go for a walk.
What do we see? (point to eyes)
Squirrels scampering up a tree;
(run fingers up opposite arm)
Leaves falling to the ground;
(flutter fingers)
Birds flying southward bound; (pre-
tend to fly)
Children walk quickly to school.
(walk fingers quickly)
Wearing warm sweaters because it's
cool. (shiver)

17. Playing football is such fun.
We catch the ball, and then we run.
(pretend to catch and run)
Down the field, in and out, (move
hands in and out)
Make a touchdown, and the fans will
shout. (hold arms straight above
head)

18. Two little black birds sitting on a
hill. (lift pointer fingers)
One named Jack. (wiggle pointer)
One named Jill. (wiggle other
pointer)
Fly away Jack. (put first pointer
behind back)
Fly away Jill. (put other pointer
behind back)
Come back Jack. (bring first
pointer in front again)
Come back Jill. (bring second
pointer in front)
Traditional

19. Mr. Frisky Squirrel plays hide and
seek (cover eyes)
As he looks around the tree trunk:
PEEK! (peek)
Is he looking at you or me? (point
to friend, then to self)
Now he's looking all around.
Whissh! (slide hands together)
He's up the tree in a bound!

20. Whiskey, friskey, hippity hop:
Up he goes to the tree top. (hold
arm up)
Whirly, twirly, round, and round:
(move arm in circle)
Down he scampers to the ground.
(bring arm down)
Furly, curly, what a tail:
Tall as a feather, broad as a sail.
(extend arms vertically and hori-
zontally)
Where's his supper?
It's in the shell.
Snappity, crackity, out it fell!
Traditional

21. These are the brown leaves flutter-
ing down. (flutter fingers)
And this is the tall tree bare and
brown. (spread arms to form
tree)
This is the squirrel with eyes so
bright, (place fists together at
chest)
Hunting for nuts with all his
might. (place hand over eyes)
This is the hole where day by day
(form circle with fingers)
Nut after nut he stores away.
(place finger through circle)
When winter comes with its cold and
storm, (shiver)
He'll sleep curled up all snug and
warm. (pretend to sleep)
Louise M. Oglevee

LANGUAGE DEVELOPMENT

1. THREE OF THESE BELONG TOGETHER: Display four items, of which three relate to
autumn and one relates to another season of the year. Children tell which ones
belong together and why. Actual items or pictures can be used. For example,
use football, football tee, football helmet, and baseball.
Variation: Display pictures of seasons. Children identify fall pictures.

2. AUTUMN:
    A. Place picture of a fall tree on flannel board. Have children cut autumn pictures from magazines and place under the fall tree. Have each child explain why it is associated with autumn.
    B. Make a fall season book. Glue fall pictures cut from magazines on orange construction paper. Place pictures in notebook.
    Note: During appropriate season throughout year, add additional pictures. Glue pictures on white paper for winter, green paper for spring, and yellow paper for summer.

3. AUTUMN LEAVES:
    A. What is another word for autumn? Why is this season also called fall? Discuss that leaves fall from trees in autumn.
    B. Collect two leaves that are the same size from a variety of trees. To flatten leaves, press in a book between layers of paper toweling. Glue one leaf from each pair onto a large piece of construction paper for a display paper. Beside each leaf write the name of the tree from which it came. Laminate the display paper with clear self-adhesive plastic. Laminate remaining leaves on both sides with clear self-adhesive plastic. Cut leaves from the plastic leaving a 1/2" border around each leaf. Place matching leaves in a box. Place display paper on table. Discuss each leaf's shape, vein structure, color, and name. Adult asks child to select a leaf from the box. Child identifies leaf and places it on matching leaf of the display paper.
    C. Laminate two leaves from each tree, one big and one little. Place big leaves on table and little leaves in box. Child selects little leaf and places it on the matching big leaf.

4. LITTLE RED RIDING HOOD: Place fruits and vegetables in basket. Adult pretends to be Little Red Riding Hood with basket of fruits and vegetables she has harvested. Adult removes, displays, and describes each food. Items are replaced in basket. Adult then gives clues to "goodie" in basket. Children identify food described.
    Variations:
    A. Instead of produce, use pictures cut from magazines.
    B. Child pretends to be Little Red Riding Hood and gives clues.

5. HARVESTING: Place pictures of trees, bushes, and vines on flannel board or poster board. Tape pictures of fruits and vegetables to appropriate plant. Each child "harvests" one item. After child picks an item, he describes it and answers questions adult asks about the item. Repeat with new child.
    Variation: Adult gives clues describing which item child is to "harvest."

6. ADJUSTING TO SCHOOL: Discuss feelings and thoughts about adjusting to school.
    A. How does school make you feel?
    B. Why do you sometimes feel afraid and alone in a new situation?
    C. How can you be friends at school? How do friends make you feel?
    D. What does your mother or father do while you are at school?

7. HORNBOOK: Cut a rectangle from center of brown construction paper leaving a 1/2" frame. Mount on white construction paper. Print alphabet on the white paper. Tape a ruler or paint stick to the back for a handle.
Note: The first country to provide free public schools for all children was the United States. In these early schools paper and books were scarce; therefore, children learned each lesson from paper pasted on the hornbook.

8. FOOTBALL:
   A. What games do people play in the fall?
   B. Display pictures of football players involved in a variety of poses. Describe the actions and introduce following words: pass, catch, run, tackle, kick, and punt.
   C. Discuss football equipment, uniforms, and playing field.
   D. Discuss how each child feels about football.

9. PEOPLE PREPARE FOR COLD WEATHER IN FALL:
   A. People wear sweaters and warmer clothing in fall. Why?
   B. People store food for the cold months. Why?
   C. People make their homes snug and warm. They install storm windows and doors, check heating systems to insure proper functioning, drain hoses so they will not freeze, and cut wood for fireplaces.

10. WHAT DO ANIMALS DO IN THE FALL?
    A. Where do some birds go in the fall? Why?
    B. What do squirrels do in the fall? Why?
    C. What do other animals do? Bears grow fat and prepare for a dormant period during cold winter months.

11. BOOKS:
    Down Come the Leaves--Bancroft
    Little Red Hen--Domanska
    When Autumn Comes--Fox
    Follow the Fall--Kumin
    The Curious Chipmunk--Lakey
    Now It's Fall--Lenski
    The Apple Book--Martin
    Let's Find Out About School--Shapp
    Let's Find Out About Fall--Shapp
    Autumn Harvest--Tresselt
    Emily's Autumn--Udry
    Autumn--Wood

GAMES AND SOCIAL ACTIVITIES

1. NAME GAME: (Tune--"Twinkle, Twinkle Little Star")
       Hello children, here we are,
       At preschool from near and far.
       Today we are going to play a game.
       Please stand when I call your name.
   Note: This can be used when attendance is taken.

2. HOW DO YOU DO? (Tune--"If You're Happy and You Know It")
       Good morning, (child's first and last name).
       How are you?
       Good morning, (child's first and last name).
       How are you?
       How are you this special day?
       We're glad you came to play.
       Good morning, (child's first and last name).
       How are you?
   Adult shakes child's hand as verse is sung. Repeat with new child.

3. FIND A FRIEND AT SCHOOL: (Tune--"Farmer in the Dell")
        I'll find a friend at school. I'll find a friend at school.
        Heigh ho the derry oh, I'll find a friend at school.
        We'll skip around the room. We'll skip around the room.
        Heigh ho the derry oh, we'll skip around the room.
    Sit in circle. One player walks around outside of circle while first two lines
    are sung. Child then chooses a friend. The two friends hold hands and skip
    around the circle while remainder of verse is sung. First player returns to
    circle, and game is repeated with second player walking outside the circle.
    Continue until all have had a turn to choose a friend.
    Variation: Instead of "skip" ask player to choose action. Examples are run,
    walk, hop, and jump.

4. SQUIRRELS IN TREES: Space children around room in groups of three. One to
    three children should not be placed in a group. They will serve as extra
    squirrels. In each group, two children arch hands over third child to make
    trees. The third child is the squirrel. When adult says, "Change trees." all
    squirrels (including extras) run to new trees. Only one squirrel is allowed in
    each tree. Squirrels not finding trees wait for next call to find a tree.
    Change positions of squirrels and trees so that all children are squirrels.
    Variation: Squirrels can hop, walk, or slide to trees.

5. A-HUNTING WE WILL GO: (Traditional)
        A-hunting we will go.
        A-hunting we will go.
        We'll catch a fox,
        And put him in a box,
        And then we'll let him go.
    Two players face one another, grasp hands, and raise arms over head to make an
    arch. Remaining players form line and walk under arch, singing verse. At the
    words, "We'll catch a fox," the two players drop arms and trap a player inside.
    At end of song fox is released. Repeat.

6. LOOK AND SEE:
        1-2-3 Open your eyes.
        What is missing?
        Who's so wise?
    Adult places fall items on table. Children close their eyes, and adult removes
    one item. Children open eyes when adult recites verse. Child guessing item
    can choose object to remove when game is repeated.

7. CLAP OR STAMP: Adult names item. If item relates to autumn, children clap.
    If it does not relate to autumn, they stamp their feet. Repeat with new item.
    Examples are: Adult says "football," and children clap. Then adult says
    "basketball," and children stamp their feet.

8. SCARECROW: (Group project) Tie ends of pant legs and ends of shirt sleeves
    with string. Stuff with newspaper. Insert broom handle through clothes.
    Place end of broomstick into pail filled with sand. Make facial features on
    paper sack with crayons, paint, or paper. Stuff sack with newspaper. Place
    stuffed sack over stick and secure open end with string.

9. NAME TAGS: (Group project) Make uncolored baking clay by mixing 2 cups flour, 1 cup salt, and 1 cup water. Roll clay to 1/8" thickness. Cut clay into shapes with cookie cutters. Make a hole in the top of each shape. Bake at 300° for 30 minutes or until dry. When cool, paint shapes. When paint dries, write one child's name on each shape with permanent felt-tipped pen. Thread yarn through hole and tie into circle large enough for name tag to be hung around neck.
    Variations:
    A. Use paper instead of clay for tags. Paper tags can be taped to shirts. They can be color-coded to match the teacher's name tag or the child's classroom. (Place colored tag on door of room.)
    B. Provide small stickers or pictures cut from catalogs or old story books. Child selects one picture and glues it to tag. Child who cannot read uses picture to identify his tag.
    Note: Name tags are helpful during the first weeks of the new school year. Provide a special place so tags can be left at school. Encourage each child to find his own name tag when he returns.

10. HELPER CHART: Glue a cookie, napkin, and cup on a chart to indicate duties to be performed at snack time. Glue an envelope at the bottom of the chart. Place all children's names in the envelope. Remove and place a name by each item to indicate who will be helper. Rotate so all have an opportunity to help.

CREATIVE DRAMATICS AND MOVEMENT

1. YEAR ROUND LEAVES: Pretend you are leaves holding tight to a branch. All summer you worked hard making food for the tree. Now it's time to stop so the tree can rest. It's getting cold. The wind blows. You sway in the breeze. The stem loosens and falls from the branch. You drift slowly to the ground. Now pretend to be a person stepping on the leaves. Crunch. Rake the leaves into a bunch. Place leaves in a basket and carry them away. Next spring mix leaves in soil to make it rich.

2. TWIRLING LEAF: Dramatize the following verse:
        The autumn wind blows and blows. Ooo, ooo, ooo.
        The leaves shake and shake, then fly into the sky so blue.
        They whirl and whirl around, then twirl and twirl around.
        But when the wind stops, the leaves sink slowly to the ground.
        Lower, lower, lower and land quietly without a sound.

3. LIKE LEAVES IN WINDY WEATHER:
        Like leaves in windy weather, dance and twirl together.
        Whosh, whirl around. Then gently float to the ground.

4. AUTUMN LEAVES: Dance to music of "Autumn Leaves" recorded by Roger Williams.
    Variation: Use variation of LEAF BOOKMARK (see page 2). Wave leaves to music.

5. THIS IS WHAT WE DO AT SCHOOL: (Tune--"Mulberry Bush")
    Dramatize the following song:
        This is the way we go to school, go to school, go to school.
        This is the way we go to school so early in the morning.
    Second verse--This is the way we paint a picture . . .
    Third verse--This is the way we play outside . . .
    Fourth verse--This is the way we build with blocks . . .
    Fifth verse--This is the way we eat our snack . . .

6. FOOTBALL PROP BOX: Cover a cardboard box with colorful paper. Paste pictures of football players to paper. Place in the box a helmet, sweat shirt, football jersey, football, shoulder pads, and football tee. Allow time for creative play.

7. BIRD FLYING SOUTH: Fold piece of construction paper in half. Starting at fold, draw half a bird. Cut along lines. Attach string to bird and fly to music. Pretend to fly south.

8. ANIMALS' FALL ACTIVITIES: Pretend you are animals in the fall of the year. First be a bird flying south for the winter. Dramatize the following verse:
    The birds are flying in the sky,
    Flying south for winter is nigh.
    Fly away little birdies in the sky. Goodbye.
What would you see as you were flying south? Dramatize answers if possible. Now pretend to be a bear. Bears grow fat during the autumn and prepare for a long winter's rest. Dramatize the following verse:
    The big bear lumbers slowly through the wood,
    Eating roots, seeds, fruit, and honey--sooo good.
    She's getting fat to prepare for winter.
    When it's cold, in her cave she'll slumber.
Squirrels prepare for winter by collecting nuts.
    Gray squirrel sits whisking his tail in the tree top.
    He scampers to the ground: hippity hop, hippity hop.
    He wrinkles and crinkles his nose
    While eating a nut he holds in his toes.
    When winter comes, where do you suppose he will be?
    Sleeping snug in his home, a hole in the tree.

9. TEDDY BEAR: Dramatize the following traditional verse:
    Teddy bear, teddy bear, turn around.
    Teddy bear, teddy bear, touch the ground.
    Teddy bear, teddy bear, show your shoe.
    Teddy bear, teddy bear, skiddoo! (kick feet)

10. GOING ON A BEAR HUNT: Children repeat each line after adult. Alternate slapping hands on thighs for beat. Dramatize motions.
    Going on a bear hunt.
    I'm not afraid.
    Got my gun.
    Coming to a river.
    Everybody swim.
    Going on a bear hunt.
    I'm not afraid.
    Got my gun.
    Coming to a tree.
    Everyone climb the tree.
    Is there a bear over there?
    No!
    Is there a bear over there?
    No!
    Climb down the tree.
    Going on a bear hunt.
    I'm not afraid.
    Got my gun.
    Coming to a clearing.
    Walking across the clearing.
    Going on a bear hunt.
    I'm not afraid.
    Got my gun.
    Coming to a cave.
    Is there a bear in the cave?
    YES!!
       (perform following verses quickly)
    Running through the clearing,
    Climbing up the tree,
    Climbing down the tree,
    Swimming through the river,
    Run home and lock the door.
       (perform following verses slowly)
    Went on a bear hunt.
    Had my gun.
    I wasn't afraid.

PHYSICAL DEVELOPMENT

1. WORM THROUGH APPLE: Players stand in a line close together with feet approximately 18" apart. One child is the worm who wiggles through legs.

2. CATCH THE HARVEST: Use bean bag for fruit or vegetable. Toss bean bag into the air and catch it in bread basket or nonbreakable bowl.
    A. Toss the "apple" (bean bag) in the air to different heights of 1 to 5 feet and catch "apple" in basket.
    B. Toss the "apple" in the air, sit down while the "apple" is in the air, and catch it while sitting.
    C. Toss the "apple" in the air, turn around, and catch it in the basket.
    Variation: Instead of bean bag, use a sock rolled into a ball.

3. FOOTBALL PLAYER EXERCISES: Do the following: jump and click heels together, run in place, and perform jumping jacks.

4. FOOTBALL THROW: Tie inner tube to end of a rope. Suspend from a swing set, clothesline, or tree. Place at eye level. Stand appropriate distance away and throw football through inner tube.
    Variations:
    A. Hike ball through tube.
    B. Kick ball through tube.
    C. Throw ball through tube while it is swinging.
    D. Change heights of tube.

5. FOOTBALL RELAY #1: Form two lines. The first child in each line holds football and runs a specified distance to a line on the floor. He touches the football to the line and runs back, handing the football to the next child. Repeat until everyone in line has completed the drill.
    Variation: When child reaches the line, he can toss or roll the football to the first child in his line.

6. FOOTBALL RELAY #2: Form two lines. The first child in each line passes or hikes the football to the child behind him. This action is repeated until the last child in the line receives the ball. He runs to the front of the line. Continue until everyone has run to front of line.

MATH

1. FALL CALENDAR: From paper, cut 30 leaves. Write number from 1 to 30 on each leaf. Use to indicate the date for the September calendar. Place correct number on calendar each day. Discuss date, day of week, and activities for day.
    Variation: Instead of leaves use footballs, football players, squirrels, or apples. Use cake to signify a birthday celebrated during the month.

2. APPLE TREE: Cut tree from brown paper. Mount tree on poster board. Laminate with clear self-adhesive plastic. Cut out and number 20 apples. Do any of the following:
    A. Tape apples to tree in numerical order.
    B. Identify number before placing apple on tree.
    C. Place apples on tree. Adult specifies by number which apple to "harvest." Child removes that apple.

3. SORTING FRUITS AND VEGETABLES: Use tubes with different diameters. Examples are waxed paper tubes or oatmeal containers with bottoms removed. Provide an assortment of fruits, vegetables, or balls. Experiment to find the correct-sized tube for each object. Roll object through tube.
Note: Many fruit and vegetable farms have a sorting machine to sort their produce according to size.

4. BEANS IN A BASKET: Number an egg carton from 1 to 12 by placing a number in the bottom of each cup. Place 80 beans in the lid of the opened egg carton. Place one bean in the cup marked 1 and two beans in the cup marked 2. Continue filling cups with the correct numbers of beans.
Variations:
   A. Instead of egg carton and beans, place nuts in plastic margarine tubs that have numbers in the bottom.
   B. Use different varieties of beans or nuts. Sort into different varieties. Place only one variety in each container.

5. MATCHING CARDS: Make set of number cards and set of object cards. Match number card with object card.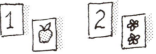

6. FOOTBALL NUMBERS: Cut pictures of football players from sport magazines and mount on large poster board. Children identify numbers on football jerseys. They can also identify colors of players' uniforms.

SCIENCE

1. WATERPLAY: Place warm water in shallow waterplay containers. While children are playing, add a few drops of red food coloring. After a short time add yellow food coloring. Discuss change in water.

2. LEAF BLUEPRINT: Collect a variety of leaves. Place piece of blueprint paper on a piece of cardboard. Space leaves on blueprint paper and cover with a sheet of glass. Place in bright sunlight for several minutes. Remove glass and wash the blueprint paper with clear water. Allow to dry. Contrast shapes of leaves. Discuss that different trees and plants have different types of leaves. Leaves are one characteristic used to identify a tree or plant. Make a booklet of leaves and their blueprints. Label each leaf.

3. THERMOMETER: Since fall brings cooler weather, chart the temperature on a graph. If children are unable to read numbers, the thermometer can be divided into cold, cool, warm, and hot.

4. WEATHER CHART: Divide a cardboard circle into four sections. In each section draw a picture of different types of weather. Use sun, clouds, rain, and snow. This can be laminated with clear self-adhesive plastic. Attach arrow to center of circle. Each day one child can move arrow to the corresponding type of weather for the day.

5. OXIDATION OF AN APPLE: Core and cut an apple into sections. Dip half of the apple sections into lemon juice and place on a plate. Place remaining sections on another plate. What happens to the apples on each plate? The apples coated with juice remain white, and the other slices turn brown. This is caused by oxidation. The lemon juice coats the apple slices with citric acid; consequently, the air does not turn these sections brown.

6. EXPLORING AN APPLE: Discuss color, size, and shape of an apple. Discuss the parts of an apple. The stem holds the apple to the tree. The outside is called the peel. How does it feel? Cut apple in half. The core and seeds are inside. The reason an apple is a fruit is because the seeds are inside the apple.
   Variation: Explore a variety of fruits and vegetables.

7. APPLE TEXTURE: The same food can have different flavors, textures, and forms.
   A. Slice fresh apples and taste. Are they soft or crunchy, dry or wet?
   B. Taste DRIED APPLES (see page 4). Compare to fresh apples. Discuss that these are another form of an apple.
   C. Make APPLESAUCE (see page 3). Talk about the changes that have occured in the apples. They are brown and soft, not white and crunchy as before.
   Variation: Use a variety of fruits and vegetables.

8. DRYING BEANS: Any bean that matures can be dried. Examples are wax, lima, and scarlet runners. Let beans dry on vine. If weather turns frosty or damp, pull bean plant or remove beans from plant and dry in a warm airy place. When pods are dry, break them open and remove seeds.

9. PLANT SEEDS FROM HARVESTED FOOD: Collect seeds from fruits and vegetables that have been harvested or purchased. Egg cartons make good seed starters. Fill cups with soil and poke a hole in the middle of each. Place a seed in each hole. Press soil over holes. Set in a sunny window. Water as necessary. Transplant to larger container after seeds have sprouted.

10. HIBERNATION: Many animals, including frogs, hibernate when the weather turns cold. These animals find sheltered places and become so still that they appear to be dead. They breathe very slowly; their heartbeat slows; and their bodies become cold or even freeze. Place a frog in a deep container of water. Gradually add ice so water temperature becomes colder. The frog should become less active as its body temperature drops nearer to that of the water. When frog becomes quite still, take it from the water and place it where it will warm gradually. What happens?

MUSIC

1. FALL: (Tune--"Frère Jacques")
        Leaves are falling, leaves are falling
        On the ground, on the ground.
        Hear the fall sounds, all around.
        Fall is here. Winter's near.

2. LITTLE LEAVES: (Tune--"Ten Little Indians")
        1 little, 2 little, 3 little leaves,
        4 little, 5 little, 6 little leaves,
        7 little, 8 little, 9 little leaves.
        Blow them all away. Whoof!

3. GOOD MORNING SONG: (Tune--"Brownie Smile")
        I awoke this morning, ate my breakfast early.
        I dressed by myself and to school I hurry.
        School, school, school, here I am today.
        Now I am ready to read and sing and play.

4. HICKETY TICKETY: (Found on page 12 of *Experience Games Through Music, for the Very, Very Young, for the Very Young*, by Sister Fleurette Sweeney, S.C.H. and Margaret Wharram, © 1973, Richards Institute of Music Education and Research.)

      Hickety Tickety Bumblebee,
      Can you sing your name to me?
      (child's name), (child's name).

5. ZIP-A-DEE-DOO-DAH-NAME:

      Zip-a-dee-doo-dah, zip-a-dee-day, can you sing your name today?
      My name is (child's name), zip-a-dee day. I can sing my name today.

Adult points to child while group sings first line. Child sings second line. Repeat pointing to new child.

6. LITTLE CABIN IN THE WOODS: (Traditional)

      Little cabin in the woods,
      Little man by the window stood,
      Little rabbit hopping by
      Frightened as he could be.
      "Help me, help me, help me," he cried.
      "Before the hunter shoots me dead."
      Little rabbit come inside safely to abide.

Dramatize song as it is sung.

7. HOP OLD SQUIRREL: (Traditional)

      Hop old squirrel, Eideldum, Eideldum.
      Hop old squirrel, Eideldum dee.
      Hop old squirrel, Eideldum, Eideldum.
      Hop old squirrel, Eideldum dee.

Variations:
  A. Replace "hop" with run, skip, walk, hide, peek.
  B. Replace "old squirrel" with little bird or old frog.

8. WAY DOWN YONDER IN THE PAWPAW PATCH: (Traditional)

      Where, oh where, is little (child's name)?
      Where, oh where, is little (child's name)?
      Where, oh where, is little (child's name)?
      Way down yonder in the pawpaw patch.
      Picking up pawpaws, putting them in her basket.
      Picking up pawpaws, putting them in her basket.
      Picking up pawpaws, putting them in her basket.
      Way down yonder in the pawpaw patch.

Variation: Name of fruit or vegetable can be substituted for "pawpaws."

FIELD TRIPS

1. APPLE ORCHARD
2. VISIT FROM A FOOTBALL PLAYER IN UNIFORM
3. NATURE WALK: Give each child a paper sack so he can collect fall treasures of leaves, grass, small sticks, weeds, flowers, and bird nests. Fall is the best time for exploring bird nests as they lose their camouflage with changing colors and falling leaves. Another advantage of nest hunting in fall is that young families are not disturbed since they've grown and left the nest. A nest can be taken because new nests will be built in the spring.

HALLOWEEN

The name HALLOWEEN comes from the Christian holy day All Hallows' Eve, which is the night before All Saints' Day. The modern celebration of Halloween, celebrated on October 31, has been influenced more by ancient custom than by Christian belief. Imaginary creatures and ghost stories originated from the ancient Celtic people, who believed that on this night evil spirits roamed the earth to play tricks on people. Costumes and jack-o'-lanterns were believed to protect people from these evil spirits. Children also dressed in costumes on All Souls' Day and went from house to house begging for soul cakes, from which comes the custom of trick or treat. Today this holiday is primarily for children who dress in Halloween costumes and go trick or treating.

CONCEPTS TO BE TAUGHT

1. Black and orange are common Halloween colors.
2. Pumpkins harvested during autumn are carved into jack-o'-lanterns.
3. Children dress in costumes and go trick or treating from door to door.
4. Scary creatures, costumes, and stories associated with Halloween are only fantasy and are not to be feared.
5. Halloween safety and ways to have fun without harming other people or property are important aspects of this holiday.

ART ACTIVITIES

1. SCRAP PAPER JACK-O'-LANTERN: Draw a circle on black construction paper. Paint circle with glue. Tear scraps of orange paper into small pieces. Arrange scraps on glue. Add torn scraps of yellow paper for eyes, nose, and mouth.

2. JACK-O'-LANTERN: Provide a round piece of orange construction paper and a variety of smaller shapes for facial features. Select small shapes and glue onto circle to make jack-o'-lantern face.

3. 3-D PUMPKIN: Fold lightweight orange paper into three equal sections. Cut round corners. Unfold and tape two ends together. Color or paste shapes on one side to form face of jack-o'-lantern.

4. STUFFED PUMPKIN: Stuff a paper bag half-full with crushed newspaper. Twist the remainder of the bag into a thick stem. Secure stem with masking tape. Paint pumpkin and add facial features of jack-o'-lantern.

5. FUNNY FACE VEGETABLE: Use squash, potato, turnip, or gourd. Make jack-o'-lantern face with felt-tipped pens, felt, yarn, and buttons.
    Note: String Christmas lights around several "funny faces" placed in a row.

6. APPEARING GHOSTS: Adult draws ghosts with white crayon on white paper. Children then paint paper with dark watercolors or diluted tempera paint wash. Encourage child to paint entire page. Ghosts appear through paint.

7. STRING PAINTING GHOST: Dip string in white paint. Place end of string at center top of dark-colored construction paper. Wiggle string while pulling downward on paper.
    Variation: Hold string at center top. Pull string tight and move other end of string back and forth over paper.

8. FOOT GHOST: Step on white paper. Trace around shoe. Use crayon or felt-tipped pen to make face.

9. 3-D GHOST: On dark paper draw or paint a scene of Halloween night. To create ghost, paste center of white facial tissue to drawing.
    Variations:
    A. Paint a picture of a pumpkin patch instead of a night scene.
    B. Use S-shaped styrofoam packing pieces for ghosts.
    C. Paste a white circle over tip of the facial tissue for ghost's head. On circle, draw a face with crayon or felt-tipped pen.

10. TISSUE GHOST: Roll a facial tissue or aluminum foil into a ball and place in the center of another tissue. Attach string, twister seal, or rubber band below ball to secure head. Leave ends free. Glue two small black circles on face to make eyes.

11. CLOTHESPIN GHOST: Paint round-top clothespin white. Make two dots for eyes with felt-tipped pen. Glue two sleeves cut from paper to body.
    Note: Prongs of clothespin will fit over side of nut cup filled with treats.

12. GHOSTLY POP-OUT CARD: Fold a piece of black paper in half for the card. From white paper, cut a ghost almost as tall and half as wide as the card. Fold ghost down the center. Unfold ghost and card. Lay ghost inside card, matching folds. Folds should bend in opposite directions. Tape sides of ghost to card. When card is opened, the ghost pops out.

13. WITCH MOBILE: Cut three orange circles and one black triangle from construction paper. Use strips of yarn for hair. Draw witch's face on one circle. Glue hair and triangular hat to face. Place witch's head face down on table. Place remaining circles below head approximately 1" apart. Place end of string in center of bottom circle. Extend string through center of all circles and triangle. Tape string to each shape.
    Variation: Instead of yarn, use construction paper hair. Fold a piece of paper accordion-style. Cut folded paper into narrow strips.

14. EGG CARTON WITCH: From egg carton, remove a section which contains four adjoining cups and two large protrusions for witch's nose and chin. Glue two round circles into the top cups for eyes. For hair, glue yarn on top of the section. Cut triangle for hat and larger triangle for body from black construction paper. Staple hat and body to face.

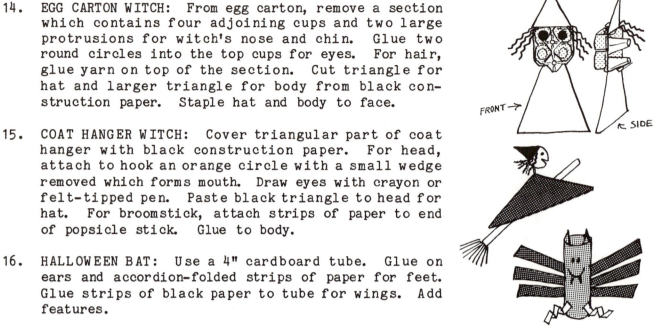

FRONT →   ← SIDE

15. COAT HANGER WITCH: Cover triangular part of coat hanger with black construction paper. For head, attach to hook an orange circle with a small wedge removed which forms mouth. Draw eyes with crayon or felt-tipped pen. Paste black triangle to head for hat. For broomstick, attach strips of paper to end of popsicle stick. Glue to body.

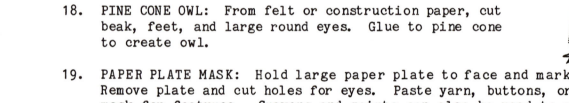

16. HALLOWEEN BAT: Use a 4" cardboard tube. Glue on ears and accordion-folded strips of paper for feet. Glue strips of black paper to tube for wings. Add features.

17. BAT: Paint spring clothespin black. Allow to dry. Use rectangle of black tissue paper for wings. Gather wings at center. Clip clothespin to center of tissue paper wings.

18. PINE CONE OWL: From felt or construction paper, cut beak, feet, and large round eyes. Glue to pine cone to create owl.

19. PAPER PLATE MASK: Hold large paper plate to face and mark location of eyes. Remove plate and cut holes for eyes. Paste yarn, buttons, or paper scraps onto mask for features. Crayons and paints can also be used to make features. Tie yarn or elastic string to holes which have been punched in opposite sides of plate.

20. GROCERY BAG MASK: Cut sections from sides of large brown sack so sack will fit on shoulders. Slip bag over head and mark location of eyes. Remove bag and cut holes for eyes. Make details with crayons, felt-tipped pens, paint, or construction paper.

21. TRICK OR TREAT BAG: Glue precut Halloween figures on paper lunch bag. For handle, fold long strip of paper several times. Staple handle to opposite sides of bag.
Variation: Decorate bag with orange and black crepe paper.

22. HALLOWEEN NIGHT PAINTING: Paste dark-colored tissue paper over white construction paper. Place a small amount of bleach in a container. Dip cotton-tipped swab into bleach and draw on tissue paper. Place several layers of newspaper under paper to protect table. Wear smocks to protect clothing.

23. PAPER TOWEL DIP: Fold paper towel several times. Dip paper towel into red-colored water and then into yellow-colored water. Open towel carefully and allow to dry. Red, orange, and yellow designs will appear on paper. Mount on construction paper if desired.

24. MOON PAINTING: Use circular-shaped objects. Examples are lids, spools, and sponges cut into half-circles or crescent shapes. Dip into orange, yellow, or white tempera and press on dark paper.

COOKING ACTIVITIES

1. TOASTED PUMPKIN SEEDS: Carve pumpkin and remove seeds. Clean seeds and dry on a paper towel. If desired, the seeds can be soaked in salted water overnight (1 1/2 teaspoons salt per 2/3 cup water). Place dry seeds in shallow baking pan. Dot with margarine. Sprinkle with salt if seeds were not soaked overnight. Bake at 350° for 20 to 30 minutes until brown. Stir occasionally. Variation: Combine 1 1/2 tablespoons melted margarine and 1 teaspoon Worcestershire sauce. Pour this mixture over 2 cups seeds. Mix well and bake in shallow pan at 250° for one hour. Stir occasionally.

2. CHEESE ON CRACKERS: Cut American cheese slices into round shapes and place on cracker. If desired, cut small features from cheese or use raisins to make jack-o'-lantern.

3. CHEESE PUMPKINS: 8 ounces cream cheese
                        16 ounces American cheese
   Cut cheeses into 1/2" cubes and let stand at room temperature until softened. Blend together. Shape into 1" balls. Place a raisin or slice of green pepper on the top for pumpkin stem.

4. VEGETABLE CHEESE SOUP: 10 ounces frozen mixed vegetables
                           10 1/2 ounce can condensed cream of chicken soup
                           1 soup can of milk
                           1 cup shredded cheddar cheese
   Cook vegetables as directed on package. Drain. Stir milk and soup into vegetables. Heat, stirring occasionally. Serve. Sprinkle with cheese.

5. JACK-O'-LANTERN SANDWICHES: Place cooked hamburger patty on half of a hamburger bun. Cover patty with a round slice of cheese. Make jack-o'-lantern face using green and black olives cut crosswise, slivers of green pepper, pickle spears, or pimento.
   Variations:
       A. Omit bun. Serve only hamburger patty.
       B. Omit patty. Place cheese on bun or English muffin. Melt cheese in oven.

6. SAND-WITCH: Spread filling between two square slices of sandwich bread. Cut crust from two adjacent sides for face. For hair, place lettuce on filling and extend beyond bread. Decorate with carrot nose, pickle for mouth, and cross-sections of green or black olives for eyes.

7. GHOST PANCAKES: 1/2 cup whole wheat flour   1 egg, beaten
                    1 1/2 cups rolled oats   1 teaspoon oil
                    1 tablespoon baking powder   1 tablespoon honey
                    1 teaspoon salt   1 1/2 cups milk
   Stir dry ingredients together in a large bowl. Beat egg and honey with fork. Combine with oil and milk. Add to dry ingredients. On hot griddle, pour batter in long streaks to form ghosts. Batter will be thin. When cooked, ghosts will puff up! Serve. Decorate with applesauce, bananas, raisins, or blueberries.

8. ORANGE BREW: 1 cup milk   10 to 12 ice cubes
                  1 cup water   1 teaspoon vanilla
                  6 ounces concentrated orange juice
Whip ingredients in blender until frothy.
Note: If desired, drink with straw decorated with
pumpkin cut-out. Slit the pumpkin in two places and
insert straw through slits.
Variation: Use ingredients to make popsicles. (Refer to SICLES on page 168.)

9. APPLE CIDER: Pour 10 cups apple cider or juice into percolator coffee pot.
Place in coffee pot basket: 1 cinnamon stick, 2 whole cloves, 2 whole allspice. Perk cider. Serve warm. Decorate with apple wedge.

10. HAYSTACK SALAD: Mix together: 2 1/2 cups grated carrots; 15 ounces garbanzo
beans, drained; and 2 tablespoons plain yogurt. Serve chilled.

11. ORANGE MUFFINS: 1 cup orange juice   1/3 cup salad oil
                      1 package yeast   2/3 cup honey
                      1 tablespoon honey   1 cup flour
                      1 cup whole wheat flour   1/2 teaspoon salt
                      1 egg   1 teaspoon vanilla
Warm juice to 110°. Add yeast, 1 tablespoon honey, and flour. Set in warm
place until bubbly (10 to 15 minutes). Beat egg. Combine remaining ingredients with egg. Stir egg mixture into yeast mixture. Fill cups of muffin tin
half-full. Place in 150° oven for 40 minutes. Remove. Preheat oven to 350°.
Bake 20 minutes.

12. COCONUT-APRICOT CANDIES: 1/4 pound dried apricots   2 teaspoons orange juice
                             3/4 cup unsweetened coconut 1 tablespoon honey
Grind apricots in food grinder. Mix with remaining ingredients. Shape into
balls about 1" in diameter.

FINGERPLAYS

1. See my pumpkin round and fat.
     (make circle with fingers)
   See my pumpkin yellow.
   Watch him grin on Halloween.
     (point to smiling mouth)
   He's a very funny fellow.
                    Author Unknown

2. Do you know my friend Jack? (point
     to friend)
   When I wave to him, (wave)
   He doesn't wave back. (shake head)
   But he has a friendly grin on his
     face so bright, (smile)
   Which makes it seem less dark on
     Halloween night.
   Before we adjourn, I'd like you to
     learn (point to friend)
   Jack's last name is O'Lantern!
     (form circle and smile)

3. I have a jack-o'-lantern (form cir-
     cle with hands)
   With a candle in.
   He's a very happy fellow.
   See his jack-o'-lantern grin.
     (narrow circle to half circle)

4. Jack-o'-lantern, jack-o'-lantern,
     (form circle with fingers)
   You are such a funny sight
   As you sit there in the window,
     (form square with fingers)
   Looking out at the night. (point
     to eyes)
   You were once a yellow pumpkin
   Growing on a sturdy vine.
   Now you are a jack-o'-lantern.
     (form circle with fingers)
   See the candle light shine. (place
     finger in center of circle)
                         Lois Holt

5. Five little jack-o'-lanterns sitting on a gate. (five fingers)
    First one said, "My it's getting late." (hold up fingers)
    Second one said, "Sh-h-h, I hear a noise."
    Third one said, "Oh, it's just some silly boys."
    Fourth one said, "They're having Halloween fun."
    Fifth one said, "We'd better run."
    Oooooo went the wind, out went their lights,
    And away they all scampered on Halloween night. (move fingers behind back as if running)
                            Author Unknown

6. I made a jack-o'-lantern for Halloween night. (form circle)
    He has three crooked teeth, but he won't bite. (point to teeth and shake head sideways)
    He has two round eyes, but he cannot see. (circle eyes)
    He's a jolly jack-o'-lantern, as happy as can be.
    Mary Jackson Ellis & Frances Lyons

7. I am a pumpkin, big and round. (form circle)
    Once upon a time, I grew on the ground.
    Now I have a mouth, two eyes, a nose. (point to features)
    What are they for, do you suppose? (shrug shoulders)
    When I have a candle inside shining bright,
    I'll be a jack-o'-lantern on Halloween night.
                            Mabelle B. McGuire

8. I am the great pumpkin. Wow, what a sight!
    I have teeth, but I won't bite. (point to teeth and shake head)
    I have eyes so I can see (point to eyes)
    To spread Halloween happiness.
    Ha, ha, giggle-ee!

9. If I were a witch, I'd ride on a broom, (pretend to ride broom)
    And scatter ghosts with a zoom, zoom, zoom! (motions with arms)
                            Author Unknown

10. A funny old woman in a pointed cap, (hands form a pointed cap above head)
    On my door went rap, rap, rap. (knock)
    I was going to the door to see who was there, (fingers walk)
    When off on her broomstick, she rode through the air. (move hand through air)
                            Don Peek

11. An old witch on Halloween night
    Knows how to scare. Oh, what a fright!
    Fee! Fie! Foe! Fum! (whisper)
    BOOOOOOOOOOOOO (clap)
    Then do you know what I do?
    SKIDOO! (jump and fall on floor)

12. I am the witch's cat,
    Meow, meow, meow.
    My fur is black as darkest night.
    My eyes are glaring, green and bright. (point to eyes)
    I am the witch's cat,
    Meow, meow, meow.
                            Author Unknown

13. Coal black cat with humped-up back, (hump back)
    Shining eyes so yellow. (point to eyes)
    See him with his funny tail; (make tail)
    He's a very funny fellow.
                            Author Unknown

14. A cute little ghost named Waldo White (signify small)
    Gave all the children a terrible fright. (act frightened)
    "Why," said Waldo, "Are you scared of me"? (shrug shoulders)
    "I'm a friendly ghost, as friendly as can be."
    The children knew that he was right. (shake head vertically)
    When he danced and sang--that Waldo White! (dance)

15. See my great big scary eyes. (hold fingers around eyes)
    Look out now for a big surprise.
    Oo-oo-ooo (walk like ghost)
    I'm looking right at you.
    BOO!
                            Author Unknown

16. One little witch did a dancing jig.
(raise respective fingers)
Two little witches wished they were
big.
Three little witches jumped up and
down.
Four little witches went to town.
Five little witches on Halloween
night
Jumped on their broomsticks and
flew out of sight.

17. An owl sat watching in a tree, (sit
with thumbs under arms)
Just as wise as he could be, (point
to side of forehead)
Watching tricksters from door to
door run, (make fingers run)
Trick or treating and having fun.
(pretend to knock)
After he had watched the whole
scene, (encircle eyes with fingers)
He said, "Whooo, it's Owl-o-ween!"

18. Mr. Owl perched in a tree. (place
hands under arms)
"Whooo goes there?" he said to me.
(point to self)
I looked high up in that oak, (look
upward)
But could not find the owl that
spoke. (shake head sideways)
In the sky I saw that bird. (pretend to fly)
"Whoo, whooo, whooo," was all I
heard. (place hand behind ear)

19. Witches, ghosts, and goblins:
What a scary sight! (act frightened)
See the happy jack-o'-lantern.
(form circle)
It must be Halloween night. (shake
finger)

20. A pretty princess wears a crown.
(form circle above head)
Bunny's ears flop up and down.
(place hands above head, move
hands up and down)
A beautiful ballerina dances to and
fro. (move arms above head)
A funny clown laughs, "Ho, ho, ho."
Two green eyes shine from a cat.
(form circles around eyes with
fingers)
A scary witch wears a pointed hat.
(form point with arms above head)
Jack-o'-lanterns shine so bright.
(form large circle)
Happy children on Halloween night!

21. Goblins and spooks, ghosts and
witches,
Go door to door giving their
pitches, (pretend to knock)
"Trick or treat,
Trick or treat,
Trick or treat."
Show me a trick, (do trick)
And I'll give you a sweet. (hold
out hand)

22. Heigh ho for Halloween,
Scary creatures can be seen:
An old witch with a crooked hat;
(form point with arms above head)
Wings flap quickly on a bat; (pre-
tend to fly)
A spider walking with eight feet;
(raise eight fingers)
While ghosts and goblins quietly
creep. (whisper and place finger
over lips)
Tiptoe, tiptoe, BOO!

LANGUAGE DEVELOPMENT

1. HALLOWEEN DISCUSSION: Discuss thoughts and feelings about Halloween.
   A. How do you look when wearing a mask or costume?
   B. How does a costume or mask make you feel?
   C. Are you sometimes afraid of costumes or masks?
   D. Which costumes are funny, scary, sad, and happy?
   E. Do you become a different person when you wear a costume or mask?
   F. Halloween costumes can be removed. They are not real but only represen-
       tations of characters.

2. HALLOWEEN SAFETY: Discuss the following:
   A. Wear costumes which fit properly.
   B. Use facial make-up when possible since masks often obstruct vision.
   C. Wear light-colored clothing, fluorescent colors, or dark costumes that have bright patches.
   D. Go trick or treating with an adult or friend.
   E. Carry a light to guide the way.
   F. Stay in a familiar neighborhood.
   G. Walk on sidewalks and cross streets properly.
   H. Have parents inspect treats before eating them.
   I. Be careful of burning candles in jack-o'-lanterns.

3. MYSTERY BAG: Explain what a mystery is. Put a number of objects without sharp edges in a large bag. Examples are unsharpened pencil, bead, block, and sponge. One player reaches into bag for an object and tries to describe it without looking. He then guesses what the object is and removes it to see if the guess was correct. Repeat until all have had a turn.
   Variation: Adult describes object in bag, and players try to guess what it is.

4. HAUNTED HOUSE: On poster board, draw picture of haunted house with windows and doors. Cut three sides of each window or door so it will open and close. Attach to house: ghosts, jack-o'-lanterns, witches, and bats. Create story about the haunted house. The story could be about a family of ghosts. Emphasize descriptive words. Examples are dark, mysterious, or spooky.
   Note: Discuss that haunted houses are make-believe.

5. SOMEONE'S KNOCKING AT MY DOOR:
   > Funny creatures dressed on Halloween
   > Will rap, rap, rap or doorbell ring.
   > When they do, I hurry to greet
   > Who has come to trick or treat.

   Children wear Halloween costumes. Recite poem. Adult then describes one child's costume. Children guess who adult is describing.
   Variations:
   A. Instead of adult, child gives description of Halloween costume.
   B. Children do not wear costumes. Adult describes Halloween character. Children guess character.

6. GHOST CARD GAME: Make a set of cards with pictures of Halloween. Make a matching set. Spread all cards face down on table. Players take turns turning two cards at a time. The first player to see two, matching, overturned cards says, "Boo!" and takes both cards. Play until all cards are matched.
   Variation: Make pairs of cards that are associated. Examples are pumpkin/jack-o'-lantern, witch/broom, cowboy/cowboy hat, owl/tree, and princess/crown. The first player to recognize association says, "Boo!" He then explains how the two are associated.

7. BECOMING A CLOWN: Tell story about adult who wanted to have a Halloween party and who wanted to dress as a clown. Show how to become clown while dressing, applying make-up, and pretending to be clown. Afterward, remove costume. This helps children understand that Halloween characters are not real but are only people dressed in costumes.
   Note: Be aware of children's reactions, as this may frighten them. Children have difficulty distinguishing fantasy from reality.
   Variation: Do the above as flannel board story by dressing felt person as clown.

8. WITCH'S BREW: Draw large pot on poster board. Stand poster board on table. Children sit on floor in front of table. Adult explains, "The witch is boiling some brew. A witch uses a variety of things in her stew. Listen and tell what objects are in the brew from the noises they make." Adult makes noises behind poster board, and children guess what makes each noise. Examples are beaters beating, hands clapping, or bell ringing.

9. SKALA KAZAM-WITCH MAGIC: Pretend to be a witch and perform magic. Display pictures related to Halloween. Discuss each picture. Place "magic" scarf over pictures. Remove one picture when lifting scarf and saying, "Skala Kazam." Players tell which picture disappeared.
   Variation: Instead of pictures, use objects.

10. WHAT IS A SHADOW? Discuss shadows. Go outdoors and discover own shadow. Adult says verse, and children do actions.
   > If I walk, my shadow walks.
   > If I run, my shadow runs.
   > And when I stand still, as you can see
   > My shadow stands beside me.
   > When I hop, my shadow hops.
   > When I jump, my shadow jumps.
   > And when I sit still, as you can see,
   > My shadow sits beside me.
   >   Author Unknown
   Try to change shape and length of shadow. Discuss other ways shadows can be made. Shadows can be made in bright light or at night when the moon is shining bright. Discuss fears about shadows. Give explanations for shadows to help remove fears.

11. HALLOWEEN FAVORS: Discuss that candy is frequently received as Halloween treats. (Refer to SUGAR FACTS on page 104 and SUGAR CONTENT IN FOODS on page 105.) The following are suggestions for treats to be given in place of candy:
   A. STICKERS: Give Halloween stickers, scented stickers, stars, notebook reinforcement holes, or shapes cut from gummed paper.
   B. PLAY DOUGH PUMPKIN: Make orange PLAY DOUGH (see page 84). Roll into small ball. Place ball in a plastic bag. Twist and tie open end with green yarn or ribbon. Attach label saying, "PLAY DOUGH." Recipe for play dough can be included on label.
   C. UNSHARPENED PENCIL OR ELBOW STRAW: Add pumpkin cut-out (see page 20).
   D. PENNY JACK-O'-LANTERN: Cut pumpkin from orange construction paper. To make jack-o'-lantern, tape two pennies for eyes and three for mouth.
   E. JACK-O'-LANTERN CRAYON: Preheat oven to 375°. Place crayon chips in paper-lined muffin tin. Turn oven off, and place muffin tin in oven for five minutes or until chips melt. Remove from oven and allow to harden. Remove paper. Place crayon in plastic bag. Tie open end with green yarn. Glue paper features to bag for jack-o'-lantern.
   F. AIRPLANE WITCH: Fold paper airplane using black construction paper. Staple precut witch's face and hat to front of plane.
   G. SMALL MAGNET
   H. PURCHASED PARTY FAVOR
   I. PLASTIC FINGER RING
   J. SMALL BALL
   K. SCRATCH PAD
   L. TOOTH BRUSH
   M. PURCHASED PLASTIC SOLDIER OR COWBOY
   Note: Items not given can be saved for the following Halloween.

GAMES AND SOCIAL ACTIVITIES

1. **HALLOWEEN CARNIVAL:** Instead of trick or treating on Halloween, plan a carnival. When entering carnival, each child donates a bag of sugarless gum, wrapped popcorn balls, peanuts in shells, or HALLOWEEN FAVORS (see page 24). These are used as prizes for games below. Give each child a trick or treat bag to collect prizes. Start groups at different booths and move clockwise around room.

   A. **BATS FLY:** Make fishing pole by attaching string to wooden dowel. Tie a magnet to loose end of string. Attach paper clip to black paper bats. Place bats in tub. Player fishes for bat and makes it fly into sack.

   B. **WORMS IN WITCH'S BREW:** Use a large kettle with 4" of water which contains a small amount of black tempera. In kettle, place rubber worms (found at sporting goods stores), colored rubber bands, or S-shaped styrofoam packing pieces. Player reaches into kettle, grasps a handful of "worms," and counts them. A treat is received for each "worm" counted.

   C. **FEED THE JACK-O'-LANTERN:** Make a jack-o'-lantern on the outside of a box. Remove large mouth. Player tosses bean bags into mouth. A treat is received for each bag that enters Jack's mouth.

   D. **SEARCH FOR PIRATES' TREASURE CHEST:** Player searches for treasure by completing obstacle course. Examples for course are walk plank on balance beam, climb steps, wiggle through chairs, and crawl through tunnel made by covering table with sheet. Player then receives a treat from treasure chest located at end of obstacle course.
   Note: String yarn through obstacle course ending at treasure chest. Children follow yarn to complete course.

   E. **RAT IN HIS HOLE:** Player stands beside quart jar and drops clothespins or rubber rats into jar. A treat is received for each rat in hole.
   Note: Rubber rats can be found in pet stores with cat toys.

   F. **WITCH'S RING TOSS:** Stand broom between two chairs or in pail. Cut rings from plastic bleach bottle. Cut bottom from bottle with a knife. Cut 1" above bottom opening to form ring. Make several. Player tosses rings at broom from designated distance established according to ability of child. A treat is received for each ring on broom handle.

   G. **SQUIRT JACK:** Place plastic tarp under and behind jack-o'-lantern. Have pail of water and extra candles to replace soaked ones. Light candle inside Jack. Player uses squirt gun to extinguish flame. A treat is received when Jack is "in the dark!"

   H. **BOB FOR APPLES:** Attach whole or sliced apple to string suspended from climbing equipment or broomstick held by two adults. Player holds hands behind back and catches apple with teeth. Apple is given for treat.

   I. **TRICK OR TREAT:** Adult stands behind a door. Child knocks on door and adult opens it. Child says, "Trick or treat." Adult has child do a trick before he receives a treat. Examples of tricks are jump, hop, make an animal noise, or count to ten.

   J. **SHAVE JACK:** Inflate and tie end of orange balloon. Paint jack-o'-lantern face on it. Cover balloon with shaving cream. Player shaves Jack with a bladeless razor. A treat is received if Jack does not break.

   K. **MAKE-UP BOOTH:** (Refer to CLOWN PARTY on page 190.)

   L. **CATCH THE GHOST:** Inflate a white balloon for ghost. Do not tie end. Player releases balloon and tries to catch the ghost before it touches the ground. A treat is received for catching the ghost.

   M. **PUMPKIN PUSH:** Place inflated, round, orange balloon at starting line. At signal, player kicks balloon to finish line. A treat is received for crossing finish line.

2. WHAT TIME IS IT, MRS. WITCH? One player is Witch, who stands in center of room. Remaining players form line on one side of room. Adult asks, "What time is it, Mrs. Witch?" If Witch says, "Midnight," players run across to other side of room. Those tagged by Witch stay in center to help Witch tag other players. Repeat until all but one child is tagged. Last child then becomes Witch.

3. WITCH ON HALLOWEEN: (Tune--"Farmer in the Dell")
    The witch on Halloween, the witch on Halloween,
    Heigh ho, let's trick or treat, the witch on Halloween.
Second verse-- The witch chooses a goblin.
Third verse--The goblin chooses a bat.
Fourth verse--The bat chooses a cat.
Fifth verse--The cat chooses a ghost.
Sixth verse--The ghost says, "Boo!"
Seventh verse--They all screech and scream.
Stand in circle. Players hold hands and move clockwise while singing first verse. Adult chooses witch who stands in center of circle. At end of second verse, the witch chooses a goblin, who joins him in the center of the circle. Continue until all characters are chosen.

4. HOOKEY SPOOKY: (Tune--"Hokey Pokey")
    Put your right hand in, take your right hand out.
    Put your right hand in and shake it all about.
    Do the Hookey Spooky and everybody shout,
    "That's what it's all about. BOO!"
Stand in circle. Players do motions for first two lines. As third line is sung, children turn around. As fourth line is sung, players slap thighs twice, clap hands twice, and raise hands above head. Repeat, using other parts of the body.
Variations:
    A. Instead of the last two lines, use: Do the Hookey Spooky and hoot like and owl, "That's what it's all about. HOOT!"
    B. Give each child a black or orange crepe paper streamer.

5. PASS THE PUMPKIN: Sit in circle. One player sits, with eyes closed, in the center of the circle. When the music starts, remaining players pass a small pumpkin or ball around circle. When music stops, the player holding the pumpkin conceals it in his hands. Other players pretend to be holding pumpkin. Player in the center is given three turns to guess who has the pumpkin. Child holding pumpkin then goes to center of circle. Repeat.

6. SHADOW CHASE: Go outside on a sunny day and chase each other's shadows.

7. PAPIER MÂCHÉ JACK-O'-LANTERN: (Group project) Inflate and tie end of round balloon. Soak strips of newspaper in liquid starch. Apply to balloon until it is completely covered. Smooth as many wrinkles as possible. Allow to dry for two or three days. Paint orange and decorate as jack-o'-lantern.
Variations:
    A. To use as piñata, leave small area at top uncovered. After papier mâché dries, pop balloon and fill with treats. (Refer to PIÑATA on page 29).
    B. Instead of jack-o'-lantern, make witch face. Attach WITCH HAT (see page 28).

8. HALLOWEEN MURAL: (Group project) Cover table or floor with a large piece of butcher paper. Make available different colors of tempera paint. Paint mural about Halloween. Work in shifts with a large group of children.

CREATIVE DRAMATICS AND MOVEMENT

1. HALLOWEEN FACES AND FEELINGS: Facial expressions can reveal feelings to others. Make faces in front of mirror that suggest feelings and appearances related to Halloween. Examples are spooky, scary, ugly, sad, happy, and angry. Halloween masks also depict feelings. Wear different masks and look into mirror. (Refer to HALLOWEEN DISCUSSION on page 22.)

2. A VISIT TO A HAUNTED HOUSE: Pretend to visit a haunted house. Huddle together and tiptoe quietly through the woods to the house. "Whoo-whoo"! Who made that strange noise? Don't be afraid. It's only an owl. Slowly open the door to the haunted house. "Creak"! Enter and push away the cobwebs. Look! There's a staircase. Let's climb the stairs. There's a door at the top. Open it carefully. AH-H-H! There's a GHOST! Close the door. Run down the stairs. Open the front door. Scamper through the forest. Run home and lock the door. Whew, safe at last.

3. HALLOWEEN WALK: Form line on one side of room. Cross room in following ways:
   A. Fly like a bat.
   B. Gallop like a cowboy on a horse.
   C. Hop like a bunny.
   D. Roll like a pumpkin.
   E. Dance like a princess.
   F. Creep like a cat.
   G. Walk like a skeleton.
   H. Float like a ghost.
   I. Stomp like a monster.

4. LET'S BE WITCHES:
   > The witch rides on her broom
   > Going here and there--zoom, zoom.
   > Sometimes she rides fast and sometimes she rides slow,
   > Watching Halloween fun below. Oooooooooooooooooo!

   Place yardstick or broom between legs and pretend to be witch flying while verse is recited. Encourage conversation to describe how it feels to fly, what the speed of flight is, and what might be seen on Halloween.

5. HALLOWEEN CHATTER: Make following sounds: cackle like a witch, screech like a cat, hoot like an owl, and make a spooky noise like a ghost.

6. SHADOW THEATRE: Hang sheet and place a bright light behind it. One child goes behind curtain and pantomimes a character or simple act. Others guess what character he is portraying or what he is doing. Adult can help child decide what to do if necessary.
   Variation: Players shut eyes while adult selects someone to go behind the sheet. Remaining players guess to whom the shadow belongs.

7. PAPER BAG OWL: From construction paper cut nose, eyes, and wings. Glue features to brown paper lunch sack to make owl. Use for hand puppet.

8. FINGER PUPPETS:
   A. JACK-O'-LANTERN: Draw and cut out jack-o'-lantern about the size of a quarter. Attach to narrow paper ring that will fit top part of finger.
   B. PEANUT SHELL GHOST: Use elongated half of peanut shell. Draw face on shell with felt-tipped pen. Place shell over tip of finger.
   Develop creative stories about puppets.

9. COSTUME BOX: Adult prepares a box with masks, costumes, and accessories. Allow children to experiment with items. This may ease the fears of some of the children. The following can be made for the costume box.

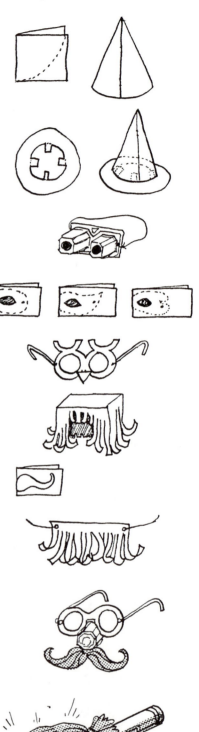

A. BASIC CONE HAT: Fold 12" x 24" paper in half and cut out quarter circle. Open and roll half-circle into cone. Adjust to fit head. Staple or tape together. Make into clown hat by adding pompons, yarn, or paper designs.

B. WITCH HAT: Make BASIC CONE HAT from black construction paper. Cut out large circle for brim. Place cone hat in center and trace around bottom of cone. Draw tabs inside circle and cut out inner circle, leaving tabs. Tape tabs to inside of cone.

C. EGG CARTON MASK: Cut holes in bottom of two adjoining cup sections of egg cartons. Staple elastic string to sides or tie strings to holes punched in sides of mask.

D. BASIC MASK: Fold 3" x 8" piece of construction paper in half. Starting at fold, draw half mask. While mask is folded, cut mask from paper and cut holes for eyes. Open mask. Tie strings through holes punched in sides of mask.

E. OWL MASK: Fold plastic holder from six-pack cans of pop in half and staple at center. Wrap pipe cleaner around each side of mask. Bend pipe cleaners to fit around ears. Tape construction paper nose to mask.

F. PAPER BAG WIG: Use large paper bag that fits over head. Cut a large rectangle from front section of bag for face. Fringe bottom of bag. Curl fringe by rolling tightly around a pencil.

G. MUSTACHE: Fold construction paper. Starting at fold, draw half a mustache shape. Cut shape from paper. Tape mustache above upper lip.

H. BEARD: Fold piece of construction paper in half and fringe bottom edges. Curl fringe by rolling tightly. Punch hole in each side and tie strings through holes.

I. MASTER DISGUISE: Cut two sections from plastic six-pack holder. Wrap pipe cleaner around each side of glasses. Bend pipe cleaners to fit around ears. Staple an egg carton cup to bottom of "eyeglasses" for nose. Staple MUSTACHE (listed above) to bottom of "nose."

10. FLASHLIGHT GOBLIN: Cut facial features from bottom of paper bag. Line the inside base of bag with orange crepe paper. Insert a flashlight into the bag. Twist open end of bag around flashlight's handle, leaving switch uncovered. Secure with rubber band. Turn on flashlight. Wave lighted goblin in darkened room to appropriate background music.

PHYSICAL DEVELOPMENT

1. PUMPKIN THROW: Place plastic pumpkin container on floor. Stand designated distance from pumpkin and attempt to throw bean bag or small ball into container.

2. JACK-O'-LANTERN CATCH: With felt-tipped pen, make jack-o'-lantern features on an inflated orange balloon. Place balloon in kitchen funnel which is held in hand. Toss balloon into air and catch it with the funnel when it falls.

3. MONSTER STOMP: With an ice pick, punch a hole in opposite sides of a 16 ounce can. Thread rope that is 60" long through the holes and tie the ends of the rope together to make a handle. Repeat with second can. Stand with one foot on top of each can. Pull rope handles taut and attempt to walk on cans.

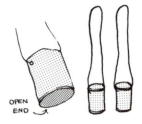

4. WITCH'S BROOM: Use broomstick or stick that is at least three feet long. Hold stick in front of body with both hands. Step over the stick with one foot and then the other. Lift the stick behind body until it is above head. Move stick in front of body to starting position. Repeat.

5. WITCH'S BROOM RELAY: Divide into two lines. The first player in each line places a broom between his legs and rides it to a designated location. He turns around and rides it back to the next player in line. Repeat until all have had a turn.

6. PIÑATA: (Refer to Variation A. of PAPIER MÂCHÉ JACK-O'-LANTERN on page 26.) Fill piñata with treats. Hang piñata from ceiling. Sit on floor a safe distance away. One child is handed broomstick, turned around three times, and given three attempts to break piñata. Repeat until piñata is broken and everyone receives a treat. If desired, blindfold older children.

MATH

1. SHAPES: Make bat, witch, cat, or jack-o'-lantern with circles, squares, triangles, and rectangles. Identify shapes in Halloween symbol.

2. JACK-O'-LANTERN DOT-TO-DOT: Adult prints numbers from 1 to 12 in a large circle. In center of circle draw eyes, nose, and mouth. Draw stem on top of circle. Child connects dots in numerical order.
   Note: This can be laminated with clear self-adhesive plastic. Child connects dots with crayon. Erase crayon and picture can be reused.

3. PUMPKIN DIMENSIONS: Display pumpkins of several sizes and shapes. Discuss:
   A. Which pumpkin weighs the most? Which weighs the least? Place pumpkins in order from lightest to heaviest. Weigh pumpkins on scale to see if order is accurate. Introduce following words: heavy, light, scales, pounds, and ounces.
   B. Which pumpkin is the tallest? Which is the shortest? Measure with a yardstick to determine accuracy. Introduce following words: inches, height, length, tallest, shortest, and yardstick.

4. TRICK OR TREAT MAP: Child cuts from paper a small home which he decorates. Adult writes home address above door. Place homes on simple map. Adult identifies home address of each child. Use map to indicate route when pretending to go trick or treating. When each child's "home" is reached, he can identify home, address, or numbers in address, depending on his ability.
Variation: Place picture of child in door of his "home."
Note: Learning addresses is a difficult concept for young children and needs to be reinforced through repetition.

5. FELT PUMPKIN: Cut pumpkin from orange felt. Have variety of black felt shapes in box for features. Include half-circles, crescents, ovals, triangles, circles, and squares. Adult instructs child to make face of jack-o'-lantern, using particular shapes. For example, "Decorate jack-o'-lantern using two triangles for eyes, square for nose, and crescent for mouth."
Variation: Draw jack-o'-lantern model using outlines of shapes for features. Match features of felt pumpkin with model.

6. MR. SKELETON: Display skeleton decoration which can be purchased or drawn. Count number of ribs, leg bones, arm bones, and bones in hands.

7. CAT'S WHISKERS: Attach various colored whiskers to cat's face. Count number of whiskers. Also count number of a particular color of whiskers. Remove whiskers and repeat using different number of whiskers.

8. TRICK OR TREAT SACK: Place treats in paper sack. Count items as they are removed from bag. Items can also be categorized. Examples of categories are nuts, fruit, and trinkets.

SCIENCE

1. HOW PUMPKINS GROW: Make a pictorial chart showing the following sequence:
   A. Remove seed from harvested pumpkin. Plant seed in ground.
   B. Sun and rain help seed to grow.
   C. Seed grows into vine.
   D. Vine flowers.
   E. Tiny green pumpkins begin to grow where flowers grew on vine.
   F. Pumpkins grow larger and turn orange.
   Discuss various stages of growth.

2. EXPLORING A PUMPKIN: Cut into the top of the pumpkin in a circular fashion. Remove top by pulling on stem. Remove soft pulp from pumpkin with spoons or hands. Discuss how it feels. Is it wet or dry? How does it smell? Remove seeds from stringy pulp and place in a separate bowl to roast at a later time. (Refer to TOASTED PUMPKIN SEEDS on page 19.) Are seeds large or small? Are they wet or dry? Are they slippery? Cut jack-o'-lantern features. Display in room.
   Variation: Instead of making jack-o'-lantern, cut pumpkin into sections. Remove meat from pumpkin and cut into cubes. Place half of the cubes in a small amount of boiling water. Cook for 7 to 8 minutes or until tender. Drain. Compare raw and cooked pumpkin.

3. WITCH'S MAGIC POTION: Pretend to be a witch with a magic potion. Sprinkle pepper in bowl of water and watch it float. Put a drop of soap in the water and watch what happens to the pepper. It should float away. Is this magic? No. The oil in the soap causes the pepper to move.

4. FIRE AND AIR: Discuss that fire needs air just as people and plants do. Light a small candle and cover it with a clear glass jar allowing no air to enter. What happens? Why? Place a candle in a jack-o'-lantern before the features are cut. Light the candle and replace top of pumpkin. After a few minutes, remove top and examine extinguished candle. Light candle in pumpkin after the features are cut. The candle burns because air comes through the holes in the face of the jack-o'-lantern.

5. MOON: Explain that the moon is the earth's nearest satellite and nearest heavenly body. It revolves around the earth and provides the earth with reflected sunlight. Observe the moon. Discuss colors of the moon. The moon appears orange on the horizon because sun rays travel a long distance through the atmosphere. The dust and moisture in the air screen the other colors in the spectrum. The moon appears white during the day because it is seen against a light background. It appears yellow at night because it is seen against a dark background. Make flannel board pictures showing phases from new to full moon. Discuss that moon only appears to change shape. The phases of the moon are caused by changes in the relative positions of the earth, moon, and sun. The sun always shines on half of the moon. However, the lighted part is not always visible from earth.

6. FLASHLIGHTS: Explain that flashlights are helpful when trick or treating. Experiment with a flashlight. Switch it off and on. Take it apart. Discuss the parts of a flashlight. Does it work without batteries? How must the batteries be inserted for it to operate?

7. SHADOWS: Direct light toward wall. Experiment with shadows in following ways:
   A. Make a shadow crisp and dark. Make a shadow pale and fuzzy.
   B. Pick a spot on the wall or floor. Guess where to place finger so that the shadow touches the spot.
   C. Make a big shadow. Make a small shadow. Make a round shadow.
   D. Use various objects to create shadows. Does the same object always cast the same shadow?
   E. Find a partner. Try making the shadows of your fingers touch. Make shadows shake hands without physically shaking hands with your partner.
   F. Mark a spot on the floor. Start with your hand close to the floor and touch the spot with the shadow cast by your finger. Move your hand away from the floor. Can you move your finger and still have the shadow touch the spot?
   Variation: Give each child a flashlight to experiment with shadows.

8. BATTY ECHO: Explain why bats can fly at night and not bump into things. While flying, a bat constantly produces high-pitched squeaks that are beyond the range of human hearing. These sound waves bounce off objects in its path and are reflected back to the bat's sensitive ears. This sound is called an echo. Experiment with echoes. Stand in a big empty auditorium or hall facing a solid wall. Stand as far away from the wall as possible so the sound of the voice and the echo will not overlap. Make a loud sound and listen for the echo.
   Note: A bat's instinct enables it to interpret echoes, judge the distance to the obstacle, and avoid it.

9. GHOUL STEW: Place bowl of cooked macaroni and dry macaroni beside shallow containers partially filled with water for waterplay. Experiment with different textures of macaroni. What happens to macaroni when it is added to water?

MUSIC

1. THREE LITTLE PUMPKINS: (Tune--"Ten Little Indians")
      One little, two little, three little pumpkins
      Rolled down the lane like funny bumpkins.
      Had their faces carved and thought they were somethin's:
      Funny Halloween jack-o'-lanterns.

2. THREE LITTLE WITCHES: (Tune--"Ten Little Indians")
      One little, two little, three little witches,
      Flying over haystacks, flying over ditches,
      Slide down the moon without any hitches.
      Heigh ho, Halloween's here.
                                    Marjorie Barrows

3. ONE LITTLE GOBLIN: (Tune--"Mary Had a Little Lamb")
      One little goblin hopping up and down,
      Hopping up and down, hopping up and down.
      One little goblin hopping up and down,
      For this is Halloween.
   Second verse--Two little skeletons walking down the street . . .
   Third verse--Three little witches flying through the air . . .
   Fourth verse--Four little ballerinas dancing to and fro . . .

4. THE GREAT PUMPKIN: (Tune--"Did You Ever See a Lassie?")
      I am the Great Pumpkin, Great Pumpkin, Great Pumpkin.
      I am the Great Pumpkin. Come dance with me.
      For your friends are my friends, and my friends are your friends.
      I am the Great Pumpkin. Come dance with me.
   Dance as verse is sung.

5. BOO, BOO: Sing "boo" instead of the words of a familiar song.
   Variation: Instead of "boo," use ooo, hoot, or whoo.

6. ECHO: Adult says a word, sings a phrase, makes a simple rhythmic pattern on a tambourine or drum, or claps hands. In response, the children try to duplicate the pattern.

7. SCREECHING CAT: Inflate a balloon. Release air gradually by holding stem of balloon with index finger and thumb of each hand, stretching stem as wide as possible. Stretch stem in different directions. Listen to the different sounds.

FIELD TRIPS

1. PUMPKIN PATCH: Visit a pumpkin field. Explain how pumpkins grow on vines. If possible, pick a pumpkin to take home. Observe different colors of pumpkins.
2. TRIP TO FRUIT STAND OR STORE to purchase pumpkins.
3. GROUP TRICK OR TREATING: During day dress in costumes. Go as group to various homes in neighborhood or to a nursing home. (Make arrangements in advance.)
4. HALLOWEEN PARADE: Dress in costumes and parade for parents or other groups of children.

THANKSGIVING

Pilgrims landed at Plymouth Rock on the Mayflower in 1620. Their first winter in America was hard, and the Pilgrims nearly starved. The Wanpanoag Indians and Squanto, a Patuxet Indian, taught the Pilgrims how to plant seeds, prepare foods, speak the Indian language, and find fishing places. Everyone at Plymouth Colony worked hard to store food and prepare for the next winter.

In the autumn of 1621, Governor William Bradley decided to have a feast to give thanks for the plentiful harvest which consisted of Indian corn, barley, pumpkins, beans, squash, sweet potatoes, apples, maple syrup, wild fruit and berries. Hunters brought many wild turkeys and water fowl; fishermen caught cod and bass; and Indian hunters brought five deer. Ninety Indians and their chief, Massosoit, feasted with the colonists for three days to celebrate the first THANKSGIVING. Today Thanksgiving is celebrated on the fourth Thursday in November. This American holiday is a time for family and friends to have bountiful dinners and to give thanks.

CONCEPTS TO BE TAUGHT

1. Thanksgiving is a time for giving thanks.
2. Today this holiday is celebrated by having dinner with family, relatives, and friends.
3. Turkey is usually served for Thanksgiving dinner.
4. Indians and Pilgrims, who had worked together, celebrated the first Thanksgiving many years ago.
5. Indian tribes differ in their locations, ways of living, customs, and language.

ART ACTIVITIES

1. THANKSGIVING COLLAGE: Tear or cut pictures from magazines and catalogs of "Things I'm Thankful For." Paste pictures onto paper.

2. THANKSGIVING FEAST: Tear or cut pictures of food from magazines for "My Thanksgiving Feast." Paste pictures onto a paper plate.

3. POPCORN COLLAGE: Place popped corn and dried tempera into small bags. Shake bags to color popcorn. Create designs, pictures, and decorations by gluing colored corn onto paper.
   Variation: Use unpopped colored kernels of popcorn.
   Note: Although most tempera is nontoxic, popcorn should not be eaten.

4. CORNUCOPIA: Cut 3" long wedge from one end of a small cardboard tube. Tape or staple cut edges together. Cover roll with yarn or cord soaked in glue. Allow to dry. Fill with CLAY FRUIT (listed below). Paint, if desired.
Variation: Cut and decorate a half-circle of construction paper. Tape or staple edges together.

5. CLAY FRUIT: Roll uncooked baking clay (2 cups flour, 1 cup salt, and water to consistency desired) into small balls for oranges and apples. Roll small cylinder to make banana. Place on shallow baking pan. Bake at 300° for 20 to 30 minutes until dry. Paint fruit.

6. PINE CONE TURKEY: Glue paper feathers to large end of pine cone for tail. Attach construction paper head to small end. Use paper, pipe cleaner, or yarn to make wattle.
Variation: Use colored chenille pipe cleaners for tail.

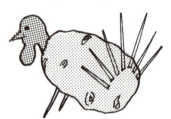

7. POTATO TURKEY: Insert colored toothpicks into potato for tail feathers. Use sandwich toothpicks for legs. Color eyes, wattle, and beak on cardboard head. Tape toothpick to head and insert toothpick into front of potato.
Variations:
  A. Use apple instead of potato.
  B. For tail, use strips of orange peel. Attach with toothpicks.
  C. Use cupcake liner folded in half or construction paper half-circle for tail. Make slit in body and insert tail.

8. HAND TURKEY: Lay hand on paper. Spread fingers. Trace around hand. Add eye, beak, and wattle to outline of thumb. Brightly color rest of outlined fingers for tail feathers. Add legs below outline of palm.

9. HAND PRINT TURKEY: Paint each finger on hand a different color. Paint thumb and palm brown. Press hand on paper. Add features.

10. GEOMETRIC TURKEY: Glue a large brown circle onto paper. Add small brown circle for head, orange triangles for beak and feet, and colorful elongated triangles for tail feathers.
Variation: Use paper plate for body.

11. PAPER BAG TURKEY: Stuff a lunch bag half-full of newspaper. Tie a string in the middle of the sack. Color the open end and cut into 1/2" wide strips for tail feathers. Cut to, but not through, string. Make a cardboard head and tape to bag.

12. LOG CABIN: Glue popsicle craft sticks onto paper to make cabin. Color with crayons to complete details.

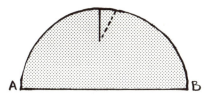

13. TEEPEE: Cut half-circle from paper. Color or paint with Indian symbols. Cut along dotted line of triangle for door. Fold along solid line. Overlap corner A with corner B. Staple.

14. BLOCK PRINT SYMBOLS: Adult prepares potato. Use a potato cut in half. Cut INDIAN PICTOGRAPH (see page 42) 1/8" into flat surface of potato. Remove background by cutting to design from the outer edge of the potato. Prepare several potatoes with different designs. Holding top half of potato, child dips design into paint and presses onto DRUM, SHIELD, BEARSKIN, or JACKET (located below).

15. INDIAN DRUM: Cover oatmeal container or coffee can with paper. Decorate. Make drumstick by sticking sharpened pencil into small rubber ball.

16. INDIAN SHIELD: Use circular pizza cardboard or circle cut from heavy paper. Attach strip of cardboard to back for handle. Decorate with Indian designs.

17. INDIAN BEARSKIN: Cut "bearskin" from a large piece of brown wrapping paper or brown sack. Decorate with Indian symbols.

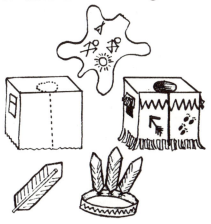

18. INDIAN JACKET: Cut large brown sack along dotted lines as shown in diagram. Fringe edges of jacket and decorate with Indian symbols.

19. INDIAN HEADBAND: For band use strip of brown paper. Cut feathers from construction paper. Tape feathers to straws. Tape or staple feathers to band. Adjust band to fit head. Staple.
    Variations:
    A. Use strip of felt for band. Attach feathers and tie band around head. Let ends of band hang down back.
    B. Use real turkey, chicken, or pheasant feathers.
    C. Cut feathers from newspaper comics. Glue feathers to heavier paper.
    D. Cut feathers from sample wallpaper books.

20. WAMPUM NECKLACE: Cut piece of yarn 25" in length. Tie one rigatoni to end. Wrap other end of yarn with tape to make needle. String with rigatoni. Tie ends to form necklace. Rigatoni can be painted with watercolors, if desired.
    Variations:
    A. For needle, tie yarn to looped end of bobby pin.
    B. Attach 2" piece of pipe cleaner to yarn for needle.
    C. Instead of rigatoni, use wagon wheel macaroni, doughnut-shaped cereal, pieces of colored paper, or 1" pieces of straw.
    D. Instead of painting, color rigatoni before it is strung. Place rigatoni in colored water, remove, spread on waxed paper, and allow to dry.

21. CLAY POTTERY: Make pottery from uncolored baking clay (2 cups flour, 1 cup salt, and water to desired consistency). Place on shallow baking pan and bake at 300° for 20 to 30 minutes or until dry. Paint.

22. SAND PAINTING: Mix dry tempera with fine sand. Make several colors. Paint glue on paper and sprinkle sand over glue. Remove excess sand.
    Variation: Use cornmeal or salt instead of sand.

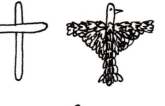

23. THUNDERBIRD: Glue two popsicle sticks together to form a cross. Glue real or paper feathers onto cross, leaving top part of cross for head. Glue paper head to top of cross. Add facial features.

24. GOD'S EYE: Glue two popsicle sticks to form a cross and allow to dry. Tie long piece of yarn to center. Wrap yarn around one piece of cross. Go to next stick and weave around it in the same way. Continue until most of the cross is covered. Tie yarn at end.

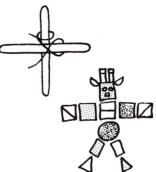

25. *KACHINA* DOLL: Draw a large stick-figure person on construction paper. Glue different-colored shapes onto figure. Examples of shapes are square, oval, diamond, and crescent. Add facial features.

26. TOTEM POLE: Decorate cardboard tubes with colored paper, paint, crayons, or felt-tipped pens. Faces can be made using three-dimensional features. Variations:
    A. Make two 1/2" slits on opposite sides in bottom of decorated tube. Insert another decorated tube in slits. Continue to desired height.
    B. Decorate tube with something symbolic of child or family. Examples are snapshot, activities, work, achievements, or animal that has characteristic with which person identifies.

COOKING ACTIVITIES

1. NAVAJO FRY BREAD: 1 cup flour   2 teaspoons baking powder
                      1 cup whole wheat flour   1/2 teaspoon salt
   Mix ingredients with enough warm water to form dough like pie crust. Knead until pliable. Pat and flatten pieces of dough into 8" circles. The thinner the dough is, the better the fry bread is. Heat 1" of oil in an electric skillet. Fry dough until lightly browned on one side. Turn and brown other side. Drain on paper towels. Eat with honey or maple syrup.

2. SUCCOTASH: Combine lima beans and corn. Heat.

3. NO-BAKE FEAST: When cooking facilities are not available, try this menu for a Thanksgiving feast: TURKEY AND VEGETABLE KABOBS
                            POPCORN GORP
                       CRACKERS AND BUTTER
            APPLE SLICES WITH JELLIED CRANBERRY SAUCE
    A. TURKEY AND VEGETABLE KABOBS: Cube thick-sliced turkey purchased from delicatessen. Cut a variety of vegetables into pieces. Examples of vegetables are bell peppers, cucumbers, and zucchini squash. Spear on sandwich toothpicks. Add cherry tomatoes, if desired.
    B. POPCORN GORP: Mix any of the following: popped popcorn, raisins, nuts, popped wheat, sunflower nuts, cereal, pumpkin seeds, or dried fruit.
    C. CRACKERS AND BUTTER: Place one tablespoon heavy cream in baby food jar. Secure lid. Shake jar vigorously until cream thickens into butter. Remove excess liquid. Serve on crackers.
    D. APPLE SLICES WITH JELLIED CRANBERRY SAUCE: Slice apples and serve with dip of jellied cranberry sauce.

4. FEAST FOR SEVERAL GROUPS OF CHILDREN: Each group prepares one recipe below. All children eat together. TURKEY
CORN AND SQUASH CASSEROLE
SWEET POTATO
CRANBERRY SALAD
CORNBREAD
PUMPKIN DESSERT

A. TURKEY: Roast turkey or chicken until meat thermometer registers 195°.
B. CORN AND SQUASH CASSEROLE: 16 ounces cream corn
1/2 cup crushed Ritz® crackers
1/8 teaspoon sage
1 cup sliced zucchini squash

Mix first three ingredients. Place in baking dish. Top with squash. Sprinkle with salt, pepper, and margarine. Bake at 375° for 45 minutes.

C. SWEET POTATO: Give each child a 3/4" cross-section of a cooled prebaked sweet potato. Peel with fingers. Eat whole or serve mashed.
D. CRANBERRY SALAD: 8 ounces whole cranberry sauce
1/2 cup chopped nuts
1 cup seedless grapes or seeded Tokay grapes
1/2 cup whipped topping

Combine first three ingredients. Chill. Fold in whipped topping.

E. CORNBREAD: 4 ounces margarine   1/2 teaspoon baking powder
2 tablespoons sugar   8 ounces cream corn
2 eggs   1/4 cup shredded Monterey Jack cheese
1/2 cup flour   1/4 cup shredded Cheddar cheese
1/2 cup yellow cornmeal

Cream margarine and sugar. Add eggs. Add dry ingredients. Combine with remaining ingredients. Bake in 8" x 8" pan at 300° for 35 minutes.

F. PUMPKIN DESSERT: 1 package cinnamon graham crackers
3 tablespoons margarine   1/2 teaspoon salt
1 envelope unflavored gelatin 1 teaspoon cinnamon
1/2 cup cold water   1 teaspoon vanilla
1/2 cup pumpkin   1 quart vanilla ice milk

Make crumbs of crackers. Add melted margarine to crumbs. Press in bottom of 8" x 8" pan. In saucepan, soften gelatin in water. Add pumpkin, salt, and cinnamon. Stir over low heat until gelatin dissolves. Pour mixture into bowl. Fold in softened ice milk. Spoon over crust. Freeze.

FINGERPLAYS

1. Thank you for the world so sweet.
Thank you for the food we eat.
Thank you for the birds that sing.
Thank you, God, for everything.
Amen.

Mrs. E. R. Leatham

2. I am very thankful
For my family whom I love,
For my friends,
And for my neighbors,
And for the Lord above.

3. On Thanksgiving Day we say,
"Thank you, Lord, as we pray
For food, health, and joy
For every little girl and boy.
Help us do the things we should,
To be to others kind and good
In all we do, in all we say,
To grow more loving every day."

4. God is great. God is good.
And we thank Him for our food.
Amen.

Author Unknown

5. Thank you, Lord, for all the things
    That you have shared with me:
    The sky above, the earth below,
    And the churning sea.

6. For my family and my friends,
    For the food I eat too,
    Thank you, Lord, for all you do.

7. For health and food,
    For love and friends,
    Father, we thank Thee.
                        Author Unknown

8. I bow my head
    To thank Thee. God,
    For this good bread.

9. On Thanksgiving we have a special
        treat:
    Turkey and dressing are sooooo good
        to eat. (pretend to eat)
    Ummmmmmmmmm! (rub stomach)

10. Every day when we eat our dinner,
    Our table is very small. (palms of
        hands close together)
    There's room for father, mother,
        sister, brother, and me--that's
        all. (point to each finger)
    But when it's Thanksgiving Day and
        the company comes,
    You'd scarcely believe your eyes.
        (rub eyes)
    For that very same table stretches
        until it is just this size!
        (spread hands wide)
                        Author Unknown

11. We go to Grandma's on Thanksgiving
        Day.
    Mom helps cook while we run and
        play. (pretend to run)
    When dinner is ready, I wash my
        face, (pretend to wash face)
    Then sit at the table in my special
        place. (sit)
    After we say the blessing, (fold
        hands)
    We eat lots of turkey and dressing.
        (pretend to eat)
    For dessert we always have a treat,
    Because pumpkin pie is so good to
        eat. (rub stomach)

12. The turkey gobbles when he talks
        (open and close hand)
    And waddles when he walks. (put
        hands under arms, move elbows)
    He scratches the ground with his
        feet, (scratch palm of hand)
    When looking for food to eat.

13. Mr. Turkey sits on the fence post.
        (sit)
    Now he looks like he's ready to
        boast, (stand)
    As he gives his tail a fling, (wig-
        gle hip)
    I think I hear him say, (place hand
        behind ear)
    "If I want to be Turkey King
    After Thanksgiving Day,
    I think I'd better run away!" (run
        fingers behind back)

14. Wild turkeys eat berries and
        scratch for seeds (pretend to eat
        and scratch palm of hand)
    While hiding quietly in the weeds.
        (place finger on lip)
    They sleep all night in a tree,
        (close eyes, pretend to sleep)
    And fly away if frightened by me.
        (pretend to fly)

15. The big turkey on the farm is so
        very proud. (form fist)
    He spreads his tail like a fan,
        (spread fingers of other hand
        behind fist)
    And struts through the animal
        crowd. (move two fingers of fist
        as if walking)
    If you talk to him as he wobbles
        along,
    He'll answer back with a gobbling
        song,
    "Gobble, gobble, gobble . . ."
        (open and close hand)

16. Mrs. Turkey, a pretty fat hen,
        (curve arms at side, stand tall)
    Lives with other turkeys in a pen.
    They spend the day talking turkey
        talk, (open and close hand)
    "Gobble, gobble, gobble."
    Strutting proudly as they walk,
    Wobble, wobble, wobble. (place
        hands under arms, move elbows)

17. Mr. Turkey took a walk one day in the very best of weather. (walk fingers)

He met Mr. Duck along the way (walk fingers of other hand)

And they both talked together,

"Gobble, gobble, gobble." (first hand opens and closes)

"Quack, quack, quack." (second hand opens and closes)

"Goodbye." (first hand opens, closes)

"Goodbye." (second hand opens and closes)

And they both walked back. (walk both hands behind back)

Don Peek

18. Our turkey is a big fat bird (curve arms at sides)

Who gobbles when he talks. (open and close hand)

His red chin's always drooping down. (point to chin)

He waddles when he walks. (place hands under arms, move elbows)

His tail is like a spreading fan. (link thumbs, spread fingers)

And on Thanksgiving Day, he sticks his tail up in the air

And whoosh, he flies away! (move hands as if flying)

Thea Cannon

19. Five little Pilgrims on Thanksgiving Day: (hold up five fingers)

The first one said, "I'll have cake if I may." (lower five fingers and then raise respective finger)

The second one said, "I'll have turkey roasted."

The third one said, "I'll have chestnuts toasted."

The fourth one said, "I'll have pumpkin pie."

The fifth one said, "Oh, cranberries I spy."

But before they ate any turkey or dressing,

All of the Pilgrims said a Thanksgiving blessing. (fold hands)

"Five Little Pilgrims" reprinted from *RHYMES FOR FINGERS AND FLANNELBOARDS* by L.B. Scott and J.J. Thompson, Copyright 1960, with permission of Webster/McGraw Hill.

20. Pilgrims landed the Mayflower fleet.

Indians helped them plant food to eat. (hold fingers behind head)

When crops were harvested and stored away, (pretend to harvest)

Pilgrims thanked the Indians in a special way

By sharing a feast on Thanksgiving Day. (rub stomach)

21. A teepee is quite a home, (form triangle with hands)

Especially for Indians who must roam. (place fingers behind head)

When it is time for them to go

And hunt the mighty buffalo, (pretend to shoot bow and arrow)

They pack their teepees, sticks and all, (pretend to pack)

Then build them again straight and tall. (form teepee with hands)

22. Indians of the Great Plain lands

Could talk by using only their hands. (hold up hands)

They could say, "Good day," and not even move a lip. (refer to GOOD and DAY in SIGN LANGUAGE on page 43)

Thank you, Indians, for this talking tip! (refer to THANK YOU in SIGN LANGUAGE on page 43)

23. The Indian brave proudly wears

Three bright feathers in his hair. (place three fingers behind head)

Each is worn for one good deed:

Yellow, when he took the lead

By running at his fastest speed; (hold up finger for each color)

Blue for hunting in the wood;

And red for being honest and good.

24. Great Spirit, help me never to judge another (shake head sideways)

Until I have walked in his moccasins for two weeks. (raise two fingers)

Sioux Indian Prayer

25. Good manners I show (point to self)
Wherever I go. (make two fingers
   walk)
"Excuse me, please," and "thank
   you," (three fingers)
Are just a few words
I should know. (point to self and
   shake head vertically)

26. Please take my advice
When someone does a deed that's
   nice.
Say, "Thank you very much."
That's a nice finishing touch!

27. When my meal is through, (rub stom-
   ach)
And I have other things to do,
"Excuse me, please." is the cue.

LANGUAGE DEVELOPMENT

1. ROUND ROBIN PRAYER: Discuss Thanksgiving is a special time to give thanks.
Pilgrims gave thanks for their plentiful harvest and food. Adult leads a
prayer. When adult finishes, each child adds something for which he is thankful. This could be done at snack time.

2. SHOPPING FOR THANKSGIVING: Adult pretends he is shopping for Thanksgiving and
fills sack with pictures of edible and nonedible items needed for the dinner.
As he places each item in the sack, he describes it. After all pictures are in
the bag, the adult describes one picture again. Child that identifies the item
receives the picture. Continue until all children have a picture.

3. GOING TO GRANDMA'S HOUSE: Display a chart with a
picture of a picnic basket, suitcase, and toy box.
Tell story about going to Grandma's house for
Thanksgiving. Ask players what they should take.
As players list items, they should also indicate
where the items should be packed. Write names of
items under appropriate container.

4. TODAY AND YESTERDAY: Display two pictures of Thanksgiving feasts--one of today
and one of the first Thanksgiving. Discuss the following:
   A. How are the dinners alike? How are they different?
   B. What foods did the Pilgrims eat? What foods do you eat on Thanksgiving?
   C. Discuss different eating utensils. Pilgrims ate with hands or wooden
      spoons instead of silverware. They also used mugs instead of glasses.
   D. Which are the Indians? Which are the Pilgrims?
   E. Did the Indians and Pilgrims dress differently? How did they dress?
   F. Who comes to Thanksgiving dinner at your house?
   G. For what were the Pilgrims thankful? For what are you thankful?

5. PILGRIMS: Discuss the following:
   A. Pilgrims came to America because they wanted to live as they desired
      which they could not do in England.
   B. They sailed across the sea in a ship called the Mayflower. This trip
      took a long time (approximately three months).
   C. When they landed in America, there were no homes or stores so they had to
      build shelters and grow their own food.
   D. Pilgrims had the first Thanksgiving dinner to give thanks for their
      bountiful harvest which consisted of corn, barley, pumpkins, beans,
      squash, sweet potatoes, apples, maple syrup, wild fruit, and berries.

6. COOPERATION OF INDIANS AND PILGRIMS: Discuss cooperation and sharing. Explain that the Pilgrims and Indians helped one another.
    A. The Indians gave Pilgrims their corn because the corn the Pilgrims brought from England would not thrive in America.
    B. Indians taught the Pilgrims how to grow food, cultivate the land, hunt, and find fishing places.
    C. Both contributed to the first Thanksgiving feast.

7. HUNTING: Name animals the Indians and Pilgrims hunted. Examples are beaver, bear, deer, moose, elk, geese, ducks, turkeys, and buffalo. Indians used skins for clothing, blankets, shelter, and moccasins. Do members of your family hunt today? What animals do they hunt? Share experiences about hunting.

8. AMERICAN INDIAN: Discuss the following:
    A. Indians lived in America many centuries before white men first came.
    B. Columbus called Indians this name because he thought he reached India.
    C. Indians believed that land belonged to everyone. Indians respected the earth and believed in maintaining a balance in nature.
    D. There are many tribes of Indians who had different life styles, customs, and languages.
    E. Indians are known for the many beautiful things they make. Examples are jewelry, pottery, rugs, blankets, baskets, and sand paintings.

9. INDIAN HOMES: Discuss the fact that the geographic placement of Indians influenced their life styles and living environments.
    A. Plains Indians lived in traditional teepees which could be moved easily as they followed the large herds of buffalo that grazed on the plains.
    B. Eastern Woodland Indians lived in areas that were wooded. Their homes were made of tree bark and were called longhouses. Five to twenty families lived in one longhouse.
    C. Southwest Indians lived in an area where it was hot, dry, and few trees grew. They built large community homes called pueblos which were made from sun-dried bricks.
    D. Pacific Northwest Indians lived in forests, on the coast, and near rivers. These Indians were whalers, fishermen, and hunters.

10. VOCABULARY:
    A. GOD'S EYE (Pueblo)--a sacred decoration which represented the "eye of God" that brought good fortune, luck, health, and long life
    B. HOMINY (Algonguian)--food prepared by hulling kernels of maize
    C. *KACHINA* DOLL (Hopi *Katsina*)--small wooden doll representing a spirit
    D. MAIZE (Spanish)--Indian corn
    E. MOCCASIN (Algonguian)--a soft heelless shoe
    F. PAPOOSE (American Indian)--infant
    G. SQUAW (Algonguian)--American Indian woman
    H. SUCCOTASH (American Indian *misickquatash*)--beans and kernels of sweet corn cooked together
    I. TEEPEE (Dakota)--tent used by most of the tribes of the Great Plains
    J. TOBOGGAN (Algonguian)--a long, flat-bottomed seat
    K. TOTEM POLE (Algonguian *ototeman*)--a pole or post carved and painted with totems symbolic of a family or clan
    L. TRAVOIS (Canadian French)--platform mounted on trailing poles for bearing a load
    M. WAMPUM (Algonguian *wampumpeage*)--small beads made of shells and used by Indians for money and ornaments

11. INDIAN PICTOGRAPHS: Indians wrote with pictographs. Display examples and guess what symbols denote.

hunt   morning   noon   evening

teepee   campfire   rain

deer   bird tracks   river

look   man   woman   mountain

hear   horse tracks   talk together

12. SIGN LANGUAGE: There are more than 600 Indian dialects. Indians of the Great Plains developed sign language for easy communication. Teach children simple sign language.
    A. I: Touch side of eye with right index finger.
    B. YOU: With right index finger, point to person.
    C. HAVE: Hold right fist in front of neck with thumb up. Move fist forward turning wrist so thumb points to person you wish to indicate.
    D. GOOD: Place right hand with palm towards floor at left breast. Keep arm horizontal and move hand away from body, swinging upward.
    E. DAY: Fold arms in front of chest with right arm on top of left. Raise both hands until fingers point upward.
    F. SUNRISE: Hold right hand at center of body. Form semicircle with index finger and thumb. Raise it even with shoulders.
    G. GOOD MORNING: Do signs for SUNRISE, DAY, and GOOD.
    H. COME: Curve right index finger and motion toward body.
    I. SIT: Place right fist over left fist. Lower fists in a quick motion.
    J. THANK YOU: Hold both hands shoulder high, palms facing outward. Bring hands down pointing toward the person you are thanking.

GAMES AND SOCIAL ACTIVITIES

1. PLEASE, THANK YOU, YOU'RE WELCOME: Discuss that Thanksgiving is a special time to give thanks and to be polite. Practice being polite. One child has an object. Adult selects another child who asks the first child for the object using, "please" and "thank you." First child gives second child the object and says, "You're welcome." Continue until all have had a turn.

2. FLYING FOOD SAUCERS: Cut pictures of food from magazines or garden catalogs. Paste pictures on center of paper plates making sets of two plates which have the same food. Sail the paper plates into the air. One player is chosen to be Food Taster, who walks into the array of plates and selects one plate. Food Taster tells what food is on the plate and chooses someone to find the matching "flying food saucer." Repeat until all plates are matched.
   Variations:
    A. With larger groups, the Food Taster can select two or three plates with different pictures of food so several children can play at one time.
    B. Instead of food, use shapes, colors, or numbers.

3. FEAST: Place several kinds of food on a plate. Use plastic food or pictures of food. First player pretends to eat food, removing one item of food at a time. Replace food on plate and choose child to remove food in same order. Repeat game until all have had a turn.

4. TURKEY CHASE: Sit in circle. Use two balls, the first to indicate the turkey and second to signify the farmer. Different-colored balls can be used. First ball is passed around the circle as fast as possible. Shortly after, start second ball around circle in same direction. The object of the game is to make the second ball overtake the first.

5. TURKEYS AND HUNTERS: Divide players into two groups. One group pretends to be hunters. The other group pretends to be turkeys. Hunters are in the woods. They hunt and finally fall asleep. Only one hunter remains awake to watch for turkeys. The turkeys, who have been hiding in trees (designated place), creep from their hiding places. As they approach, the hunters awaken and chase the turkeys back to their trees. Turkeys that are caught become hunters.

6. INDIAN TOSSING GAME: Use six walnuts. Paint each nut a different color. Toss nuts into can or box from designated distance established according to ability of player. Player identifies color before throwing each walnut. Repeat with a different player tossing the nuts.

7. PASS THE STONE: Two teams of Indians sit on floor in lines facing each other. Members of one team cover their hands with a blanket. While adult beats a drum, the team passes a stone from one Indian to the next under the blanket. When adult stops beating drum, players stop passing the stone. Adult chooses a member of the opposite team to guess which player has stone. If he guesses correctly, his team receives stone and blanket. The game is repeated.

8. INDIAN GUESSING GAME: Use two identical sticks. Mark end of one stick. Hold one stick in each hand. Place hands behind back and shuffle sticks. Bring hands to front of body, covering marked end with hand. Another player tries to guess which stick has the mark.
Note: Indians used two identical pieces of bone to play this game of chance.

9. SIGN LANGUAGE GAME: Sit in circle. One player in center of circle motions with hand for another player to come to center of circle. Two players shake hands, and the first player leaves center of circle. Repeat until all players have had a turn.
Note: There seems to be a fascination for the fact that the entire game is played silently.

10. THANKSGIVING FEAST: Invite parents. Each family contributes one food traditionally served at family gatherings, from ethnic or religious background, or on the first Thanksgiving. During meal, each family shares history of dish. For place cards, decorate TOTEM POLES (Variation B from page 36). Write name on each totem pole. For centerpiece use PINE CONE TURKEY or CORNUCOPIA filled with CLAY FRUIT (see page 34). Pretend it's the first Thanksgiving.

11. PILGRIM AND INDIAN DWELLINGS: (Group project) Create following:
    A. INDIAN PUEBLO: Gather different-sized boxes and arrange like an Indian pueblo on piece of plywood. Cover boxes with thin, brown, salt clay. Use toothpicks or twigs for ladders and outlines of doors and windows.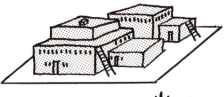
    B. BIRCH BARK TEEPEE: Cut large circle from brown paper bag. Glue white crepe paper over circle. Draw lines on circle with brown felt-tipped pen for bark markings. Remove wedge from edge of circle. Roll into cone and tape. Glue three toothpicks to top of cone.
    C. INDIAN LONGHOUSE: Cover shoe box with "birch bark" paper described above. Invert box and cut door from side.
    D. LOG CABIN: To create flat surface, depress and tape top of one-half gallon milk carton. Lay carton on its side. Glue long pretzel sticks to long sides of carton. Cover small ends with brown paper. Fold piece of brown paper in half and tape to carton for roof.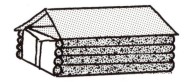

CREATIVE DRAMATICS AND MOVEMENT

1. SHOPPING FOR THANKSGIVING DINNER: Use empty food boxes, egg cartons, milk cartons, and margarine tubs. Place items on shelves or table. Child chosen as store owner can wear apron and operate toy cash register. Remaining children pretend to shop using play money. Store owner places purchased food in grocery bags.
Variation: Instead of cash register, use muffin tin or box with attached lid.

2. POPCORN: Pretend to be a small round kernel of popcorn with a little water inside. You are placed in a popcorn popper. You are becoming hotter and hotter. The water inside starts to expand. Finally you POP into a fluffy popcorn which bounces up and down.

3. CORNMEAL PLAY DOUGH: Mix 2 1/2 cups flour with 1 cup cornmeal. Add 1 tablespoon oil and 1 cup water. More or less water can be added to make desired texture. Dough has a grainy texture. Use for "pretend" baking and cooking.

4. TURKEY WADDLE: Trace and cut along outline of turkey. Cut out the two small circles. Place first two fingers through the holes. Make turkey waddle and say, "gobble, gobble." Allow time for creative play with turkey.

5. MAYFLOWER MODEL: Build a model of a ship with large blocks, planks, and boxes. Use this model to re-create the voyage of the Mayflower to America.
Variation: Wooden rocking boat can be used as ship.

6. PILGRIM AND INDIAN ROLE PLAYING: Divide group into Pilgrims and Indians. Indians dress in INDIAN JACKETS and accessories (see page 35). Pilgrims dress in hats and collars listed below. Dramatize the first Thanksgiving.

   A. PILGRIM HAT: From blue construction paper cut a 12" circle. Cut along dotted lines leaving brim and top of hat as shown in diagram. Fold top of hat forward along dotted line. To make buckle, fold 3" square of yellow paper in half. Cut a rectangle from the fold leaving an edge 1/2" in width. Open and glue buckle to hat above fold.

   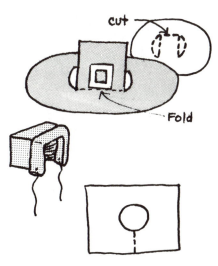

   B. BONNET: Remove top two-thirds of large paper bag. Cut one narrow side from bag. Fold bottom and sides of bag several times to form cuff. Punch a hole in each side of bonnet. Tie ribbons or string through holes.

   C. PILGRIM COLLAR: Use rectangular piece of white paper. From center, remove circle that is diameter of neck. Cut to hole from edge of paper beginning at middle of long side. Slip collar over head.

7. PILGRIMS AND INDIANS: Pretend to be Pilgrims sailing on the Mayflower. It takes a long time to cross the ocean. How does it feel to be on a ship? What do you do while on the ship? Oh, there's land! Pretend to row to land in small boats. What must you do to live on this land since there are no homes or stores? The Indians help. They show you how to plant, fish, and hunt. What do you hunt? What do you plant? Now it's autumn and it's time to harvest all the vegetables. Prepare a feast. What will you have? Invite your Indian friends who have helped you.

8. LOG CABIN OR INDIAN PUEBLO: Use large appliance box for log cabin or Indian pueblo. Allow time for creative play.

9. CLASSROOM TEEPEE: Color or paint Indian designs or symbols on an old sheet. Tape a hula hoop to floor. Run strings from hoop to bent coat hanger hanging from ceiling. Cover with sheet. Use completed teepee to inspire impromptu play. Teepee can also be used as special area for Indian stories, poems, or songs.
    Variation: Place sheet over table for teepee.

10. SIGN LANGUAGE: One player pantomimes a simple word with his hands. Examples are big, small, walk, run, moon, look, square, round, and bounce. Other players guess the word.
    Variation: Each child draws an Indian symbol on one section of a large piece of paper. When symbols are completed, place the paper on the wall. Each child can then tell about his picture.

PHYSICAL DEVELOPMENT

1. OVER THE RIVER: Place two strings parallel on floor approximately one foot apart. Pretend this is the river which must be crossed to reach Grandma's house for Thanksgiving dinner. Object is to jump across the "river" without falling into the "water" (stepping between the strings). Place strings farther and farther apart.

2. TURKEY FEATHER BLOW: Use a straw to blow feather around room.
    Variations:
    A. Place a line on the floor with masking tape. Blow feather along line.
    B. Have a relay race blowing the feather.

3. SAILING ON MAYFLOWER: (Tune--"Row, Row, Row Your Boat")
    Sail, sail, sail the Mayflower
    Slowly across the sea.
    Merrily, merrily, merrily, merrily
    Pilgrims now are free.
    Two children sit facing one another. Partners hold hands, bend knees, and press against each other's feet. Rock back and forth while singing verse.

4. BUFFALO HUNT: Explain that the Plains Indians rode horses to hunt for buffalo. Gallop by stepping forward on one foot and bringing other foot beside it. The same foot always steps forward while the other foot follows but never passes it. Practice galloping around the room or outside.

5. INDIAN JUMP-TO-BEAT: Place two broomsticks on floor. Children form line on one side of sticks. An adult sits at each end of the sticks, holding a stick in each hand. They steadily beat sticks on floor in unison, making each fourth beat louder. First child jumps into center of sticks on fourth beat. Child then jumps to opposite side on next fourth beat. Continue with next child in line until all have had a turn.

6. SIT INDIAN-STYLE: Sit with arms and legs crossed. Try to stand without uncrossing arms or legs.

7. INDIAN STICK GAME: Tie a knot in one end of a string that is 16" long. Thread string through small hole poked in bottom of a paper cup so knot is inside cup. Tie other end of string to end of a straight stick that is approximately one foot in length. Player holds opposite end of stick, swings cup, and attempts to catch it on the top of the stick.
Note: Indians used a cup made from wood or bark.

8. INDIAN HOOP GAME: Make a circle with masking tape, a rope, or use a hula hoop. Player stands a designated distance from circle with back to hoop. Sticks that are a little shorter than the diameter of the hoop are tossed over shoulder. Object is to land sticks inside the hoop.
Note: Indians made a hoop by bending a green stick. They notched and tied the ends of the stick together.

MATH

1. SETTING THANKSGIVING TABLE: Count number of people to attend Thanksgiving feast. Set table while counting number of glasses, napkins, plates, and silverware needed. Provide too many of one item. Count number of extra items. Provide too few of another item. Ask how many additional items are needed.

2. POPCORN NUMBER CHART: Make a number chart with the numerals clearly written. Glue corresponding number of popped popcorn beside each number.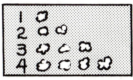

3. SORTING POPCORN: Make popped corn different colors. (Refer to POPCORN COLLAGE on page 33.) Combine popped corn. Child categorizes popcorn by colors.

4. TO GRANDMA'S HOUSE: Make a path to Grandma's house. The road should be approximately 1" wide and divided into 1" sections. To make a spin card, divide a 6" cardboard square into four sections by drawing two lines from corner to corner. Write one number from 1 to 4 in each section. For pointer, cut one end of a 3" x 1" piece of cardboard to a point. Make a hole 1/2" from straight end of pointer. Push a paper fastener through the hole and through a hole in the center of the cardboard square. Take turns spinning to determine how many sections to advance. Use large buttons for markers. Object is to reach Grandma's house.
Variation: Color each section of road with red, blue, or yellow. Make spin card using primary colors. Player spins and moves to matching color on road.

5. MATCHING FEATHERS: Hang paper turkey without tail feathers on wall. Make tail feathers by cutting pairs of large matching feathers from sample wallpaper books. Place one of each pair on wall for turkey's tail. Place remaining feathers in a box. Each child draws a feather from box and matches it to corresponding feather on turkey. Discuss colors and patterns in wallpaper.

6. FEATHER COUNT: Explain that an Indian was given a feather for each achievement he attained. Tape feathers to construction paper headband while telling of one Indian's achievements. Count number of feathers. For example: "Squanto did three brave deeds on Monday (add three feathers to band) and one on Tuesday (add one feather to band). How many feathers does he have?

7. STRINGING BEADS: Make card to indicate sequence for stringing beads or colored spools. Cards can be laminated for protection. String beads to match sequence. Beads can be strung by matching color, shape, or both. Increase number of beads on card according to stringer's ability.

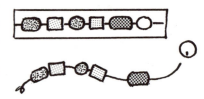

8. TACTILE NUMBERS: Adult draws outline of large-sized number on paper. Make number 1" wide. Child paints number with glue. Sprinkle with cornmeal, sand, or aquarium gravel. Remove excess. Repeat with different number.
Variation: Refer to SAND NUMBERS AND SHAPES (see page 179).

9. INDIAN NUMBER GAME: Color one side of a popsicle stick. Drop popsicle stick on ground. If colored side lands upward, a bead or uncooked macaroni is received. If uncolored side is upward, nothing is received. At end of game, count number of beads received. Stick and beads can be kept in a small plastic tube with lid so that game can be carried and played anywhere.

10. INDIAN CHERRY STONE GAME: Use six cherry or plum stones. Paint one side of each stone black and the other side white. Put stones in a bowl or box and shake. Count number of black sides showing. Repeat.

SCIENCE

1. BUTTER TASTE TEST: Compare taste and color of purchased butter with home-made butter. (Refer to CRACKERS AND BUTTER on page 36.) Explain that salt and food coloring have been added to the purchased butter. Add salt and yellow food coloring to home-made butter. Taste and compare again.

2. CORNMEAL PLAY: Place cornmeal in shallow waterplay containers. Use plastic containers, spoons, and measuring cups for pouring and measuring. Place newspapers on floor and under containers for easy clean-up.

3. CORN: Display ears of Indian corn, field corn, and popcorn. Discuss differences. Indians liked bright colors and so they preferred Indian corn. Corn is America's oldest and largest crop. Corn is a plant that grows on a stalk. Each kernel of corn has a strand of silk attached to it to make it grow. Show pictures of cornstalk. Shuck ear of corn. Contrast corn that has been popped, creamed, canned, frozen, and made into cornmeal. Explain that Indians ground corn to make cornmeal. Pop popcorn and eat it for snack. Indians made popcorn for Pilgrim children in earthen jars over fire. They served the popcorn with maple syrup.

4. TURKEY: Display pictures of a wild and a domestic turkey. Discuss that turkeys are large birds. There are both wild and domestic turkeys. Wild turkeys are greenish bronze in color. Wild turkeys fly and sleep in trees. Pilgrims hunted wild turkeys for their Thanksgiving feast. A turkey's head and neck are bare. The red skin hanging from a Turkey's neck is called a wattle. Turkeys eat insects, seeds, berries, and tender plants. Discuss the sound a turkey makes.

5. WISHY WISHBONE: Place a wishbone in a bottle. Pour some vinegar in the bottle covering the wishbone. Leave the wishbone in the bottle for 24 hours. Remove the bone. It will feel and bend just like rubber.
Note: The calcium in the bone is chemically changed by the acid in the vinegar. In its new form the calcium is not rigid but flexible.

48

6. ANIMAL, BIRD, OR FISH: Mount three envelopes on large piece of cardboard.
Glue picture on each envelope to designate category. Provide pictures of
animals, birds, or fish. Sort into proper categories.

7. BARK ON TREES: Discuss that the bark of a tree is its outer covering on the
trunk and stems. Different trees can be distinguished by their bark. Bark was
used by the Indians for homes, canoes, and drums. Compare bark on different
trees.

MUSIC

1. IF YOU'RE THANKFUL: (Tune--"If You're Happy and You Know It")
      If you're thankful and you know it, clap your hands.
      If you're thankful and you know it, clap your hands.
      If you're thankful and you know it, then your face will surely show it.
      If you're thankful and you know it, clap your hands.
Variation: In place of "clap your hands," use: stomp your feet, turn around,
or shout hooray.

2. JOHNNY APPLESEED: (Words by Frances Frost)
      The Lord's been good to me.
      And so I thank the Lord
      For giving me the things I need:
      The wind, and the rain, and the appleseed.
      The Lord's been good to me.

3. THANKSGIVING DAY: (Traditional song written by Lydia Maria Child)
      Over the river and through the wood, to Grandfather's house we go;
      The horse knows the way to carry the sleigh through the white and drifted
      snow.
      Over the river and through the wood, oh, how the wind does blow!
      It stings the toes and bites the nose as over the ground we go.
      Over the river and through the wood, to have a first-rate play;
      Hear the bells ring, "Ting-a-ling-ling!" Hurray for Thanksgiving Day!
      Over the river and through the wood, trot fast my dapple gray!
      Spring over the ground like a hunting hound, for this is Thanksgiving
      Day.
      Over the river and through the wood, and straight through the barnyard
      gate,
      We seem to go extremely slow: it is so hard to wait!
      Over the river and through the wood, now Grandmother's cap I spy!
      Hurray for the fun! Is the pudding done? Hurray for the pumpkin pie!

4. POPCORN SONG: (Tune--"I'm a Little Teapot")
      I'm a little popcorn in a pot,
      Heat me up and watch me pop.
      When I get all fat and white, then I'm done,
      Popping corn is lots of fun.
                          Clare Cherry

5. TURKEY GOBBLE: (Tune--"London Bridge")
      The turkey talks, "Gobble, gobble,
      Gobble, gobble, gobble, gobble."
      The turkey walks, wobble, wobble,
      All day long.

6. MR. TURKEY: (Tune--"Brownie Smile")
   "Where is Mr. Turkey?"
   I thought while at play.
   I guess he's in the barnyard,
   Behind the stack of hay.
   "Gobble, gobble, gobble," I can hear him say,
   "I won't come out till after Thanksgiving Day!"

7. BEAT THE TOM-TOM: Listen and move to the beat of the drum in the following ways:
  A. Walk to a slow steady beat.
  B. Run to a fast steady beat.
  C. Skip to a long beat followed by a short beat.

8. INDIAN DANCE: Dance to drum beat which is four steady beats with the last beat emphasized. For example: boom, boom, boom, BOOM. On the first beat move right foot up and tap it on floor. Repeat with second and third beats. On fourth beat, bring right foot flat on floor. Repeat alternating feet.

9. INDIANS LIKE TO BEAT THEIR TOM-TOMS: (Tune--"Ten Little Indians")
   Indians like to beat their tom-toms.
   Indians like to beat their tom-toms.
   Indians like to beat their tom-toms.
   Ten little Indian boys and girls.
Variations: In place of "beat their tom-toms," use:
  A. Ride their ponies.
  B. Go hunting.
  C. Substitute suggestions from singers.

10. WALK AND HOP: (Tune--"Ten Little Indians")
   Walk and hop and walk and hop now.
   Walk and hop and walk and hop now.
   Walk and hop and walk and hop now.
   Ten little Indian boys and girls.
Variations:
  A. Hop on one foot then the other.
  B. Lift one foot then the other.
          Clare Cherry

11. RECORD: "Things I'm Thankful For" from *Holiday Songs and Rhythms* by Hap Palmer Educational Activities, Inc., Box 392, Freeport, New York 11520.

F IELD TRIPS

1. TURKEY FARM
2. POTTERY STUDIO
3. INDIAN SITE OR MUSEUM WITH INDIAN ARTIFACTS
4. VISIT FROM AMERICAN INDIAN IN AUTHENTIC INDIAN DRESS

CHRISTMAS

CHRISTMAS, celebrated by Christians throughout the world, commemorates the birth of Jesus Christ nearly 2000 years ago. The word "Christmas" is derived from the English term *Christes masse*, meaning Christ's Mass. There are many different Christmas traditions and customs throughout the world. Many of these customs have pagan origins, but for people everywhere Christmas is a season of joy and a time for giving to others.

American customs come from many places. Santa Claus has a Dutch origin and was developed from a real person, St. Nicholas. St. Nicholas, the patron saint of school boys, would bring gifts to the children. The idea that Santa Claus comes down the chimney originated in Norway, where children hung their stockings on the mantel. When pagans of Northern Europe became Christians, they incorporated their sacred evergreens in the celebration by decorating the trees with nuts and candles. They sang Christmas carols while dancing around the Christmas tree.

CONCEPTS TO BE TAUGHT

1. Christmas Day is celebrated on December 25.
2. Christmas is the day Christians celebrate the birth of Jesus Christ.
3. Symbols include Christmas trees, wreaths, holly, candles, bells, stars, sleighs, stockings, reindeer, elves, and Santa Claus.
4. Colors used at Christmas are red and green.
5. Traditional Christmas activities include caroling, making and giving gifts, sending cards to family and friends, and enjoying festive dinners and parties.

ART ACTIVITIES

1. FIRST CHRISTMAS: With chalk draw picture of the first Christmas. Dip chalk into water before drawing to make colors more brilliant.

2. BABY JESUS IN MANGER: Make manger by pushing thumb into center of 2" ball of baking clay. (For baking clay, refer to CLAY ORNAMENTS on page 53.) To make baby, roll 1" clay ball into cylinder shape. Pinch clay one-third from end, forming neck. Bake items in 300° oven for 20 to 30 minutes until dry. Place dry grass in manger for hay. Lay baby in manger.

3. WHAT CAN I GIVE FOR CHRISTMAS? Cut pictures of Christmas gifts for a family member from old catalogs. Glue gifts onto precut paper stockings.

4. TUBE SANTA: Create Santa by gluing red paper, white yarn, and cotton onto cardboard tube.

5. CONE SANTA: Cut half-circle from red construction
paper. To make cone, overlap corners A and B.
Staple. Draw face near pointed end. Glue a circle
of cotton around face. Attach cotton ball to tip of
cone.

6. CHRISTMAS STOCKING: Cut large red stocking from construction paper. Provide a
variety of materials to decorate stocking. Examples are cotton balls, colored
popped corn, macaroni, cereal, glitter, crayons, and felt-tipped pens.
Variation: Add a few drops of food coloring to salt. Shake. Moisten stocking
with water. Sprinkle colored salt over stocking. Remove excess.

7. LIGHTING THE TREE: Cut a tree from construction paper. Use a cotton-tipped
swab to dab glue on tree. Sprinkle glitter on tree. Remove excess glitter.

8. CHRISTMAS TREE: Cut two identical triangles from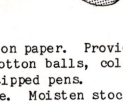
green construction paper. Slit one triangle from
bottom to center and the other from point to center.
Glue onto triangles any of the following: gummed
stars, sequins, felt pieces, rickrack, or small
pictures. Slide two slits together and tree will
stand.

9. 3-D TREE: Cut paper towel tubes into 1" rings.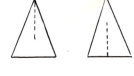
Glue rings together in a tree shape. Paint tree
green.

10. MACARONI WREATH: Cut hole in center of paper plate. Glue different shapes of
macaroni onto ring of plate. Cover with gold or green spray paint.
Variation: Instead of macaroni use peach pits, small pinecones, half walnut
shells, dried weeds, and flowers. Attach evergreen sprigs or crepe paper bow.

11. CANDLE: Color, paint, or cover with aluminum foil a
cardboard tube and a small paper plate. Glue con-
struction paper flame to one end of tube. Apply
glue to other end of tube and stand tube in center
of plate. Allow to dry.
Variation: Glue several tubes onto cardboard strip.

12. ANGEL: Make face on end of white cardboard tube.
Fold piece of white paper and cut wings from fold.
Open paper and glue wings to tube. Make halo by
bending one end of pipe cleaner into circle. Bend
circle forward. Attach other end to top of tube.
Variations:
    A. Use white construction paper triangle instead of tube.
    B. For wings, trace around hands. Cut.
    C. For wings, fold cupcake liner in half and glue onto tube.

CHRISTMAS TREE ORNAMENTS:

13. HANGERS for ornaments listed on following pages:
    A. Use metal ornament hook.
    B. Open paper clip into S-shape.
    C. Thread yarn, ribbon, or string through hole in ornament. Tie ends to-
       gether to make loop.
    D. Bend pipe cleaner into S-shaped hook.

14. CONSTRUCTION PAPER ORNAMENT: Cut Christmas shape from construction paper or Christmas card. Punch hole in top and attach hanger. Decorate with glitter.

15. PINE CONE ORNAMENT: Place small amount of white tempera in shallow container. Roll pine cone in paint to cover tips of cone. Allow to dry. Wrap pipe cleaner around cone. Make hook with other end of pipe cleaner.

16. ALUMINUM ORNAMENTS: Use aluminum foil cake pans, pie plates, or aluminum frozen food containers for following ornaments.
    A. Draw design on aluminum. Cut out design. Punch hole in top and attach hanger.
       Variation: Punch holes in ornament with paper punch to create interesting lighting effect.
    B. Cut 1" x 6" strip from aluminum. Wrap strip around pencil and remove pencil. Punch hole in end of foil and attach hanger.
    C. Draw spiral on aluminum. Cut along line. Punch hole in one end and attach hanger.

    D. Cut circle or free-form shape from aluminum. Fringe edge of shape. Bend alternate sections of edge forward and backward.

17. SATELLITE: Crush aluminum foil into ball. Stick colored toothpicks through ball.

18. CLAY ORNAMENTS: For following ornaments use uncolored baking clay (2 cups flour, 1 cup salt, and water to desired consistency). Place ornaments on shallow baking sheet and bake at 300° for 20 to 30 minutes until dry.
    A. To make candy cane, roll clay into long rope. Curve one end. When dry, paint red stripes on the cane. Tie red ribbon to cane, if desired.
    B. To make dangling beads, form clay into balls. Use pencil for making holes through center of balls. When dry, tie one ball to end of string. Wrap tape around other end of string to make needle. Thread 2 to 4 additional balls. Remove tape and tie string to HANGER (see page 52).
    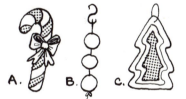
    C. Roll clay to 1/8" thickness. Cut out shape with cookie cutter. Poke hole in top before baking so that string can be threaded through hole. When dry, decorate with glitter or paint.
    D. Create free-form decoration. Poke hole in top before baking. Paint when dry.

19. BELL: Invert paper or styrofoam cup. Glue rickrack, gummed stars, small pieces of felt, or small pictures onto cup. Poke two holes in center top of bell. Thread string through holes and tie ends to make loop.
    Variations:
    A. Attach jingle bell by placing bell in center of string that is 10" long. Place two ends of string together and tie a knot 2" above bell. Poke two holes in top of cup and thread loose ends of string through holes. Tie knot in string close to cup. Tie ends of string to make loop.

    B. Cover cup with aluminum foil.
    C. Paint egg carton cup for bell.

20. CANDY CANE: Cut 9" square from white paper. With
    red crayon, draw lines according to diagram. Roll
    into tube starting at A. Tape B to center of tube.
    Roll one end around pencil. Remove pencil.

21. PIPE CLEANER ORNAMENT: Create ornament by twisting together different-colored
    pipe cleaners.

22. WREATH: Dip rigatoni in water mixed with food col-
    oring. Dry on waxed paper. String 3 to 5 rigatoni
    with curling ribbon. Tie strands together and curl
    ribbon by pulling ends over blade of scissors.
    Variation: String uncolored rigatoni. Spray with
    silver or gold paint after stringing.

23. CHAINS:
    A. Cut 1" strips from brightly colored pictures in magazines. Glue one
       strip into circle. Thread another strip through circle, overlap ends,
       and glue. Continue interlocking circles to make chain.
    B. String popped corn, cranberries, cereal, colored rigatoni, styrofoam
       packing, or pieces of drinking straws to make garlands for tree.
    C. String colored cotton balls. To color cotton, place dry tempera and
       cotton balls in bag. Shake.
    D. Squeeze aluminum foil into long rope and hang on tree.

GIFTS:

24. CHRISTMAS CARD: Fold piece of construction paper in half to make card. Deco-
    rate front of card in the following ways:
    A. Cut picture from an old Christmas card. Glue it on card.
    B. Make collage from old Christmas cards. Glue onto doilies and then onto
       front of card.
    C. From front of card cut out shape of Christmas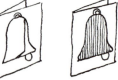
       tree, bell, or candy cane. With crayons or
       felt-tipped pens, color grooves of white cor-
       rugated paper. (Liners from potato chip cans
       can be used.) Glue corrugated cardboard to
       inside front of card.
    D. From front of card cut out shape for stained glass window. Glue pieces
       of colored tissue paper onto piece of paper. Glue paper to inside front
       of card.
    Child dictates as adult writes message inside card.

25. WRAPPING PAPER:
    A. Place two sheets of white tissue paper together. Fold many times until
       it is approximately 2" x 4". Dip corners into dishes of water that have
       been colored with food coloring. Carefully open and allow to dry on
       newspaper.
    B. Cut sponge in star shape. Attach sponge to spring clothespin. Dip
       sponge into paint. Block print onto tissue paper.
    C. Color or paint white tissue paper.

26. PLACEMATS: Cut red or green poster board into 12" x 18" pieces. Cut designs
    from old Christmas cards and arrange designs on the poster board. Glue and
    allow to dry. Cover each placemat with clear acrylic spray or laminate with
    clear self-adhesive plastic.

27. NAPKIN RINGS: Cut 1" sections from cardboard tubes. Glue precut felt strips over rings. Glue small bows or precut holly leaves to rings.
Variation: Cover rings with aluminum foil.

28. COASTERS: Place lid from margarine tub over old Christmas card. Try to center picture. Trace around outside of lid. Cut out circle. Glue circle from card to inside of lid. Cover with clear acrylic spray or laminate with clear self-adhesive plastic. Make several.
Variation: Use as an ornament by punching a hole in the top. Glue and sprinkle glitter around edge of lid, if desired. Attach HANGER (see page 52).

29. BATH SALTS: Fill baby food jar 3/4 full with Epsom salt. Add small amounts of perfume and food coloring. Secure lid and shake. Cover rim of lid with lace, ribbon, tape, or rickrack. Place gummed Christmas seal on top.

30. FELT PIN: Cut 4" tree from green felt. Glue small scraps of felt, fabric, or yarn to tree. Pin tree to shirt or blouse.

31. DRIED FLOWER TERRARIUM: Place small amount of modeling clay in lid of baby food jar. Arrange dried flowers and weeds with stems approximately 1" long in clay. Place baby food jar over dried arrangement and secure lid. Glue red ribbon around edge of lid.

32. PRETTY POT: Cut squares of fabric with pinking shears. Paste the fabric pieces on clay flower pot. Cover the entire pot. Shellac or cover with clear acrylic spray. Place small potted plant inside the pot.

33. SURPRISE BALL: Wrap yarn or crepe paper around a trinket. Continue to wrap until a large ball is formed. Secure end of paper or yarn with gummed star or tape.

34. POMANDER BALL: With a toothpick, poke holes into an orange, apple, lemon, or lime. Fruit should be ripe, firm, and unbruised. Press a clove into each hole until fruit is almost covered. Cut cheesecloth or nylon netting into a square large enough to wrap the fruit completely. Place fruit onto cloth. Sprinkle cinnamon over fruit. Enclose fruit in cloth and tie ribbon around cloth. Hang the ball. As the fruit dries, it shrinks, becomes lighter, and the sweet smell will develop and grow stronger. If the sweet smell becomes weak, sprinkle the ball lightly with water, and the smell will return.

35. CANDLE HOLDER: Use lid from spray can that has a small circular rim inside. Decorate lid by gluing rickrack, braid, or other trimmings to the outside. Place candle in rim.

36. STAINED GLASS CANDLE: Paint outside of baby food jar with liquid starch. Cover jar with various-colored pieces of tissue paper. Paint tissue paper with liquid starch. Allow to dry. Place a small purchased candle inside jar.
Note: For safety, paper should not extend beyond rim.

37. PHOTO PIN: Cut small circle from cardboard to fit snugly inside of bottle cap. Glue photo of child's face on outside of bottle cap. To wear, place cap on outside of shirt or blouse, put cardboard circle on underside of garment, and push into cap.
Variation: Glue magnet on inside of bottle cap and place on refrigerator or metal file cabinet.

38. GIFT CERTIFICATE: Child can do something for others as a special gift. Examples are giving hug every day, picking up playroom, or making a special art project. Draw picture of special gift. Adult writes at bottom of picture:
I (child's name) give you (description of gift).
Merry Christmas
(child's name)
Child can write or scribble name after Merry Christmas.

39. BATIK HANDKERCHIEF: Draw picture with crayon on white handkerchief. Iron handkerchief to set crayon.

40. DECORATIVE TISSUE BOX: Glue different shapes of macaroni to unopened tissue box. Do not glue on perforated section which is removable. Cover box with silver or gold spray paint. Allow to dry. Remove perforated section.

41. PET ROCK: Select a favorite rock. Rock can be left natural or painted to become a "designer rock." Place rock in a jar or box. If desired, child can dictate instructions about care of the rock to adult who writes information on card titled "How to Care for Pet Rock."
Variation: Rock can be given as a paper weight.

42. PENCIL HOLDER: Glue sample wallpaper pieces, rick-rack, yarn, and cloth scraps onto empty juice or soup can.
Variation: Decorate as a person by attaching felt or cloth strips for arms and legs. Make face on top part of can. Yarn can be used as hair.

43. YUMMY GIFT: Place GORP (see page 57) in baby food jar. Secure lid. Glue red ribbon around edge of lid.

COOKING ACTIVITIES

1. APPLE SANTA: Core apple. Cut apple into cross sections and dip into lemon juice. For face, place one section on lettuce leaf. Use one-fourth slice for hat. Decorate with raisins, grapes, pineapple chunks, dried fruit, flaked coconut, or cottage cheese.

2. APPLE STAR: Cut apple in half crosswise. Observe Christmas star formed by seeds. Cut apple into wedges and dip into peanut butter.

3. CHRISTMAS STAR SALAD: 5 pineapple tidbits
1/4 cup cottage cheese
lettuce leaf
On lettuce leaf, arrange tidbits in a circle with points outward to form a star. Spoon cottage cheese in center of tidbits.
Variations:
    A. Instead of pineapple tidbits, use round slice of cheese cut into wedges.
    B. Mix crushed pineapple with cottage cheese.
    C. Sprinkle cottage cheese with one tablespoon of blueberries.

4. ORANGE STRAW SIPS: Roll an orange on table until soft. Cut a small slit in orange. Insert a stiff straw. Drink natural juice. Cut orange into sections. Eat fiber.

5. HOLIDAY COOLER: 20 ounces unsweetened frozen strawberries
                     46 ounces pineapple juice
                     lime sherbet
Puree strawberries in blender. Combine in pitcher with pineapple juice. Pour into glass. Top with dollop of lime sherbet.

6. CHRISTMAS COCKTAIL: Serve tomato juice, hot or cold, with a dash of celery salt. For decoration, add celery stalk with leaves.

7. YUM YUM TREE: Attach with toothpicks to styrofoam cone any of the following: cherry tomatoes, strips of green pepper, unpeeled cucumber sections, unpeeled orange sections, or pineapple chunks. Eat with CHRISTMAS VEGETABLE DIP (listed below).
   Variations:
   A. Serve as kabob by skewering several of above on one toothpick.
   B. Instead of styrofoam cone, use half of peeled cucumber for base.

8. CHRISTMAS VEGETABLE DIP: 1 cup sour cream   10 ounces frozen chopped spinach
                            1 cup mayonnaise   1 package Knorr Vegetable Soupmix
Cook spinach according to package directions. Drain. Mix together with remaining ingredients. Chill. Serve with vegetables.

9. CHEESE BALL: 4 ounces Cheddar cheese   1 teaspoon Worcestershire sauce
                5 ounces Colby cheese   1/2 teaspoon cayenne pepper
                4 ounces cream cheese   chopped nuts
                8 ounces American cheese
Grate cheeses. Let stand at room temperature until soft. Mix together all ingredients except nuts. Form small individual balls. Roll in nuts.
Variation: Form one cheese log. Chill. Slice to serve.

10. CHRISTMAS RICE: Prepare rice according to box directions, substituting chicken broth for water. Add frozen peas to rice five minutes before it is cooked. Garnish with cherry tomatoes.

11. GORP: Mix together any of the following to make gorp: raisins, carob chips, unsalted nuts, cereal, and coconut flakes.

12. SANDWICH YULE LOG: Remove crust from slice of whole wheat bread. Flatten bread with rolling pin. Spread with favorite filling. Roll into log.

13. YULE LOG: 1 cup cereal (shredded wheat, granola)   1 tablespoon milk
              1 tablespoon honey   toasted wheat germ
              1 tablespoon peanut butter
Grind cereal in blender. Combine honey, peanut butter, and milk. Blend with cereal. Add milk as necessary to roll into log. Cover log with wheat germ. Refrigerate in covered container. Slice to serve.

14. SUGARPLUMS: 2 cups pitted prunes   1 tablespoon orange juice
                1 teaspoon grated orange rind   1/2 cup flaked coconut
Grind prunes. Add orange rind and juice. Form into walnut-sized balls. Roll balls in coconut. If mixture is too dry, add more juice.
   Variations:
   A. Instead of prunes, use one of the following dried fruits: apples, apricots, dates, raisins, figs, or any combination of the dried fruits.
   B. Instead of flaked coconut, roll balls in toasted wheat germ.

15. FUDGE: 1/2 cup honey   2 cups (total) mixture of chopped nuts,
           1/2 cup peanut butter   sunflower nuts, sesame seeds
           1/2 cup carob powder   1/2 cup flaked coconut
           1/2 cup raisins or dates
    Heat honey and peanut butter. Add carob. Stir. Remove from heat. Add re-
    maining ingredients. Pour into greased 8" x 8" pan. Refrigerate.

16. BROWNIES: 1/4 cup oil   1 cup wheat germ
               2/3 cup brown sugar   1/4 teaspoon baking powder
               2 teaspoons vanilla   1/4 cup carob
               2 eggs, beaten   1/4 cup sunflower nuts
               3/4 cup + 2 tablespoons nonfat dry milk granules
    Combine first four ingredients. Add dry ingredients, except nuts. Place in
    greased 8" x 8" pan. Sprinkle nuts on top. Bake at 350° for 25 to 30 minutes.
    Do not overbake.

17. STARDUST TREES: 1/3 cup honey   1/3 cup nonfat dry milk granules
                     3/4 cup peanut butter   2 1/2 cups 100% bran cereal
                     3 tablespoons margarine 3 tablespoons sesame seeds
    Combine first three ingredients. Blend well. Add milk and cereal. Stir.
    Press in bottom of 8" x 8" pan. Sprinkle with sesame seeds. Press seeds into
    surface. Chill one hour. Cut into triangles.
    Variation: Toasted sesame seeds can be used. Place seeds in non-stick pan.
    Stir constantly over medium heat until toasted.

FINGERPLAYS

1. The Christmas story we are living,
   Makes this a special time for giv-
     ing. (pretend to give)
   We give and do things for others:
     (point to others)
   For our father, mother, sisters,
     and brothers. (raise four fin-
     gers)
   What can I give? Let's see . . .
     (place finger on side of head)
   I can give a lot of ME! (point to
     self)

2. Two small hands that touch in
     prayer, (fold hands in prayer)
   A golden halo in her hair, (make
     circle above head with hands)
   On her back, two silver wings:
     (two fingers)
   Once each year my angel brings
   The Christmas story back to me
   While she rests upon my Christmas
     tree. (form triangle)
   "The Angel On My Christmas Tree" re-
   printed from *RHYMES FOR FINGERS
   AND FLANNELBOARDS* by L.B. Scott
   and J.J. Thompson, Copyright 1960,
   with permission of Webster/McGraw
   Hill.

3. On the very first Christmas night,
     (raise one finger)
   A wondrous star shone big and
     bright. (open and close fingers
     above head)
   It marked the spot where the Baby
     lay, (cradle arms)
   So kings and shepherds could come
     to pray. (fold hands in prayer)

4. What can I give Jesus, small as I
     am? (place finger on side of
     head)
   The shepherd gave Him a baby lamb.
   The wise men gave Him precious
     gold. (form circle)
   The angels sang of His glory un-
     told. (form circle above head)
   Mary and Joseph gave their loving
     care. (cradle arms)
   But what can I give? My heart to
     share! (place hand over heart)

5. Santa Claus is a chubby old elf
     (form large circle)
   Who slides down our small chimney
     in spite of himself. (lower body
     while wiggling)

6. Santa Claus is jolly and plump.
   (form large circle)
   He spreads joy--he's no grump.
   (shake head sideways)
   When he laughs, he "ho, ho, hos,"
   And says, "MERRY CHRISTMAS," wherever he goes.

7. Santa's sometimes called Kris
   Kringle.
   His merry eyes--oh how they twinkle. (point to blinking eyes)
   His nose and cheeks are red as a
   rose, (point to nose and cheeks)
   Which match all his bright red
   clothes. (point to clothes)
   Wearing a white beard and boots of
   black, (point to chin and feet)
   He's a jolly elf carrying his sack.
   (pretend to throw sack over
   shoulder)
   When he laughs, he "ho, ho, hos,"
   From the tip of his hat to the ends
   of his toes. (point to head and
   toes)

8. Jingle, jingle, jingle--there's
   excitement in the air. (pretend
   to ring bell)
   Jingle, jingle, jingle--Christmas
   time is here.
   Thump, thump, thump--I hear a reindeer hoof. (tap floor)
   Jump in bed, pull the covers high:
   (jump, cover eyes)
   Santa's on the roof!! (point upward)

9. When Santa comes to my house,
   (point to self)
   I'm always sound asleep. (lay head
   on hands with eyes closed)
   Oh, to be a little mouse
   So at him I could peek. (open one
   eye)

10. Here is the chimney. (make fist
    enclosing thumb)
    Here is the top. (place palm of
    other hand on fist)
    Open the lid, (quickly remove top
    hand)
    And out Santa will pop. (pop up
    thumb)

                    Author Unknown

11. Little elves help Santa make toys
    for girls and boys. (pretend to
    hammer)
    Dolls and trains and airplanes
    bring children many joys.
    (spread arms wide)
    Oh, to see the old North Pole be-
    fore the Christmas trip,
    Santa would be standing proud with
    hands upon his hips. (stand tall
    with hands on hips)

12. This little elf likes to hammer.
    (pretend to hammer)
    This little elf likes to saw.
    (pretend to saw)
    This little elf likes to splash on
    paint. (pretend to paint)
    This little elf likes to draw.
    (pretend to draw)
    This little elf likes best of all,
    To put the cry in the baby doll.
    Mama, mama.

                    Marguerite Gode

13. Five little bells hanging in the
    hall. (raise fingers)
    The first one said, "Ring me slow."
    The second one said, "Ring me
    fast."
    The third one said, "Ring me last."
    The fourth one said, "Ring me like
    a chime."
    The fifth one said, "Ring me at
    Christmas time."

                    Mary Jackson Ellis

14. Five Christmas stockings hanging in
    a row. (five fingers)
    When Santa comes--guess what?
    (place finger on side of head)
    They'll be filled from tip to toe!
    (point to head and toes)

15. There's a special present on the
    shelf.
    I made it with care and wrapped it
    myself. (pretend to make and
    wrap package)
    I'll take it home and put it under
    the tree. (form triangle with
    fingers)
    On Christmas Mom will open it and
    see (look surprised)
    That it contains a lot of love from
    me. (point to self)

16. There are many secrets at Christmas
time (place finger over mouth and
whisper)
Wrapped with pretty paper, ribbon,
and twine. (pretend to wrap)
They are hidden in closets out of
the way,
Marked, "Do not open till Christmas
Day." (shake finger sideways)

17. I wish Christmas would last and
last and last. (point to self)
It takes soooo long to come;
(spread arms and shake head sideways)
Then it's over so fast. (clap
hands)

18. My Christmas tree glistens bright
(form triangle)
With shiny balls and twinkling
lights. (open and close fingers)
At the very top is an angel in
flight, (circle over head)
Greeting people on a wintry night.
(shiver)

19. Come and trim our Christmas tree
(form triangle)
Till it glistens bright.
First we'll string some popcorn
chains, (pretend to decorate
tree)
Then some tinsel bright.
Now for color hang some balls (form
circle with hands)
And a twinkly light, (open and
close fingers)
So we can dance and sing
On a Merry Christmas night.
Marguerite Gode

20. A little Christmas tree, (make a
small triangle)
A bigger Christmas tree, (form a
larger triangle)
A great big Christmas tree, (make
large triangle with arms pointed)
Now let's count the trees:
One, two, three. (hold three fin-
gers)
Three trees I see.
Author Unknown

21. Outside there's a pine tree, standing straight and tall. (stand
tall)
It needs no decorations--nature's
done it all: (shake head sideways)
Pinecones on its branches with
icicles glistening bright, (extend arms sideways)
Snow upon its needles and birds at
rest from flight. (form wings
with arms)
I see it from my window and take
the time to say, (point to eyes)
"Thank you, Lord, for the beauty of
this Christmas Day."

22. Umm, the smell of Christmas is
everywhere I go: (point to nose)
Evergreens and holly and pretty
mistletoe, (form triangle with
fingers)
Gingerbread and cookies and fresh
pumpkin pie, (rub stomach)
Smoke is in the chimney, curling to
the sky. (raise finger with
circling motion.

23. I have a friend named Candy Cane.
(point to self and then form a
candy cane with fingers)
We go dancing down Sugarplum Lane.
(dance with fingers)
While we're doing the peppermint
twist, (twist hips)
We blow each other a candy kiss.
(blow a friend a kiss)

24. Little Jack Horner sat in a corner,
Eating his Christmas pie. (pretend
to eat)
He stuck in his thumb and pulled
out a plum (point thumb downward
and then upward)
And said, "What a good boy am I."
(point to self)
Traditional

25. Twinkle, twinkle, little stars,
(open and close fingers)
Santa comes tonight.
Twinkle, twinkle, little stars,
Make his journey bright!

LANGUAGE DEVELOPMENT

1. CHRISTMAS SYMBOLS: The following symbols can be used for discussion or with a Christmas calendar. To make calendar: Mount envelopes that are numbered from 1 to 25 on bulletin board. In each envelope, place a picture or small replica of one of the symbols below. A statement about the significance of that symbol can also be included. Make a tree which will be decorated with the symbols. On December 1, one child removes picture from envelope numbered 1 and places it on the tree. Adult then reads statement or has discussion about the symbol. Continue until December 25, when a picture of Baby Jesus is placed on the tree.

   A. CHRISTMAS COOKIES originated with pre-Christian Romans, who gave sweet cakes to their senators.

   B. MINCE PIE, full of spices and fruits, represents the choice and exotic treasures of the East.

   C. PLUM PUDDING was made by an English king who was stranded in a blizzard on Christmas Eve. He wanted a special holiday dish, so he mixed together all the edibles he had.

   D. WASSAIL is a salutation of "Be in health," or "Here's to you." It is a mixture of mulled eggs, curdled cream, apples, nuts, and spices. It was drunk from a bowl with much ceremony while exchanging Christmas greetings.

   E. HOLLY is a shrub with clusters of red berries and stiff, glossy, sharp-pointed leaves which remain green throughout the year. Ancient people thought its greenness was a promise the sun would return to earth another year. Early French and English people hung it over the door indicating a home in which Christ abided.

   F. MISTLETOE is a sprig of an evergreen plant hung at Christmas time. By custom, men can kiss women standing under it. A legend states that a girl who receives no kisses under the mistletoe by the end of the year will not marry in the new year.

   G. POINSETTIA is a flower brought to the United States by Dr. Poinsett, first minister to Mexico. In Mexico it was a wild, small, unimposing weed.

   H. EVERGREEN TREE was decorated by pagan people at the feast of the winter solstice. The evergreen was a sign that winter would end and warmth would return.

   I. CHRISTMAS TREE LIGHTS represent Christ as being the "Light of the World." Lights also represent stars. Candles were first used for lights.

   J. TINSEL are thin strips of metal foil. A legend tells that parents trimmed a tree while children were sleeping. Spiders who wanted to see the tree crept all over it, leaving cobwebs. The Christ Child came to bless the tree. He loved the spiders but knew the parents wouldn't feel the same. He touched the webs and they turned silver.

   K. ICICLES: An old story gives a reason for trimming trees with icicles. The Christ Child took shelter for the night under a pine tree. When the tree realized it was caring for the Christ Child, tears of happiness fell from its branches. They froze into icicles.

   L. CANDLES: Candlelight symbolizes the light that Jesus brought to earth.

   M. GIFTS: The source of this custom is Wise Men giving gifts to Baby Jesus.

   N. CARDS: For many years private notes of good wishes were sent at Christmas time. In 1843, Sir Henry Cole had artist John Horsley design a card especially for Christmas. One thousand copies were printed, and the custom of sending printed cards began.

   O. CHRISTMAS SEALS: A Danish postal clerk sold Christmas stamps to show that users had given to a worthy cause.

   P. CAROLING comes from Italian *"carolare,"* a medieval custom of singing and dancing around a Christmas tree. Early carols weren't sacred enough for singing inside a church so caroling was done outside.

1. CHRISTMAS SYMBOLS: (continued)
    Q. SAINT NICHOLAS was a generous and kind bishop who would bring presents to children and needy people.
    R. REINDEER was the animal chosen by St. Nick to pull his sleigh.
    S. STOCKING: St. Nick heard of a poor family that he wanted to help. In order to remain anonymous, he tossed gold down the chimney. It fell into a stocking that was hung there to dry.
    T. YULE LOG: Before the Christian era the English thought the sun stood still for 12 days at the end of the year. A log was cut that was large enough to burn throughout this period and burn away the last year's evil.
    U. BELLS: Church bells rang to announce the coming of Jesus.
    V. SHIPS: Some countries, separated by water from the Holy Land, adopted this symbol at Christmas to bring the story of Jesus' birth closer.
    W. ADVENT WREATH: Four candles are placed on a wreath. One candle is lit each Sunday before Christmas in anticipation of the arrival of Christ.
    X. CRÈCHE is a manger scene representing Jesus' place of birth.
    Y. JESUS: Christmas is the celebration of Jesus' birthday.
Variation: The following symbols can be substituted to explain the CRÈCHE:
    A. STAR: The Star of Bethlehem guided the Wise Men to Baby Jesus.
    B. ANGEL told the shepherds of the birth of Jesus.
    C. DONKEYS, LAMBS, AND COWS were humble beasts close to Jesus at his birth.
    D. CAMELS were animals the Wise Men rode when they visited Baby Jesus.
    E. THREE WISE MEN came to see Jesus bearing their best treasures: gold, a precious metal associated with the power of kings; frankincense, a resin from a rare and sacred tree used as incense; myrrh, a resin from a shrub used in making perfume.
    F. SHEPHERDS were the men who tended sheep and came to honor the Baby Jesus.
    G. COW'S MANGER is the place where Baby Jesus slept.
    H. JOSEPH is the husband of Mary.
    I. MARY is the mother of Jesus.
Note: The following can be used on December calendar after Christmas Day: STAR, ANGEL, CAMELS, THREE WISE MEN, AND SHEPHERDS.

2. FEELINGS AT CHRISTMAS TIME: During the Christmas season many feelings and emotions are experienced. Discuss:
    A. When do you feel excited? When do you feel happy?
    B. Why do you sometimes feel sad at Christmas? Do you miss people you love and cannot be with during the Christmas holidays?
    C. Are you ever jealous during the season?
    D. Do you become impatient during this season waiting for Christmas Day?

3. CHRISTMAS IS A TIME FOR GIVING and doing things for others. Discuss:
    A. What can be given at Christmas? Presents do not have to be purchased but can be made.
    B. Doing things for others is also an act of giving. Give examples.
    C. How does it feel when someone opens a present you've given them?
    D. The reason for giving is to show family and friends love and affection.
    E. The most important aspect of giving is the thought and not the present.
    F. Read and discuss *The Little Drummer Boy* by Ezra Jack Keats.

4. CHRISTMAS ACTIVITIES: Have children share personal experiences about things they do with their families at Christmas time.
    A. How does your family decorate your home for Christmas?
    B. What else does your family do to prepare for the holidays?
    C. When are presents exchanged? Where does Santa leave his presents?
    D. Where is Christmas dinner eaten and with whom?

5. HOLIDAY HELPERS:
    A. Discuss that many people work to make the holidays more pleasant. For
        example, postal workers deliver cards and packages.
    B. Survey parents and relatives to discover if their jobs change during the
        holidays. Include homemakers in the survey.
    C. Discuss ways children can make holidays a more pleasant time.
    D. Place large box in corner for Baby Jesus' manger. Place straw beside
        box. Explain that every time a child does a kind deed, he can place a
        handful of straw in the manger to "make Baby Jesus' bed more comfort-
        able."

6. LETTER TO SANTA: Children dictate to adult or write letter to Santa telling
    him what they want for Christmas.
    Variation: Call Santa on telephone.

7. BELLS: (Mabelle B. McGuire)
            Up in the tower there's a carillon of bells.
            Each of the eight a Christmas story tells.
            One bell tells of the star so bright
            That shone over Bethlehem that first Christmas night.
            Two bells tell of the two who sought
            Room in Bethlehem but found it not.
            Three bells tell of the Three Wise Men
            Who made a long journey to Bethlehem.
            Four bells tell of the innkeeper who said,
            "Use my manger for the Babe's bed."
            Five bells tell of the angels whose song
            Assured the shepherds nothing was wrong.
            Six bells tell of the shepherds who gazed
            At the beautiful Baby and were amazed.
            Seven bells tell of the doves that cooed
            A lullaby in that stable rude.
            Eight bells tell the story again
            Of how Jesus came to the world of men.
    This verse can be used as a flannel board story. Make eight bells and display
    at appropriate times. Discuss what the story means.

8. SANTA'S BAG: Use pillowcase, plastic trash bag, or paper sack for Santa's bag.
    Children are Santa's helpers. Each helper finds one item in the room to put in
    Santa's bag. Helpers return to circle with items selected. Each helper de-
    scribes the item he has and then places it in the bag. After all items are in
    the bag, helpers recall what is in Santa's bag. Remove the items as they are
    named. Items that are not mentioned can be described by an adult. Helpers
    then guess item that is described.

9. BOOKS:
    Christmas Is a Time for Giving--Anglund
    On Christmas Eve--Brown
    A Christmas Story--Chalmers
    Nine Days to Christmas--Ets
    How the Grinch Stole Christmas--Geisel
    Rudolph, the Red Nose Reindeer--Hayden
    The Animals' Merry Christmas--Jackson
    The Little Drummer Boy--Keats
    How Spider Saved Christmas--Kraus
    A Visit From St. Nicholas--Moore
    The Night Before Christmas--Moore
    The First Christmas--Trent

GAMES AND SOCIAL DEVELOPMENT

1. GUESS WHO: Adult describes a Christmas character, and children guess who it is. For example: "He is jolly, wears red and white clothes, and brings toys to girls and boys. Who is he?" Children answer, "Santa Claus."

2. DANCE AROUND THE CHRISTMAS TREE: (Tune--"Ring Around the Rosie")
   Dance around the Christmas tree,
   Bright with twinkling lights.
   Whirl around. Twirl around.
   All fall softly down.

Stand in circle. Hold hands and circle clockwise. Twirl and fall while saying appropriate lines.

3. SANTA, SANTA DOWN THE CHIMNEY: (Tune--"Bluebird, Bluebird Through My Window")
   Santa, Santa, down the chimney,
   Santa, Santa, down the chimney,
   Santa, Santa, down the chimney,
   To bring a special toy.

Stand in circle. Join hands and raise them in the air. One player is Santa. While group sings verse, Santa weaves around the players in the circle. When singing stops, Santa stands in front of child nearest him and sings, "What kind of toy do you want?" The child answers, "I want a (kind of toy)." All players then sing, "(child's name) wants a (kind of toy)." Child then becomes Santa, and the game is repeated.

4. WHAT IS IN THE CHRISTMAS PRESENT?
   What is in the Christmas present? (form fist)
   Something exciting, no doubt! (cover fist with other hand)
   I open the lid and a sound comes out! (adult creates sound when removing hand from fist)
   What is it?

Adult recites the verse. Sounds adult could make are "toot, toot" for horn; "varoom" for motor vehicle; "quack, quack" for duck. Afterward, children guess what object is being imitated. Repeat, using different sound.
Variation: Choose a child to create the sound.

5. CHRISTMAS SECRETS:
   Christmas secrets are such fun.
   In this present is a special one.
   I'll give some clues to what's inside.
   Then you guess what the box does hide.

Place several items in box. Adult says verse. Then adult describes one item in box. Players guess what is described. Display item. Repeat.

6. SANTA AND ELVES:
   All do as I do.
   All do as I do.
   All do as I do.
   Ho, ho, ho, ho, ho, ho.

One child is chosen to be Santa, who does action. For example, pretend to make toys or feed reindeer. Other children who are elves do the same action. Repeat, choosing a new Santa.

7. MUSICAL BELL GAME: Sit in circle. Pass a bell around circle while adult plays Christmas music. When the music stops, the person holding the bell rings it as directed by the adult. Examples of directions are ring the bell two times, ring the bell with your left hand, or ring the bell behind your head.

8. STAINED GLASS WINDOW: (Group project) Cut shapes from many colors of transparent cellophane. Attach cellophane pieces to window using clear tape. Cover entire window.
Variation: Use colored tissue paper in place of cellophane.

9. SANTA MOBILE: (Group project) Cover coat hanger with red paper. Glue cotton balls to top. Cut eyes from blue paper. Eyebrows, mustache, and beard can be cut from white paper and covered with cotton. Hang pieces from coat hanger with string.

10. DECORATE CHRISTMAS TREE: (Group project)
    A. Decorate evergreen tree with CHRISTMAS TREE ORNAMENTS (see pages 52 to 54).
    B. Place an evergreen tree made of construction paper on the bulletin board. Decorate tree with rickrack, buttons, and gummed Christmas seals. Cut or tear items from a catalog to place under the tree as presents.

11. CLASSROOM WREATH: (Group project) Decorate individual cups of an egg carton with paint. Mount sections on cardboard base cut into the shape of a wreath. This can be used as December calendar by dating each cup and mounting it to the base each day until Christmas.

12. CHRISTMAS PROGRAM: Give Christmas program for parents and grandparents. Program can include singing Christmas songs and doing fingerplays. Serve cookies and candies made in COOKING ACTIVITIES (see pages 56 to 58). At end of program Santa can come and listen to what each child wants for Christmas. Some guidelines to follow include:
    A. Emphasis should be on children enjoying program and not on executing songs and poems properly.
    B. Program should be simple, short, and in familiar surroundings.
    C. Children and parents can sing carols together.

13. THANK YOU CARD: After Christmas a thank you card can be made. Adult writes "Thank You, (person's name who gave present)" on outside of card. Child draws picture of gift for which he is thankful on inside of card. Give card to person who sent the gift.

CREATIVE DRAMATICS AND MOVEMENT

1. BLOCK STABLE: Build a stable with blocks, boxes, and planks. Dramatize animals that might be found in a stable.

2. SANTA MOVES: When Santa is in a small space like the chimney, he makes small movements. Make small movements as does Santa in the chimney. When Santa is on the roof, he has more space so he can make big movements. Show how Santa would move when he had a large amount of space.

3. REINDEER:

> "Come Dasher, Dancer, Prancer, and Vixen.
> Come Comet, Cupid, Donner, and Blitzen."
> Santa said, "My reindeer number eight.
> We need to go. We can't be late!
> It's dark this Christmas Eve night.
> We need someone to carry a light.
> Rudolph, of course, you'll be fine.
> Now my reindeer number nine."

For antlers, trace around hands. Cut. Attach to headband. Adjust band to fit head. Dramatize verse.

4. STAND-UP REINDEER: Trace and cut out reindeer outlined on page. Fold head downward on dotted line. Fold body in different directions on dotted lines to form Z so reindeer will stand. Color features. Allow time for creative play.

5. THE LITTLEST CHRISTMAS TREE:

> Once there was a small evergreen who wanted to be a Christmas tree. (Adult lays six pieces of green construction paper on floor to form tree by placing three for base, two in middle, and one for top of tree.) People came into the forest and cut all the big trees around the little tree. They took them home for Christmas trees. Now the littlest tree was very sad and lonely because no one wanted him for a Christmas tree. He cried big tears which formed into icicles because it was cold (place icicles on tree). It was very close to Christmas, and it started to snow. Snowflakes fell on the littlest tree (place snowflakes on tree). On Christmas Eve there came a chipmunk who was hungry and looking for food. He saw two pine cones that lay under the littlest tree (place pine cones at bottom of tree). These made a welcome Christmas feast for the hungry little chipmunk. As he was eating the seeds in the pine cones, a star rose just above the little tree (place star at top of tree). The chipmunk looked at the little tree and discovered it was the prettiest Christmas tree ever. They both had a very merry Christmas.

Give every child one of the following items cut from construction paper. Give one child a star and two children each a pine cone. Give each remaining child either a snowflake or an icicle. Adult tells story and children add items to tree as they are mentioned in the story.

6. WHAT I FOUND UNDER THE CHRISTMAS TREE: Say verse and dramatize action.

> I found a ball under the Christmas tree.
> And this is the way it bounced for me!
> Bounce, bounce, bounce.
> And this is the way it bounced for me.

Variations: In place of "ball . . . bounced," use the following:
   A. Doll . . . and this is the way he talked to me. Ma-ma-ma-ma.
   B. Top . . . and this is the way it spun for me. Spin, spin, spin.
   C. Rocking horse . . . and this is the way it rocked for me. Rock, rock, rock.
   D. Piano . . . and this is the way it played for me. Tra-la-la-la.
   E. Horn . . . and this is the way it tooted for me. Toot-toot-toot-toot.

7. WRAPPING PRESENTS: Child goes "shopping" in classroom for toy or gift for teacher. Child wraps gift with newspaper and masking tape. Place giver's name on gift. Gifts are placed under the tree. Children watch as adult opens presents. Adult watches twinkle in child's eyes as joy of giving is expressed. Adult's "thank you" will set an example for children to follow at Christmas.
Variation: Divide into pairs. Each child selects and wraps gift for partner.

66

8. GIFT SHOP: Prepare dramatic play area as gift shop. Provide cash register, play money, shopping bags, and gifts. Examples of gifts are books, cooking utensils, hats, and clothes. Gift boxes, newspaper, and tape can be provided to wrap presents.

9. TOYSHOP WINDOW: Adult says verse and children dramatize motions.
   Look through the window of this toyshop.
   See the bunny. Wind it up and it will hop.
   There is a drum you can bang, bang, bang.
   There are shiny cymbals to clang, clang, clang.
   There is a soldier marching straight and tall.
   See the funny rag doll. Stand it up, and it will fall.
   The baby doll says, "Ma-ma-ma."
   Wind the little flying bird. It sings, "La-la-la."
   Oh, what a surprise it would be
   To find these toys under MY Christmas tree.

10. CANDLE FLAME: Light a candle. Gently blow candle and observe how it flickers. Now imitate the movement of the flame. Raise one finger to represent flame. Move finger in same direction as flame of candle. Drop finger when flame is extinguished.
    Variation: Try this movement with arms, legs, or entire body.

11. TWINKLE, TWINKLE LITTLE STAR: (Ann and Jane Taylor)
    Twinkle, twinkle, little star. How I wonder what you are.
    Up above the world so high like a diamond in the sky.
    Twinkle, twinkle, little star. How I wonder what you are.
    Lie on floor and stretch arms and legs out to represent the points of the star. Encourage movement through blinking of the eyes, swaying back and forth, or wiggling fingers as this familiar verse is sung.

12. DANCE OF THE SUGARPLUM FAIRIES: Play "The Dance of the Sugarplum Fairies" from Tchaikovsky's *Nutcracker Suite*. Dance to tempo of music.

13. MY CHRISTMAS GIFT: One player dramatizes a gift that he received for Christmas. Other players try to guess what the gift is.
    Variation: Describe gift instead of dramatizing gift.

PHYSICAL DEVELOPMENT

1. SANTA DOWN THE CHIMNEY: Remove narrow ends from a long box that is a little wider than a child. Lay box on floor. Move through the box like Santa would wiggle down a chimney.
   Variation: Tape several boxes together.

2. REINDEER MOVEMENT: Discuss that reindeer are hitched together when pulling Santa's sleigh. They must all move at one time. What would it be like to be attached to a partner and move together? Hold hands with a partner. Adult gives directions to walk, run, hop, or skip.
   A. Instead of holding hands hold a scarf, string, or rope with partner.
   B. Move together to music.
   C. Form line of "reindeer" with pairs of children holding hands. Outside hands hold rope which reaches from first child to last child in line. Adult gives directions as above.

3. CHRISTMAS LOG ROLL: Lie on the floor with arms to the sides and attempt to roll body a certain distance without moving arms.

4. HOPSTARS: Place 8" paper stars on floor to form a straight line, square, star, or constellation. Indicate starting star and path to be followed to the finishing star. This can be done by letters, numbers, or verbal instructions. Hop from one star to another until path is completed.
Variation: Walk, jump with two feet, skip, or gallop through path.

5. RING THE CHRISTMAS BELL: Hang a bell from the ceiling. Throw a bean bag or sponge ball and try to "ring the Christmas bell."

6. STOCKING FUN: Put on and remove a pair of old socks. This can be played as a relay race. Each child on the team must put on socks, remove, and give socks to next team member.

7. JACK BE NIMBLE: (Traditional)
   Jack be nimble, Jack be quick,
   Jack jump over the candlestick.
Sit in circle. Place a cardboard roll or wooden block for the candlestick in center of circle. One child is chosen to be Jack, who jumps over the candlestick while verse is recited. Choose new Jack and repeat.
Variation: Form line and take turns jumping over a wooden block. After all have had a turn, increase height by adding additional blocks. Repeat.

MATH

1. HOW MANY DAYS TILL CHRISTMAS?
   How many days till Christmas?
   It seems a long, long spell.
   But with this jolly Santa,
   There's an easy way to tell.
   Each evening from his middle
   A peanut take away,
   And when there are no more,
   Tomorrow will be Christmas Day!
Cut 3 1/2" x 18" strip from red felt or construction paper. Cut corners from one end to form pointed hat. From white felt or construction paper, cut the following: two 1/2" circles for top of hat and nose (white pompons can also be used); two 1" circles with small triangle removed from each for eyes; a mustache; and a beard with a small hole removed at top for mouth. From black felt or construction paper, cut two boots and one 1" circle to be cut in half and used for pupils of eyes. Glue together to make Santa. Glue seven peanuts below beard for buttons. If desired, type poem on heavy white paper and attach to Santa's hat. Punch hole in top, thread red ribbon through hole, and tie to make a loop so Santa can be hung on doorknob or wall. Do this project one week before Christmas. Remove one peanut each day.

2. CHRISTMAS BELL:
> It seems the Christmas season
> Is the longest time of the year.
> How many days before Old Santa will appear?
> Take a link from this bell
> When the Sandman is at the door.
> And Christmas Eve will be here
> When there are no more.

Cut 1" strips of red and green construction paper. Glue one strip into circle. Thread another strip through circle, overlap ends, and glue. Add a loop for each day until Christmas. Attach bell to end of chain. Write poem on bell or below bell if desired. Remove one loop each day until Christmas.
Variation: Write a direction on each loop. When loop is removed, complete direction. Example of direction is, "Place icicles on Christmas tree."

3. PAPER CHAIN PATTERNS: When making paper chains (directions given above) begin a pattern. For example, make two red loops followed by one green loop. Complete the chain with the same pattern. Progress to more difficult patterns.

4. PRESENTS:
> Christmas is a time to give and share.
> Select the gifts and package them with care.
> Find some round boxes and square boxes, too.
> A rectangular box for a bat will do.
> Place gifts in boxes that are the right size.
> Wrap them with a pretty Christmas disguise.

From felt, cut squares, circles, and rectangles of different sizes for boxes. Cut from a Christmas catalog a picture of a gift that will fit in each box shape. Attach flannel to back of picture. Each child is given a box or gift. As adult recites verse, children place boxes on flannel board at appropriate times. At end of verse, children match gift shapes to appropriate boxes.

5. TREE MOBILE: Arrange various lengths of long green rectangles from shortest to longest. Discuss concepts of short and long. When arranged attach string to center of each rectangle with tape to make mobile.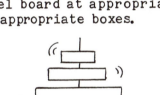

6. STACKING TREE: From green construction paper, cut 4 to 5 half-circles making each half-circle larger than the previous one. To make each half-circle into cone, overlap corners A and B. Staple. Fringe bottom edge of each cone, and curl fringe by rolling it around a pencil. Stack cones from largest to smallest.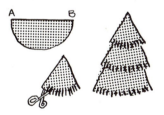

7. CHRISTMAS TREE DECORATIONS:
> Let's decorate the Christmas tree. We'll make it bright and gay.
> But I will surely need your help to make it look that way.
> Place red balls everywhere, then some of pretty blue.
> Yellow adds bright color--purple and orange do, too.
> Add a splash of pink and then some of green.
> Now isn't it the grandest tree that you have ever seen?

Lay six pieces of green construction paper on floor to form tree by placing three for base, two in middle, and one for top of tree. Give each child a paper ball that is one of the colors mentioned in the verse. Place balls on tree when color is read in the poem.

8. COUNTING REINDEER:

    (1-2-3-4-5) prancing reindeer were ready to go.
    They wanted to leave early because of ice and snow.
    "Hurry," Santa said to the others, "for this is the day."
    (Three) more reindeer make the eight we need to pull our sleigh."

This activity can be done on flannel board or with REINDEER (see page 66).
Tell how many reindeer it will take to make eight. Change number of reindeer
waiting. For example, "(1-2-3-4-5-6) prancing reindeer . . ." and "(Two) more
reindeer . . ."

9. STAR: Make two equilateral triangles. Glue triangles together, forming a star. Discuss that the
   sides of the triangles are the same size.

10. STAR COUNT: Display pictures of familiar constellations. Count the stars in
    each constellation. Which constellation has the greatest number of stars?
    Which has the fewest?

SCIENCE

1. SLENDER SANTA: Follow directions to make Santa look
   chubby and plump again. Trace and color diagram of
   Santa. Tape picture against outside of a clear
   glass. Santa should look inward. Fill glass with
   water. Look through water to observe Santa. Now
   see his "broad face and little round belly."
   Note: The curve of the glass distorts the perimeter
   of the figure outward. Also, looking at something
   through water makes it appear 25% larger.

2. REINDEER: Display picture of reindeer. Reindeer
   live in the northernmost parts of Europe, Asia, and
   America. American species are called caribou.
   Reindeer pull sleds and provide meat, cheese, and
   milk. Their hides are used for clothing and blankets. They have heavier
   bodies than most deer. The legs are shorter and thicker. Their feet, which
   are called hoofs, are wide for support in the snow. Reindeer have antlers.
   Their hair is thick and is grayish brown with white on their bellies.

3. BELLS: Compare the sounds of many kinds and sizes of bells. Discuss why the
   sounds are different. There are many uses for bells. Examples are church
   bells, doorbells, fire alarms, telephones, chimes, and musical instruments.

4. GLASS + WATER = MUSIC: Fill glasses with different levels of water. Tap the
   glasses with a spoon and listen to the variation in tones. The glass with the
   smallest amount of water will have the highest-pitched sound.
   Variation: Fill pop bottles with different amounts of water and blow across
   the top of the bottle.

5. THE COLOR GREEN: Fill two baby food jars with water. Add several drops of
   blue food coloring to the first jar and several drops of yellow food coloring
   to the second jar. Secure lids to jars. Hold jars to light. Place one jar in
   front of the other and look through both jars. What color do you see?
   Variation: Place primary colors in jars. Allow time to experiment and discover what combinations will make different colors.

6. STARS: Discuss:
    A. What is a star? Stars are suns which are giant clusters of hot gases burning in the heavens. Many stars are bigger than our sun but are so far away that they appear to be small.
    B. Why do stars twinkle? Light from the stars passes through the air, and the movement of the air makes the stars appear to twinkle. In outer space the astronauts have told us the stars do not twinkle because there is no air.

7. CONSTELLATIONS: A long time ago, people imagined that groups of stars in the sky made pictures of animals, people, and things.
    A. On pieces of blue construction paper, paste silver stars to form constellations. Display.
    B. Punch holes in the bottom on a can to form constellations. Shine flashlight through can and project image of constellation on wall. Below are examples of some constellations.

Ursa Major--Big Dipper

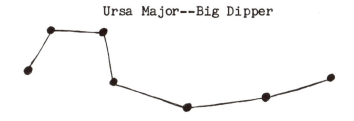

Scorpius

Ursa Minor--Little Dipper

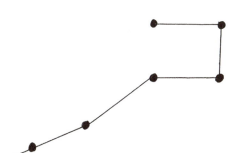

Bootes

Libra

Phoenix

MUSIC

1. MARY HAD A BABY, MY LORD: (Tune--"Kumbaya")
   Mary had a Baby, My Lord. Mary had a Baby,
   Mary had a Baby, My Lord. Mary had a Baby,
   Mary had a Baby, My Lord. Mary had a Baby,
   Oh Lord, Mary had a Baby.
                                    Traditional
   Second verse--Where was He born, My Lord? Where was He born?
   Third verse--Born in a manger, My Lord. Born in a manger.
   Fourth verse--What did Mary name Him, My Lord? What did Mary name Him?
   Fifth verse--She named Him Jesus, My Lord. She named Him Jesus.

2. WE WISH YOU A MERRY CHRISTMAS: (Traditional)
   We wish you a Merry Christmas, we wish you a Merry Christmas.
   We wish you a Merry Christmas and a Happy New Year.
   Second verse--Let's all do a little clapping . . . to spread Christmas cheer.
   Third verse--Let's all do a little jumping . . . to spread Christmas cheer.

3. HERE STANDS A LOVELY CHRISTMAS TREE: (Tune--"Mary Had a Little Lamb")
   Here stands a lovely Christmas tree, Christmas tree, Christmas tree.
   Here stands a lovely Christmas tree so early in the morning.
   Second verse--Here is a horn for the Christmas tree . . .
   Third verse--Here is a drum for the Christmas tree . . .
   Fourth verse--Here stands a lovely Christmas tree . . .

4. MY PEPPERMINT STICK: (Tune--"Brownie Smile")
   Oh, I took a lick of my peppermint stick, and I thought it tasted yummy.
   It used to be on my Christmas tree, but I like it better in my tummy.
                                    Author Unknown

5. ANGEL'S HARP: Cut a 4" to 5" oval from the side of a two-quart milk carton.
   Place different sizes of rubber bands around the carton. The bands should
   stretch over the oval opening. Pluck the bands with fingers. Notice the
   different sound from the different-sized bands.
   Variations:
       A. Raise a band with a pencil and pluck it. Higher notes are heard when the
           band is tighter.
       B. Place rubber bands around a cake pan instead of milk carton.

6. JINGLE BELLS: Ring bells to the beat of *Jingle Bells* while singing the song.
   Variations:
       A. Instead of singing, play the record *Jingle Bells*.
       B. In place of bells, use shakers. To make one shaker: place macaroni, dry
           beans, rice, or coins in plastic egg (hosiery container) or can with lid.

7. DRUMMER BOY: Play the record *The Drummer Boy*. March to music while beating
   drums which can be made from oatmeal boxes.

FIELD TRIPS

1. CAROLING
2. VISIT SANTA CLAUS: Visit Santa at department store or have Santa come to
   school.
3. CHRISTMAS DISPLAYS: View Christmas displays in store windows.

WINTER

In the Northern Hemisphere, WINTER begins in mid-December and ends in mid-March. During this season the days grow shorter, and the nights grow longer. The southern part of the United States has milder winters characterized by warmer weather and rain instead of snow. Cold weather abounds in the northern states during the winter months.

The cold weather causes many changes in the environment. Water freezes and forms ice, snow, sleet, and icicles. Most plants and animals become dormant and rest. The only plants that grow and remain green are called evergreens. People's life styles also change. They protect themselves from the cold and enjoy a variety of indoor activities and winter sports.

CONCEPTS TO BE TAUGHT

1. Winter is the season that comes between autumn and spring.
2. In some places the weather turns cold during winter causing snow and sleet.
3. Plants and animals adapt to cold winter weather in many ways.
4. In cold weather people need to wear heavier warmer clothing.
5. People enjoy a variety of activities and sports during the winter months.

ART ACTIVITIES

1. SNOWFLAKE: Fold square paper in half. Fold in half again. Fringe edges by cutting or tearing. Open.
   Variations:
   A. Fold square into quarters. Fold into triangle by folding on dotted line. Cut design in edges.
   B. To make round snowflake, use circle instead of square.
   C. Instead of fringing, cut small triangles into edges.

2. GLITTERY SNOWFLAKE: Make snowflake as above. Cover with a solution of glue mixed with water. Sprinkle with glitter. Remove excess.

3. HONEYCOMB SNOWFLAKES: Glue Honeycomb® cereal on blue construction paper to make snowflake design.
   Variation: Glue edges of Honeycomb® cereal together to make snowflake.

4. SPATTER PAINT SNOWFLAKE: Cut a large circle from black or blue construction paper. Fold in half and open. Dip brush into white tempera paint that is thinner than normal. Hold brush over paper, being careful not to touch brush to paper. Shake brush allowing paint to fall randomly. Fold on original crease and press. Open and symmetrical design appears.
Variation: Place white and blue tempera on brown paper. Fold and press.

5. WHIPPED SOAP PAINTING: Mix soap flakes and water in a mixing bowl. Beat with egg-beater until mixture is frothy, but not stiff. Apply mixture to paper with easel brush or tongue depressor to create design.
Variation: Add food coloring or tempera to whipped soap flakes.

6. SOAP SCULPTURE: Add small amount of water to soap flakes to make soap clay. Create free-form sculpture from clay. Use toothpicks to attach pieces of sculpture together. (To use as soap bar, remove toothpicks.)
Note: This is an unbelievably messy project. Therefore, cover floor and table with newspaper. Place waxed paper on newspaper. Put soap clay on waxed paper.

7. SNOWMAN: Create a snowman by gluing cotton balls or circular-shaped pieces of styrofoam packing onto paper. Make features with yarn, bits of fabric, construction paper cutouts, or felt-tipped pens. Spatter picture with white tempera to create snow. (Refer to WINTER TREE, Variation A.)

8. SNOWMAN'S FACE: Glue buttons, seeds, beans, bits of paper, fabric, or yarn on a paper plate to create features of snowman's face. Glue construction paper hat to top of head.

9. FROST-ON-WINDOW: Use rectangular construction paper for window. Draw two lines dividing paper in half lengthwise and crosswise. Place glue on window. Sprinkle with glitter.
Variation: Moisten construction paper window. Sprinkle with salt.

10. SNOWY DAY PICTURE: Place a small amount of bleach in a container. Using a cotton-tipped swab, paint with bleach on a dark piece of paper.
Note: Paint shirts and close supervision are necessary.
Variation: Cut hexagon-shaped sponge piece. Clip onto clothespin. Dip into white paint. Paint on dark construction paper.

11. WINTER SCENE: Draw winter scene on brightly colored construction paper using crayons. When finished, cover entire piece of paper by rubbing with side of white chalk.
Variation: Draw scene using white chalk on black construction paper.

12. SNOWFALL SHAKER: Place household cement in center of baby food jar lid. Stick green plastic leaves with stems 1" long in cement. When dry, fill baby food jar with water. Pour 1 to 2 teaspoons of silver glitter into water. Coat inside rim of lid with glue and secure lid to jar. Invert jar when glue dries. Shake jar to make "snow" appear.

13. WINTER TREE: Glue twig on construction paper to represent a tree during winter. Glue cotton balls around base of tree for snow.
Variations: Instead of cotton balls:
A. Dip brush into white tempera paint that is thinner than normal. Hold brush over paper, being careful not to touch brush to paper. Shake brush allowing paint to fall randomly.
B. Cover paper with glue. Sprinkle holes punched from white paper on glue.
C. Cook macaroni stars. Place moist stars on construction paper.

14. BARK AND PINE CONE ARRANGEMENT: Glue pine cone and dried weeds or flowers on a piece of bark. Use landscaping bark or bark that has fallen from dead trees.

15. PAINTING WITH PINE BOUGH: Use small pine bough for paintbrush. Place a small bough beside each container of tempera paint that is a different color. Dip end of pine bough in paint and apply to paper. When finished, one of the pine bough brushes can be taped to corner of picture.
Variation: Dip side of pine cone in paint and brush cone across paper. Use a variety of colors to create an interesting design.

16. BEAR IN WINTER: Tear a semicircle from the edge of a styrofoam cup. Decorate cup with felt-tipped pens or paint to create a cave. Glue a brown pompon inside rim of cup for the bear.
Variation: Instead of pompon, use brown cotton ball. To make, place cotton ball and dry brown tempera in bag. Shake.

17. WINTER FABRIC COLLAGE: Glue cloth scraps to paper to make a design or form a collage.
Variation: Cut cloth scraps into shapes. Glue to paper to make design.

18. MITTENS: Cut two mittens from construction paper. Attach a mitten to each end of a long piece of yarn. Color mittens.
Variation: Draw around each hand to make mittens. Cut.

19. KERCHOO: Make a face on a paper plate. Glue facial tissue to nose and mouth.

20. WINTER SPORTS COLLAGE: Cut pictures of winter sport activities from magazines. Mount on white construction paper.

21. SKIER: Glue two popsicle sticks parallel on a piece of paper for skis. With chalk draw picture of skier on skis.
Variation: Instead of skier, make ice skater. Use two short pieces of pipe cleaner that have been curved on one end for ice skates. Glue to paper. Draw picture of skater on skates.

22. SLEIGH: Poke two pipe cleaners through the bottom of an egg carton cup on opposite sides. Curve one end of each pipe cleaner. Paint.

23. PUDDING PAINTING: Mix instant pudding following the directions on the box. Place on top of a table that has been washed. Fingerpaint with pudding. When desired picture is obtained, place piece of paper on pudding picture and press. Remove paper. A reverse picture of design on table will appear. Allow to dry.

COOKING ACTIVITIES

1. BANANA SNOWMAN: Place three round slices of banana on top of lettuce leaf to form snowman. Use pecan half for hat and raisins for features. Sprinkle with coconut for snow.

2. BANANA PUDDING: 4 ripe bananas
                      1 1/2 cups applesauce
                      4 tablespoons peanut butter
Mash bananas. Mix with remaining ingredients. Chill. Sprinkle with cinnamon.
Variation: Instead of above recipe, place banana slices in applesauce.

3. SNOW CONE: Freeze orange, apple, or grape juice in ice cube trays. Place five juice cubes in blender. Start and stop blender several times. Pack crushed ice into paper cup.
Note: To make a slush, add a little water while blending.
Variation: Place 1/2 cup water and several ice cubes in a blender. Start and stop blender until ice is crushed. Pack crushed ice into paper cup. Combine 6 ounces frozen concentrated juice with 3/4 cup water. Stir and pour over crushed ice.

4. SNOWFLAKE MACAROONS: 2 egg whites   1 cup rolled oats
                          1/3 cup honey   1/2 cup grated coconut
Beat egg whites in small bowl until stiff. Combine warm honey and oats in another bowl. Mix well. Add coconut. Fold in egg whites. Drop by spoonfuls onto lightly greased cookie sheet. Bake at 300° for 25 to 30 minutes.

5. SNOWFLAKE SWIRLS: Flatten a refrigerator biscuit. Cover with any of the following: applesauce, peanut butter, cheese, or sesame seeds. Roll into log. Slice into fourths. Bake according to package directions.

6. GRANOLA-PEANUT BUTTER BARS: 1/2 cup honey
                                 2/3 cup peanut butter
                                 3 cups granola
Heat honey to boiling. Boil one minute. Remove from heat. Mix with peanut butter until well blended. Add granola. Press into buttered 9" x 9" pan. Cool. Cut into squares.

7. HOT CINNAMON OATMEAL: 2 cups water   1/2 teaspoon vanilla
                          1/2 cup raisins   1 teaspoon cinnamon
                          1 cup rolled oats   1/4 cup sesame seeds
Combine water and raisins in a saucepan. Bring to boil. Gradually add oats and stir. Add vanilla and cinnamon. Cook ten minutes. Pour into bowls and top with seeds. Serve with milk.

8. BIRDSEED BREAD: 2 cups biscuit baking mix   2 tablespoons sesame seeds
                     1/2 cup cold water   2 tablespoons sunflower nuts
                     2 tablespoons margarine
Heat oven to 425°. Form soft dough with baking mix and water. Pat dough on ungreased cookie sheet forming a 10" circle. Melt margarine and brush circle with it. Sprinkle sesame seeds and nuts in circle. Firmly press seeds into dough with rubber spatula. Cut circle into twelve equal wedges (like a pie). Bake for 15 to 20 minutes or until golden brown. Serve warm. Bread will break into wedges.

9. HOT CAROB DRINK: 2 tablespoons carob powder   2 cups milk
                      1 tablespoon honey   1/2 teaspoon vanilla
                      1/2 cup water
Boil carob powder, honey, and water. Stir constantly. Reduce heat. Add milk and vanilla. Serve warm.

10. CHILI: 1 1/2 pounds hamburger   46 ounces tomato juice
            1 tablespoon dried onion   10 ounces tomato paste
            1 pound can of pork and beans 2 teaspoons chili powder
Brown hamburger and onion. Drain excess grease. Add remaining ingredients, and simmer for one hour.

11. SNOWY DAY SOUP: 10 3/4 ounce can condensed cheddar cheese soup
                      1 soup can milk
                      2 teaspoons lemon juice
                      7 ounces tuna, drained and flaked
                      1/2 teaspoon dry minced onion
   Blend soup and milk until smooth. Add remaining ingredients and stir. Heat to
   boiling. Stir occasionally.

12. MIX AND MATCH SOUPS: Combine two canned soups. Heat to boiling, stirring
    occasionally. Try these combinations.
       A. 1 can cheddar cheese soup, 1 can tomato soup, and 2 soup cans water
       B. 1 can chicken and stars soup, 1 can cream of chicken soup, and 1 1/2 soup
           cans water
   Variation: Have each child bring a vegetable from home for soup. Wash, cut,
   and combine all ingredients in pan. Add canned beef broth and water as necessary. Cook.

13. SOUP GARNISHES: Use any of the following:
       A. Crackers
       B. Grated cheese
       C. Popcorn or popped wheat
       D. Toasted bread cut into circles, diamonds, hearts, or child's initials
       E. Cooked pasta (alphabet shapes, spaghetti rings, or star noodles)
       F. Fried bacon bits
       G. Cereal (use doughnut shapes or wheat squares)
       H. Round slices of processed cheese cut with jar lids or cookie cutters
           (place on soup to make a floating snowman)

                              FINGERPLAYS

1. Who makes us dress in our winter
       suits?
    Who causes us to wear our boots?
       (point to feet)
    Who comes on a cold, wintry night?
       (shiver)
    Who decorates the windows white?
       (form square)
    Who makes the trees glisten in the
       lane (form triangle over head)
    And taps on our windows with his
       icicle cane? (tap)
    MR. JACK FROST!

2. My little nose (point to nose)
    Is red as a rose.
    Jack Frost kissed it. I suppose!
       (blow kiss)

3. Snowflakes falling, falling down,
       (flutter fingers)
    The wind blows them round and
       round. (circular motion)
    They whip and whirl in the air
    Then land softly everywhere.

4. Watch the little snowflakes flutter
       to the ground. (flutter fingers)
    They look like tiny diamonds and
       hardly make a sound. (hold fin-
       ger over mouth and whisper)

5. When I heard my mom call, (hands
       encircle mouth)
    "Time to come in for a nap."
    What should I do with my snowball?
       (pretend to hold snowball)
    Ahh, I'll put it in my stocking
       cap. (pretend to put ball in
       cap)
    Beside my bed it lies,
    Waiting until I wake up to play.
    Zzzzzzzzzzz as I sleep, (pretend to
       sleep)
    My snowball begins to weep. (rub
       eyes)
    When I wake from my nap, (stretch)
    There is a puddle under my cap!
    I guess snow doesn't like it warm
       (shake head sideways)
    Because then it changes form.

6. The North Wind blew. Whoo-ooo.
   It rattled the windows. (make
      square with fingers)
   It swept down the flue. (swoop
      down with hand)
   The great trees groaned (hold hands
      over head and sway)
   As the North Wind moaned,
   Whoo-ooo-ooo.

   Author Unknown

7. It is a cold winter day. (shiver)
   We will stay inside to play.
   Snow, snow is all around. (flutter
      fingers)
   Listen to the windy sound: (hand
      to ear)
   Ooooooooooooooooooooo.
   No friends outside to be found.
      (shake head sideways)

8. Snow is on the housetop. (make
      point with fingers for roof)
   Snow is on the ground. (point to
      ground)
   Snow is on the mountain. (make
      mountain with arms)
   Snow is all around. (move hands in
      big circle)

   Mary Jackson Ellis
   and Frances Lyons

9. Here is a chimney, (tuck thumb in
      fist)
   Here is the top, (other hand on top
      of fist)
   Take off the lid: (remove hand)
   Out smoke pops. (pop up thumb)

10. It's fun to walk in the sparkling
      snow (walk)
    And hear my boots go crunch.
       (place hand behind ear)
    I play so hard.
    Soon I'm wet and tired (shiver and
       look tired)
    And ready for hot soup with lunch.
       (rub stomach)

11. Oh, how I love to ski in the sun
       (form circle above head)
    While its warm rays tan my nose.
       (point to nose)
    It would be nice if that sun above
    Could do the same for my toes!
       (rub toes)

12. Here's a hill (make hill with left
       arm)
    All covered with snow.
    We'll get on our sled
    And ZOOM! Down we'll go! (swoop
       right hand downward)

    Author Unknown

13. Snow, snow has fallen today.
       (flutter fingers)
    Come, let's go out to play. (mo-
       tion to come)
    We'll roll three balls--large, me-
       dium, and small (three fingers)
    And build a snowman, proud and
       tall. (form snowman in air,
       stand tall)
    Then play a game before we freeze.
       (shiver)
    I'd like to play fox and geese.
       (point to self)
    We can make angels with lovely
       wings. (move arms up and down)
    Lie down and give your arms a
       fling.
    After awhile we'll surely tire,
    So we'll go inside and sit by the
       fire. (sit)

14. Five little snowmen, happy and gay.
       (hold up respective fingers)
    First one said, "What a beautiful
       day."
    Second one said, "We'll never have
       tears."
    Third one said, "We'll stay for
       years."
    Fourth one said, "But what will
       happen in May?"
    Fifth one said, "Look, we're melt-
       ing away."

    Mary Jackson Ellis

15. Five little snowmen, standing in a
       row, (hold up fingers)
    Each with a hat (point to head)
    And a bright red bow. (make bow
       under chin)
    Five little snowmen dressed for a
       show. (hold up fingers)
    Now they are ready. Where will
       they go?
    Wait till the sun shines. (make
       circle above head)
    Soon they will go
    Down through the field with the
       melting snow.

    Author Unknown

16. I built a snowman the other day.
    (form snowman with hands)
    Then I ran off to play. (make
    fingers run)
    The sun was warm, the day was
    bright. (form circle in air)
    When I came home--oh, what a
    fright! (look surprised)
    All that was left of his poor soul
    (shake head sideways)
    Was a floppy hat and two lumps of
    coal. (point to head, raise two
    fingers)

17. I built a little snowman. (form
    outline of snowman)
    He had a carrot nose. (point to
    nose)
    Along came a bunny. (move two fin-
    gers up and down)
    And what do you suppose?
    That hungry little bunny (rub stom-
    ach)
    Looking for his lunch,
    Ate that snowman's nose: (point to
    nose)
    Nibble, nibble, crunch! (open and
    close hand)
                              Author Unknown

18. I built a snowman out of three
    balls--1-2-3. (three fingers)
    One ball was small, one middle-
    sized, and one as big as can be!
    (form three circles, each larger)

19. Let's make a big white snowman.
    (raise hands above head)
    Roll three snowballs, 1-2-3, (raise
    three fingers)
    And pat them very hard. (pat)
    Put a big one on the bottom, (pre-
    tend to build snowman)
    Next one of middle-size,
    A smaller one is for his crown.
    Use two rocks for his eyes. (point
    to eyes)
    Place a floppy hat upon his head.
    (pat head)
    Let's use a scarf of the brightest
    red.
    Now that our snowman looks his
    best,
    Let's sit down and take a rest.

20. The warm south wind is taking a
    nap. (pretend to sleep)
    Zip up your coat and put on your
    hat. (pretend to zip and put on
    hat)
    So Mr. North Wind won't nip at your
    toes, (point to toes)
    Put on warm boots and warm winter
    clothes. (pretend to dress)
    Put on your gloves to protect your
    fingers. (pretend to put on
    gloves)
    Now Mr. North Wind's cold won't
    linger. (shake head sideways)

21. "Oh, Mom," I said on a snowy day.
    "Must I wear my boots to play?"
    (point to boots)
    "Of course, dear," was what she
    said, (shake head vertically)
    "And your hat, your scarf, and your
    mittens red." (point to head,
    neck, and hands)

22. Mom knit me a pair of mittens,
    (hold hands in front of body)
    A hat and scarf to match. (point
    to head, pretend to wrap scarf
    around neck)
    But when I am dressed from head to
    toe, (point to head and toe)
    The door I can hardly unlatch.
    (shake head sideways)

23. I like to play in the snow, (flut-
    ter fingers)
    But every time I want to go,
    I hear my mom say, (hand to ear)
    "It's a very cold day, (shiver)
    Bundle up, zip up, (pretend to
    dress)
    Boots, gloves, and hat on."
    After I dress from here down,
    (point to head then toe)
    I feel as clumsy as a clown. (act
    clumsy)
    Dressing up sure is a bummer!
    (shake head sideways)
    Why isn't there snow in summer?

24. A cold is a contagious disease.
So when you need to sneeze, (shake
finger)
Cover your mouth and nose, please.
(cover mouth and nose)

25. Little birds, when winter comes,
(make wings with arms)
Have no food at all. (shake head
sideways)
Make a feeder for our feathered
friends.
Then place it in the treetop tall.
(raise hands above head)

26. Mr. Woodchuck hibernates. (pretend
to sleep)
In his winter home he waits and
waits.
While he's asleep, he doesn't eat.
(shake head sideways)
Now don't you think that's quite a
feat? (point to friend)
But in the spring when the earth's
aflower,
He looks for food in field and
bower. (place hand above eyes)

LANGUAGE DEVELOPMENT

1. WEATHER GAME: (Tune--"Bluebird, Bluebird, Through My Window")
    Weatherman, weatherman, what will the weather be?
    Weatherman, weatherman, what will the weather be?
    Weatherman, weatherman, what will the weather be,
    On this wintry day?
Sit in circle. While verse is sung, child chosen as weatherman skips around
inside of circle distributing pictures of winter weather that have been mounted
on construction paper. Pictures can include activities that relate to weather
conditions. Weatherman then asks for one child to step into circle and describe picture. Weatherman sits in empty space. After describing picture,
child chooses another to describe his picture. Continue until everyone has described picture.

2. SNOWMAN FLANNEL BOARD:
    Roll a large snowball upon the ground.
    Upon it place a medium-size ball that is round.
    Add a small ball and a hat for his head.
    Around his neck, tie a scarf that's red.
    Use a carrot for his nose and coal for his eyes.
    Now we have a snowman who looks so wise!
Cut the following from felt: a small, medium, and large white circle for
snowman; two black squares for coal; orange triangle for nose; rectangle with
square for hat; and a red strip for scarf. Give each child one item. Adult
recites poem, and children place items on board at appropriate time.

3. PLANTS IN WINTER: Observe plants and trees in winter. Discuss how they look
and what happens to them.
    A. The plants and trees that remain green and grow are called evergreens.
    B. Many trees and bushes are bare. They appear to be dead but are only
       resting. Their roots, which serve as food storage places, are protected
       by dirt and snow.
    C. The tops of some plants which are above ground die. Their bulbs or roots
       are alive but are dormant.
    D. Some plants die in the cold weather. These plants live only one year and
       are called annuals.
Note: Where winters are warmer and it rains instead of snows, plants bloom and
grow all year round.

4. THE LITTLEST TREE: (Thea Cannon)
         Down deep in the forest where trees grow so tall
         Stood one little fellow, the smallest of all.
         The trees waved their branches and rustled their leaves,
         But the smallest of all just stood stiff in the breeze.
         When winter winds howled, the tall trees were afraid
         And dropped all their leaves till there was no more shade.
         The smallest of all just stood brave and grew tall
         And kept his green coat when snow started to fall.
         During the winter months 'twas easy to see
         The smallest of all was the loveliest tree.
   Tell as flannel board story. Use several felt trees that have leaves, several
   that are bare, and a smaller evergreen tree. Place items on flannel board at
   appropriate time.

5. WHERE ANIMALS GO IN THE WINTER? Draw a mural of the forest in winter. Attach
   pictures of different animals to show where they spend their winter. For
   example, place bear in cave. Use following discussions about animals in winter.

6. HIBERNATION: Many animals, birds, and insects find sheltered places and hibernate during the cold winter months. True hibernators almost stop living. They
   stay in a very deep sleep without eating or drinking. They breathe very
   slowly, their heartbeats slow, and their body temperatures drop. This dormancy
   saves energy while maintaining body functions essential to survival.
   A. Many insects reproduce during winter and hibernate as larvae, grubs,
      eggs, or cocoons that are attached to bark, twigs, or under rocks. These
      insects become frozen solid during this time.
   B. Turtles and frogs bury themselves in mud. They may become partially
      frozen.
   C. Snakes and lizards find shelter in holes or rocky dens and hibernate.
   D. Birds that hibernate include chimney swifts, quail, grouse, and some
      hummingbirds. Some hummingbirds migrate south.
   E. Prairie dogs, badgers, woodchucks, ground hogs, and some mice hibernate
      from 4 to 7 months.

7. ANIMALS THAT SLEEP IN WINTER: Many animals are less perfect hibernators. They
   sleep most of the time but waken on warm winter days to eat and drink.
   A. Bears sleep in caves but may be seen on warm winter days looking for food
      and water. Cubs are usually born in January or February.
   B. Squirrels, chipmunks, and some mice intermittently arouse and eat stored
      food and nuts.
   C. Raccoons find hollow trees or logs and sleep during cold winter months.
   D. Skunks find dens or holes and also sleep for prolonged periods.

8. OTHER ANIMALS IN WINTER: Some hardy creatures live as actively as in summer.
   A. Birds that remain have a difficult time finding food. We can help birds
      by making BIRD FEEDERS (see page 89) and throwing crumbs to them on snowy
      days. Discuss that feathers help birds to stay warm.
   B. Rabbits, deer, and mice must search even harder for food. They eat dried
      plants and tree bark. They grow thicker coats as protection from the
      cold.
   C. Bobcats, wolves, and foxes grow lean as food is difficult to find. They
      also grow heavier coats.
   D. Some rabbits, owls, and weasels turn white in winter to match the snow.
   E. Bees and ants seal the entrances to their hives and nests. They live
      from food stored in the summer.

9. PEOPLE IN WINTER: Discuss activities in which children and their families are involved during the winter months. The following can be included:
    A. Vacationing to warmer climates
    B. Indoor projects such as sewing, reading, and games
    C. Playing basketball, ice hockey, or outdoor winter sports
    D. Jobs that make winter more pleasant (For example, clearing sidewalks)
    E. Enjoying a fire in the fireplace
    F. Enjoying the snow in different ways

10. OUTDOOR FUN: Display pictures of outdoor winter activities such as sledding, tobogganing, skating, skiing, snowshoeing, or enjoying the snow. Discuss:
    A. What is happening in each picture?
    B. What clothing is worn for each activity? What equipment is used?
    C. How many people participate in each activity?
    D. What part of the body is most important in performing each activity?
    E. Which activities require skill and practice?
    F. Who has participated in each winter activity?

11. WINTER HEALTH AND SAFETY: Discuss:
    A. Dress appropriately on cold days by wearing warmer clothing. Additional clothing can also be worn for protection against the cold. Examples are hats, boots, mittens, gloves, scarfs, and coats. Why are these articles worn? Discuss where to put articles after they are removed and why.
    B. People are more likely to catch colds and flu during cold winter months. Remember to cover mouth when coughing to keep germs from spreading.
    C. Play outside for short periods of time during cold weather. If hands become numb, warm them by placing in cool water.
    D. Remember streets and sidewalks can be slippery with ice or snow. People shovel snow from sidewalks to make them safer. City and state highway departments clear snow from streets with snowplows. They also sand streets.
    E. Listen carefully for cars. Hoods and scarfs may reduce ability to hear.
    F. Go sledding in a safe place. Don't slide on streets or in places where there are trees to bump.

12. STOP AND TELL: Adult begins a story and stops in the middle. Children tell the ending. For example, "One day it was snowing. The children went out to play and . . ." Children tell rest of story.

13. BOOKS:
    All Ready for Winter--Adelson
    Animals in the Winter--Bancroft
    Winter Sleeping Wildlife--Barker
    Big Tracks, Little Tracks--Branley
    The Indoor Noisy Book--Brown
    The Winter Noisy Book--Brown
    Josie and the Snow--Buckley
    Bear Weather--Chaffin
    Hamilton Duck--Getz
    When Will It Snow?--Hoff
    The Snowy Day--Keats
    I Like Snow--Lenski
    Carruthers--Marshall
    White Snow, Bright Snow--Tresselt

GAMES AND SOCIAL ACTIVITIES

1. JACK FROST:
   Teacher: "Jack Frost is here today."
   Children: "How do you know?"
   Teacher: "He bit my (nose)."
   Children: "Oh, oh, oh."
   While saying last line, children rub their noses. Repeat, using different parts of the body.

2. FREEZE: Players march in time to music. The leader stops the music. Players "freeze" or stand perfectly still. At first it might be necessary to say, "Freeze." when the music stops. Later the signal of the music stopping should be enough. There is no contest to this game. No one is withdrawn for not conforming. The object is to see if everyone can "freeze" at the right moment. If one player doesn't understand, he can stand beside the leader and watch the others. He can "freeze" by leader. Then he can join the other players.
   Variation: Instead of standing still, players can squat.

3. WHO HAS THE ICE CUBE? Sit in circle. Enclose an ice cube in a small plastic bag. One child is chosen to be Jack Frost. He goes to center of circle and hides eyes. Remaining players pass bag around circle while music is playing. When music stops, players stop passing ice cube. Jack Frost tries to guess who has ice. Child with ice cube becomes Jack Frost, and game is repeated.

4. SNOWMAN FOLLOW THE LEADER: Play follow the leader in the snow.
   Variation: When a new snow has fallen, adult can go outside and make footprints in the snow. Children follow adult's footprints when they come outside.

5. COME AND FOLLOW ME IN A LINE: (Tune--"Mary Had a Little Lamb")
   Come and follow me in a line, me in a line, me in a line.
   Come and follow me in a line, we will go this way.
   Form line. Sing verse while following leader who can walk, hop, or skip around room. At the end of the verse, the leader "freezes" in an unusual or peculiar position. Followers "freeze" in the same position. Change leaders and repeat.

6. FOX AND GEESE: Make a path with foot tracks in the snow. The path is a circle divided into fourths or eighths. In the center make a small circle to be used as the pen for the geese. To play the game, select one child as the fox. The remaining players are geese. The fox and geese must stay on the paths. The geese are safe in the pen. There can only be two geese in the pen at one time. The fox tries to catch a goose. When a goose is caught, the goose becomes the fox. The game is repeated.

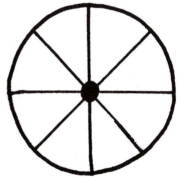

7. MATCHING TEXTURES: Cut two pieces from the same fabric. Use different fabrics. Examples are wool, felt, velvet, and tweed. Place one piece of each fabric in a bag. Present child with a piece of fabric. After he has touched the fabric, he reaches into the bag and locates its mate.

8. SNOW CLAY: Use equal parts of Elmer's® School Glue and liquid starch. Place starch in a disposable container. Add glue and mix until it forms a ball. Remove ball and knead until putty-like consistency is reached. (Mixing and kneading takes a considerable amount of time.) Allow time for creative play. Store in plastic bag or covered bowl in refrigerator.

9. PLAY DOUGH: Combine in saucepan 1 cup flour, 2 teaspoons cream of tartar, and 1/2 cup salt. Combine 1 cup water, 1 tablespoon vegetable oil, and food coloring. Slowly stir liquid into flour mixture. Cook for three minutes over medium heat until mixture pulls away from sides of pan. Cool slightly. Allow time for creative play. Store at room temperature in covered container.
    Note: This is one of the best experiences you can provide for a child. Play dough allows for release of energy and tensions in a socially acceptable manner. It increases manipulation skills. It allows creativity and is intriguing to children at all levels of development.

10. INDOOR SAND PLAY: If indoor sand table is not available, line a sturdy cardboard box with a large trash bag. Fill bag with several inches of sand. Bag can be closed with twister after use. Use buckets, shovels, trowels, funnels, sieves, rolling pins, stones, ladles, dump trucks, combs, or plastic containers. The following can also be made:

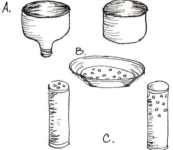

    A. FUNNEL: Use large, plastic, bleach bottle. Cut across the middle. Use top as funnel and bottom as bucket.
    B. PIE TIN SIEVE: Punch holes in the bottom of a pie tin.
    C. CAN SIEVE: Punch holes in top or sides of a tennis ball or potato chip can. Vary size and number of holes in each can.
    Variation: Use birdseed instead of sand.

11. INDOOR SNOW PLAY: If unable to go outside to play in snow. bring snow indoors. Fill waterplay containers with snow. Provide spoons, measuring cups, molds, plastic containers, pails, and shovels.
    Variation: Add a few drops of food coloring to snow.

12. SNOWMAN: (Group project) Go outside and make a snowman. Items that can be used to decorate snowman are a carrot, scarf, old hat, stick, rocks, coat, or charcoal.

13. SNOW SCENE: (Group project) Cover the inside of a large gift box lid with cotton. Use a mirror for a frozen pond. Small twigs and evergreen branches can be used for trees. Add plastic or play dough animals and figures.

14. PINE CONE GARDEN: (Group project) Place household cement in center of a small aluminum pie tin. Stand pine cone in cement. Sprinkle rye grass seed in the "leaves" of the pine cone. Pour 1" of water into pie tin. Keep water at this level by adding water when necessary. Pine cone will absorb water, and soon the grass will start to grow. Trim with scissors to make an attractive garden.

15. FROSTY WINDOW MURAL: (Group project) Cover window with Glass Wax® and let dry. With fingers, draw design on wax.

CREATIVE DRAMATICS AND MOVEMENT

1. SNOWFLAKES: (Tune--"Mary Had a Little Lamb")
         Snowflakes falling gently down.
         Whirling round, twirling round.
         Slowly falling to the ground.
         Landing softly without a sound.
    Make snowflakes according to diagram. Attach snowflakes to strings. Use when dramatizing this verse.

2. WALKING IN THE SNOW: Dramatize motions while adult says verse.
   Walking, walking in the snow. First walk quickly on tiptoe.
   Lift your left foot, then your right. Raise them to the tallest height.
   Now slide, now glide, just like a skater from side to side.
   Shuffle, shuffle, shuffle your feet. Make a circle until ends meet.
   Round and round and round you go. Now you can skip fast or very slow.
   Watch your step; don't slip. Oh no! Down you go!

3. SNOW FUN: Pretend to be a snowflake and float slowly through the air. Now Mr.
   North Wind blows you quickly through the air. Finally, you fall silently on
   the ground. Children come outside to play in the snow. They roll you and your
   snowflake friends into a ball. The children make a snowman. Now stand and
   pretend to be that snowman. It's cold. You stand straight and tall. The sun
   shines and the temperature warms. You slowly begin to melt. It becomes hotter
   and hotter, and you become smaller and smaller. Finally you melt into a puddle
   of water.

4. BEAR IN WINTER: Pretend to be a bear. Walk like a bear by bending your knees
   and touching your hands to the floor. Look for a warm cave because it is
   becoming colder. Curl up and go to sleep until the weather is warmer. Now
   awaken slowly from your winter's nap. Stretch your body. You are very hungry.
   It is time to leave the cave and to hunt for food.

5. WINTER SCARVES: Hold scarf or paper streamer that matches a color mentioned in
   the following verse. When color is mentioned, wave scarf.
   Winter scarves come in every hue. So wave your scarf on your color cue.
   Start with a pretty blue. Wave it high in the sky. Thank you.
   And next is a bright color red, often the color of a winter sled.
   Then comes yellow, too; wave a circle like the moon so new.
   The green is like the evergreen trees, swaying in the winter breeze.
   Purple is a majestic sight. Wave it high like the mountain's height.
   Wave all the scarves with colors bright. They are such a pretty sight!

6. WAVING SCARF: Wave a scarf or paper streamer to different tempos of music.

7. DRAMATIZE WINTER ACTIVITIES: Name activities and things that happen in winter.
   Dramatize responses. Responses can include sledding, skiing, snowmobiling,
   shoveling snow, bears sleeping, snow falling, and people wearing coats.

8. SKATER'S WALTZ: Play the familiar "Skater's Waltz" and pretend to be a skater.

PHYSICAL DEVELOPMENT

1. SHOVEL SNOW: Go outside and use small shovels to clear snow from sidewalks and
   paths on playground.

2. SNOW SCULPTURE: Go outside and mark an area of snow with a stick for each
   child. Use snow in area to create sculpture. After sculptures are created,
   have a "Show and Tell" time. The sculptures can be as simple as a ball or as
   complex as a snow castle.

3. SNOW ANGEL: Lie on back in snow or on floor. Place arms at sides and legs
   together. Keeping elbows straight, move arms up and down in snow. Keeping
   knees straight, open and close legs. Stand and admire the "angel" created in
   the snow.

4. SNOWBALL FIGHT: If it's too cold outside, have a "snowball" fight inside. Old newspapers can be torn, formed into balls, and thrown. A fort can be made from cardboard boxes or blocks.

5. DRESSING SKILLS: Teach basic dressing skills by preparing the following:

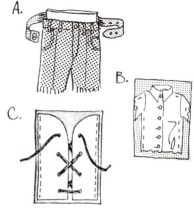

   A. Cut legs from child's pants. Insert stiff cardboard in top portion of pants to retain shapes. Thread belt through loops and buckle. This can be used for zipping, snapping, and buckling.
   B. Cut front of child's shirt, leaving buttons and buttonholes. Staple sides to artist canvas panel. Use for buttoning.
   C. Staple two pieces of vinyl to heavy cardboard as shown in diagram. Punch matching holes along inside vertical edge of each piece of vinyl. Provide long shoelace for lacing and tying.

   Variations:
   A. Place winter clothes in cardboard box for children to dress themselves or to dress dolls. Examples are mittens, gloves, scarves, boots, hats, sweaters, and jacket.
   B. Prepare a dressing book using sturdy fabric such as canvas or vinyl. Plan pages and do the necessary sewing before assembling book. Include a page for each dressing skill. Examples are large button and buttonhole, large zipper, large snap, and belt with belt buckle.

6. MITTENS: (Marie Louise Allen)
         Thumbs in the thumb place,
         Fingers all together:
         This is the song we sing
         In mitten weather.
   Learn to put on mittens using this verse.

7. COAT:
         My coat is open on the floor.
         I stand at the tip-top.
         In the armholes go one hand and one more.
         Then it's over my head--flip-flop.
         I did it myself! Now I'm out the door.
   Adult recites verse, while child dons coat. On floor, place coat with front facing upward. Child stands at top of coat, places hands in armholes, and flips coat over head. Coat will slip on easily.

8. BASKETBALL: Stand in circle and take turns trying to throw ball into a basket placed in center of the circle.
   A. For basket use box or place circle on floor with masking tape.
   B. Instead of basketball, play "snowball" toss. Toss styrofoam snowballs or newspaper rolled into balls into a large, black, top hat.

9. SLEDDING: Flatten a large cardboard box. Make holes in two corners on one narrow end of box. Holes should be 3" from edge. Thread a rope through the holes making a handle for the sled. Pull box as a sled.

10. HOCKEY: Use a cardboard box for the goal, a sponge ball or sock rolled into a ball for the puck, and a yardstick or old broom for the hockey stick. Each player hits puck across room and into goal. To make it seem like skating on ice, play in stocking feet on hard smooth-surfaced floor.

MATH

1. TEAR A SNOWFLAKE: Use a large piece of white paper or computer paper. Tear a tiny snowflake, an enormous one, a long narrow one, a short fat one, and a round one. Paste the snowflakes on a piece of paper or attach to a string and hang as a mobile. Discuss shapes.

2. SNOWMAN: Give each child three different-sized white circles and a dark piece of construction paper. How many snowballs do you have? What are the shapes of the snowballs? Which circle is largest? Which is the smallest? Build a snowman by gluing circles in order from largest to smallest. Discuss top, middle, and bottom. Use black squares for eyes, orange triangle for nose, and red oval for mouth. Discuss color and shape of features.

3. BUTTONS FOR SNOWMAN: Use ten pieces of tagboard. Draw a snowman without a hat on each piece of tagboard. Put sets of buttons on each snowman from 1 to 10. Cover with clear self-adhesive plastic. Cut ten top hats from paper. Mark each with a number from 1 to 10. Match each hat with corresponding snowman that has same number of buttons.

4. COLOR GRADATION: Divide a primary or secondary color of tempera paint into two containers. Paint a popsicle stick with the color. Paint additional popsicle sticks different tints and shades by doing the following:
    A. Add small amount of white paint to first container to make a lighter color or a tint. Paint popsicle stick. Continue process until five different tints are painted on sticks.
    B. Add small amount of black paint to second container to make a darker color or a shade. Paint stick. Continue process until five different shades are painted on sticks.
Paint sticks with clear acrylic spray. Arrange sticks in order from lightest to darkest. Discuss lighter, darker, tint, and shade.
Variations:
    A. Experiment with paint to make shades and tints.
    B. Use paint chips available in paint stores.

5. MATCHING MITTENS: Draw a set of mittens along the vertical edge of paper. Color a different design on each mitten. Draw a matching set on other side of paper but alter sequence. Laminate with clear self-adhesive plastic. Child draws a line with crayon connecting the matching pairs of mittens. Crayon can be erased so activity can be repeated.
Variations:
    A. Match pairs of mittens that have been placed in a box.
    B. Cut pairs of mittens from construction paper, wallpaper books, or cloth. Place in box. Match the pairs of mittens.
    C. Instead of mittens, match boots or shoes.

6. TRACKS: Cut footprints or animal tracks from paper. Make half the footprints red and half blue. Place on floor, alternating colors. Tie red ribbon to one leg of child and blue ribbon to other leg. Walk through tracks matching color on leg with color of track.

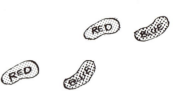

Variation: Place numbers or letters on footprints. Walk through pattern following consecutive numbers or letters.

SCIENCE

1. SNOWFLAKES: Go outside when it is snowing. Catch a snowflake on hand. How does snow feel? Responses could include soft, wet, and cold. Place dark construction paper outside in cold weather or in refrigerator to cool it so snowflakes will not melt as quickly. Catch snowflakes on paper. Look at snowflakes through a magnifying glass. Compare shapes. Discuss:
   A. No two snowflakes are exactly alike. All snowflakes are six-sided (hexagonal).
   B. What is snow? Snow occurs when ice crystals form around tiny dust particles in the air.
   C. What would happen if the air were warmer? It would rain instead of snow.
   D. What happens to snow when it melts? It waters outside plants and trees. Melting snow in the mountains where the heaviest snow falls runs into reservoirs where water is stored for use in homes and schools.

Measure to determine how much snow has fallen. Let measured snow melt to determine how much moisture or actual water was in the snow.

2. SNOW, WATER, AND ICE: Experiment with snow in the following ways:
   A. Give each child a paper cup to fill with snow. Bring cups inside and discuss changes as snow melts. What is happening to the snow? Why is it melting? Has it decreased in volume?
      Variation: Bring a pan of snow inside. Mound snow in pan. Discuss changes.
   B. Fill two identical containers with snow. Bring containers inside. Spread snow from one container evenly to cover bottom of a 9" x 13" cake pan. Mound snow from second container in center of another 9" x 13" pan. Discuss which will melt first. Why? Observe.
   C. Place a pan of the melted snow in the freezer or outside if temperature is below freezing point of 32° Fahrenheit. Note changes after it forms into ice. It will expand. Discuss that water freezes when it becomes very cold.

3. ICE: Experiment with ice cubes. Examples are: place ice cube beside another ice cube; place it on floor; lay it on open hand; hold it in closed hand; place it in mouth and chew; place it on plate and sprinkle salt over it; and place it in a cup of hot water. Discuss:
   A. The solid form of water is ice.
   B. Which ice cube melted first? Why?
   C. How is ice melted when it forms on sidewalks, streets, and car windows?
   D. Why does water remain frozen on an indoor ice skating rink?
   E. Is water that comes from a faucet always a liquid? Would ice ever come from a faucet? No. Why?

Variation: Put a mitten on one hand. Hold ice cube in each hand. Which is colder? This is why mittens are worn.

4. FROST: Frost is the form of water found in a deep-freeze. Observe frost outdoors or in freezer with magnifying glass. There are three basic types of frost: tabular or flakes, spikes, and feathery.

5. SEE YOUR BREATH: Blow breath in hand. How does it feel? The breath is warm. Blow breath outside when it is cold. What happens? The water vapor in the warm breath condenses when it is cooled by the cold air and makes steam.

6. THERMOMETERS: There are many kinds of thermometers. Display candy, weather, meat, oven, and refrigerator thermometers. Explain how they are used. How are they alike? How are they different? Register outside temperature with weather thermometer. Register temperature indoors. Note changes. What causes this? It is cold outside and warm inside. How did the room get warm? Feel heat coming from heat registers. Explore the furnace to see from where the heat comes. Discuss that pipes carry heat to rooms.

7. BIRD FEEDERS: Explain that many birds migrate to warmer climates because food becomes scarce in colder areas. Birds that remain have a difficult time finding food. People can help birds by making bird feeders and throwing crumbs to birds on snowy days. Hang feeder outside in a location where birds can easily be observed feeding.

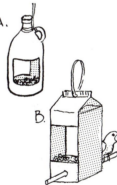

   A. BOTTLE BIRD FEEDER: Cut a large rectangle from both sides of a large, plastic, bleach bottle. Fill bottom with birdseed. Tie string through handle and around neck of the bottle.

   B. MILK CARTON BIRD FEEDER: Cut windows from opposite sides of milk carton leaving 2" at the bottom. To make a perch for the bird, place a pencil through the sides of the carton at the bottom. Punch a hole in the top. Tie string through hole and make loop. Spray paint, if desired. Place birdseed in bottom of carton.

   C. SCANDINAVIAN BIRD FEEDER: Place in frying pan one pound suet cut in small pieces. Cover pan and melt suet over low heat. Cool. Mix with 1/2 cup birdseed. Spoon into milk carton. Place in refrigerator overnight. When suet has hardened, remove carton. Tie suet with string like wrapping a package. Tie ends of string around branch of tree.
   Note: It is a tradition to share the Christmas feast with the birds in Norway, Denmark, and Sweden.

   D. PINE CONE BIRD FEEDER: Tie string to pine cone and form loop with remaining string. Roll tips of pine cone in peanut butter or honey. When covered, roll cone in birdseed. Cover with plastic wrap if children are going to take the feeder home.

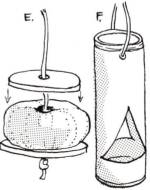

   E. DOUGHNUT BIRD FEEDER: Punch hole in center of two plastic lids. Place doughnut between lids. Tie knot in one end of cord. Thread other end through lids and doughnut. Tie loose end to tree.

   F. POTATO CHIP CAN FEEDER: Cut two triangular-shaped holes in opposite sides of potato chip can. Make bottom sides of triangles parallel to bottom and 1" from bottom of can. Punch two holes in top of can on opposite sides. Lace string through holes. Tie string in loop. Place birdseed in bottom of can.

8. FABRIC: Cold temperatures require warmer clothing. Various types of fabric can be displayed and examined with a magnifying glass. Note differences.

9. COLDS AND COUGHS: Discuss that people can give their colds to others by spreading germs. Germs are tiny invisible organisms that cause disease. They are carried on the hands and in the mouth and nose of a sick person. When the person coughs or sneezes, tiny droplets of water are sprayed into the air. These droplets contain germs. To demonstrate this, fill spray bottle with water. Spray water into air and into facial tissue. Explain that germs carried by a sick person act in the same way as the spray of water from the bottle. Discuss good health habits which can prevent the spread of colds. Examples are:
    A. Covering mouth with facial tissue when coughing or sneezing.
    B. Disposing of facial tissue into trash container.
    C. Washing hands frequently when sick.
    D. Staying in bed away from others.

10. CRYSTAL GARDEN: Place pieces of charcoal in a shallow bowl or 9" x 9" glass pan. Mix together 1/4 cup ammonia, 1/4 cup noniodized salt, and 1/4 cup liquid bluing. Pour this solution slowly over the pieces of charcoal. If desired, sprinkle garden with food coloring. Almost immediately the crystals will start forming. Do not move the container or shake it because the crystals are very fragile and will crumble. Cover bare spots with a little more ammonia. Look at crystals with a magnifying glass. Compare crystals to snowflakes.

                              MUSIC

1. COME SING A SONG OF WINTER: (Tune--"Did You Ever See a Lassie?")
         Come sing a song of winter, of winter, of winter.
         Come sing a song of winter: the cold days are here.
         With winter winds blowing and rosy cheeks glowing,
         Come sing a song of winter: the cold days are here.   Author Unknown

2. A-SLEDDING WE WILL GO: (Tune--"A-Hunting We Will Go")
         A-sledding we will go, a-sledding we will go.
         We'll hold on tight and sit just right,
         And down the hill we'll go. Wheeeeeeeee!   Author Unknown

3. CHILDREN PUT YOUR COATS ON: (Tune--"Did You Ever See a Lassie?")
         Children put your coats on, your coats on, your coats on.
         Children put your coats on--one, two, and three.
            (Continue using clothing children are putting on. Finally sing:)
         Children now are dressed, are dressed, are dressed.
         Children now are dressed. Let's go out to play.   Author Unknown

4. KERCHOO: (Tune--"Oats, Peas, Beans. and Barley Grow")
         When I have to go KERCHOO,
         Do you know what I always do?
         My hankie covers both mouth and nose
         And into my hankie my kerchoo goes. KERCHOO!   Author Unknown

                           FIELD TRIPS

1. WINTER WALK: Go for a walk and try to identify animal tracks in the snow. Note differences in size and depth of tracks.

VALENTINE'S DAY

VALENTINE'S DAY honors two different saints named Valentine. However, customs for the holiday have nothing to do with the lives of these saints. The customs come from the ancient Roman festival called Lupercalia, which took place on February 15. The festival honored Pan, the Roman god of nature, and Juno, the goddess of women and marriage. During this festival young people drew names from a box and exchanged gifts.

Gradually the custom of giving gifts was replaced by sending cards. Today Valentine's Day, celebrated on February 14, is a time to display love and affection. People send cards, candy, or flowers as valentines to their sweethearts, friends, and family.

CONCEPTS TO BE TAUGHT

1. Valentine's Day is celebrated on February 14.
2. It is a time to show affection to family and friends by sending and receiving cards, gifts, and flowers.
3. Valentine colors are red, white, and pink.
4. Hearts and cupids are Valentine symbols.
5. Love and friendship can be expressed in many ways. Examples are sharing, helping, and talking or playing with each other in kind ways.

ART ACTIVITIES

1. HEART: Fold paper in half. Draw half a heart starting and ending at fold. Cut along line. Open.

2. DOILY: Fold square of white paper in half. Fold in half again. Cut small triangles from edges. Open.

3. STAINED GLASS HEART: Place red, pink, and white crayon shavings between two pieces of waxed paper or in waxed paper sandwich bag. Cover with newspaper. Adult presses with warm iron to melt crayon chips. Allow to cool. Cut heart shape from center of construction paper. Tape waxed paper behind heart-shaped hole.
Variations:
   A. Fold construction paper in half to make card. Cut heart shape from front of card. Tape "stained glass" behind the heart-shaped hole.
   B. Cut "stained glass" into heart shape. Attach string to create mobile.

4. TISSUE PAPER HEART: Cut heart from construction paper. Crumple small squares of tissue paper and glue to heart.

5. HEART HAT: Fold paper in half. On one half of paper, draw a heart with top touching the fold. Cut. Staple points of two hearts to 1 1/2" strip of construction paper. Adjust strip to fit head. Staple. If desired, write name on heart.

6. FAN: Glue a doily onto a colored paper circle of the same size. Add a heart in the center. Decorate heart. Glue popsicle stick to back of paper circle.
Variation: Write on heart, "You're FANtastic."

7. VALENTINE SACHET: Spray perfume on cotton ball. Glue ball to upper area of large round doily. With cotton inside. fold doily in half forming a half-circle. Staple together at top. Glue small bows and tiny hearts to sachet.
Variation: Use two heart-shaped doilies. Place one doily on construction paper. Trace and cut. Glue paper heart onto doily. Glue perfumed cotton ball to center of paper heart. Attach second doily to paper heart. To hang, punch hole in top of heart. Thread ribbon or yarn through hole. Tie ends of ribbon.

8. VALENTINE SMILE BUTTON: Make a happy face on a heart shape with crayons or felt-tipped pens. Pin or tape onto shirt or blouse.

9. LOVE BEADS: Cut piece of yarn 25" in length. Tie 1" piece of straw to one end. Wrap other end of yarn with tape to make needle. Thread half of yarn with 1" pieces of straw. Then thread with paper heart that has hole punched in top center. Continue adding pieces of straw. Tie ends of yarn together to make necklace.
Variation: For needle, tie yarn to looped end of bobby pin.

10. VALENTINE FLOWER: Place the bottom tips of 3 to 5 red hearts together. Glue a small circle over the tips for the center of the flower. Attach stem and use green hearts for leaves.

11. HEART MOBILE: Make different sizes of hearts. Attach hearts to string.

12. HEART PEOPLE AND ANIMALS: Create people or animals by gluing together various sizes of hearts cut from white, pink, and red paper. For facial features use tiny hearts, chalk, crayons, or felt-tipped pens. Examples are fat cow, thin lady, and sad-faced man.
Variations:
    A. Accordion-fold strips of paper. Glue strips to hearts for arms and legs.
    B. Instead of gluing hearts together, attach with string to make mobile.

13. **VALENTINE BUTTERFLY:** Cut two red hearts and two smaller white hearts. Matching bottom points of hearts, glue white hearts to top of red hearts. Overlap and glue the bottom tips of the hearts. Twist a red and white pipe cleaner together. Glue to center of hearts to form butterfly's body. Leave 1" of pipe cleaners untwisted at ends for antennae.

14. **VALENTINE CARD:** Fold piece of construction paper in half. Glue any of the following materials to front of card.

Pictures from magazines	Rickrack	Glitter
Paper hearts	Doilies	Feathers
Paper cupids	Yarn	Tissue paper
Paper arrows	Lace	Fabric scraps
Photo of child	Net	Old valentine cards

Variation: Instead of card, make collage by gluing materials to piece of paper.

15. **VALENTINE SACK:** Decorate pink or white lunch sack with crayons, felt-tipped pens, or materials found in VALENTINE CARD (listed above). Write child's name on sack.
Variation: Instead of sack use shoe box.

16. **VALENTINE BASKET:** Cut two large hearts from red, pink, or white construction paper. Staple sides and bottom of hearts together. Attach strip of construction paper for handle. Decorate with materials from VALENTINE CARD. This makes a nice valentine present for Mom when filled with flowers listed below:

    A. Make VALENTINE FLOWER (see page 92) and use pipe cleaner for stem.
    B. Roll cotton balls in dry tempera and attach pipe cleaners for stems.
    C. Paint individual cups of an egg carton. Attach pipe cleaners for stems.
    D. Cut or tear flowers from colorful paper. Glue to pipe cleaners.
    E. Use VALENTINE CARNATION (see page 105).
Note: If desired, place drop of perfume on each flower for fragrance.

17. **YARN DESIGN:** Dip red yarn in glue or liquid starch. Place on paper to make design. Allow yarn to dry. Glue colored tissue paper to center of design.
Variations:
    A. Instead of tissue paper, paint or color center of the design.
    B. To make mobile, place yarn on waxed paper or aluminum foil instead of paper. When yarn dries, remove it from waxed paper or foil. Hang.

18. **CREATION PAPER:** Adult draws a different heart shape in a different location on each piece of paper. Give one paper to each child. Encourage use of imagination to incorporate shape into drawing.
Variations:
    A. Cut a small heart-shaped hole in the paper.
    B. Draw shape, line, letter, or number on paper.
    C. Use different-shaped pieces of paper.

19. **DRIBBLE DESIGN:** Add red food coloring to salt. Shake. Dribble glue onto paper to make design. Sprinkle colored salt onto wet glue. Remove excess.
Variations:
    A. Instead of dribbling glue, spread glue over a heart shape.
    B. Instead of dribbling glue, dab glue onto paper with cotton-tipped swab.

20. VALENTINE PAINTING: Paint with red, white, and pink tempera onto red, white, or pink heart-shaped paper.
Variations:
    A. Add salt to paint. The salt sparkles when it dries.
    B. Instead of tempera, paint with ketchup. This can also be used for fingerpainting.

COOKING ACTIVITIES

1. RED GELATIN HEARTS: 3 envelopes unflavored gelatin
                        1/4 cup cranapple juice, boiling
                        2 3/4 cups cranapple juice, cold
Dissolve gelatin in boiling juice. Add cold juice. Stir. Pour into shallow baking pan. Chill. When gelatin is set, cut with metal, heart-shaped, cookie cutter. Hearts are eaten with hands.
Note: Trimmings can be used in other salads, snacks, or desserts.

2. SWEETHEART SALAD: 16 ounces cherry pie filling   2 sliced bananas
                      13 ounces pineapple tidbits, drained
Combine all ingredients. Chill and serve.

3. LOVE JUICE: 2 cups chilled pineapple juice
                 10 ounces unsweetened frozen strawberries
                 2/3 cup nonfat dry milk granules
                 8 ice cubes
Combine all ingredients in blender. Blend until ice cubes are crushed.

4. PINK TOMATO JUICE COCKTAIL: 4 cups tomato juice   dash of soy sauce
                                 1 cup plain yogurt   1/4 teaspoon celery seeds
Mix ingredients. Chill and serve.

5. VALENTINE MILK SHAKES: 10 ounces frozen strawberries
                            4 cups cold milk
Combine fruit and milk in blender. Blend until smooth and frothy.
Variation: Instead of strawberries use frozen raspberries or cherries.

6. CRANBERRY NOG: 1/2 cup cranberry juice
                    1/2 cup plain yogurt
                    1/2 teaspoon unsweetened strawberry soft drink mix
Combine all ingredients. Serve chilled.

7. PIZZA HEARTS: Using a heart-shaped cookie cutter, cut shape from toasted whole wheat bread. Spread with pizza sauce. Sprinkle with shredded Mozzarella cheese. Broil until cheese melts.

8. HEART SANDWICHES: Use a heart-shaped cookie cutter to cut a heart from a slice of whole wheat bread. Spread with favorite sandwich filling.
Variation: Cut a heart from a slice of cheese. Serve on bread or cracker.

9. FROZEN CANDY CUP: 8 ounces plain yogurt
                       1 cup frozen, whole, unsweetened strawberries
Whip yogurt and berries in blender. Place paper cupcake holders in muffin tin. Fill cups 1/4 full. Freeze.

10. VALENTINE MUFFINS: 1 egg   1/4 cup sugar
                          1 cup milk   1 tablespoon baking powder
                          1/4 cup salad oil
                          2 cups flour
                          12 small, frozen, unsweetened strawberries

Beat egg, milk, and oil with fork until blended. Mix dry ingredients together. Add to egg mixture. Stir until blended. Batter will be lumpy. Spoon batter into 12 paper-lined muffin cups. Fill each 1/3 full. Place thawed strawberry in each cup. Top with enough batter to fill each cup 2/3 full. Bake at 400° for 20 to 25 minutes.
Variation: Instead of strawberries, use 1/2 teaspoon of strawberry preserves in each muffin.

11. HEALTHY HEART CAKE: 1 1/2 cups flour   1 teaspoon soda
                          1/2 cup wheat germ   1 teaspoon salt
                          1/2 cup nonfat dry milk granules   1 1/4 cups oil
                          1 1/2 cups sugar   4 eggs, beaten
                          1 teaspoon unsweetened, strawberry, soft drink mix
                          2 cups frozen unsweetened strawberries

Thaw and drain strawberries. Mix together dry ingredients. Add remaining ingredients. Combine. Pour batter into one square 8" pan and one round 8" pan. Bake and cool. Cut round cake in half and place on adjoining sides of square cake to form heart shape.

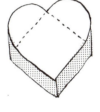

FINGERPLAYS

1. Snip, snip, snip the paper. (pretend to cut)
Paste, paste, paste the paper (pretend to paste)
Press, press, press the paper. (pretend to press paper)
Here's a valentine for you! (pretend to give card to friend)
              Marion Grayson

2. I'll cut red paper into a heart. (pretend to cut)
I'll paste lace on the outside part. (pretend to paste)
I'll give it to a friend of mine.
Will you be my valentine? (point to friend)

3. A piece of bright red paper.
Scissors and doilies, too. (open and close fingers like scissors)
Snip, paste, and PRESTO! (clap)
Here's a valentine for you. (point to a friend)

4. Won't you "bee" my valentine (point to friend)
And buzz away with me. (pretend to fly)
We'll bumble along together
Because you're my Honey Bee. (throw kiss)
Bzzzzzzzzzz!

5. To each and every friend of mine (point to friends)
I'll send a lovely valentine. (pretend to hand out valentines)
Mom, Dad, Sis, and Brother, too. (four fingers)
Will receive a heart that says, (form heart with fingers)
"I love you." (point to friend)

6. I feel topsy. (tilt to one side)
I feel turvy. (tilt to other side)
I feel absolutely fine.
Thank you for my valentine. (point to friends)

7. Cards, flowers, and candy (three
   fingers)
   Make valentines that are dandy.
   But a special gift that means a lot
   (stretch arms outward)
   Is a smile and a loving thought.
   (smile and point to head)

8. On Valentine's Day
   We give love in a special way.
   (hands at heart then extend outward)
   We care for family and friends.
   (point to friends)
   We share ourselves and gifts we
   send. (pretend to give gift)
   We express kind words and deeds
   (fingers to lips)
   And help with each other's needs.

9. On February fourteen
   Love and affection can be seen
   (point to eye)
   If we can do this for one day,
   (raise one finger)
   Then let's make it stay (shake head
   up and down)
   Every day of the year
   For those far and near. (point far
   and near)

10. The first valentine is trimmed in
    lace. (form heart)
    The second valentine has a funny
    face. (make funny face)
    The third valentine says, "I love
    you." (point to friend)
    The fourth valentine is forever
    true.
    Put them in an envelope. (pretend
    to put in envelope)
    Deliver door to door. (pretend to
    knock)
    How many friends are happy? (point
    to friends)
    1-2-3-4. (four fingers)

11. Let's give love in a special way
    (cross arms over chest and spread
    outward)
    By what we do and what we say.
    (point to mouth)
    We can share our toys with others.
    (pretend to give toy to friend)
    Say, "please" and "thank you" to
    sisters and brothers.

12. Valentine in the box sits so still.
    (squat)
    Won't you come out? Yes, I will!
    (jump up)

13. I love all my friends, this is
    true. (place hand over heart)
    But for my valentine, I'll choose
    you! (point to friend)

14. Do you know what this is? (form
    heart with fingers)
    Yes, a heart. Pretend it's mine.
    (point to self)
    I'll put it on paper and make a
    valentine.
    Into an envelope it will go, (pre-
    tend to stuff envelope)
    With address written clear. (pre-
    tend to write)
    Soon you'll pull it out and read,
    (pretend to take out card)
    "To my valentine so dear."
    That's you! (point to friend)
                        Mabelle B. McQuire

15. I treat my friends (point to
    friends)
    How I like them to treat me.
    (point to self)
    That's the Golden Rule, you see.
    (raise index finger)
    If I'm kind and polite, (point to
    self)
    My friends will treat me right.
    (point to friends)
    Everyday will be such fun.
    Love is good for everyone. (place
    hand over heart)

16. I send a smile to friends I meet.
    (fingers to smiling lips)
    It will return a special treat.
    A smile is like a boomerang.
    It comes right back in a while
    When your friend returns your
    smile. (fingers to smiling lips)

17. When friends come to visit me
    (point to self)
    I am as polite as I can be.
    When I share my toys (pretend to
    give)
    It fills my heart with many joys.
    (hand to heart)

By watching what we do & say that is the love we send

Love one another

96

18. A happy smile I'll send to you.
    (point to friend and smile)
    Put it on and wear one, too. (fin-
    gers to smiling lips)
    Pass it around to all you meet.
    (point to friends)
    Happiness will flow to all you
    greet. (smile and wave)

19. How much do you love me? (point to
    friend and self)
    A bushel and a peck and a hug
    around the neck, (hug)
    That's how much I love you!
                              Traditional

20. Let's have a happy day. (smile)
    Let's give our love away. (hands
    over heart, then extend arms)
    Let's share our love at play.
    Let's take turns and have fun.
    Let's share our love with everyone.
    (point to friends)
    That's the way friendships are won.
    (hold hands)

21. My friends are here to play.
    (point to friends)
    We'll have a zip-a-dee-doo-dah day!
    (fling arms wide above head)

LANGUAGE DEVELOPMENT

1. DISCUSSION ABOUT FRIENDS:
   A. What is a friend?
   B. How do you become a friend to someone?
   C. Discuss the phrase, "Do unto others as you would have them do unto you."
   D. How do you show love and affection? On Valentine's Day cards, gifts, and
      flowers are sent to family and friends. Love can also be expressed by
      sharing, helping, saying kind words, doing kind deeds, and being consid-
      erate of one another.

2. VALENTINE SYMBOLS:
   A. HEART symbolizes love and emotion.
   B. CUPID, Greek god of love and beauty, is represented as winged boy with
      arrow.
   C. ARROW was shot by Cupid to make people fall in love.
   D. RED symbolizes warmth and feeling. It is associated with the heart.
   E. WHITE is associated with bridal apparel.
   F. LACE is used for bridal veils. This inspired its use on Valentine's Day
      as a symbol of romance.
   G. FLOWER is a love token. A rose is the flower most closely associated
      with love.
   H. BIRDS associated with this holiday include dove (a symbol of peace and
      romantic love) and lovebird (a small parrot that is greatly attracted to
      its mate). Ancient people thought birds chose their mates on Valentine's
      Day.
   I. HAND symbolizes courtship. A man often asked a lady "for her hand."

3. MAIL CARRIER: Place pictures related to Valentine's Day into envelopes. Examples of pictures are family members, house, envelope, stamps, mailbox, flowers,
   and valentine. Discuss that on Valentine's Day cards and letters are sent as
   expressions of love and friendship. One player is selected to be the mail
   carrier who hands one envelope to another player. The player opens the envelope and describes the picture. Remaining players guess what the picture is.
   Player who described the picture then becomes the mail carrier, and the game is
   repeated until all have had a turn being the mail carrier.
   Variation: Place all children's names in an envelope. Adult draws one name
   and gives clues about child. Players guess "mystery person." Continue until
   all children's names are drawn.

4. **VALENTINE STORY SEQUENCE:** Adult draws several pictures that depict the steps of a process from beginning to end. For example, make valentine, place valentine in an envelope, and mail valentine. Glue each picture on an individual card. Place cards in sequential order.

5. **VALENTINE STORY:** Child dictates creative story about Valentine's Day to adult. Variations:
   A. Write story as group project.
   B. Instead of story, create a valentine poem.
   C. Instead of story, make love-o-gram by writing creative message inside VALENTINE CARD (see page 93).

6. **FOLDING HEART STORY:** Tell the following story while making a heart from a folded piece of paper. Draw items on paper according to diagram.

   Sally and Jim lived at A (make A). Grandma lived at B (make B). They decided to make a map of the path to Grandma's around the lake (draw lake). They walked around the lake (draw half heart starting at A and ending at B). When they arrived at Grandma's, they took scissors and cut along the path they had walked (cut along line). They opened it and gave the valentine to Grandma!

   Author Unknown

7. **MOVING VALENTINE:** Set decorated valentine box on table. Move a valentine in relationship to box according to directions given by adult. Examples are under, behind, in front of, and at the side of the box.

8. **VALENTINE SAYINGS:** Fold piece of construction paper in half. Use one of the following ideas to decorate card. Discuss word usage and meaning of each saying.
   A. "You light up my life!" Use an outline of a light bulb.
   B. "You're priceless!" Use "For Sale" column from newspaper.
   C. "You'll always be NEWS with me." Use section of newspaper.
   D. "For Mom, my need-le never end." Give package of needles as gift.
   E. "Dad's an old smoothie--never rough on me." Use sand paper and satin.
   F. "I'd like a Corn-er in your heart." Place corn in corner of a heart.
   G. "Where have you Bean all of my life?" Use a bean seed.

9. **BOOKS:**
   A Friend Is Someone Who Likes You--Anglund
   Love Is a Special Way of Feeling--Anglund
   Let's Be Friends--Bryano
   Do You Want To Be My Friend?--Carle
   May I Bring a Friend?--De Regniers
   Play With Me--Ets
   T.A. for Tots--Freed
   What Do You Say Dear?--Joslin
   George and Martha--Marshall
   I Learn About Sharing--Roorback
   Making Friends--Scheck
   I Don't Like It When Friends Come to Visit--Sherman
   The Giving Tree--Silverstein
   One Is Good, Two Are Better--Slobodkin
   A Friend Is Aimie--Steiner
   I'd Rather Stay With You--Steiner
   Do You Know What I'll Do?--Zololow

10. REFERENCE BOOK:
    Hearts, Cupids, and Red Roses--Barth

GAMES AND SOCIAL ACTIVITIES

1. A-TISKET, A-TASKET: (Adapted from traditional verse)
        A-tisket, a-tasket,
        A red and yellow basket:
        Sent a valentine to my friend,
        And on the way I dropped it.
        One of you has picked it up
        And put it in your pocket.
   Sit in circle. While verse is sung, Player A walks around circle with a bean
   bag or felt heart. He drops heart behind Player B when fourth line is sung.
   Player B takes the heart and chases Player A around the circle to the empty
   space. Repeat.
   Variation: Carry bean bag or felt heart in basket.

2. RING TO MY LOVE: (Tune--"Mary Had a Little Lamb")
        I sent a ring to my love, to my love, to my love.
        I sent a ring to my love on Valentine's Day.
   Sit in circle. Thread small ring onto long piece of cord or string. Tie ends
   of cord to make circle the approximate size of the circle made by players. One
   child stands in center of circle. Remaining players pass ring around circle
   while singing verse. When the verse is finished, players stop passing ring,
   and one player holds it in his hand. Child in center guesses which player has
   the ring. Player holding the ring then replaces child in center, and game is
   repeated.

3. HEART WALK: Cut matching pairs of hearts from various colors of construction
   paper. Place one heart of each pair in a box. Tape remaining hearts to floor
   in a circle. Players walk on circle of hearts to music. When music stops,
   each player stands on one of the hearts. One heart is drawn from box, and
   player standing on matching heart chooses heart from box for the following
   walk. Repeat.

4. BE MY VALENTINE:
        1-2-3-4-5-6-7-8 (circles rotate in opposite directions)
        Who will be my Valentine mate?
        Please stop and stand in place. (circle stop)
        Turn around, look me in the face. (inside players turn and face outside
        players)
        Let's clap our hands and slap our knees. (clap hands, slap knees)
        Be my Valentine, would you please? (give partner a hug)
   Divide players into two equal groups. Form two circles with one circle inside
   the other. Recite verse and do actions.

5. I HAVE A VALENTINE JUST FOR YOU: (Tune--"Skip to My Lou")
        I have a valentine just for you. I have a valentine just for you.
        I have a valentine just for you. I'll give you my heart, my darling.
   Sit in circle. While verse is sung, one player walks around outside of circle
   with paper heart. At end of verse, player gives heart to closest child. That
   child gives the first player a hug or handshake. Game is repeated with second
   player walking around outside of circle.

6. VALENTINE, LISTEN: Children do action when adult gives command that is preceded by word, "valentines." If command does not begin with word "valentines," players should not do action. For example, Adult says, "Valentines stand." and players stand. Adult says, "Sit." and players do not sit.

7. WHO WAS SO KIND?
   Can you guess who was so kind,
   To bring you a pretty valentine?
One player sits on a chair facing away from remaining players. Remaining players each have a construction paper valentine. Adult chooses one player who quietly places his heart behind the chair and returns to place. Everyone hides heart and recites verse. Player sitting in chair guesses who brought the valentine. Player then takes heart and joins remaining players. Player who brought heart sits in chair. Repeat game.
Variation: Use only one valentine. Adult gives player heart to deliver.

8. MARY FINDS A FRIEND: (Tune--"Farmer in the Dell") Found on page 65 of *Experience Games Through Music, for the Very, Very Young, for the Very Young.* by Sister Fleurette Sweeney, S.C.H. and Margaret Wharram, © 1973, Richards Institute of Music Education and Research.
Children sit in a circle. One child (Mary) walks or skips outside the circle, while everyone sings:
   Mary finds a friend. Oh Mary finds a friend.
   Heigh ho the derry oh, Mary finds a friend.
At the cadence, Mary takes the hand of the child nearest her (Linda), and asks, "Will you be my friend?" or "Will you come with me?" *The next verse is "Linda finds a friend." The game continues until all have joined the long "train" of friends. The two ends join to make a circle. Everyone skips around in the circle singing:
   We all found a friend. We all found a friend.
   Heigh ho the derry oh, we all found a friend.
*Note: Linda answers Mary saying, "Yes, I will." Linda·walks around circle with Mary singing next verse.

9. FRIEND OF MINE: (Tune--"Mary Had a Little Lamb")
   Will you be a friend of mine, a friend of mine, a friend of mine?
   Will you be a friend of mine and (action) around with me?
   (Child's name) is a friend of mine, a friend of mine, a friend of mine.
   (Child's name) is a friend of mine who (action) around with me.
                        Author Unknown
Sit in circle. One player moves around circle doing action. Examples of actions are skipping, hopping, and running. Player stops by another child, and both players move around circle. First player then sits in circle, and game is repeated with second child moving around circle doing different action.

10. WHICH FRIEND IS MISSING? Players hide their eyes, and adult taps one player who quietly leaves the room. Adult then asks remaining children, "Which friend is missing?" Remaining players guess who is missing. Repeat.
Variation: Instead of one child, two or three children leave at one time.

11. HEART STABILE: (Group project) With string attach hearts to a small branch of a tree. Stand tree in a flower pot filled with dirt or plaster of Paris.

12. VALENTINE EXCHANGE: (Group project)
    A. Tape VALENTINE SACKS (see page 93) to wall. Place sacks in a line at children's eye level.
    B. Child can sign name on back of valentine card. If child cannot print, the parent can write child's name on back of each card.
    C. To simplify valentine exchange, do not address the envelope. When giving valentines, drop one valentine in each sack.
    D. After all valentines are distributed, each person takes his bag and opens his cards. Replace valentines in sacks to insure safe delivery home.

CREATIVE DRAMATICS AND MOVEMENT

1. POST OFFICE: Discuss mailing valentines to friends, and then play post office. Materials needed include large blocks to make post office, large box for mailbox, table and chairs for writing, old valentines, envelopes, pencils, stamps, play money, stamp and stamp pad, large lady's shoulder bag to be used as mail carrier's bag.

2. ACTIVITY ADAPTED FROM VALENTINE CUSTOM: In a valentine box, place pictures of different people. Examples of pictures are Indian, clown, baby, barber, fire fighter, police officer, and mail carrier. First player draws one picture from the box and dramatizes person on picture. Remaining players try to guess what person he is depicting. Continue until all have drawn a picture from box.
Note: In Austria, Hungary, and Germany, priests had young men draw names of saints from a valentine box. The young men were to pattern their lives after these saints.

3. DID YOU EVER SEE A VALENTINE? (Tune--"Did You Ever See a Lassie?")
        Did you ever see a valentine, a valentine, a valentine?
        Did you ever see a valentine go this way and that?
        Go this way and that way, go this way and that way.
        Did you ever see a valentine go this way and that?
One player is chosen to be Valentine. Valentine does motion, and remaining children do same motion. Valentine chooses another to be leader. Repeat.
Note: HEART HAT (see page 92) can be worn for this activity.

4. VALENTINE PUPPETS: Make the following puppets come alive in a creative way.
    A. VALENTINE CARD PUPPET: Place two holes large enough for fingers in bottom of a valentine card that has an animal or person on it.
    B. HEART PUPPET: Cut out a 3" paper heart and a 1" paper heart. Make two finger holes in top of large heart. Draw face on small heart. Overlap pointed ends of hearts and glue. Accordion-fold strips of paper. Glue strips to hearts for arms.
    C. LOVE BUG: Make face on bottom of lunch sack with paper hearts, crayons, and felt-tipped pens. For antennae, accordion-fold strips of paper and attach to face. Glue small hearts on ends of strips. Attach a heart to each side of sack. Place hand in bag. Open and close hand in fold to make bug "talk."
    Variation: A special valentine message can be written under the bag flap. When the love bug "talks," his message will be visible.

5. VALENTINE MASK: From red construction paper cut a heart that is larger than child's face. Cut holes for eyes. Draw remaining features with crayon. Attach a 1" strip of doily or glue cotton around outside edge of heart. Attach a popsicle stick to bottom point of heart. Write an appropriate phrase on the forehead of the mask. For example, "Guess who wants to be your valentine?"

6. CREATIVE VALENTINE DANCE: Divide players into two equal groups. Form two circles with one circle inside the other. Circles rotate in opposite directions to music. When music stops, inside players turn and face outside circle. Player across from each person in opposite circle is partner. Music is played again, and partners create dance or march.
Note: In England, it was believed the first man a lady would see on Valentine's Day would be her husband. Some girls would keep their eyes shut until their favorite man would come to their homes.

7. FRIENDS: Dramatize following verse:
        Let's be friends on this Valentine's Day.
        We'll show love in many a way.
        I'll blow you a kiss. Catch it in your hand.
        Throw it back. Watch it land.
        Now partner, let's dance to a lively band.
        It's so nice to have a friend like you,
        Not just for today, but the whole year through!

8. HEART BEATS: Glue a heart shape cut from red construction paper on the end of an oatmeal container. Pat end of container with hand, creating own heart beat. Pretend to sleep and create slower heart beat. Pretend to run and create faster heart beat.

PHYSICAL DEVELOPMENT

1. FOLLOW THE HEART: Place masking tape on floor in shape of a large heart. Move on tape in the following ways:
    A. Walk, skip, hop, or jump along tape.
    B. Walk with one foot on tape and the other inside heart.
    C. Walk with one foot on tape and the other outside heart.
    D. Jump inside heart.
    E. Jump outside heart.

2. BEAN BAG TOSS: Cut heart-shaped holes in one side of a large box. Stand appropriate distance away and throw two socks rolled together or bean bags into holes in various ways. Bags can be tossed overhand or underhand. They can also be hiked like a football.
Variations: Instead of box, use one of the following:
    A. Use bowls or pans of different sizes for targets.
    B. Tape heart-shaped targets on the floor.
    C. Draw a heart-shaped target on butcher paper and place on floor.

3. BOWLING--FALLING HEART: For bowling pins use plastic bottles, milk cartons, or tennis ball cans. Place a heart on top of one bowling pin. One child is pin setter. Bowler holds ball until pin setter is ready. Bowler rolls ball, trying to knock down heart pin. Give extra points if heart pin has fallen.

4. HAND PINPRICK: Lay hand on paper. Trace around hand. Poke holes in outline of hand with paper clip that has one end bent outward.
Note: Pins or needles were used to make valentine cards by this method because it gave the appearance of lace.

MATH

1. VALENTINE ORDERING: Cut hearts that are progressively larger. Paste each heart on a square. Arrange hearts according to size.

2. VALENTINE SORTING BOX: Place hearts that are different sizes and colors in a box. Sort hearts according to size, color, or both.

3. VALENTINE NUMBER CARDS: Make set of number cards from 1 to 10. Cut out 55 paper hearts. Give one card to each child. Adult calls a number. Child having that number card places the correct number of hearts on it. Repeat, using a different number.
Variation: Instead of number cards, make number chart. Write numerals on one side of chart. Glue corresponding number of hearts next to each number.

4. MATCHING SHAPES: Cut out various shapes including hearts. Outline each shape on a piece of paper. Place shapes used for outlining on table. Place corresponding shape on outline.

5. HEART DOMINOES: Make a number domino set using hearts instead of dots. Play by matching dominoes that have equal numbers of hearts on adjacent sides.

6. CALENDAR TOSS: Place large calendar of February on the floor. Take turns tossing marker, button, bottle cap, or coin onto calendar. Identify number on which marker lands.

7. BROKEN HEART PUZZLE: Cut large heart from red paper. Write a saying or draw a picture on it. Example of saying is, "I go to pieces over you." Cut the heart in 3 to 6 pieces for a puzzle. Place pieces in an envelope with a note saying, "Please put the pieces of my heart together, and I'll be your valentine." Put pieces of heart puzzle together.
Variations: Instead of heart:
    A. Use a different shape.
    B. Cut picture from magazine. Make into puzzle.
Note: Cover picture before it is cut with clear self-adhesive plastic, and puzzle will be more durable.

8. COUNTING VALENTINES:
        Valentines, valentines, how many do I see?
        Valentines, valentines, count them with me.
        I have red ones, orange ones, yellow ones, too.
        I have green ones, purple ones, and some that are blue.
        Valentines, valentines, how many do I see?
        Count them with me! 1-2-3-4-5 . . .
Give each child a red, orange, yellow, green, purple, or blue heart. While adult says verse, children place hearts on flannel board at appropriate time. Count number of hearts and identify different colors when verse is finished.

9. VALENTINE PARTNERS: Divide into two equal groups. Each group forms line on one side of room. Adult calls name of one child from each group. The two children named meet in center of room. If they are wearing the same color, they are matched as partners and go to designated area. If children are not wearing the same color, they return to respective sides of room until their names are called again. Partners are kept for following activity. Examples of activities that follow are dance, walk, or snack.
Variation: Instead of colors, match shapes or numbers that are found on paper taped to shirt or necklace worn by each child.

10. VALENTINE DRAW: Write numbers on slips of paper. Write each number twice. Wrap each slip of paper in aluminum foil and form ball. Float foil balls in container of water. Each person draws ball from water, unwraps paper, and finds partner with matching number.
Note: In England, a girl wrote names of boys on slips of paper, wrapped them in clay, and dropped them into water. As the clay fell away, the paper rose to the surface. The first name to arise would be the girl's future mate.

SCIENCE

1. RED GELATIN PLAY: Place congealed red gelatin into shallow containers. Use small plastic containers and measuring cups when playing with gelatin. Discuss changes in texture of gelatin.

2. WET RED HEART: Fill clear glass bowl with red-colored water. Place a white heart in the bottom of a clear drinking glass and add crushed paper. Can a wet red heart be made by placing the glass upside down in the red water? Place inverted glass in bowl below water level. If glass is not tilted, paper will remain dry due to trapped air inside glass. Tilt glass slightly, keeping rim below water level. Observe bubbles. This is the trapped air escaping.

3. HUMAN HEART: The heart is located inside the chest. It is a muscle which is about as big as a person's fist. Inside the body are many tubes called arteries and veins. The heart pumps blood through these tubes. Blood carries oxygen from the heart to all parts of the body. Listen to own heartbeat with a stethoscope. Describe the sound. Run quickly. Listen to the heart again. It is beating faster because more oxygen is needed by the body.
Variation: Compare and contrast human heartbeat to heatbeat of guinea pig. Discuss that all animals have a heart.

4. SUGAR FACTS: Candy is frequently received as a Valentine gift. Discuss:
   A. Sugar is a simple carbohydrate which provides the body with quick energy. It has no nutrients--only calories. If these calories are not used for energy, they are stored in the body as fat.
   B. Sugar consumed when eating fruits, vegetables, and grains is complex carbohydrate. It takes longer to digest and provides energy for a longer period. The body receives calories plus nutrients from these foods. Carbohydrates are needed for energy and for the brain to function properly. Carbohydrates received in the complex form are more nutritious.
   C. Some people think honey is a health food. It is also sugar.
   D. Sugar causes dental problems. Its effect will be lessened if the mouth is rinsed with water or teeth are brushed after sugary foods are eaten.
   E. It is necessary to know what sugar is before intake can be reduced. Compare the different types of household sugar. Examples are granulated sugar, brown sugar, powdered sugar, cubed sugar, honey, corn syrup, maple syrup, and molasses. Discuss color and texture of each.

5. SUGAR CONTENT IN FOODS: Demonstrate the amount of sugar in different foods. Display servings of foods listed below. Place beside the food a sugar cube for each teaspoon of sugar contained in the serving. Teaspoons of sugar are in parenthesis.

8 ounces presweetened soft drink (5)	2 tablespoons chocolate sauce (7)
12 ounces carbonated cola (8)	1/2 cup ice cream (2 1/2)
8 ounces chocolate milk (6)	1/2 cup sherbet (9)
2 ounces peanut brittle (7)	1/2 cup chocolate pudding (4)
2 ounces fudge (9)	1/2 cup gelatin (4 1/2)
1 stick gum (1/2)	1/4 cup whipped topping (1)
1/2 cup Old Fashion Quaker® Oats (1/4)	1 glazed doughnut (6)
1 cup Cherrios® (1/4)	6 Ritz® crackers (1/2)
1 cup Post Toasties® (1/2)	1 slice bread (1/3)
1 cup All Bran® (1)	1 tablespoon ketchup (1)
1 cup Apple Jacks Cereal® (3)	1 tablespoon peanut butter (1/4)

6. VALENTINE CARNATION: Leave carnation out of water for 1 to 2 hours until it starts to wilt. Cut 1" from stem. Place carnation in red-colored water made by adding red food coloring to water. Cover 6" of stem with water. Observe what happens to carnation. Discuss how plants receive water.

7. VALENTINE TERRARIUM: Make a terrarium. Cover the bottom of an empty aquarium or glass bottle with 1 1/2" fine gravel. Place 4" of soil in container. Plant small plants in soil. Water plants and place in sunny area. Discuss that plants need sun, air, water, and soil to grow. Add small paper hearts glued to pipe cleaners to terrarium for decoration.
Note: This can be given as a special valentine present to Mom or as a valentine surprise to someone in a hospital or nursing home. Emphasize the pleasure growing plants can be to someone who cannot go outside to observe growing plants.

MUSIC

1. IT ISN'T ANY TROUBLE: (Tune--"Battle Hymn of the Republic")
    It isn't any trouble just to s-m-i-l-e.
    It isn't any trouble just to s-m-i-l-e.
    So smile when you're in trouble.
    It will vanish like a bubble.
    If you only take the trouble just to s-m-i-l-e.
                    Author Unknown
Variations: Instead of "s-m-i-l-e . . . smile," use:
  A. G-i-giggle-e . . . giggle . . .
  B. Ha, ha, haha, ha . . . laugh . . .

2. JOY: (Tune--"Row, Row, Row Your Boat")
    I've got joy in my heart, joy in my heart today.
    Joy, joy, joy, joy, down in my heart to stay.
Variation: Instead of "joy," use love.

3. IF YOU'RE HAPPY AND YOU KNOW IT: (Traditional)
    If you're happy and you know it, clap your hands.
    If you're happy and you know it, clap your hands.
    If you're happy and you know it, then your face will surely show it.
    If you're happy and you know it, clap your hands.
Variation: Instead of "clap your hands," sing stamp your feet, turn around, or sit on the floor.

4. DO YOU HAVE A VALENTINE? (Tune--"Muffin Man")
   Do you have a valentine, a valentine, a valentine?
   Do you have a valentine to call your very own?
   Oh yes, I have a valentine, a valentine, a valentine.
   Oh yes, I have a valentine to call my very own.

5. I HAVE A GREAT BIG MESSAGE: (Tune--"Brownie Smile")
   I have a great big message.
   It isn't very new.
   It has three words,
   And it says, "I love you!"
                                    Author Unknown

6. MAGIC PENNY: (By MALVINA REYNOLDS © Copyright 1955, 1958 by Northern Music
   Co., New York, N.Y. USED BY PERMISSION ALL RIGHTS RESERVED)
   Love is something if you give it away, give it away, give it away,
   Love is something if you give it away, you end up having more.
   It's just like a magic penny, hold it tight and you won't have any.
   Lend it, spend it, and you'll have so many, they'll roll all over the
   floor.
   For love is something if you give it away, give it away, give it away,
   Love is something if you give it away, you end up having more.

7. HERE IS A MESSAGE JUST FOR YOU: (Tune--"Twinkle, Twinkle Little Star")
   Here is a message just for you.
   It is old and not so new.
   But it says what I want it to.
   Only three words but they are true.
   I LOVE YOU is what they say,
   Please be mine on Valentine's Day.

8. THE MORE WE GET TOGETHER: (Tune--"Did You Ever See a Lassie?")
   The more we get together, together, together,
   The more we get together, the happier we'll be.
   For your friends are my friends, and my friends are your friends.
   The more we get together, the happier we'll be.
                                    Traditional
   Variations:
      A. The more we play together . . .
      B. The more we work together . . .
      C. The more we share together . . .
      D. The more we care for others . . .

9. RECORDS:
      A. "Love, Love, Love, Love" from *Songs of Joy* by Diane Hartman, Joy, Box 58,
         Aspen, Colorado 81611
      B. "Valentine Song" from *Holiday Songs and Rhythms* by Hap Palmer, Educa-
         tional Activities Inc., Box 392, Freeport, New York 11520

FIELD TRIPS

1. POST OFFICE: Mail valentines to parents.
2. NURSING HOME: Take VALENTINE TERRARIUM (see page 105) as a surprise valentine
   present.

EASTER

EASTER is the Christian holy day commemorating the resurrection of Jesus Christ.
This holiday occurs in the springtime and is associated with the rebirth of nature
and the renewal of life. The date of Easter varies from year to year. It is held
on the first Sunday after the occurrence of the first full moon following March 21,
or spring equinox. The earliest possible date is March 22, and the latest is
April 25.

Easter customs are based on Christian and pagan tradition. The word "Easter" comes
from Anglo-Saxons, who held a festival each April for *Eastre*, the dawn goddess of
light and spring. The egg was a symbol of birth and a new beginning. The custom of
coloring and exchanging eggs started with the ancient Egyptians. Rabbits symbolize
abundance of new life. The story of the Easter bunny developed in fifth century
Germany from this belief.

CONCEPTS TO BE TAUGHT

1. Easter is a Christian holiday.
2. It occurs in the spring and is a celebration of new life.
3. Easter occurs on Sunday.
4. Symbols for this holiday include colored eggs, Easter bunny, lilies, and crosses.
5. Traditional Easter colors are pastels and purple.

ART ACTIVITIES

1. DYED EASTER EGG: Prepare dye by mixing 1 teaspoon food coloring, 1 tablespoon
   vinegar, and 1 cup hot water. Dip HARD-COOKED EGG (see page 110) in mixture
   until desired color is reached.
   Variations:
   A. Use commercial Easter egg dye to make dye mixture.
   B. Dip egg in dye mixture to which 1 tablespoon of oil has been added. The
      addition of oil gives the egg a marbled appearance.
   C. Before dyeing egg, color it with crayon.
   D. Glue decorations to dyed or undyed egg. Examples are gummed stars,
      Easter seals, reinforcement rings, rickrack, yarn, sequins, or pieces of
      comic strips from newspapers.
   E. Instead of dyeing, color egg with felt-tipped pens.
   Note: When egg is dry, place a drop of oil on hands. Rub over egg to set
   color. This is not necessary when oil has been added to dye mixture.

2. EASTER EGG STAND: Cut 1" ring from a cardboard tube. Decorate outside of
   ring. Place DYED EASTER EGG (see page 107) in stand.
   Variation: Use egg carton cup section for stand.
   Note: Stand can be used for drying egg.

3. STYROFOAM EGG: Cut egg shape from styrofoam meat tray. Decorate with yarn,
   tissue paper, ribbon, and fabric scraps.

4. EGG SHELL COLLAGE: Save shells from colored Easter eggs. Crumble shells.
   Glue onto paper.
   Variation: Spread glue over paper. Sprinkle shells on glue.

5. PAPER EGG: Cut egg shape from construction paper. Decorate as follows:
   A. Use EGG SHELL COLLAGE (listed above).
   B. Paint with purple or pastel colors.
   C. Use chalk from EASTER PICTURE (see page 110).

6. COTTON TAIL BUNNY: Draw a bunny on paper. Attach cotton ball for tail.

7. EGG CARTON BUNNY: Remove one cup section from a
   foam egg carton. Invert cup. Glue cotton ball to
   one end of cup. Glue precut bunny ears to other
   end. Add features for face.
   Variations:
   A. Make pair of bunnies by decorating two adjoin-
      ing egg carton sections.
   B. From paper egg carton, cut a section which
      contains one cup and two long protrusions.
      Cut bunny ears from protrusions. Add facial
      features to outside front of cup.

8. FLUFFY BUNNY: Glue two cotton balls together. Add paper ears and features.
   Variation: Glue two cotton balls together on paper to make bunny. Make several if desired. Color or paint surrounding scene on paper.

9. PAPER PLATE BUNNY: Fold white paper plate in half.
   Staple or tape top of arch. Glue cotton ball to one
   end. Add precut ears to other end. Add features
   for face.
   Variation: Attach two paper plates together. Make
   face of bunny on top of plate. Attach ears and bow
   tie to face. Place feet and cotton ball tail to
   bottom of second plate.

10. BUNNY BANK: Tape two foam drinking cups together.
    Cut 1" slit in top cup. Glue ears, bow tie, and
    cotton ball tail to bank. Add facial features.

11. FLAPPER BUNNY: Fold square piece of paper in half
    to form triangle. Cut along solid line shown in
    diagram. Fold along dotted line. Add facial fea-
    tures with crayon. Attach cotton ball for tail.

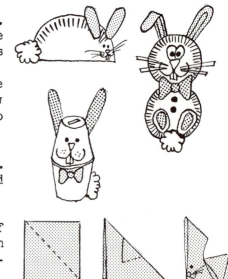

12. EGG BUNNY: Cut 3/4" x 9" strip of white construction paper. Form strip into circle and staple for base. Cover plastic egg (hosiery container) with pieces of pink and white tissue paper dipped in liquid starch. Set egg in base and allow to dry. Add a cotton tail, paper ears, and whiskers. Color eyes with black felt-tipped pen.
Variation: Instead of bunny, make chick by covering egg with yellow tissue. Fringe narrow edge of 1" x 3" piece of orange paper and attach to base for tail. For beak, fold small diamond-shaped paper in half and attach to egg. Add eyes with felt-tipped pen.

13. COTTON BALL CHICK: Color cotton ball by placing it in sack of dry yellow tempera. Shake. Fold a small diamond-shaped paper in half and glue to ball for beak. Make eyes by punching circles from blue construction paper with paper punch. Glue eyes onto chick. Place chick in half of plastic egg (hosiery container) that has been filled with grass.
Variations:
    A. Use egg carton cup instead of plastic egg.
    B. Instead of placing chick in egg, glue two balls together on construction paper. Draw beak and legs on paper with orange crayon to form chick.
    C. Instead of chick, make duck. Glue two cotton balls together for body. Glue paper bill, eyes, and wings to cotton balls.

14. CHICK IN EGG: Cut egg from white construction paper. Cut jagged line through center of egg. Attach two halves to construction paper with paper fastener so egg will open and close. Open egg and draw chick between halves.

15. FOLDED EASTER CARD: Fold construction paper on each side so ends will meet at the center. Cut round corners to make egg. Decorate outside of egg shell like an Easter egg. Color chick or Easter picture on inside center section of egg.

16. EASTER BUNNY BASKET: Draw and cut ears from open end of flattened, white, lunch bag. Add facial features to unfolded side of bag. Unfold bag and attach paper strip for handle.

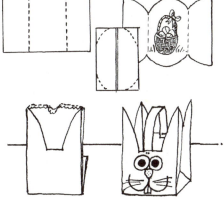

17. MILK CARTON BASKET: Cover bottom half of milk carton with construction paper. Staple cardboard handle to carton. Decorate.
Variations:
    A. BUNNY: Cover carton with pink or white paper. Add ears, facial features, and cotton tail.
    B. DUCK: Cover carton with yellow paper. Glue paper wings, bill, and eyes to basket.
    C. FLOWER BASKET: Glue paper scraps or tissue flowers to basket.

18. CONSTRUCTION PAPER BASKET: Cut along dotted lines of 9" square of paper as shown in diagram. Fold and staple corners. Staple strip of paper to opposite sides for handle. Decorate.

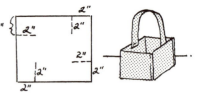

19. BERRY BASKET: Use a plastic, mesh, berry basket. Hook pipe cleaner to top edge of basket on opposite sides to form handle. To make grass, tear strips from newspaper comics.

20. EASTER BONNET: Punch hole on side of paper plate. Punch another hole on opposite side. Tie 24" long ribbon or yarn in each hole. Decorate hat with ribbon, bows, and yarn.
    Variation: Glue small paper cup to center of plate. Decorate hat with paper or plastic flowers, tissue paper, and ribbons.

21. STAINED GLASS CROSS: Cut a cross from the center of a piece of purple paper. With permanent felt-tipped pens, color a piece of clear plastic that is large enough to cover cross. Allow each color to dry before using a different color. Tape plastic to back of purple paper.
    Variations:
      A. Place white paper behind plastic.
      B. Instead of plastic, color white piece of paper with felt-tipped pens.
      C. Instead of plastic, sprinkle crayon chips on a piece of waxed paper. Cover the waxed paper which is the same size. Place between paper or fabric. Adult presses with warm iron to melt chips.

22. EASTER PICTURE: Make sugar water using one part sugar to three parts water. Soak chalk in solution for five munutes. Draw picture of Easter activities using chalk. Keep chalk wet by dipping it in the solution.

COOKING ACTIVITIES

1. HARD-COOKED EGGS: Place 6 eggs in a saucepan. Add enough cold water to cover eggs. Heat until water boils. Cover pan and cook on low heat for 15 to 20 minutes. Water should not boil. Place eggs in cold water to prevent further cooking. Peel and slice eggs crosswise. Serve slices on crackers.

2. DEVILED EGGS: 6 hard-cooked eggs   4 tablespoons sour cream or mayonnaise
                  salt and pepper   2 teaspoons prepared mustard (optional)
   Peel eggs and slice each in half lengthwise. Place yolks in a bowl. Mash yolks. Add remaining ingredients. Mix. Place mixture into egg whites.

3. SCRAMBLED EGGS: 6 eggs   salt and pepper
                    6 tablespoons milk   1 tablespoon margarine
   Break egg into a small bowl to make certain it is fresh. Pour egg into bowl. Repeat process with remaining eggs. Add milk. Add salt and pepper to taste. Mix well with wire beater or fork. Melt margarine in skillet. Pour egg mixture into skillet and cook over low heat. Lift cooked eggs with spatula so uncooked eggs can flow to bottom of skillet. Cook until eggs are set. Remove from heat and serve.
   Variation: Fold into egg mixture 1/2 cup cooked ham that has been diced.

4. GREEN EGGS AND HAM: 4 eggs   1 tablespoon margarine
                         1/4 cup milk   1/4 cup diced ham
                         2 tablespoons frozen spinach, thawed
Combine first three ingredients in blender. Melt margarine in electric fry
pan, coating entire surface. Add egg mixture. Set control on low setting.
Cover. Cook until egg is almost firm. Sprinkle lengthwise across center of
omelet 1/4 cup diced ham. Using a spatula, flip one side of omelet over the
ham. Flip the other side over center also. Slice to serve.
Note: Before making the omelet, read the book *Green Eggs and Ham* by Dr. Seuss.

5. GELATIN EGG: 1 envelope unflavored gelatin
                  1/4 cup fruit juice, boiling (not pineapple)
                  3/4 cup cold fruit juice
Rinse egg. Poke hole in each end of egg with ice pick. Break yolk inside egg
with ice pick. Blow out inside of egg. Rinse inside of egg. Let stand until
dry. Place masking tape over smaller hole. Dissolve gelatin in boiling juice.
Add cold juice. Fill egg shell with gelatin using glass measuring cup. Place
egg in egg carton. Chill. After gelatin is congealed, crack and remove shell.

6. WHOLE WHEAT COOKIES: 1 teaspoon baking powder   1/2 cup margarine
                         1/2 teaspoon baking soda   1/2 cup honey
                         1/2 teaspoon nutmeg   1 teaspoon vanilla
                         2 cups whole wheat flour   1 egg
                         1 tablespoon nonfat dry milk granules
                         1 tablespoon grated lemon or orange peel
Combine dry ingredients. Cut margarine into flour mixture. Beat honey, peel,
vanilla, and egg. Add to flour mixture. Mix well. Roll dough 1/4" thick on
cookie sheet. Cut with egg-shaped cookie cutter made by removing both lids
from tuna can and bending rim into egg shape. Remove excess dough from cookie
sheet. Decorate with COOKIE PAINT. Bake at 375° for 8 to 10 minutes.
Variations:
A. Shape dough into small ovals. Flatten lightly. Decorate. Bake.
B. Instead of COOKIE PAINT, frost with BANANA FROSTING. Decorate.

7. COOKIE PAINT: Blend one egg yolk with 1/4 teaspoon water. Divide among sev-
    eral small containers. Add small amount of food coloring to each container.
    Paint designs on cookies with paintbrush before baking. If paint thickens,
    thin with a few drops of water.
    Variation: Use evaporated milk instead of egg yolks and water.

8. BANANA FROSTING: 2 tablespoons margarine   2 tablespoons plain yogurt
                      2 tablespoons honey   1 cup nonfat dry milk granules
                      1 teaspoon vanilla   1 small banana, mashed
Cream margarine and honey. Add remaining ingredients. Stir. Spread.
Variation: Omit banana, use 1/2 cup dry milk, and add a dash of cinnamon.

9. PURPLE EASTER SHAKE: 1 can frozen grape juice   2 cups vanilla ice milk
                         1 cup milk
Blend juice and milk until smooth. Add ice milk. Blend.

10. BUNNY SALAD: Make bunny by decorating pear half with any of the following:
     raisins, prunes, mandarin oranges, uncooked spaghetti, cheese strips, carrot
     strips, or celery strips.

11. BUNNY FOOD: Spread lettuce or cabbage leaf with any of the following: peanut butter; peanut butter and raisins; cottage cheese; tuna or egg salad; slice of turkey, chicken, or roast beef; sticks of carrot, celery, pickle, green pepper, or cheese; mixture of chopped apples, raisins, and nuts; mixture of grated carrots, raisins, and crushed, drained pineapple. Roll lettuce or cabbage around filling.

12. BUNNY CAKE: 1/4 cup wheat germ or whole wheat flour   1 teaspoon cinnamon
                 3/4 cup flour   2/3 cup oil
                 1/4 cup nonfat dry milk granules   1/2 teaspoon salt
                 1 teaspoon baking soda   3/4 cup sugar
                 1 1/2 cups grated carrots   2 eggs

Mix together dry ingredients. Add remaining ingredients. Bake in 9" x 2" round pan at 350° for 30 to 35 minutes. Let cool before removing from pan. Cut in half. Frost in two sections with BANANA FROSTING (see page 111). Place frosted tops together and stand cake on flat edge. Frost cake and sprinkle with coconut. Add ball of cheese for tail and cut paper features.

Variation: Double recipe. Bake cake in two round 9" cake pans. Remove cake from pans. Cut one cake according to diagram. Attach two side pieces to top of second round cake for ears. Attach center piece to bottom for tie. Frost and sprinkle with coconut. Use cereal and paper cut-outs for features.

FINGERPLAYS

1. Easter is a new beginning.
   Flowers are growing. (bring hands together and spread above head)
   Birds are singing. (move arms up and down)
   Church bells are ringing. (pretend to ring bell)

2. An Easter bonnet on my head, (point to head)
   New shoes upon my feet, (point to feet)
   I go to church on Easter morn.
   And quietly find my seat. (sit)

3. Here is the church. (place back of hands together and interlock fingers, place palms together)
   Here is the steeple. (point index fingers upward)
   Open the doors and here are the people. (open palms)
   They come to church on Easter Day.
   This is how they pray. (pray)

4. Easter is the time of year
   When families come from far and near. (indicate far and near)
   We go to church on Easter Day (form steeple with hands)
   To give thanks and to pray. (fold hands to pray)

5. We celebrate Easter everyone knows
   Because this is the day Jesus rose. (raise arms)
   For this we give thanks and pray (fold hands)
   On this very special Easter Day.

6. Pink, yellow, green and blue.
   I color my eggs every hue. (form oval)
   Peter Rabbit will hide them all (extend two fingers)
   In the flowers and grass that's tall (hold hand above head)
   So I can gather them on Easter Day (pretend to gather eggs)
   In my Easter basket, and then we'll play!

7. When I awoke on Easter Day (yawn)
   I saw a basket, bright and gay.
   (rub eyes)
   Inside upon the grass so green
   Was a darling stuffed bunny--
   The prettiest I've seen. (two
   hands above head)
   Next to the bunny in colors galore
   Were Easter eggs which numbered
   four. (four fingers)
   One was red. One was blue.
   Another was bright yellow,
   And the last was a purple hue.
   The Easter Bunny came last night.
   (shake head vertically)
   My basket is proof. What a de-
   light! (clap hands)

8. Humpty Dumpty sat on a wall.
   (place fist on arm)
   Humpty Dumpty had a great fall.
   (drop fist)
   All the king's horses and all the
   king's men
   Couldn't put Humpty together again.
   (shake head sideways)

   Traditional

9. Three eggs sat on by Mother Hen
   (three fingers)
   To keep them warm and then--(place
   fist in cup of other hand)
   Crack, crack, crack,
   Peep, peep, peep,
   Three baby chicks softly cheep.
   (raise three fingers)

10. Mother Hen came looking for her
    chicks so small. (indicate
    small)
    It was feeding time in the barn-
    yard.
    Would they hear her call? (hand
    behind ear)
    Scratch, scratch, scratch.
    Peep, peep, peep.
    Her baby chicks were sleeping
    In a fluffy yellow heap. (pretend
    to sleep)

11. Mr. Easter Rabbit goes hip, hop,
    hip. (extend index and middle
    finger and make hand hop)
    See how his ears flip, flop, flip.
    (place hands on head and move
    them forward and backward)
    See how his eyes go blink, blink,
    blink. (blink eyes)
    See how his nose goes twink, twink,
    twink. (wiggle nose with finger)
    Stroke his warm coat soft and fur-
    ry. (stroke fist)
    Hip, hop, hip, he's off in a hurry.
    (extend two fingers and hop)
                         Author Unknown

12. My rabbit has two big ears (hold up
    index and middle fingers)
    And a funny little nose. (join
    other two fingers and thumb)
    He likes to nibble carrots, (open
    and close fingers and thumb)
    And he hops wherever he goes.
    (make hand hop)
                         Margaret Stant

13. Pinky is a rabbit. (hold up index
    and middle finger)
    His tail is fluffy white.
    Hop, hop, hop, goes Pinky
    All the day and night. (hand hops)
                         Mary Jackson Ellis
                         and Frances Lyons

14. Here is a bunny with ears so funny.
    (hold up index and middle finger)
    And here is his hole in the ground.
    (make hole with other hand)
    When a noise he hears, he picks up
    his ears (extend two fingers)
    And hops in his hole in the ground.
    (jumps fingers into hole)
                         Traditional

15. Mr. Rabbit has a habit (extend two
    fingers)
    That is very cute to me.
    He wrinkles up and crinkles up
    His little nose at me. (wrinkle
    nose)
    I like my little rabbit,
    And I like his brother.
    And we have a lot of fun
    Making faces at each other. (make
    faces)
                         Dixie Willson

16. Mr. Bunny, Mr. Bunny, won't you
stop, stop, stop? (two fingers)
"No," said Mr. Bunny, "I must hop,
hop, hop. (make fingers hop)
Easter is coming, and there is lots
to do. (open arms wide)
Eggs must be colored green, pink,
and blue. (form oval)
I'll tie each basket with a pretty
bow. (pretend to tie bow)
Children are waiting so I must go!"
(extend fingers, make hand hop
behind back)

17. Here comes a bunny--hippity, hop,
(extend two fingers and hop)
With ears so funny--floppity, flop.
(place hands on head and move
them forward and backward)
For danger he can quietly sniffity,
sniff. (wiggle nose)
Then he quickly hides in a jiffity,
jiff! (quickly hide two raised
fingers behind back)

18. Here's a little bunny. (extend two
fingers)
Here's a green cabbage head. (form
fist with other hand)
"I wish I had some breakfast,"
The little bunny said.
So he nibbled and he nibbled, (open
and close hand)
Then cocked his ears to say, (move
extended fingers)
"I think it's time that I was
Hopping on my way." (make hand
hop)
                    Traditional

19. Little Bo-Peep has lost her sheep
(ten fingers)
And can't tell where to find them.
(hide hands behind back)
Leave them alone, and they will
come home (show hands)
Wagging their tails behind them.
(wiggle fingers behind back)
                    Traditional

20. Ducks at the park swim here and
there. (move hand in zigzag
motion)
When we toss bread to show we care,
(pretend to toss bread)
Their heads go in the water, (point
fingers downward)
Their tails go in the air! (point
thumb up)

21. Easter duck and Easter chick
Easter eggs with chocolate thick,
(form oval with fingers)
Easter hats for one and all, (place
hand on top of head)
Easter bunny makes a call. (extend
two fingers, make hand hop)
Happy Easter always brings
Such a lot of pleasant things.
                    Elsie Parrish

22. New clothes and hats of pink and
blue, (point to clothes and head)
Baby animals at the zoo,
Flowers bloom and robins coo.
(raise hands above head, form
wings with arms)
Easter welcomes spring anew!

LANGUAGE DEVELOPMENT

1. EASTER ACTIVITIES: Display pictures related to Easter. Discuss different ways
people celebrate Easter. The following are some examples:
    A. Attending church services
    B. Wearing new clothes and Easter bonnets
    C. Watching Easter parades
    D. Decorating and hunting Easter eggs
    E. Having Easter dinner with family and friends (Ham or lamb is often served
       with this meal.)
    F. Decorating with Easter lilies
Ask children to share their personal experiences and family activities at
Easter. Discuss what each likes best about the holiday.

2. RENEWAL OF LIFE: Easter is partially a celebration of new life. Examples are:
    A. BABY ANIMALS: In the spring many animals bear their young. Baby rabbits, chicks, and ducklings are closely associated with Easter.
    B. EGG: An egg symbolizes new life.
    C. FLOWERS: At this time the grass begins to turn green, and dormant plants start to grow again.

3. EGG SOUNDS: Fill each plastic egg (hosiery container) with a different material. Examples are salt, rice, macaroni, and buttons. Tape containers closed. Shake each one. Discriminate between soft and loud sounds.
    Variation: Fill two containers with same material. Make several pairs and place all containers on table. Shake containers to find pair that makes the same sound.

4. EASTER BONNET: Tell the following story. At (A) in story draw diagram A on paper. Add additional features to initial sketch at points indicated in story.

    When Mary woke on Easter morning, she saw a beautiful Easter bonnet lying on her dresser (A). On the top of the bonnet was a large bow (B). The center of the bow was decorated with a soft white pompon (C). Mary reached for the two silk ties so she could wear her beautiful bonnet (D). Suddenly it hopped into the air and flipped. (Invert paper.) Do you know what her bonnet was? It was the Easter bunny!

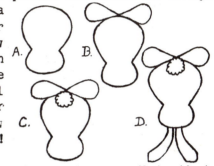

5. TALK TO MR. BUNNY: Display a stuffed rabbit. Describe the bunny. Note that the bunny has long ears so he can listen. Have each child talk to Mr. Bunny. Ask the following questions:
    A. What would you tell Mr. Bunny about school?
    B. What would you tell Mr. Bunny about your family?
    C. What question would you like to ask Mr. Bunny?
    Variations:
    A. Instead of a stuffed animal, use a rabbit puppet.
    B. Talk to a different animal.

6. BUNNY WHISKERS: Make variation of PAPER PLATE BUNNY (see page 108). For nose, attach large round circle. Cut slits through plate on sides of circle that are large enough for whiskers. Cut paper strips for whiskers. Write several directions on each whisker. Insert whiskers in slits. Child pulls one whisker and completes tasks written on whisker. Examples of tasks are touch your nose and hop three times.

7. BABY ANIMALS SAY:
        Little woolly lamb likes to sleep, play, and walk.
        Pet it gently; it will talk, "baa, baa, baa."
    Second verse: Little downy duckling . . . "quack, quack, quack."
    Third verse: Little fluffy chick . . . "peep, peep, peep."
    Fourth verse: Little furry kitten . . . "meow, meow, meow."
    Adult recites first three lines of verse, and children add sound that baby animal makes. Continue with animals the children name.

8. BABY ANIMALS AND THEIR PARENTS: Make two sets of cards. One set should contain pictures of baby animals. The other set should have pictures of babies' parents. Match each baby animal to its parent. Discuss the names of the baby and parent animals. Examples are duck-duckling, sheep-lamb, horse-colt, cow-calf, chicken-chick, goose-gosling, cat-kitten, and dog-puppy.

9. THE UGLY DUCKLING: Read *The Ugly Duckling* by Hans Christian Andersen. Discuss the following:
   A. Why didn't the other ducklings like the Ugly Duckling?
   B. Can we tell things about people by the way they look or dress?
   C. Often at Easter we buy new clothes. Do new clothes change us or make us different?
   D. Outer appearances are not as important as the way we feel inside.

10. Books:
    Home for a Bunny--Brown
    The Golden Egg Book--Brown
    What's Inside the Egg?--Garelick
    The Tale of Peter Rabbit--Potter
    Happy Easter--Wiese
    The Bunny Who Found Easter--Zolotow
    Mr. Rabbit and the Lovely Present--Zolotow

11. REFERENCE BOOK:
    Lillies, Rabbits, and Painted Eggs--Barth

GAMES AND SOCIAL ACTIVITIES

1. EASTER EGG HUNT: One player hides plastic eggs or peanuts in shells. These can be hidden indoors or outdoors. After all eggs are hidden, remaining players hunt for eggs, using baskets from EASTER ACTIVITIES (see pages 109 to 110).

2. PICKING UP EASTER EGGS: (Tune--"Way Down Yonder in the Pawpaw Patch")
        Where, oh where, are the Easter eggs?
        Where, oh where, are the Easter eggs?
        Where, oh where, are the Easter eggs?
        Out here in our back yard.
        Picking up (color) eggs, put them in the basket.
        Picking up (color) eggs, put them in the basket.
        Picking up (color) eggs, put them in the basket.
        Out here in the back yard.
   While singing first part of verse, players place hands above eyes and search for eggs. Players then pretend to gather eggs and place them in a basket. Change color of eggs and repeat verse.
   Variation: Sing while having EASTER EGG HUNT (listed above).

3. WILL YOU BE A BUNNY FOR ME? (Tune--"Muffin Man")
        Will you be a bunny for me, a bunny for me, a bunny for me?
        Will you be a bunny for me on this Easter Day?
   Form two lines. Players at front of line hop down center in different ways while everyone sings verse. Examples of hopping are with two feet, on one foot, big leaps, and small hops.

4. BUNNY HOPPED DOWN THE ROAD: (Tune--"The Bear Went Over the Mountain")
        Easter bunny hopped down the road. Easter bunny hopped down the road.
        Easter bunny hopped down the road to see who he could see.
        He saw (child's first and last name). He saw (child's first and last
        name).
        He saw (child's first and last name) and gave him an Easter egg.
    Sit in a circle. One child is Bunny, who hops around circle holding an Easter
    egg. After fourth line is sung, Bunny stops and faces closest player. At end
    of verse he gives the player the egg. Repeat, with player holding egg becoming
    Bunny.

5. BUNNY COMES TO MY HOUSE: (Tune--"Bluebird, Bluebird Through My Window")
        Easter bunny comes to my house.
        Easter bunny comes to my house
        Easter bunny comes to my house.
        To bring a pretty Easter egg.
    Sit in circle. Bunny walks around outside of circle and stops in front of
    nearest player at end of verse. Bunny asks child, "What color Easter egg would
    you like?" Child answers, "I would like a (color) egg. Everyone sings,
    "(child's name) would like a (color) egg." Child then becomes Bunny, and game
    is repeated.
    Variation: Bunny holds basket with different colored eggs in it. He gives
    child the color of egg he likes. When child becomes Bunny, he receives basket
    and places his egg in it.

6. RABBIT'S LUNCH:
        Peter Rabbit went hoppity hop, hoppity hop, hoppity hop.
        Into McGregor's garden without a stop; hoppity hop, hoppity hop.
        For lunch he crunched on a (carrot) top
        Peter ran home without a stop; hoppity hop, hoppity hop.
    Sit in circle. One child is rabbit who hops around inside of circle. At end
    of verse, the child he is standing closest to becomes Rabbit. Rabbit tells
    what kind of vegetable he would like to eat from the garden. Verse is repeated
    with vegetable substituted for carrot.

7. DUCK, DUCK, GOOSE: Sit in circle. One player walks around outside of circle,
    touching head of each player, designating each a "Duck." Then he touches a
    player and calls him a "Goose." Goose chases him around circle to empty place.
    Goose then walks around circle, and the game is repeated.
    Variation: If the player is caught before he reaches safety, he must sit in
    center of circle until another player is caught to replace him.

8. LITTLE LOST DUCK: Adult chooses a Mother (or Father) Duck to leave room.
    After she has left room, adult chooses a Little Lost Duck. Everyone covers his
    mouth with his hands. Mother Duck returns and says, "Where is my little lost
    duck?" The Little Lost Duck quacks, and Mother Duck tries to guess who it is.
    Little Lost Duck then becomes Mother (or Father) Duck. Repeat.

9. WHAT AM I? Adult tapes on one child's back a picture of baby animal. Remain-
    ing children give clues to child until he names animal. Repeat.
    Variation: Tape a picture on each player's back. Players walk around room and
    ask questions that can only be answered by "yes" or "no." Each player contin-
    ues asking questions until he knows the animal that is attached to his back.

10. EASTER SEAL COLLAGE: (Group Project) Draw a large egg shape on the bulletin
    board. Stick Easter seals to egg for decoration.

11. EGG TREE: (Group project) Use a branch of a budded tree. Place branch in a coffee can full of sand. Keep sand moist, and tree will bud. Attach string to PAPER EGGS or STYROFOAM EGGS (see page 108). Hang eggs on tree.
Variations:
   A. Poke hole in each end of an uncooked egg. Break yolk. Blow into hole to remove inside of egg. Decorate shell. Glue or tape string to egg. Hang on tree.
   B. Make tree for each individual by placing small branch in center of empty spool of thread. Attach eggs.

CREATIVE DRAMATICS AND MOVEMENT

1. WHAT CAN YOU DO, MR. RABBIT? (Tune--"Frère Jacques")
      What can you do, Mr. Rabbit, here at school, here at school?
      I can (wiggle my nose). I can (wiggle my nose)
      Here at school, here at school.
One player stands in front of group and does action which is sung in verse. Examples of actions are wiggle my ears, hop on two feet, and chew my carrot. Repeat with different leader choosing new action.

2. CAN YOU BE A BUNNY? Pretend to be an Easter bunny and look a little funny. Make your pink nose wrinkle, wrinkle, wrinkle. And your cottontail wiggle, wiggle, wiggle. Make your long bunny ears flop, flop, flop. Over there is a carrot--to it hop, hop, hop. And eat the carrot--crunch, crunch, crunch. Now, little bunny, you are ready to rest after such a big lunch!

3. BUNNY EARS: Adjust paper band to fit head and staple. Cut two bunny ears from white or pink construction paper. Tape or staple ears to headband. Wear headband and pretend to be bunny.
Variation: Punch hole on side of paper plate. Punch another hole on opposite side. Tie 24" long yarn in each hole. Inflate and tie two, long, narrow balloons for ears. Make two slits in top of plate. Place tied ends of balloons through slits. Tape tied ends to underside of plate.

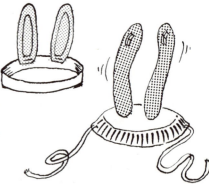

4. BUNNY HOP: Wear BUNNY EARS (listed above) and paint whiskers on face. Use cotton ball for tail. Play record of *Bunny Hop*. Discuss what this music makes you want to do. Examples are hop, skip, and leap. Move to music in that manner.

5. HATCHING DUCK: Pretend to be a baby duck inside a large white egg. You are tired of being so cramped inside the egg. Peck with your bill against the shell. Soon it begins to crack. You peck and peck until you are able to see outside the egg. Poke your head through the shell. Look around. What do you see? Push one wing and then the other through the hole. Step from the egg-shell. Shake your feathers dry. Waddle down to the pond and drink the cool clear water. Your brothers and sisters have come to join you. What fun you have swimming in the pond.

6. MOVEMENT OF BABY ANIMALS: Dramatize the following: waddle like a duck, hop like a bunny, walk like a chick, frolic like a lamb, and gallop like a colt.

PHYSICAL DEVELOPMENT

1. EGG ROLL: Place plastic egg (hosiery container) on floor. Blow egg across room or a designated distance.
   Variation: Roll egg with part of body. Examples are nose, elbow, and foot.

2. PICK UP COTTON EGGS: Using tongs or tweezers, pick up cotton balls from one basket and place in another basket.
   Note: The activity develops motor coordination necessary for cutting with scissors.

3. PETER COTTONTAIL'S BUNNY TRAIL: Pretend to be Peter Cottontail moving through obstacles on bunny trail to deliver Easter eggs. Examples of obstacles and ways to overcome them are:
   A. Jump over or weave through blocks.
   B. Circle around, weave through, or crawl under chairs.
   C. Jump or walk through tires.
   D. Crawl through boxes.
   E. Climb steps and come down slide.
   F. Walk on balance beam.
   G. Walk on two strings that are 6" apart.
   H. Walk on rope that is curved like a winding stream.

4. PETER RABBIT'S TAIL: Draw outline of Peter Rabbit on large piece of paper. Draw circle marking location of rabbit's tail. Glue paper to side of box. Stand rabbit upright. Make tail by rolling two white socks together. Toss socks at rabbit. Object is to throw tail as close to circle as possible.

5. HOP, HOP, HOP: Hop in different ways while saying verse.
   Be a funny bunny and hop, hop, hop.
   Now all tired bunnies should stop, stop, stop.
   Then lift one foot and hop again.
   Bunnies turn around and count to ten. 1-2-3-4-5-6-7-8-9-10

6. EASTER BUNNY: (Tune--"Frère Jacques")
   Easter bunny, Easter bunny,
   Hop, hop, hop, hippity hop.
   Easter bunny rabbit, Easter bunny rabbit,
   Hop, hop, hop, hippity hop.
   Variations: Instead of "hop, hop, hop, hippity hop," use:
   A. On right foot, hippity hop.
   B. On left foot, hippity hop.
   C. With big leaps, hippity hop.
   D. In one place, hippity hop.
   E. Hop backwards, hippity hop.

7. ANIMAL WALK: Form line and do the following:
   A. DUCK: Squat and tuck hands under arms to make wings. Swing one foot ahead. Shift weight to that foot. Swing other foot forward. Shift weight to that foot. Continue waddling across room.
   B. CHICKEN: Squat. Hold legs below knees and walk.
   C. BUNNY: Hop.

119

MATH

1. **EASTER EGG COUNT:** Place colored plastic eggs in Easter basket. Count how many eggs are in basket. Remove red eggs and place them in second basket. Count red eggs. Continue with each color. Count how many eggs it takes to fill the second basket.
    Variation: Use wooden beads for eggs.

2. **GOOD EGG:** Arrange chairs in a circle with seats facing outward. Cut eggs from paper and number each consecutively. Tape one egg to each chair. Players walk around chairs to music. When music stops, players sit on chairs. Adult calls a number. Player sitting on chair with that number is called a "good egg." Adult gives player a paper egg which has the same number written on it. Continue until all children have received an egg.

3. **MY FINE HEN:**
    Hickety, pickety, my fine hen, lays eggs on her nest in a pen.
    The farmer comes everyday to see what my fine hen doth lay.
    Place felt hen and felt eggs on flannel board. Recite verse. Count the number of eggs the hen laid. Repeat using different number of eggs.

4. **OVAL:** Feel sides of oval cut from cardboard. Place cardboard oval on paper. Trace around it with a crayon and cut outline. Discuss:
    A. This is an oval. It is the shape of an egg.
    B. Describe characteristics of an oval. Notice that it is larger at one end.
    C. Compare oval to other shapes.

5. **WHOLE AND CRACKED EGGS:** Cut several eggs from the same color of poster board. Cut jagged line through the center of each egg. Make each cut different. Place pieces in basket. Put eggs together by matching correct two pieces of each egg.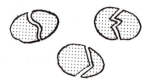

6. **ORDINAL NUMBERING:** Display five plastic eggs in rings cut from cardboard tubes. Count eggs using ordinal numbers: first, second, third, fourth, and fifth. Players cover eyes while adult hides a bean in one egg. Players uncover eyes. Adult asks, "Is the bean in the first, second, third, fourth, or fifth egg?" Players respond using ordinal numbers.

7. **MISSING EASTER EGG:** Display several plastic eggs, each a different color. Players close eyes. One egg is removed. Players open eyes and guess which egg is missing. Identify by color.
    Variation: Set eggs beside bunny. When players uncover eyes, they guess which egg the bunny hid.

8. **HUNGRY BUNNIES:**
    Once there was a family of bunnies who were hungry. They hopped to the garden and found a basket filled with carrots. Each bunny wanted a carrot to eat. Were there enough carrots for each bunny to have his own? Were there any extra carrots?
    While telling story. adult places felt bunnies and felt carrots on flannel board. At end of story children answer questions. Repeat story changing number of carrots and bunnies. Sometimes have equal number of rabbits and carrots, sometimes have too many carrots, and sometimes have too few carrots.

9. BABY BUNNIES: (Author Unknown)
    "My bunnies now must go to bed,"
    The little mother rabbit said.
    "But I will count them first to see
    If they have all come back to me. 1-2-3-4-5 . . ."
A group of players squat on floor as baby bunnies. One player is chosen to be
Mother Rabbit. Adult or Mother Rabbit says verse. Mother Rabbit then counts
the baby bunnies. Repeat, using new mother and a different number of babies.

SCIENCE

1. LATVIAN EASTER EGG: Use colored outer skins from purple or yellow onions.
Place 7 to 11 skins on a 10" square cloth. On top of onion skins arrange
design materials. Examples are grass, leaves, flower petals, tape, gummed
stars, and string. Center egg on design materials. Wrap cloth tightly around
egg. Tie with a twister seal. Place wrapped egg in a saucepan and cover with
water. Heat to boiling. Lower heat and simmer for 20 minutes. Cool. Untie.
Observe changes in color. The color of dye received from the onion skins
varies depending upon the number of skins used and the length of cooking time.
Onion skins and other plants are used to dye yarn and fabric.
Note: Several eggs can be cooked together. Wrapped eggs may float. Eggs need
to be submerged or turned frequently while cooking.

2. HUMPTY DUMPTY:
    Humpty Dumpty sat on a wall.
    Humpty Dumpty had a great fall.
    All the boys and girls
    And all the women and men
    Guessed how he'd land,
    On the top or bottom end.

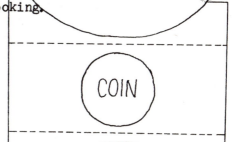

Trace and cut diagram from construction paper. Tape a coin where indicated.
Fold on dotted lines. Tape round ends together. Use Humpty Dumpty to dramatize poem. Discuss why Humpty Dumpty always lands on bottom end: the weight
of the coin causes the heavier end to land first.

3. COMPARING EGGS: Display a raw egg and a hard-cooked egg. Can they be distin-
guished by looking, feeling, or shaking? Break the raw egg into a cup. Describe and discuss color and texture. Peel the hard-cooked egg. Discuss color
and texture. Slice hard-cooked egg. Compare the two types of eggs.

4. HATCH CHICK IN INCUBATOR: Place unhatched chick in incubator. Discuss:
    A. What is inside the egg?
    B. How will the chick hatch?
    C. What will he look like?
    D. How big will the chick be?
    E. How do we care for the baby chick?
Observe chick hatching. Care for baby chick.

5. RABBIT: Bring a rabbit to school for observation. Discuss characteristics of
the rabbit and how to care for him. The following are some guidelines: Keep
rabbit in wire cage at room temperature. Keep cage clean. Feed rabbit vegetables or rabbit pellets and water. Do not lift rabbit by ears. Rabbits can be
kept outdoors if there is sufficient shelter from sun and wind.

6. THE COLOR PURPLE: When making DYED EASTER EGG (see page 107), experiment with the following: Fill one container with red dye mixture and second container with blue dye mixture. Dip one egg in red dye and one egg in blue dye. Observe color of each egg. Dip dyed eggs in opposite dye mixture. Discuss change in color. Mix red and blue dye mixture. Dip an undyed egg into mixture and observe color. Discuss that red and blue mixed make purple.

MUSIC

1. THE LITTLE HEN LAID SOME EGGS: (Tune--"The Bear Went Over the Mountain")
    The little hen laid some eggs. The little hen laid some eggs.
    The little hen laid some eggs. Cluck, cluckity, cluck.
    Second verse: Some of the eggs we do eat . . . crack, crackity, crack.
    Third verse: The other eggs go in the dye . . . plop, plopity, plop.
    Fourth verse: Easter eggs go in the basket . . . click, clickety, click.

2. BUNNIES: (Tune--"My Bonnie Lies Over the Ocean")
    All bunnies have pink shiny noses, and this is the reason, my friend.
    All bunnies have pink shiny noses. Their powder puff's on the wrong end.
                        Author Unknown

3. DID YOU EVER SEE A BUNNY? (Tune--"Did You Ever See a Lassie?")
    Did you ever see a bunny hop, a bunny hop, a bunny hop?
    Did you ever see a bunny hop this way and that?
    Hop this way and that way. Hop this way and that way.
    Did you ever see a bunny hop this way and that?
    Variations: Instead of "bunny hop" use duck waddle, lamb frolic, and chick scratch.

4. SIX LITTLE DUCKS: (Traditional)
    Six little ducks that I once knew: three were fat, and skinny were two.
    But the one little duck with the feathers on his back,
    He ruled the others with his "quack, quack, quack!"
    Down to the water they would go: wibble wobble, wibble wobble, to and fro.
    But the one little duck with the feathers on his back,
    He ruled the others with his "quack, quack, quack!"
    Home from the water they would come: wibble wobble, wibble wobble, ho ho hum.
    But the one little duck with the feathers on his back,
    He ruled the others with his "quack, quack, quack, quack, quack, quack."
    He ruled the others with his "quack, quack, quack."

5. EASTER PARADE: Model EASTER BONNETS (see page 110) to record *Easter Parade*.

FIELD TRIPS

1. HATCHERY
2. PARK TO FEED DUCKS
3. FARM TO OBSERVE BABY ANIMALS
4. PET STORE

SPRING WEATHER

Many changes in nature occur during the spring months due to SPRING WEATHER. In the northern United States, the temperature warms causing ice and snow to melt. As a result, rivers and streams swell. The ground also thaws which aids sprouting plants and greenery.

In some areas rain and wind occur more frequently. Spring rainstorms are caused by a sudden change in the temperature. Thunder and lightning often accompany these storms. Afterward, rainbows will appear if the sun begins to shine while the air is still filled with raindrops.

CONCEPTS TO BE TAUGHT

1. During the spring, the weather begins to warm in most places.
2. Wind and rain occur more frequently during this season.
3. Clouds are indicators of approaching weather.
4. People adapt to spring weather by wearing appropriate clothing.
5. Spring winds make kite flying a favorite pastime.

ART ACTIVITIES

1. CLOUD CREATION: Create clouds.
   A. Place shaving cream on blue construction paper. Sprinkle dry tempera on shaving cream to create clouds during a sunset or storm.
   B. Cut clouds from white, gray, and black paper. Glue onto paper.
   C. Paint cloud shapes.
   D. Shape cotton balls into clouds. Place on paper that is coated with glue.

2. MARSHMALLOW CLOUD SCULPTURE: Make sculpture with marshmallows and colored toothpicks.
   Variation: Use styrofoam packing pieces instead of marshmallows.

3. RAINDROP PAINTING: Place water in small juice cans or containers. Color water by sprinkling a different color of tempera into each container. Drop colored water onto construction paper with eye dropper to make raindrops.
   Variations:
   A. Color water with food coloring.
   B. Place colored water in dilution trays or cups of styrofoam egg carton.
   C. Use white paper towel or filter paper instead of construction paper.

4. RAINDROP: Cut large raindrop from white paper. Paint with watercolors.

5. RAINDROP DESIGN: Use seeds as raindrops. Drop 5 to 10 seeds on paper. Make dots where raindrops fall. Create design by connecting all the raindrops.

6. RAINDROP SPATTERING: Draw or paint spring picture on paper. Dip brush in blue tempera paint and shake over picture, allowing paint to fall in drops.
    Variation: Place glue drops on white paper. Allow to dry. Paint paper with watercolors or wash of diluted blue tempera paint.

7. RAINY DAY PICTURE: Glue cotton or styrofoam packing to piece of paper for clouds. Use rickrack for lighting. Draw picture and raindrops with felt-tipped pens or crayons.
    Variation: Use RAINDROP SPATTERING (listed above) for raindrops.

8. WET PAPER ART: Wet piece of construction paper. Paint with dry tempera or draw picture with colored chalk. When finished, allow paper to dry.

9. RAINBOW DESIGN: Fill plastic squirt bottles with water that is mixed with several drops of food coloring. Prepare several colors. Squirt colored water onto 12" x 15" section of old white sheet. A rainbow of pastel colors is the result. Allow sheet to dry.
    Variation: Do as group project. Take turns squirting colored water onto whole sheet. If weather permits, do this outdoors. After sheet has dried, display as wall hanging or cut into sections. Give one section to each artist.
    Note: Use pump-style bottles, dishwashing liquid bottles, or bottles with sprinkler tops.

10. RAINBOW: Use clear plastic lid with a wide rim. Cut lid in half. Outline arc of lid with permanent felt-tipped pen. Layer arc with different colors to form rainbow. Stand rainbow on flat side.
    Variation: Form arc on paper with side of chalk or crayon. Layer arc with different colors to form rainbow.

11. RAINY DAY PERSON: Cut umbrella from sample wallpaper books or brightly colored construction paper. Glue umbrella to another piece of paper. Cut two boots from brown or black construction paper. Attach boots to bottom of umbrella.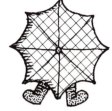

12. UMBRELLA DESIGN: Cut top of large umbrella from construction paper. Decorate with pieces of fabric or tissue paper. Mount umbrella on large piece of paper. To make handle, bend one end of a pipe cleaner to form hook and glue other end to umbrella.

13. WINDY PAINTING: Pour watery tempera paint onto paper. Blow through straw at paint to create design.
    Variation: Dip the end of the straw into thinned tempera paint. Place straw above paper and blow through straw.

14. PINWHEEL: Color paper square with crayons or felt-tipped pens. Cut two-thirds of distance from each corner to center of square. Mark X on corners as illustrated. Overlap X corners in center of square. Place thin nail through the X corners and center of square. Push nail into eraser end of pencil.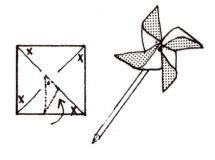

15. PARACHUTE PICTURE: Fold a cupcake liner in half for top of parachute. Glue liner to paper. With crayons draw strings of parachute, parachutist, and surroundings.
    Variations:
    A. Instead of cupcake liner, use half-circle cut from cloth or paper.
    B. Glue pieces of yarn to cupcake liner or half-circle for parachute strings.

16. KITE: Cut or tear paper to create kite of any shape. Attach short piece of yarn to kite. Tear pieces of paper and tape to yarn to make tail. Attach longer piece of yarn for kite string.
    Variation: Draw diamond-shaped kite on piece of paper. Cut or tear along lines to make kite.

COOKING ACTIVITIES

1. WHOLE WHEAT CLOUD PUFFS: 6 tablespoons margarine   2 teaspoons sugar
                             3/4 cup water   3 eggs, beaten
                             3/4 cup whole wheat flour
   Boil margarine and water in pan. Add flour and sugar. Stirring, cook until mixture forms a ball. Cool 10 minutes. Add eggs. Use 1/4 cup of batter for each puff. Drop onto greased baking sheet. Bake at 400° for 35 to 40 minutes. Immediately cut thin slice from top of puff. Remove soft center. Place lid, with inner side upward, on baking sheet. Return to oven for 10 minutes to make shells crisp.
   Note: These are delicious served with creamed hard-cooked eggs and ham.

2. CLOUD CREATURES: Tear a cloud shape from a piece of bread. Spread with cottage cheese or applesauce. Use olives, raisins, or dried fruit for features.
   Variation: Use mixture of cottage cheese and applesauce.

3. POTATO CLOUDS: Prepare instant mashed potatoes according to directions on package. Sprinkle servings with grated cheese, bacon bits, or sour cream.

4. FLUFFY CLOUD VEGETABLE DIP: 1 cup plain yogurt
                                1 tablespoon chopped black olives
                                1 teaspoon minced onion
                                1/4 teaspoon dried dillweed (optional)
   Stir together. Serve with raw vegetables. Examples are carrots, celery, green pepper, cucumber, cauliflower, broccoli, zucchini, and cherry tomatoes.

5. THUNDERCLOUD SALAD: 1 1/2 cups creamy cottage cheese   1/4 cup sunflower nuts
                        1 1/2 cups applesauce   1/4 cup dried fruit
                        1/2 teaspoon cinnamon
   Mix above ingredients together. Serve chilled.
   Variation: Serve in center of CHRISTMAS STAR SALAD (see page 56). Instead of pineapple bits, use watermelon wedges.

6. DRIZZLE DAY SUNDAE: 1 envelope unflavored gelatin   3 ice cubes
                        1/4 cup grape juice, boiling   milk
                        1 1/4 cups cold grape juice
   Mix gelatin with boiling juice. Stir in remaining juice and ice cubes. Place in clear plastic glasses. Chill until firm. Pour milk into glass, about 1/2" deep. Make tunnels around outside of gelatin with a drinking straw. Milk will drizzle into tunnels.

7. RAINBOW PARFAIT: Alternate layers of yogurt or cottage cheese with layers of different kinds of fruit in clear plastic cups. Examples of fruit are peaches, apples, plums, strawberries, and mandarin oranges.
   Variation: Omit yogurt or cottage cheese and layer fruit.

8. FLUFFY CLOUD FRUIT DIP: 1 cup plain yogurt   1/2 banana. mashed
                            2 tablespoons frozen orange juice concentrate, thawed
   Stir together. Serve with fresh fruit. Examples are apples, pears, bananas, or strawberries.

9. HEAVENLY HASH: 13 ounces pineapple chunks, drained   1/2 cup coconut
                   11 ounces mandarin oranges, drained   1/2 pint whipping cream
                   1/4 cup miniature marshmallows   1/2 pint sour cream
                   2 tablespoons powdered sugar
   Fold sour cream and sugar into whipped cream. Mix with remaining ingredients.

10. KITE SANDWICH: Make favorite sandwich using square whole wheat bread. Form kite string by extending in a line from one corner with any of the following: pickles, carrot strips, and olives.

FINGERPLAYS

1. The cold has passed. (shiver)
   It's warm at last. (make circle above head)
   Let's show a big smile. (smile)
   It's spring for awhile.

2. March winds and April showers,
   (flutter hands sideways and then downward)
   Popping up are pretty flowers.
   (raise hands above head)
   A kite flying in the sun. (form diamond with hands)
   Aren't you glad the spring's begun?
   (point to a friend)

3. What's fluffy white and floats up high (point upward)
   Like piles of ice cream in the sky?
   (rub stomach)
   And when the wind blows hard and strong, (move hands slowly through air)
   What brings the rain? (flutter fingers downward)
   What brings the snow? (flutter fingers downward)
   That showers down on us below?
   (point to friends and self)
                        Author Unknown

4. White sheep, white sheep on a blue hill. (form hill with hands)
   When the wind stops, you all stand still.
   When the wind blows, you walk away slow. (walk, with fingers)
   White sheep, white sheep, where do you go?
                        Christina G. Rossetti

5. Looking up at the clouds, what do I see? (look upward)
   A lion in a cage staring at me.
   (make claws with hands)
   It seems if I stretch with all my might, (stretch)
   I could touch the cloud all right.
   Looking up again, what do I see?
   The cage is gone and the lion is free.

6. Raindrops are such funny things.
   (flutter fingers downward)
   They haven't feet or haven't wings.
   (point to feet, pretend to fly)
   Yet they sail through the air
   With the greatest of ease (flutter fingers downward)
   And dance on the street
   Wherever they please. (move fingers as if dancing)
                        Mary Jackson Ellis
                        Frances Lyons

7. Thunder crashes. (clap hands)
   Lightning flashes. (move hands in
       air with zigzag motion)
   Rain makes puddles, (flutter fin-
       gers)
   So I can make splashes. (jump)

8. "Pitter, patter, pitter, patter,"
   Hear the raindrops chatter. (tap
       fingers on floor)
   Raindrops water trees and flowers
       (extend arms above head)
   For oh, so many hours.
   But soon the raindrops will go away
   So we can go outside to splash and
       play. (jump)

9. During spring it often showers,
       (flutter fingers)
   Or the sun shines for many hours.
       (form circle in the air)
   Both are good for the flowers.
       (extend arms above head)

10. From dark clouds the rain falls
        down. (flutter fingers)
    Soon big puddles form on the
        ground. (make circle with arms)
    Thirsty flowers raise their heads
        to say, (lift head)
    "Thank you for the showers. You've
        made my day!" (smile)

11. One spring day the big round sun
        (form circle in air)
    Winked at a cloud just for fun.
        (wink)
    That dark gray cloud thundered and
        cried, (rub eyes)
    Scattering raindrops on all out-
        side. (flutter fingers)
    But when the sun peeked out from a
        sunset low (form circle)
    Together they both made a gay rain-
        bow! (form arch with arms)

12. After it rains, it's fun to splash
        (jump)
    In puddles, small rivers, and
        streams.
    Often the sun peeks through the
        clouds, (form circle with hands
        in air)
    And in the distance a rainbow
        beams. (form arch with arms)

13. Raindrops fell from the clouds one
        day. (flutter fingers)
    Then the sun peeked out and made a
        rainbow gay. (form arch with
        arms)

14. Raindrops fell on Lee.
    Raindrops fell on Paul. (flutter
        fingers)
    But they didn't fall on Sarabella:
        (shake head sideways)
    She had a huge umbrella. (pretend
        to hold umbrella above head)

15. It rains on the duck, cow, and
        horse.
    It rains on the trees and leaves,
        of course! (flutter fingers)
    It rains on a little girl and
        fella. (point to girl and boy)
    But I'm not wet. I have an umbrel-
        la! (place hands over head)

16. Who has seen the wind?
    Neither you nor I. (shake head
        sideways)
    But when the trees bow down their
        leaves, (bow)
    The wind is passing by. (move arms)
                    Christina G. Rossetti

17. Blow wind, bloooooooooow.
    Blow a breeze
    And rustle the leaves. (extend
        arms and move fingers)
    Blow a gale,
    And a boat will sail. (move hand
        through air like a boat sailing)
    Blow a strong wind,
    And a windmill will spin! (extend
        arms outward and move arms in
        circles)

18. The wind blew one March day. (move
        hands through air sideways)
    I knew the time was right.
    With string, paper, scissors, and
        paste, (pretend to cut and paste)
    I built a colorful kite. (form
        diamond with hands)
    Outside in the breezy air,
    My kite and I ran by. (move fin-
        gers as if running)
    A gust of wind nipped at my heels.
        (point to heels)
    My kite was flying high! (point up)

19. Oh, to be a kite floating in the sky! (form diamond with hands)
What a wonderful place to see birds fly by, (pretend to fly)
To touch a cloud, WOW! (pretend to touch a cloud)
And to the sun take a bow, (bow)
To float along and ride the breeze (pretend to be floating)
And take a spin whenever I please. (spin)

20. We can make a parachute billow in the air. (wave arms upward as if billowing parachute)
But if we let go, it floats down there. (point downward)

21. Bubbles, bubbles, large and small, (make large circle, then small circle)
Sailing through the air.
I reach out to catch one (pretend to catch bubble)
And POP! (clap hands)
It isn't there.

22. Blow a bubble. (blow and form circle with hands)
Catch a bubble. (pretend to catch bubble)
Look, what do I see? (pretend to look in bubble)
It looks just like me! (point to self)

LANGUAGE DEVELOPMENT

1. CLOUDS:
    A. Clouds are a visible collection of a large number of tiny water droplets or ice particles being carried by currents of air.
    B. Clouds are signs of approaching weather. Some clouds promise fair weather, and others warn of storms.
Go outside and observe clouds. How are the clouds alike? How are they different? What words could be used to describe clouds? Observe cloud shapes and discuss what objects or animals they resemble.

2. CLOUD FORMATIONS: Observe different types of clouds. Discuss:
    A. CIRRUS are thin, wispy, white clouds. They are located high in the sky and are almost entirely composed of ice crystals. Cirrus clouds often precede rain or snow.
    B. CUMULUS are white, fluffy, rounded clouds seen on a nice day. These tend to grow upwards and can turn into CUMULONIMBUS clouds on days when there are strong updrafts that cause much evaporation on the ground and moisture build-up in the air.
    C. CUMULONIMBUS are tall vertical clouds often called thunderheads. They are shaped like anvils, domes, or towers with white tops and dark bases. They normally produce lightning and heavy storms.
    D. STRATUS are low-hanging clouds spread in layers that form a gray blanket. They give the sky a hazy appearance. Stratus clouds can become fog if they rest on the ground.
    E. NIMBOSTRATUS are dark STRATUS clouds that are normally the source of steady daylong or persistent rain or snow.
Note: Cirrus, cumulus, and stratus clouds are the three basic types of clouds. There are many variations of these. Examples are cumulonimbus, cirrocumulus, cirrostratus, altocumulus, altostratus, and nimbostratus. Nimbus denotes any cloud that produces precipitation.

3. EXAMPLES OF CLOUD FORMATIONS: Display pictures of CLOUD FORMATIONS (see page 128). Make examples of each in the following ways:
    A. CIRRUS: Glue several cotton balls on blue construction paper, leaving space between each ball. After glue dries, remove cotton. Thin cotton remains.
    B. CUMULUS: Glue cotton balls onto blue construction paper. Some balls can touch to form larger clouds.
    C. CUMULONIMBUS: Draw an anvil on gray construction paper. Fill top of anvil with white cotton balls. Fill bottom of anvil with gray cotton balls, made by placing cotton balls and dry tempera in a bag and shaking. Draw rain falling from cloud.
    D. STRATUS: Color construction paper with side of gray chalk. Draw darker horizontal layers through parts of the paper.
    E. NIMBOSTRATUS: Draw dark STRATUS cloud with rain or snow falling from it.

4. RAIN: Discuss:
    A. What does the rain feel like? What does it sound like?
    B. How does the rain make you feel? Why?
    C. Sometimes during a thunderstorm, there are bright flashes of lightning and loud claps of thunder. How do these make you feel? Why?
    D. What do you think of when it rains?
    E. What do you do when it rains?
    F. What should you wear if you need to be in the rain? Why?
    G. How is the rain helpful?
    H. Where does the water go after it rains?

5. HAIL: Hailstones are small balls of ice that sometimes fall during thunderstorms. Hail falls most often between April and June. One hailstone is formed when an ice crystal falls from a cloud into warmer air and gathers water droplets. It is then swept into upper freezing air, and a layer of ice is frozen around the crystal. This continues until the hailstone becomes too heavy and falls to earth.
    A. Have you ever seen hail? What did it look and feel like?
    B. During a hailstorm watch the hail bounce. Afterwards collect some hail. Hold it in your hand. What happens to hail when it becomes warm? Why? Hail is ice that melts and becomes water.

6. LIGHTNING: Make a bolt of lightning on paper by playing the dot-to-dot game. Adult draws dot on paper. Player places pen on dot. Adult places another dot to the right of the first. Player draws line to second dot. Continue forming dots and drawing lines until a bolt of lightning is formed.

Variations:
    A. Increase length of lines and difficulty of pattern.
    B. Adult draws horizontal bolts of lightning on paper. Player traces bolts from left to right with finger. These can also be laminated with clear self-adhesive plastic. Player traces bolts with crayon. Erase crayon with tissue.
    C. Adult draws dots on paper and numbers each progressively. Player connects dots in numerical order.
Note: This activity helps develop visual, motor, and pre-writing skills.

7. WINDY LETTERS: Form a letter in the air. Players guess the letter.
Variations: Form shapes or numbers.

8. WIND: When air moves, it is wind. Wind is common in many parts of the country in the spring. Discuss the following:
   A. Can you hear the wind? What does it sound like?
   B. Can you see the wind? No. How do you know it is blowing? You can see what the wind does. Look outside. What signs of wind do you see? What direction is the wind blowing?
   C. How is the wind useful? Examples are drying clothes hung outside, moving sailboats, turning windmills, carrying seeds, and flying kites.
   D. Create a small wind by moving your hand. What other ways can you make air move?

9. RAIN, WIND, STORM: Discuss variations of these words:
   A. RAIN: drizzle, sprinkle, shower, downpour
   B. WIND: breeze, gale, tornado
   C. STORM: rainstorm, thunderstorm, hurricane

10. KITE SAFETY: Discuss these rules when making and flying kites:
    A. Make a kite from paper, plastic, or wood. Avoid use of metal.
    B. Use dry string for the kite line. Avoid wire.
    C. Fly kite in an open area away from electric wires and transmission towers.
    D. Fly kite in nice weather, not in thunderstorms.
    E. Don't try to remove a kite entangled in wires, treetops, or roofs.

11. CLOTHING: Man adapts to his environment by wearing appropriate clothing for weather conditions. The weather determines the clothing people wear. Divide poster into three sections. Draw picture of rain, wind, and sun at the top of each section. Cut pictures from magazines of different kinds of clothing. Glue to appropriate section.

12. BOOKS:
    Pitter, Patter--Baruch
    Gilberto and the Wind--Ets
    Rainbow of My Own--Freeman
    Jonathan Plays with the Wind--Gallant
    Where Does the Butterfly Go When It Rains?--Garelick
    The Wind Blew--Hutchins
    Goodbye Thunderstorms--Marine
    Curious George Flys a Kite--Rey
    Who Knows When Winter Goes?--Simon
    Follow the Wind--Tresselt
    Raindrop Splash--Tresselt
    When It Rains Cats and Dogs--Turner
    Umbrella--Yashima

GAMES AND SOCIAL DEVELOPMENT

1. SPRING--HOT OR COLD: Discuss different meanings for the word "spring." Make a coiled spring by wrapping a pipe cleaner around a pencil. Adult hides the spring, and then players try to locate it. Adult gives clues to help players determine how close they are to the spring. Examples are freezing, cold, cool, warm, hot, and sizzling. The closer the players are to spring, the "hotter" the clues become.

2. RAIN OR SHINE: To make rain or shine coin, cut 4" circle from cardboard. Cover one side of circle with blue paper and the other side with yellow paper. Yellow side represents shine, and blue side represents rain. Game is played with two players. Player that represents rain is given 30 blue 1" paper circles. Player that represents shine is given 30 yellow 1" paper circles. One player flips rain or shine coin. The player whose side is showing places one circle on the first day of a large 30-day calendar. Alternate turns for flipping coin until calendar is filled. A weather report is then given which includes the number of days of sunshine and rain for the month.

3. CLOUD GREETINGS:
    A big dark cloud races through the sky.
    He sends flashes of lightning to a cloud nearby.
    They bow to one another, roar, and thunder.
    "How do you do?" (deep voice of first child)
    "How do you do?" (deep voice of second child)
    "How do you dooooo?" (deep voice of first child)
Stand in circle. First child is chosen to be dark cloud and goes into circle. At the end of second line, first child stops near closest child. They bow to one another and exchange greetings. The second child then goes around circle as the verse is repeated.

4. WINDY WEATHER: (Tune--"Twinkle Twinkle Little Star")
    In the springtime, there's windy weather.
    When the wind blows, we all run together.
Stand in circle. Circle clockwise while singing verse. At end of verse everyone comes together in center of circle.

5. WINDY: A ping-pong ball is placed at the center of a table. A player stands at each end of table. Each player attempts to blow the ball off opponent's end of the table by being as windy as possible.

6. PARACHUTE PARTICIPATION: When playing with a real parachute, it is necessary to cooperate as a group. This is accomplished by the adult giving the commands and the players responding together. For the following activities hold edge of chute with both hands. Examples of ways to hold chute are palms down (usually works best), palms up, or one palm up and one palm down.
    A. PARACHUTE CLOUD: Everyone lifts arms, extending the arms straight up as far as possible. Hold arms fully extended until chute flutters down. When chute touches floor, lower hands, and then repeat.
    Variation: Everyone lifts arms up and pulls arms down to make chute billow. When it billows to maximum size, adult gives signal for all players to take one step forward, crouch while holding chute, and pull it over their heads.
    B. PARACHUTE RAIN OR SHINE: Players kneel around chute. Go around circle, alternately designating each child as Holder or Crawler, until everyone is named. Then adult calls, "rain" or "shine." If adult calls, "shine," Holders hold chute on floor while Crawlers crawl across the top of the chute to opposite side. If adult calls, "rain," Holders lift chute high while Crawlers crawl under chute to opposite side. After awhile, Crawlers and Holders change positions, and the game is repeated.
    Note: Parachutes can be purchased at a military surplus store. If a chute isn't available, use a blanket or sheet.

7. FOGGY DAY PARACHUTE: Stand in circle. Place teddy bear under parachute. Hold parachute and make it billow in center. (Refer to PARACHUTE PARTICIPATION on page 131.) Pretend parachute is a cloud. One player is named to retrieve the teddy bear before the "cloud" lowers and "Teddy is lost in the fog."

8. SUDSY CLOUD PAINTING: Add a minimum amount of water to soap flakes. Beat until mixture holds stiff peaks. Place in bucket. Use brush to paint fence, side of house, or slide. Remove handiwork with water from hose.
   Note: This also makes great icing for mud pies.

9. RAINDROPS AND PUDDLES: Mix several drops of food coloring with 1/4 cup of water. Experiment in the following ways:
   A. Make drops on a section of paper towel using different objects. Examples are toothpick, straw, crayon, finger, paintbrush, eyedropper, and teaspoon. Discuss size and shape of drops. Drop the colored water from 1/2" above the paper. Drop it from 6" above the paper. What differences are there in the drops?
   B. Make several drops on a piece of waxed paper. Make the drops come together to form a puddle. Add more drops to the puddle. Lead the drops with a straw to form a stream.
   C. Add drops to a full glass of water. Notice bulge at rim of glass before it overflows. Discuss that glass is "fuller than full" because surface tension holds water molecules together. Place paper on rim of glass to make water spill or flood.
   Variations:
   A. Instead of water, use other liquids. Examples are syrup, hand lotion, oil, and milk.
   B. Instead of paper towels and waxed paper, use newsprint, aluminum foil, wood, or cloth.

10. WATERPLAY: Most children enjoy playing in water. Use warm water to make the experience more pleasant. Add soap to water. Examples of soap are flakes, powder, liquid, and bar. Place waterplay container either on floor or use at child's waist level.
    A. CONTAINERS: Containers that can be used include molded, plastic, wading pool; portable baby bath; large basin, bowl, or dishpan; galvanized wash tub; bathtub; or sink.
    B. ACCESSORIES: Accessories that can be used include measuring cups; small pitchers or beakers; various-sized plastic containers; funnels of various sizes; straws and bubble pipes; plastic squirt bottles; bottles with sprinkler tops; ketchup dispensers; spoons; wire whisks; egg beaters; sponges; small plastic boats, animals, and people; meat basters; plastic eye droppers; plastic or rubber tubing. The use of glass and easily breakable plastic accessories is not recommended.
    Note: Waterplay experiences can be used to teach many concepts. Mathematical concepts of measuring and filling can be explored. Scientific principles dealing with floating, sinking, and absorbency lend themselves to experimentation. Language and communication are fostered through group waterplay. Finally, waterplay provides a social experience that accommodates every level of social development, including solitary play, parallel play, and group participation.

11. WATER PAINT: Fill juice can, bucket, or plastic container with water. Use brush to paint fence, tree, swing, slide, or sidewalk.

12. BLOW BUBBLES IN THE AIR: To make bubble solution mix 1 cup water, 1/3 cup liquid soap, and 1 table-spoon sugar. Make wand for blowing bubbles by bending end of 3" pipe cleaner back 1/4" to form hook. Attach hook to same pipe cleaner, forming a loop approximately 1/2" in diameter. Use the lower end of pipe cleaner for handle. Experiment with bubbles in the following ways:

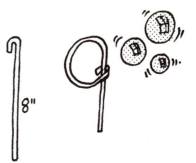

A. Blow bubbles with wand.
B. Slide the hook, making the loop of the wand as large as possible. Blow bubbles. Does a larger loop make larger bubbles?
C. Shape the pipe cleaner loop into a triangle. Does a triangular-shaped loop make a triangular-shaped bubble?
D. Remove hook from side of pipe cleaner. Will an incomplete loop make a bubble?
E. Use other items for wand. Examples are strainer, wooden bead, straw, funnel, circular ends of scissors, and juice can with both ends removed.
F. Catch a bubble on the wand. Examine the bubble. What can be seen? How are bubbles like rainbows? How are they like mirrors? Place black paper behind the bubble. Do big bubbles make you look bigger? Are you upside down? Are there two images of you in the bubble? Look at the bottom of the bubble near the wand for your image. Look at the top of the bubble. Is there a difference in your image?

Note: Many children blow too hard or touch the film of the bubble solution on the wand with their lips or fingers. In both instances the film is popped before it becomes a bubble. Experiment with blowing. Blow into hand like a strong wind and a gentle breeze. Feel the difference. To form bubble, blow like a gentle breeze. Observe flat bubble on wand. Touch the flat bubble and it is gone.

13. BLOW BUBBLES IN BOWL: Place 1/2 cup water and 1/2 teaspoon liquid soap in a bowl. Place straw in liquid and blow a pile of bubbles. What shape are the bubbles? On how many sides do the bubbles touch other bubbles?
Variations:
A. Mix one quart warm water and one cup granulated soap. Place small amount of soap mixture and straw in a juice can. Blow!
B. Add food coloring to soap mixture.
Note: Instruct children to blow through straws. This project can be difficult for smaller children, as they frequently inhale instead of blow.

14. SHAKE BUBBLES IN BOTTLE: Place small amount of water and liquid soap in a clear plastic bottle. Shake. Look at the shape and color of bubbles. Add several drops of food coloring. Shake. What color are the bubbles? Are the bubbles like a rainbow?

15. BUTTERFLY KITE: (Group project) Cut a butterfly from a large sheet of construction paper. Decorate with crayons or felt-tipped pens. Cut three narrow strips of cardboard. Glue one strip on butterfly's body. Glue remaining strips over wings, forming an X. Tie a string across bottom of X and a string across top of X. Tie the two strings together in center of X, pulling the butterfly into a curve. Attach kite string to point where two strings are tied. Kite is ready to fly.

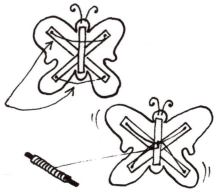

16. KITE MOBILE: Suspend KITES (see page 125) from wire hanger. Hang mobile near open window so it will fly in the wind. Observe how the wind moves the kites.

CREATIVE DRAMATICS AND MOVEMENT

1. RAINY DAY: What do you wear on a rainy day? What do you wear on your feet? What do you carry? Pretend to put on raincoat, rain hat, boots, and carry an umbrella. Open the door and go for a walk on a rainy day. Open the umbrella and hold it. Walk in the puddles and splash. Continue walk in rain to following verse:

> During April showers I hold my umbrella high
> When I go walking so it will keep me dry.
> Pitter, patter, goes the rain. Splash, splash, go my feet
> As I play in every puddle that I chance to meet.

2. THUNDER AND LIGHTNING DRAMA: Pretend to go for a walk. There are large gray clouds in the sky. Drip. Drop. Drip. Drop. Rain begins to fall. Run quickly! Lightning flashes (clap hands). Thunder roars (stamp feet). Run faster. The house is just ahead. Climb the stairs. Open the door. There is a fire burning in the fireplace. Warm your hands. Change into dry clothes. Go to sleep by the warm fire. Safe at last!

3. RAINY DAY PROP BOX: Cover a cardboard box with blue paper. Glue UMBRELLA DESIGNS (see page 124) onto box. Fill box with raincoat, slicker, rain hat, boots, and child's umbrella. Allow time for creative play.

4. BOOTS: Use two, flat-bottomed, paper bags that are slightly larger than shoes. Place a foot in each bag. Secure bags at ankles with string or rubber bands. Pretend to walk in rain and splash in puddles.

5. WINDSHIELD WIPERS: Windshield wipers are important when driving in a car when it is raining. Visibility is limited without them. Pretend to be wipers by extending arms upward and bending side to side. Dramatize following verse.

> When I'm driving with my Dad and Mom,
> And the rain comes splashing down,
> Dad presses a button and,
> SPLISH, SPLASH, SPLISH,
> The wipers come zooming on.
> Back and forth and back and forth,
> They swish across the glass.
> It's fun to watch, but it won't last long,
> For the storm will quickly pass.

6. THINGS FOUND IN THE AIR: Name things that are found in the air. Dramatize motions of each object. Examples are bird, cloud, smoke, smog, helicopter, balloon, butterfly, kite, airplane, parachute, rain, snow, sun, moon, stars, and planets.

7. MARCH WIND: Dramatize following verse:
> Five little children one March day
> Went for a walk just this way.
> The wind blew so hard and strong
> As they walked down the street.
> It turned them round and round
> And almost blew them off their feet.

8. WIND DANCE: Make wind chimes to demonstrate movement of the wind. With a hammer and nail, punch a hole in plastic scoops from coffee or soft drink mixes. Thread a string through each hole and tie. Tie strings to a wire clothes hanger. Hang mobile near an open window so it will move in the wind. Wait for a strong breeze. Create a dance to rhythm of the chimes.
   Variation: Use plastic spoons in addition to, or instead of, scoops.

9. KITE FLYING: Dramatize following verse:
    On many spring days I wish that I
    Could be a kite flying in the sky.
    I would climb high toward the sun
    And chase the clouds. Oh. what fun!
    Whichever way the wind chanced to blow
    Is the way that I would go.
    I'd fly up, up, up. I'd fly down, down, down.
    Then I'd spin round and round and round.
    Finally I'd float softly to the ground.

10. PARACHUTE DRAMATICS: Place parachute over circular climbing apparatus. Play under parachute in creative way.

11. RECORD: "Windshield Wipers" from *Songs of Joy* by Diane Hartman Smith, Joy, Box 58, Aspen, Colorado 81611.

PHYSICAL DEVELOPMENT

1. FLOATING CLOUDS: A white balloon is used as a cloud. Inflate balloon and tie. Make "cloud" float in the air by striking it from underneath with hands.

2. BLOW BALLOON, GO BALLOON: Inflate balloon. When adult says, "Go." release balloon. Watch balloon fly. Blow more air into the balloon and more wind will be released, making balloon fly longer.

3. RAINY DAY BALANCE BEAM: Do the following activities on a balance beam:
    A. Walk forward holding a child's umbrella.
    B. Walk forward with arms extended at sides.
    C. Walk forward with arms held straight over head.
    D. Walk forward to middle of board, kneel on one knee, rise, and continue to end of board.
    E. Walk forward with bean bag balanced on head, shoulder, or outstretched arm.
    F. Walk backward to middle of board, turn around, and walk backward to end of board.
    G. Walk sideways with weight on balls of feet.
    H. Walk forward and bounce a ball on floor with one hand.
    I. Walk on all fours to end of the board.
    J. Walk forward carrying a small bucket in each hand. Adult drops bean bags into each bucket as child walks.
   Variations:
    A. Mark board into four sections with colored tape, shapes, or numbers. Small goals can be achieved if child cannot reach end of beam.
    B. Instead of balance beam, use a board or masking tape placed on floor.
    C. Play music while doing activity. It may help relax children who are timid.
   Note: Encourage use of arms to maintain or regain balance.

4. **PUDDLE JUMPING:** Pretend the center of an inner tube is a puddle. Jump in tube pretending to make the water splash.
   Variations:
   A. Place several inner tubes in a line with sides touching. Jump from one "puddle" to the next.
   B. Use hula hoops instead of inner tubes.
   C. Make puddle shapes on the floor with masking tape or rope.

5. **BLOWING WIND:** Pretend to be the wind blowing by doing the following:
   A. Blow on hand with mouth open.
   B. Blow hard with lips puckered. Blow softly.
   C. Whistle while blowing.

6. **FLYING KITE:** Go outside and run with KITE (see page 125).
   Variations:
   A. Fly BUTTERFLY KITE (see page 133).
   B. Assemble and fly kite purchased from store.

7. **PARACHUTE:** Cut 12" x 12" square from a plastic bag. Punch a small hole in each corner of the square. Thread a piece of string through each hole and tie. Thread ends of strings to plastic figure of cowboy, astronaut, or soldier. Hold figure and run with chute.
   Variation: Use bottom half of plastic bread bag for parachute.

8. **PARACHUTE LAUNCH:** Place a flat rock on ground. Put a two foot long board on rock one-third the distance from one end of board. Place folded PARACHUTE on the long end of the board. Stamp on short end. The parachute will shoot in the air.

9. **CATCH THE WIND:** Two children hold opposite sides of the open end of a large trash bag. Walk into wind or run to make bag inflate.

10. **WINDMILL EXERCISE:** Stand with arms extended outward. Move arms forward and then backward in small circles, larger circles, and giant circles.

MATH

1. **RAINDROP COUNTING:** Pretend a bouncing ball is the pitter patter of raindrops falling. Players close their eyes or turn their backs while adult bounces ball several times. Players listen and count silently the number of bounces. The adult then asks one child to clap his hands and verbally count the same number of times the ball bounced. Child then becomes leader and bounces ball.
   Variations:
   A. Identify total number of bounces without clapping.
   B. Bounce the ball, pause, and then bounce the ball again. Players must identify both times the ball bounced. For example: clap three times, pause, and then clap two times.
   C. Instead of ball, pat the bottom of an oatmeal container for the pitter patter of the raindrops. Give child an oatmeal container so he can make the same pitter patter sound as the leader when responding.

2. MORE OR FEWER RAINDROPS: Divide a poster board into two sections. Place a paper cloud at the top of each section. Place a different number of paper raindrops under each cloud. Which cloud has more raindrops? Which cloud has fewer? Repeat, changing number of raindrops under each cloud.

3. RAIN GAUGE: To make rain gauge, use a tall clear container with straight sides. (Large plastic herb jars are suitable.) To side of container, tape ruler. placing smaller numbers at bottom. Put gauge in an unprotected place outdoors. Look at gauge after a rain and record rainfall. Empty gauge and replace it.
Variation: Purchase rain gauge.

4. KITE COUNTER: Draw a kite with long tail on poster board. Laminate. Number construction paper bows from 1 to 10. With masking tape attach bows to tail in sequence.
Variation: Cut 10 kites and 55 bows from paper. Mark each kite with a number from 1 to 10. Attach tail to each kite. Tape corresponding number of bows to each tail.

5. COLORED KITES: Attach different-colored kites to strings. Place kites in box with strings hanging over edge. Pull one string at a time and identify color.

SCIENCE

1. WHAT MAKES THE RAIN? The biggest source for rain is the ocean. Lakes and other water bodies also contribute to the formation of rain. The heat from the sun causes water to evaporate from these water bodies and rise into the atmosphere, where it is condensed into clouds. Precipitation is produced when the tiny water droplets become too heavy to float. so they fall to earth in the form of rain, snow, sleet, or hail. Place tea kettle on hot plate or stove. When water boils, a cloud will form just beyond the spout. The clear area near the spout is steam. Hold a pie pan filled with ice cubes in the cloud. What happens when the water vapor comes in contact with it? Why?

2. EVAPORATION: When water is heated, it evaporates (changes from liquid to gas) and becomes water vapor or steam. Experiment with the following:
   A. Sometimes the water vapor from evaporation can be seen. Observe steam from boiling water. Observe the water vapor from a cool mist vaporizer.
   B. Sometimes the evaporation cannot be seen. For example, water evaporating from a lake cannot be seen. This water rises and forms clouds. Fill pan to top with water. Set in place where pan will not be bumped. Mark water level every morning. After a few days discuss what has happened to the water level and why. The water has evaporated.
   C. Wash some doll clothes or handkerchiefs. Place them in the sun. What happens to the water? Do things dry more quickly spread out separately or packed together? Wet six handkerchiefs. Roll three into a ball and place in sun. Lay remaining hankies separately and flat in sun. Which dried more quickly? Why? The warm air reaches all parts of the flat hankies, and air surrounding hankies enhances drying time.
   D. Wipe a chalkboard with a wet sponge. Watch water on the board disappear.
   E. Dip both hands in water. Place one hand in front of fan. Which hand is cooler? Why? The moving air causes evaporation. As the water evaporates, it requires heat energy. This energy is drawn from the hand.

3. AIR CONTAINS WATER: Discuss that air contains water. Make certain the outside of a jar is dry. Fill jar with ice cubes. What happens? How did water get on the outside of the jar? Why? The air around the jar was cooled, forming water vapor.

4. WHAT MAKES LIGHTNING? Lightning is a flash of light in the sky caused by energy (electricity) being released within a cloud, between a cloud and the ground, or between two clouds. Go into a darkened room. Rub two, long, inflated balloons on clothing or fur. Hold the balloons so they almost touch. A spark will jump between the two balloons. That spark is electricity. If the balloons had been clouds, the sparks would have been lightning. Lightning is electricity we see in the sky.

5. WHAT MAKES THUNDER? Thunder is a loud noise caused by lightning rapidly heating the air which suddenly expands and contracts. Inflate a paper bag and hold the neck tightly so air cannot escape. Hit the bag with the other hand. The bag will break with a loud bang. This causes the air in the bag to suddenly contract and expand, which makes the noise. This is how thunder occurs. It takes one second for thunder to go one mile. If the time between seeing the lightning and hearing the thunder is five seconds, the thunder is five miles away. When you see lightning and hear thunder at almost the same time, the storm is directly overhead.

6. WHAT MAKES A RAINBOW? A rainbow is colored light seen in the sky when rays of the sun strike falling raindrops. Rainbows are curved because raindrops that reflect the sunlight are curved. Rainbows occur after a storm when the sun begins to shine while the air is still filled with raindrops. They occur most often in the morning or evening. Stripes of the rainbow are always red, orange, yellow, green, blue, and violet. Sometimes one color may fade out (most often blue). The red is almost always seen. Sometimes two rainbows can be observed. A rainbow is really a circle and has no end. Occasionally passengers in low-flying aircraft see rainbows that form complete circles. The bottom half of the rainbow is hidden from most observers because it is below the horizon.
    Experiment with the following:
    A. Place a small mirror in a glass of water. Place the glass of water so the sun will shine on the mirror. Turn the glass until the rainbow is reflected against the wall. Find the colors of the rainbow. The sun is made up of these colors. When sunlight hits raindrops or water, the colors are separated.
    B. Spray fine mist of water from a hose. Stand with your back to the sun. A rainbow will appear in the fine spray of the water. Stand with spray between you and the sun. Can you still see the rainbow? Why?
    C. A prism will separate colors like the raindrops. Hold a prism to light and observe the colors. Make a cardboard disk with primary colors on it in equal proportions. Thread string through center of disk. Spin disk rapidly. Colors will combine. and disk will appear to be white.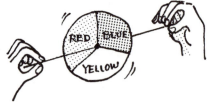

7. WIND: Wind is moving air. Experiment with any of the following to create wind: blow with mouth, inflate balloon and allow air to escape through the opening, use air pump, and use fan with several speeds. Make gentle breeze and then a strong wind. Discover what objects can be moved by the wind you create. Make chart of things the wind can do.

8. WINDMILL: Cut a vane 8" in length from corrugated cardboard. Corrugated ribs should go crosswise on the vane. Use PINWHEEL (see page 124). Push nail attached to pinwheel in narrow end of vane. Use a pole or broomstick for shaft. Hammer a second nail in the end of shaft, leaving 1" exposed. Cut 1/4" from a drinking straw and place on nail. Insert top of nail into rib of vane, balancing windmill on shaft. Place in front of a fan or take outside on a windy day. Discuss that windmills are used to create electricity and to pump water. Wind strikes the vane of the windmill. The vane acts as a rudder and swings the wheel toward the wind. The wheel turns a shaft connected to a water pump.

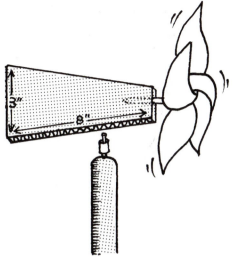

MUSIC

1. FLOATING CLOUDS: (Tune--"Frère Jacques")
   Clouds are floating, clouds are floating,
   Up so high, up so high,
   Floating up above us, floating up above us,
   In the sky, in the sky.
   Clare Cherry

2. IT'S RAINING, IT'S POURING:
   It's raining, it's pouring.
   The old man is snoring.
   He bumped his head, and he went to bed,
   And he couldn't get up in the morning.
   Traditional

3. RAIN, RAIN GO AWAY:
   Rain, rain go away.
   Come again some other day.
   Little Johnny wants to play.
   Traditional

4. COME GOOD RAIN: (Tune--"Did You Ever See a Lassie?")
   Come sing a song for rain, for rain, for rain.
   Come sing a song for rain on meadows and plain,
   With thunder calling and drops of rain falling.
   Come sing a song for rain, pitter pat.
Lift arms and stand on tiptoes. Turn to one side and then the other. Then gently fall on the floor.

5. THUNDER: (Tune--"Frère Jacques")
   I hear thunder. I hear thunder. (stamp feet on floor)
   Hark, don't you? Hark, don't you? (place hand behind ear)
   Pitter patter raindrops, pitter patter raindrops, (wiggle fingers
      downward)
   I'm wet through. (shake body)
   So are you. (point to friend)
   Traditional

6. WEATHER MUSIC: Reproduce weather sounds with musical instruments.
   A. RAIN: Strike triangle or wooden sticks with quick motions.
   B. WIND: Shake tambourine or slide mallot on xylophone.
   C. THUNDER: Clap symbols or blocks.

7. BALLOON SHAKE: Place a teaspoon of rice, sand, or beans in a balloon. Inflate balloon and tie. Shake balloon to music.

8. WIND INSTRUMENT: Make large hole near one end of a cardboard tube. Cover both ends with pieces of waxed paper which are held in place with rubber bands. Hum into large hole.

FIELD TRIPS

1. AIRPORT
2. WEATHER STATION
3. VISIT FROM A WEATHERMAN
4. VISIT FROM A PARATROOPER

SPRING

SPRING officially begins mid-March and ends mid-June in the Northern Hemisphere. In places where the weather was cold during the winter months, it begins to warm causing plants to grow once again. Spring flowers brighten gardens, trees bud, and the grass starts to turn green. Gardens and fields are planted as people become involved in outside activities during this season.

Because of the warm weather, birds return from their winter homes and build nests. Animals and insects that were dormant also reappear. Many insects produce foods we eat, pollinate plants, and kill other harmful insects which spread disease and compete with man for food. Generally, insects are more helpful than they are harmful.

CONCEPTS TO BE TAUGHT

1. Spring is the season between summer and winter.
2. In the springtime, dormant and migrating animals reappear.
3. Insects and spiders, which are plentiful in the spring, can be both helpful and harmful.
4. Seeds are planted, and plants begin to grow in the spring.
5. People enjoy outdoor activities once again as the weather becomes warmer.

ART ACTIVITIES

1. SIGNS OF SPRING: Paint signs of spring using pastel colors.

2. SEED COLLAGE: Create picture by gluing different seeds onto construction paper. Use seeds that are large in size. Examples are pinto beans, dried peas, navy beans, lima beans, and popcorn kernels.

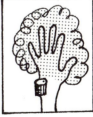

3. MAPLE TREE: Place forearm and hand, with fingers spread, on construction paper. With brown crayon, trace around forearm and hand to make tree trunk and branches. Color tree and leaves with crayons. Glue nut cup or egg carton cup to trunk for maple bucket.
   Variations:
   A. Paint hand and forearm with brown paint. Press painted area onto paper.
   B. Instead of bucket, place swing in tree. Glue two pieces of yarn from one branch. For swing seat, attach rectangular piece of paper or popsicle stick section to ends of yarn.

4. APPLE BLOSSOM TREE: Glue tree trunk cut from brown paper onto construction paper. Crumple small squares of pink and green tissue paper. Glue to tree. (For technique to apply tissue paper refer to AUTUMN TREE on page 1.)

5. EGG CARTON FLOWER: Cut an egg carton cup into a flower. Paint. Allow to dry. For stem, insert a pipe cleaner through bottom of cup. Cut construction paper leaves. Poke hole in one end of each leaf. Thread leaves onto pipe cleaner. Variation: Glue perfumed cotton ball in center of a colored, styrofoam, egg carton cup.

6. FLOWER COLLAGE: Cut or tear pictures of flowers from seed or flower catalogs. Glue onto construction paper to form flower garden. Variation: Cut or tear scraps of brightly colored construction paper. Glue onto paper to make flowers.

7. SUNFLOWER: Paint a large paper plate yellow. Glue brown cotton ball to center. To make cotton ball brown, place cotton and dry brown tempera in sack. Shake. Glue green paper stem and leaves to flower. Variations:
    A. Make flower by cutting wedges from edge of paper plate.
    B. Instead of cotton ball, glue sunflower seeds to center of plate.
Note: Make bulletin board by arranging several sunflowers above paper vase.

8. HAND TULIP: Hold fingers together on one hand. Place hand in brightly colored paint. Press hand onto paper. Dip side of hand into green paint and press onto paper to make stem. Repeat to make leaves.

9. LAYERED FLOWER: Cut graduated circles from different colors of construction paper. Arrange in order from largest to smallest. Attach by placing paper fastener through center of circles. Place paper fastener through piece of construction paper and secure. Draw stem, leaves, and vase with crayons. Variation: Instead of using paper fastener, glue circle together.

10. PUSSY WILLOW: For stem, draw straight line on piece of construction paper. Glue cotton or puffed rice on sides of stem. Variation: Use a twig for stem. Glue oval-shaped pieces of gray velveteen to sides of stem.

11. DANDELION JEWELRY: Thread blunt-ended needle with dental floss or crochet thread. Push needle through center of dandelion. Repeat. When desired length is reached for bracelet or necklace, tie ends of thread together.

12. NATURE CASTING: Flatten nonhardening modeling clay with a rolling pin. Arrange nature items on top of clay. Examples are leaves, seeds, rocks, and twigs with buds. Move rolling pin over the nature items to make an impression on the clay. Carefully remove the items. Surround the clay with cardboard 2" high. Pour plaster of Paris mixed to the consistency of pudding into the enclosure. When the plaster of Paris hardens, remove the cardboard and clay. Paint cast.

13. CATERPILLAR TO BUTTERFLY: To form caterpillar, glue cotton balls in a line on colored file card. Cut rectangle from colored tissue paper. Gather at center for butterfly wings. Attach to back of card.

14. COCOON: Mark a 1" section at the end of a popsicle stick. Wrap string that is two feet long around the marked section to form a cocoon.

15. CLOTHESPIN BUTTERFLY: Cut wings from colored tissue paper. Gather wings at center. Clip clothespin to center of tissue paper wings. Open clothespin slightly and insert pipe cleaner for antennae.
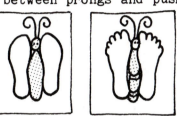
   Variations:
      A. Paint clothespin black. When dry, attach wings.
      B. Instead of tissue paper for wings, color a napkin with crayons.
      C. Use round-top clothespin for body. Place wings between prongs and push toward top of clothespin.

16. FOOT BUTTERFLY: Trace around shoes to make wings of butterfly. Draw body between wings. Add antennae. Color butterfly with crayons.
   Variation: Trace around bare feet instead of shoes.

17. BUTTERFLY BLOT: Fold piece of construction paper in half. Open. Drop bright colors of paint onto one half of paper. Close paper and press. Open.
   Variation: Use brown or black paint to make bug.

18. LADYBUG: Paint half a walnut shell red. When dry, paint black spots on shell with a cotton-tipped swab.
   Variations:
      A. Paint a smooth round rock instead of walnut shell.
      B. Make spots with black felt-tipped pen.
      C. Instead of painting spots, glue black circles made with a paper punch.

19. GRASSHOPPER: Use round-top clothespin for body. Wrap pipe cleaners around prongs of clothespin to form legs and wings. Paint or spray paint green.

20. BEEHIVE: Glue Honeycomb® cereal onto paper to represent inside or outside of beehive. Draw bees with crayons.

21. EGG CARTON CREATURES:
   A. CATERPILLAR: Use three connected egg carton cups. For antennae, make two holes in cup at one end and thread a pipe cleaner through the holes. Paint. Allow to dry. Add facial features with felt-tipped pen.
   B. WASP OR BEE: Paint CATERPILLAR yellow. Allow to dry. Make slots on sides of the center cup. Insert wings made of construction paper. To make legs, poke a hole through the two sides of each cup. Thread a pipe cleaner through holes in each cup. To cover with "pollen," place legs in dry yellow tempera.

WING
   C. BUG: Paint section or sections of egg carton for body. Glue small scraps of construction paper to body for features. Use pipe cleaners for antennae, legs, or wings.
      Variation: Glue egg carton section or sections to construction paper. Paint egg carton and paper to create bug.
   D. SPIDER: Poke four holes near open edge of egg carton cup. Thread a pipe cleaner halfway through one hole. Bend in half to form two legs. Repeat process with other holes. Paint brown or black.

22. INCHWORM: Cut circles from different colors of construction paper. Glue circles together in a line to form inchworm.

23. PLAY DOUGH BUG: Create a bug by using PLAY DOUGH (see page 84) for the body. Attach toothpicks, pipe cleaners, or paper strips for legs, wings, and antennae.

24. FLYING BIRD: Cut bird and wings from construction paper. Color bird with crayons or felt-tipped pens. Place wings through slot cut in bird's body. Variation: To make robin, cut body and wings from gray paper. Color or paint breast of robin orange.

25. BIRD NEST: Collect string, twigs, and grass. With collected items, form nest in margarine tub or bottom half of milk carton. Add cotton balls for eggs.

26. ROPE PAINTING: Cook spaghetti in boiling water until pliable. Drain. Place in cool water until ready to use. Dip strand of spaghetti in paint. To paint, wiggle spaghetti on paper.
Variations:
  A. Instead of dipping in paint, arrange spaghetti strands on paper to make collage. Starch in spaghetti will cause it to stick to paper. When dry, paint collage.
  B. Add food coloring to cool water. Arrange colored spaghetti on paper to make collage.

27. MARBLEIZED PRINT: Fill a 9" x 13" pan one-third full of water. Add 1 teaspoon salad oil to 2 tablespoons of thin tempera paint. Float this mixture on the water. Gently blow on water to make design. Place a piece of paper on top of the water. Quickly lift and observe marbleized print. Allow to dry.

28. MARBLE PAINTING: Line bottom of box with paper. Dip marble into tempera paint, remove, and place in box. Roll marble inside box to make design on paper.
Variations:
  A. Use box with clear plastic lid. Child can shake the box and see the design that is being made.
  B. Instead of marble, use hollow plastic golfball with holes.
  C. Instead of marble, use dried bean or large seed from fruit or vegetable.

29. YO-YO: Cut circle from piece of cardboard. Paint circle on both sides. Attach elastic string to circle.

COOKING ACTIVITIES

1. EDIBLE SEEDS: Discuss which seeds are used for food. Serve the following:
  A. Examine coconut and shake it. Hammer a screwdriver into the eyes of the coconut. Empty juices and taste. Open the coconut by tapping around middle with hammer. When you reach starting point, give an extra tap. Smell and taste. Compare to packaged coconut. Discuss that coconut is the largest seed.
  B. Shell and eat peas, sunflower seeds, or peanuts.

2. SEED BALLS: 1/2 cup peanut butter   1/2 cup wheat germ, toasted
                 1/2 cup honey   1 cup peanuts, chopped
                 1/2 cup carob powder   1/2 cup sunflower nuts
Combine ingredients. Roll into 1" balls. Cover with flaked coconut. Chill.

3. GRANOLA: 4 cups regular oats   1 cup sliced almonds
              2 cups raw wheat germ   3/4 cup brown sugar
              1 cup flaked coconut   1/2 cup vegetable oil
              1 cup raw sunflower nuts (optional)   1/4 cup water
              1/2 cup sesame seeds (optional)   1/2 cup raisins
    Combine first six ingredients. Mix brown sugar, oil, and water for syrup. Add
    syrup to oatmeal mixture. Place on shallow baking pan. Bake at 300° for one
    hour until brown. Stir every 15 minutes. Add raisins.
    Variation: Use dried chopped apricots instead of raisins.

4. BEAN SPROUTS: Use purchased sprouts or BEAN SPROUTS (see page 158) in the
    following ways:
        A. ORIENTAL FOODS: For example, heat can of chow mein. Add sprouts and
            serve with rice.
        B. SOUPS AND CASSEROLES: Add sprouts before serving.
        C. SALADS: Use in tossed, fruit, three-bean, or Waldorf salad. Sprouts can
            also be used as a crunchy replacement for celery in tuna or chicken
            salad.
        D. EGGS: Use in omelets, souffles, or scrambled eggs.
        E. BREADS: Grind sprouts in meat grinder and add to final kneading of
            bread. Stir into muffin, waffle, or pancake batter.
        F. SANDWICH SPREADS: For example, mix 1 cup sprouts, 1/4 cup slivered
            almonds, dash of ginger, and 2 tablespoons sour cream. Spread on bread
            or cracker.

5. BUGS ON A BRANCH: Fill celery stalk with peanut butter. Place raisins on
    peanut butter for bugs.
    Variations:
        A. Instead of peanut butter, use CHEESE SPREAD (see page 167). Sprinkle
            with paprika for ants on a branch.
        B. Instead of raisins, use peanuts.

6. VEGI-CATERPILLAR: Skewer three or four cherry tomatoes on a sandwich tooth-
    pick. Poke two holes in last tomato. Poke small celery leaves into holes.
    Presto! A caterpillar.
    Variation: Use parsley instead of celery leaves.

7. BUTTERFLY: Place carrot stick in center of lettuce
    leaf. Cut slice of pineapple in half. Arrange
    pineapple according to diagram. Add a seedless
    grape or raisin at top of carrot. Place raisins or
    grape halves on pineapple.
    Variation: Instead of pineapple, use pear cut
    lengthwise for wings.

8. LADYBUG: Use half of tomato. Place flat side of tomato on lettuce leaf. Use
    whole, black, pitted olive for head and slices of black olives for spots.

9. GRASSY SANDWICH: 1 avocado, mashed   1 tablespoon mayonnaise
                      1/2 teaspoon lemon juice   1 hard-cooked egg, diced
    Mix above ingredients together. Spread over bread or crackers. If desired,
    sprinkle with alfalfa sprouts.

10. GARDEN CUP: With a 3" cookie cutter, cut circle from a slice of whole wheat
    bread. Place in a muffin tin and bake at 400° for 8 to 10 minutes until brown.
    Add diced cucumber and alfalfa sprouts. Sprinkle with shredded Monterey Jack
    cheese. Return to oven to melt cheese.

11. TOSSED SALAD: Have each child bring one item from home for salad. Wash, cut, and combine all ingredients. Toss lightly. Serve with HONEY SALAD DRESSING.

12. HONEY SALAD DRESSING: 1/2 cup oil   2 tablespoons soy sauce
                         1/4 cup vinegar   1 tablespoon honey
    Combine ingredients. Add salt and pepper to taste. Shake well.

13. SPRINGTIME COOLER: 1 cup fresh or frozen unsweetened strawberries
                       1 cup orange juice
                       1 banana
    Combine in blender. Serve chilled.

FINGERPLAYS

1. Trees are budding. (stretch arms
       above head)
   The grass is green. (point to
       ground)
   Flower blossoms I have seen. (form
       circle with arms above head,
       sway)
   The days are warm.
   By evening it cools.
   It's time to find the garden tools.

2. Seeds, seeds of every size,
   They come in white, yellow, and
       brown.
   Some are flat, some oval, some
       round. (hold hand flat, form
       oval and circle)
   A seed so very small
   Could grow a plant very tall.
       (raise hand above head)
   The seed's color, shape, and size
   Give no clues of the plant to rise.
       (shake head sideways)

3. Little seed in the ground below
       (form small ball with body)
   Felt the warmth of the warm sun's
       glow, (rub hands over arms)
   Heard the raindrops pitter patter,
       (place hand behind ear)
   Wondered why the birds did chatter.
       (place hand on head as if ponder-
       ing)
   So the seed began to grow (pretend
       to grow)
   And poked its head up very slow!
       (lift head)
   What it saw was such a sight. (rub
       eyes)
   The plant was in a garden bright!

4. In the spring I take a seed and
       plant it in the ground. (pretend
       to plant seed)
   The warm sun shines on the world
       around. (form circle)
   Clouds gather in the sky, and the
       raindrops fall. (flutter fin-
       gers)
   The little plant sprouts above the
       ground
   And grows so straight and tall.
       (pretend to grow)

5. I dig a hole and plant a seed,
       (pretend to plant a seed)
   Cover it with dirt, and pull a
       weed. (pretend to pull weed)
   Down comes the rain and out comes
       the sun. (flutter fingers, form
       circle)
   Up grows my plant. Oh! What fun!
       (pretend to grow)

6. Inside a seed, sound asleep, (form
       fist)
   Lived a little plant, not making a
       peep. (fingers to lips)
   Mr. Raindrop knocked on the little
       seed's door, (knock)
   "Pitter, pat! You can do more."
   Mrs. Sunbeam sent a message hot,
   "Rise and shine! You can give
       a lot."
   The plant understood;
   Gave a stretch and a yawn; (stretch
       and yawn)
   Grew into a flower, pretty to gaze
       upon. (grow into flower)

7. Yellow dandelions brighten the day.
       (extend arms and sway)
   Gray dandelions, I'll blow away!
       (blow)

8. Yellow polka dots in the grass so
   green--(form small circles)
   Dad makes a fuss and says, "You're
   not to be seen." (shake finger)
   But I'd like to say, (point to
   self)
   "Dandelions make a neat bouquet!"
   (pretend to pick dandelions and
   make a bouquet)

9. Five little peas in a pea pod
   pressed, (make fist)
   One grew, two grew, and so did the
   rest. (raise respective fingers)
   They grew and grew and did not stop
   (stretch fingers wide)
   Until one day the pod went POP!!
   (clap hands)

                        Traditional

10. Beautiful spring flowers in the
    breeze (arms over head)
    Sway back and forth and rustle
    their leaves. (sway)
    Their pretty colors brighten our
    day. (smile)
    Let's pick some and make a bouquet!
    (pretend to pick flowers and make
    a bouquet)

11. Here is the beehive. (make fist)
    Where are the bees?
    Hiding inside where nobody sees.
    Look! They are coming out.
    They are all alive.
    1-2-3-4-5. (lift each finger)
    Bzzzzzzzzzzzzzzzzzzz!
                        Traditional

12. Bees make honey for me to eat, (rub
    stomach)
    And pollinate flowers that they
    meet. (form circle with arms
    above head and sway)
    Bees are busy flying everywhere,
    (move arms as if flying)
    Buzzing around here and there.
    Bzzzzzzzzzzzzzzzzzzz!

13. A creepy crawling caterpillar I
    spy. (place hand above eyes)
    Soon you'll have wings and be a
    beautiful butterfly! (pretend to
    fly)

14. Once I saw an ant hill with no ants
    about. (make fist)
    I said, "Little ants, won't you
    please come out?" (motion to
    come)
    Then as if they had heard my call,
    1-2-3-4-5 came out, and that was
    all.
                        Traditional

15. Little ladybug so prim and proper:
    (form small circle)
    All the insects love you, even the
    big grasshopper. (form big cir-
    cle)

16. Roly-poly round we go. (roll fists)
    Roly-poly roll up high.
    Roly-poly roll down low.
    Roly-poly roll around.
    And form a tight ball on the
    ground. (squat and place head on
    knees)

17. A nest for Mrs. Robin, (form cir-
    cle)
    A woodpecker's hole in a tree,
    (form circle)
    Or a birdhouse made by me: (point
    to self)
    Bird homes are all three! (three
    fingers)

18. Little robin redbreast sat upon a
    rail.
    Niddle, naddle went his head.
    (move head)
    Wiggle, waggle went his tail.
    (wiggle hands behind back)
                 Scottish Nursery Rhyme

19. Sit on the swing. Hold on tight.
    Pump your legs with all your might.
    (pretend to swing)
    Soon you'll soar high in the air
    With the wind blowing in your hair.
    (shake head)

20. It's fun to skip rope--1-2-3.
    (hold up respective fingers)
    I can do it myself or with Susie
    and Lee. (point to self and
    friend)
    The rope goes up high. (point up)
    It comes down with a thump. (hit
    floor)
    It's fun to skip rope.
    Jump, jump, jump! (jump)

147

LANGUAGE DEVELOPMENT

1. SIGNS OF SPRING: Take a short walk and note signs of spring if located in a geographical area where observable spring changes occur.
   A. Observe buds on trees and new leaves beginning to grow. What size and texture are the leaves? Are all the leaves the same color? New leaves grow because the sap starts to flow from the roots into the trunk and branches. If located in an area where maple syrup is harvested, observe sap flowing into maple buckets. This only occurs in early spring when the days are warmer and the nights are still cold.
   B. What color is the grass?
   C. Do you see any flowers? Some spring flowers include tulip, lilac, daffodil, crocus, hyacinth, and pussy willow.
   D. Observe birds that have returned from their winter homes. For example, the return of the robin is one of the first signs of spring. A robin can be identified by its reddish orange breast. Observe activities of birds. Many birds build new nests in the spring.
   E. What other animals reappear? Examples are bears, chipmunks, squirrels, snakes, and ground hogs.
   F. What outdoor activities do children enjoy in the spring? Examples are swinging, jumping rope, and playing hopscotch.

2. SEEDS: Prepare a poster board display using pictures of fruits and vegetables cut from seed packages or seed catalogs. Glue seed of each plant next to appropriate picture. For example, glue peach seed beside picture of peach. Provide box of seeds that can be matched to seeds in display. Discuss:
   A. Spring is the time people plant seeds, from which most fruits and vegetables grow.
   B. Seeds are different colors, sizes, and shapes. The size of the seed has nothing to do with the size of the plant that grows from it.
   C. Each seed contains a tiny plant, food for the plant when it begins to grow, and a seed coat to help protect the plant. Take a seed apart and discover the different parts.
   D. Seeds are found in different "containers." Examples are pods, hard shells, and fruits.

3. FROM SEED TO FLOWER: Fold a large piece of paper in half. Fold in half again. Open paper. In first section glue a seed. Rain is needed to make the seed grow. Draw rain in the second section. The sun shines on the sprouted seed to help it grow. Draw sun in the third section. Soon the plant begins to flower. Draw a flower in the last section.

4. LIFE CYCLE OF A PLANT: Draw a large chart which displays the life cycle of a plant. Discuss the plant's growth.
   A. First a seed is planted which needs air, water, food, and sun to grow.
   B. A small root grows from the seed.
   C. A small shoot appears.
   D. The young plant matures developing leaves and flowers.
   E. The flowers produce seeds, seed pods, or fruit. These seeds can be replanted, and cycle is repeated.

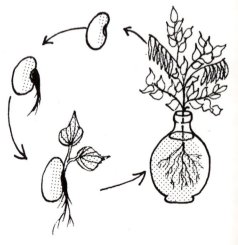

5. PLANT PARTS: Display a flower or plant and discuss different parts:

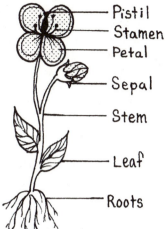

A. STEM supports the flower and leaves. The stem carries food from the roots to all parts of the plant.
B. LEAVES are flat, thin, usually green blades growing from the stem. Leaves manufacture food for the plant with the help of sunlight.
C. ROOTS are usually located beneath the ground. Roots anchor the plant. They also collect water and minerals from the soil for the plant.
D. FLOWER is the seed-producing part of a flowering plant. A flower contains petals, sepals, pistil, and stamens. The stamens hold pollen which is a powderlike substance that is usually yellow.

6. VEGETABLES: Display vegetables, using pictures or real produce. Discuss which part of each plant can be eaten.
A. STEM--celery, rhubarb, asparagus
B. LEAF--cabbage, spinach, parsley, lettuce, kale, collard
C. ROOT--beets, carrots, radishes, turnips
D. FLOWER--broccoli, cauliflower
E. SEED--peas, beans, sunflower, pumpkin, peanut
F. FRUIT--eggplant, peppers, tomatoes, squash, okra, cucumbers
G. BULB--onion
H. TUBER--potato

7. FLOWER IDENTIFICATION: Display and pass around a variety of spring flowers. Flowers can be real or pictures. Discuss name, color, shape, size, and smell of each flower. Record descriptions on piece of paper. For example, allow children to see, feel, and smell pussy willows. Describe furry blossoms. Record descriptions.

8. INSECT INFORMATION: Discuss the following facts:
A. Insects are the most numerous kind of animal in the world. They live everywhere on land, but only a few insects live in the ocean.
B. Insects are many different sizes, shapes, and colors. Fairy flies and some beetles are so small they can go through the eye of a needle. The largest insects are the Goliath beetle which is 4" in length and the Atlas moth which has a wing spread of ten inches.
C. Beetles, grasshoppers, bees, wasps, butterflies, moths, ants, mosquitoes, flies, and ladybugs are some common insects.
D. Insects come from eggs. Baby insects are usually called larvae.
E. An insect has six legs and a jointed body which consists of three distinct parts: the head, thorax or middle body, and abdomen. A good example of this is an ant.
F. Some insects have hooks and sticky pads on their feet which aid them in walking upside down or on smooth surfaces.
G. Most winged insects have four wings (two pairs).
H. Their antennae detect odors, sound waves, respond to air currents, and are used for touch.
I. Some insects are helpful. They produce foods we eat, pollinate plants, eat other insects which are harmful, and are a source of food for many animals.
J. Some insects are harmful. Mosquitoes and fleas spread disease. Other insects eat crops and destroy trees.

9. SPRING QUIZ: Mount a picture of an insect on a piece of cardboard. Make several, using different insects. Place pictures on table and identify all insects. Adult collects pictures and gives clues about one picture. When a player guesses the insect, he is given the picture. When all pictures are guessed, each player displays his picture and identifies insect.
Variations:
   A. Use pictures of vegetables or flowers instead of insects.
   B. Instead of adult collecting pictures, give one picture to each player. Adult gives clues. Player who holds picture of item described, stands and displays it to group.

10. SPIDER INFORMATION: Discuss:
   A. Spiders are called arachnids. They are not insects.
   B. Like insects, they come from eggs.
   C. Spiders have only two body parts. They have no wings or antennae. Spiders have eight legs. Six legs are used for walking, while the front pair is used for holding and moving objects.
   D. Most spiders spin webs for their homes.
   E. Spiders are helpful because they catch insects for food.
   F. It is best to observe and not touch spiders. Some spiders, like the black widow, have a very poisonous bite.

11. IMAGINATION STRETCHER: Tell a story with open-ended comparisons. Children complete sentences. For example: "Ted planted a seed that was as little as a . . . He watered it with water that was as wet as . . . The seed grew as fast as . . . The plant popped through the ground like a . . . The plant had leaves as green as . . ."

12. ROPE KNOWLEDGE: Give each player a section of rope that is five feet long. Discuss the rope. What words can be used to describe the rope? What color is it? Is it little or big? Is it rough or smooth? Is it round or square? Is it long or short? Can it make a noise? What can you do with it? Ask each child to do any of the following:
   A. Make a circle, square, oval, triangle, or rectangle.
   B. Make a long or short line. Walk, jump, or straddle the line.
   C. Make a number or letter.
   D. Make a circle. Stand inside circle. Stand outside circle. Walk around the circle. Touch the circle with different parts of the body. Examples are fingers, toes, and elbows.

13. BOOKS:
   Two Little Gardeners--Brown and Hurd
   The Boy Who Didn't Believe in Spring--Clifton
   What Is a Plant?--Darby
   The Bug Book--Dugan
   The Flower--Downer
   Things That Grow--Eggleston
   Bird Talk--Gans
   Hamilton Duck's Springtime--Getz
   Titch--Hutchins
   The Carrot Seed--Kraus
   The Growing Story--Kraus
   Spring Is Here--Lenski
   Creepy the Caterpillar--Smith
   Birds--Wildsmith

GAMES AND SOCIAL ACTIVITIES

1. I SEE SOMETHING THAT'S A SIGN OF SPRING: Adult says, "I see something that's a sign of spring." She then describes what she sees. Players guess what is being described.
   Variation: Play, "I hear something that sounds like spring."

2. NATURE HUNT: Display ten nature items. Examples are feathers, leaves, and rocks. Study display. Go outside and search for items that match those on display.

3. BUGGY GUESSING GAME: Place following parts from COOTIE® by Schaper Manufacturing Company in a bag: six legs, two antennae, one head, and one body. Remove one part from bag at a time. Attempt to guess what the finished product will be. When completely assembled discuss names and functions of the parts. Count number of legs.
   Variation: Instead of COOTIE® cut legs, antennae, head, and body from felt. Attach to flannelboard.

4. LADYBUG RACE: Place marble inside walnut shell of LADYBUG (see page 143). Hold two ladybugs on the raised end of inclined board. Release. Marbles will roll, moving ladybugs down the board.

5. ROLY-POLY: (Tune--"Row, Row, Row Your Boat")
   Roly-Poly, Roly-Poly, roll across the floor.
   Roly-Poly, Roly-Poly, come rolling back for more.
   Sit in circle. Two adults sit across from each other in circle. One child is chosen to be Roly-Poly, who stretches full length like a log with his arms above his head. Roly-Poly starts at first adult and rolls to second adult while first line is sung. Adult gives Roly-Poly a hug, and then rolls him back to first adult while second line is sung. First adult also gives him a hug. Continue around circle until all have had a turn.

6. BUTTERFLY BALLOON: To form wings, cut rectangle from colored tissue paper and gather in middle. Tape wings to center of inflated balloon. If desired, draw butterfly features on balloon with permanent felt-tipped pens. Play following:
   A. BUTTERFLY FLY: Children sit in circle. One player bats butterfly balloon to another who bats it to another. Play continues until butterfly falls to ground. Repeat using a new player to start action.
   B. BUTTERFLY COUNT: Player stands in one spot and attempts to gently hit butterfly balloon into air without moving from the area or allowing it to touch the floor. Group counts each time the butterfly is successfully hit into the air. Change players when the butterfly falls. Proceed until all players have had a turn.

7. FLYING HIGH: A leader names animals or objects making a sentence with "fly" included each time. Examples are: a robin flies; a table will fly; some insects fly. If the animal or object is able to fly, players put their hands high in the air and pretend to fly. If object or animal cannot fly, hands should be folded in lap.

8. BLUE BIRD: (Adapted from traditional verse)
   Blue bird, blue bird, through my window
   Blue bird, blue bird, through my window
   Blue bird, blue bird, through my window
   To bring me a pretty flower.
Stand in circle. Join hands and raise them in the air. One player is Blue Bird. While group sings verse, Blue Bird weaves around the players in the circle. When singing stops, Blue Bird stands in front of child nearest him and sings, "What kind of flower do you want?" The child answers, "I want a (kind of flower)." All players then sing, "(Child's name) wants a (flower named)." Child then becomes Blue Bird, and the game is repeated.
Variations:
   A. Before singing verse player chooses color of bird he would like to be. Sing verse using color of bird player chose. Play game as indicated.
   B. Ask, "What color of flower would you like to be?" instead of kind.

9. JUMPING ROPE: (Tune--"Did You Ever See a Lassie?")
   Did you ever see (child's name) jump this way and that way?
   Did you ever see (child's name) jump this way and that?
Two players hold rope ends and swing rope gently back and forth about 4" above the ground. One player jumps back and forth across rope as verse is sung. Repeat until everyone has jumped.

10. ROPE-A-DOPE-A-DO: A rope is held at the ends by two players. Holders place rope on ground. Remaining players form line and go over rope to verse.
   It's called rope-a-dope-a-do.
   Go over the rope, can you?
Repeat raising rope a few inches each time. When rope becomes too high, play game by going under rope. Hold rope several feet from ground. Recite following verse:
   It's called rope-a-dope-a-do.
   Go under the rope, can you?
Repeat, lowering rope several inches each time. Encourage creativity when going over and under the rope.

11. BUG CATCHERS: (Group project) Collect insects in any of the following:
   A. TUNA CAN CATCHER: Use two tuna cans. Remove labels and one lid from each can. Cut a wire screen that is 6" x 12". Fold each edge of screen approximately 1/4" to smooth exposed rows of wire prongs. Bend screen into a tube which will fit inside can. Staple overlapped edges. Place tube in can. Fill can with grass. Catch bug. Place second can over opening.
   Variation: Fill one tuna can with plaster of Paris. Insert plastic flowers into wet plaster. Place wire tube into plaster. Allow to dry. Other tuna can is the removable lid.
   B. BOTTLE CATCHER: Use clear plastic bottle which has a screw top lid. Perforate lid for air. Add twigs so bug will have a place to climb.
   C. MILK CARTON CATCHER: Cut windows in two opposite sides of a milk carton. Place carton in the foot of a nylon stocking. Place bug in carton. Secure top of stocking by tying knot or using twister seal.

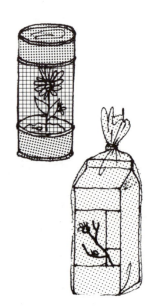

152

12. SPRING GARDEN: (Group project) Prepare a small plot of ground for a garden. Use child-size tools that are safe. Follow instructions on seed package for planting seeds. Empty seed packages can be used as row markers so growing plants can be easily identified. Continue to care for garden by watering, weeding, and harvesting crops.

CREATIVE DRAMATICS AND MOVEMENT

1. PLANTING PANTOMIME: Dramatize following verse:
   I plant a little seed in the dark, dark ground. (pretend to be seed by crouching on the floor and covering head with arms)
   Out comes the yellow sun, big and round. (remain crouching, extend arms over head and form large circle)
   Down comes the cool rain, soft and slow. (flutter fingers)
   Up comes the little flower, (pretend to be growing plant)
   Grow, grow, grow. (stretch arms above body)
                       Author Unknown
   Ask each child to describe the kind of flower he had become.

2. LITTLE FLOWER: Dramatize following verse:
   If I were a little seed planted in the ground,
   I'd stretch my roots and grow and grow;
   I'd stretch my stem and grow and grow;
   I'd blossom into a pretty flower.
   Then I'd sway back and forth as if to say,
   "I'm glad to be with you today!"

3. SPRING HAS COME: Divide the children into four groups--raindrops, sunbeams, birds, and flowers.
   "Wake up," said the little raindrops. (Raindrops rise quickly from chairs.)
   "Wake up," said the sunbeams, too. (Sunbeams rise quickly.)
   "Spring has come," sang a bird. (Birds rise and flutter wings.)
   Then the little flowers heard, (Flowers rise slowly.)
   So they all woke up and grew.
                       Lillien E. Landman

4. FLORAL ARRANGING: Provide box of plastic flowers and a variety of flower vases or containers. Allow time for creation of floral arrangements and dramatic play as a florist.

5. FUZZY LITTLE CATERPILLAR: Dramatize following verse:
   A fuzzy little caterpillar under a leaf crept.
   Round and round he spun a cocoon.
   And for a very long time, he slept.
   That fuzzy little caterpillar slowly wakening with a sigh,
   Discovered that he had wings and was a beautiful butterfly!
   He fluttered his wings and said, "That's no joke."
   And flew away to meet new folk.

6. INSECTS: Name different kinds of insects. Dramatize how each insect moves and sounds as it is named.

7. ROLY-POLY: Crawl on floor and pretend to be a roly-poly. When touched by an adult, roll into a tight ball. When adult leaves, stretch out and begin to crawl.

8. FIDDLERS THREE: The grasshopper, cricket, and katydid become fiddlers on warm evenings. The sounds are made by rubbing two wings or two legs together. Pretend to be these fiddlers:
    A. CRICKET: Make a clicker by pressing a small baby food jar lid into a larger baby food jar lid. The inside of the clicker is hollow. For example, press a meat lid into vegetable or fruit lid. Fold fingers of hands together with the clicker between palms. Squeeze palms together hard and fast. Pretend to be cricket chirping. It is getting warmer. Chirp faster. Now it is getting colder. Chirp slower.
    B. KATYDID: The katydid is the loudest and largest of the fiddlers three. Its name reveals the sound created: "katydid, katydid" or "kikak, ki-kak." Move finger over teeth of comb and pretend to be a katydid.
    C. GRASSHOPPER: Stretch rubber band around box. Rub pencil over rubber band to produce sound.

9. CREATURE CREEP: Dramatize following verse:
    Grasshoppers go jumpity jump, jumpity jump.
    Caterpillars crawl humpity hump, humpity hump.
    Playful crickets go hoppity hop, hoppity hop.
    In the springtime happy children like you
    Will jumpity, humpity, hoppity too.

10. BABY BIRDIES: Dramatize following verse:
    We are baby birdies living in a nest.
    We dream of flying when we take our rest.
    Finally one spring day we hop, hop, hop.
    And flutter our wings flop, flop, flop.
    They lift us up and then we fly.
    We fly around the sky.
    Flying very high and flying very low.
    Then in a big circle--round we go.
    Finally we soar home and go to sleep.
    We close our eyes without a peep.

11. YO-YO: Make a yo-yo by tying a piece of elastic to a plastic doughnut from a doughnut stacking toy. Move yo-yo up and down. Create tricks with it.

12. RECORDS:
    A. "Birds are Flying Through the Air" and "Growing Song" from *Learning Basic Skills Through Music* by Hap Palmer. Educational Activities Inc., Box 392, Freeport, New York 11520
    B. "Wiggle, Giggle, Wiggle Worm" and "I am a Little Flower" from *Songs of Joy* by Diane Hartman Smith. Joy, Box 58, Aspen, Colorado 81611
    C. "Swing, Swing" from *Loving and Learning* by Diane Hartman Smith. Joy, Box 58, Aspen, Colorado 81611

PHYSICAL DEVELOPMENT

1. HAPPY CHILDREN IN THE SPRINGTIME: Do the following:
    Happy children in the springtime, run to the wall.
    Happy children in the springtime, hop back one and all.
    Happy children in the springtime, skip to the tree.
    Happy children in the springtime, fly back to me.
    Happy children in the springtime, gallop to the door.
    Happy children in the springtime, sit on the floor.

2. CREATURE MOVEMENT:
    A. WORM WIGGLE: Lie on stomach. Hold arms at side. Try to move body
        forward without using hands or elbows.
    B. GRASSHOPPER LEAP: Squat with fingers touching floor. Leap upward and
        forward. Return to squatting position. Continue to leap across room.
    C. SPIDER WALK: From standing position bend so fingers are touching the
        floor. Lift one leg and arm very high in front of body and stretch.
        Take a long step. Repeat with opposite leg and arm.
    D. CATERPILLAR CREEP: Lie on floor in prone position with hands beside
        shoulders. Lift upper body by straightening arms. Bring knees forward.
        Stretch front of body forward. Lie flat. Repeat.
    E. BUTTERFLY FLUTTER: Move arms up and down as if flying. "Fly" around
        room.
    F. FLIGHT OF BUMBLEBEE: Move arms in figure-eight motion. Pretend to fly
        around room while making a buzzing sound.

3. JUMPING: Jump in the following ways:
    A. As high as possible
    B. As far as possible
    C. Backward, forward, and sideways
    D. Jump and try to turn around in the air
    E. Jump and do something in the air (for example, clap hands above head)
    F. Jump and land as quietly as possible

4. CHINESE JUMP ROPE STRETCH: Use a Chinese jump rope or a piece of elastic
    thread or elastic braid. Adult suggests movements:
    A. Stretch the rope with hands and arms.
    B. Step on rope and pull with hands.
    C. Place rope around bent knee and pull with hands.
    D. Stretch rope to music.
    Variation: Stretch all parts of body to music without the rope. Examples are
    neck, arms, fingers, waist, legs, ankles, and toes. Stretch as if still pul-
    ling the rope.

5. ARM JUMP ROPE: Clasp hands together forming a loop in front of body. Pull one
    leg through the loop and then the other. Release hands and repeat.

6. ROPE OBSTACLE COURSE: Use ropes to make obstacle course. Players can go
    through course in creative way or follow directions given by adult. Encourage
    players not to move ropes as they complete the course.
    A. Place ropes parallel to each other and one foot apart. This can be a
        path for walking, jumping, hopping, or straddling. Path can also be
        jumped across.
    B. Lay rope in a zigzag line that is to be followed.
    C. Lay rope in a straight line that is to be followed or straddled.
    D. Tie rope between two chairs that are approximately two feet apart. Jump
        over rope or crawl under rope.
        Variation: Make a series of six ropes which player alternately goes
        under and over.
    E. Make a circle with the rope. Walk around circle or jump in and out of
        circle.
        Variation: Make three circles with three ropes. Jump from one circle to
        the next.
    F. Two people hold ends of rope that is approximately five feet long. Hold-
        ers move rope back and forth like a snake. Participants jump over rope.
    G. Two people hold ends of rope and make waves by moving rope up and down,
        approximately 3" from the ground. Participants jump over rope.

7. MARBLES: Make a circle on the floor with string or tape. Place five marbles inside circle. First player holds shooter marble which is used to shoot marbles from circle. To shoot the marble make a fist. Place fist on floor with middle knuckle of fingers touching floor. Place thumb between index finger and middle finger. Place shooter marble in cup formed by index finger. Shoot marble by pushing the thumb forward. Give each player an opportunity to hit marbles from the circle.

8. HOPSCOTCH: Draw a hopscotch diagram on the sidewalk with chalk. Write a number in each box, starting with 1 and progressing in numerical order. Players hop or jump through design following the numerical order. Object is not to step on any lines. Variation: Outline hopscotch on floor with tape.

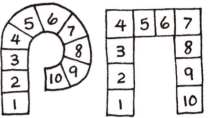

MATH

1. NEED SEED, HEED SEED: Place large seeds or beans between two players. The first player takes 1 to 5 beans. He then says to the second player, "Need seed, heed seed." The second player guesses how many seeds are in the handful. If the guess is correct, the second player receives all the seeds. Reverse roles and continue playing.

2. SEED NUMBER BOOK: Cut construction paper in half. Staple pieces together at top to make a book of 5 to 10 pages. On first page, write the number 1 and glue one seed. Continue using different number on each page until book is completed.

3. PLANTING CALENDAR: On construction paper, make a calendar to cover a four week period. Cut small brown pots and one green leaf. Plant seeds in soil. Glue a brown pot on the calendar each day while waiting for the seeds to sprout. When the first green shoot appears, glue on the green leaf. Count the number of brown pots to determine number of days until sprout appeared.

4. FLOWER GARDEN: Cut different colors of flowers from magazines. Make a "garden" with the flowers by placing the same color of flowers in the same location.

5. BUG SHAPES: Make template by cutting a shape from the middle of a margarine lid. Make several sizes of each shape. Hold template on paper and draw around inside of shape. Create bug by combining shapes.

6. LADYBUG: On flannel board, place ladybug that doesn't have any spots. Ask child to place a certain number of spots on the ladybug. For example: "Place four spots on the ladybug." Remove spots and continue, using a different number.

7. CRICKET THERMOMETER: At moderate temperatures, a male cricket will serve as a fairly accurate thermometer. He chirps at a rate that increases as the temperature rises. To determine the temperature of the air surrounding the cricket, count the number of chirps in 15 seconds and add 37. This is an approximate Fahrenheit reading!!! Jiminy Cricket!!!

8. BEEHIVE: Form a beehive by placing chairs in a circle. Players pretend to be bees in the center of the hive. Bees walk slowly to chairs and stop. Bees then walk back to the center of the hive. How could the hive be made larger? Move chairs to make a large circle. Walk to chairs and back to center of hive. Is there more or less space in the hive? What can be done to make even more space? Some bees could leave the hive. Discuss concept of space.

9. INCHWORM: Place face of inchworm on flannelboard or bulletin board. Give each child a different-colored circle. Help inchworm grow by adding circle to worm when that color is named.
   Variation: Place numbers or letters on circles.

10. BIRD HOUSE: Assemble a bird house on the flannelboard by using a circle, a square, and a triangle. Discuss shapes.

   Variations:
   A. Make several sizes of bird houses. Match the correct triangle roof with the appropriate square house.
   B. Make several sizes of birds. Place each bird near house of correct size.

11. HOPSCOTCH PATTERNS: Cut small squares from construction paper. Adult creates hopscotch pattern by arranging squares in vertical or horizontal line. Child creates matching pattern. Discuss meaning of horizontal and vertical.
   Variations:
   A. Form pattern in shape of letter. Child creates pattern and identifies letter.
   B. Instead of paper squares, use seeds to create patterns. Child pretends to plant seeds in garden by matching pattern made by adult.

SCIENCE

1. PLANTS NEED WATER: Grow two similar plants. Water one daily. Do not water the other one. Note what happens. Why?

2. PLANTS NEED SUNLIGHT: Grow two similar plants. Place one plant in sunlight. Cover the other plant with cardboard which is perforated for air. Water each plant daily. Note what happens. Why?

3. SOIL: Display sample of soil from each child's yard. Note differences in color and texture. Discuss that plants take food from the soil. Plants would die if they did not have food. Soil is prepared for planting by plowing, fertilizing, and weeding. Earthworms are helpful because they fertilize and aerate the soil when digging tunnels under the ground.

4. STARTING A PLANT: Plants can be grown from seeds, bulbs, or plant cuttings.
   A. SEED: Fill lid of an egg carton 2/3 full of soil. Plant lettuce seeds, following the planting instructions on package. Harvest lettuce greens when they are approximately 2" high. Use in TOSSED SALAD (see page 146). Variation: Cut top half from milk carton. Place rocks in bottom for drainage. Fill with soil and plant seeds.
   B. BULB: Set a narcissus bulb in a bowl of pebbles and water. Keep base of the bulb wet. Set it in a dark place until roots are formed. Move to a sunny window. In 4 to 5 days, blossoms should form.
   C. CUTTING FROM MATURE PLANT: Cut a 6" leafy stem from ivy, coleus, begonia, or philodendron. Place bottom half in glass container filled with water. Observe growing roots with magnifying glass. Transplant into soil.

5. OBSERVE GROWING PLANTS: See how plants grow by using the following methods:
   A. WATER JAR AND TOOTHPICKS: Grow sweet potato, avocado seed, beet, onion, or garlic. Stick four toothpicks around middle of vegetable and suspend it on the mouth of jar. Fill jar with water to cover the bottom part of the vegetable. Keep water at this level. Vine will begin to grow in approximately two weeks.

   B. WET PAPER TOWEL: Grow lentils, watercress, grass seeds, or green bean seeds. Line bottom of dish or cake pan with several layers of paper towels. Pour water onto paper until it is thoroughly wet. Place seeds on top of paper. Keep paper moist and keep grower in a sunny window.

   C. WATER DISH: Grow carrot top or turnip top. Cut a 1" slice from top of vegetable. Place in a shallow dish of water. Keep in sunny window and water regularly.

   D. SPONGE AND GLASS JAR: Sprout kidney beans; lima beans; corn; or seeds from pear, apple, orange, or grapefruit. Fill a clear glass jar with a sponge. Pour water over sponge to moisten thoroughly. Place a few seeds between sponge and side of jar.
   Variation: Instead of sponge, use paper towel.

6. BUDDING BRANCH: Cut budding branch from forsythia, elm, crab apple, or other fruit tree. Lightly hammer bottom 2" of branch. Place branch in container of warm water. Move it to a sunny window. In several days the buds will open.

7. GROWING BEAN SPROUTS: Many seeds sprout with excellent results. The most popular seeds for taste and the easiest to grow are mung, soy, lentil, alfalfa, and wheat. Seeds are available at supermarkets or health food stores. Buy seeds which have not been treated with chemicals, such as fungicides. Items needed are seeds, water, and quart jar with screw-top lid. Punch 8 to 12 holes in the top of the jar lid with an ice pick. Holes need to be smaller than seeds. Use the following method for growing sprouts:
DAY 1: Place seeds in jar of warm water. Secure lid. Set in dark place. Soak overnight.
DAY 2: In morning and evening drain jar. Fill with tepid water. Swirl seeds and water. Drain. Set in dark place. To insure adequate drainage and ventilation, prop jar at an angle with lid facing downward.
DAYS 3 THROUGH 7: Rinse morning and evening as indicated in DAY 2. When sprouts are desired length, set jar in sunlight. Watch them turn green! Rinse hulls away by placing on jar a lid with holes slightly larger than hulls. Hold the jar at a slight angle under running water. Swirl sprouts as the jar fills and overflows. Continue until most hulls are rinsed away. Use in BEAN SPROUTS (see page 145).

8. HONEYCOMB: Bees are the only insects that produce food eaten by man. Of the many species of bees, only the honeybee makes honey. Observe honey in honeycomb. Taste honey. The bees' nest is called a comb. It is made of six-sided cells that are wax. Beeswax is used for candles, floor waxes, polishes, plasters, ointments, and in lipstick.
Note: Honeybee colonies last through the winter. They keep warm by clustering around the queen and moving their wings rapidly.

158

9. CREATURE DISPLAY: Display creatures that have been collected in BUG CATCHERS (see page 152). Look at insects with magnifying glass. Observe similarities and differences. Discuss the following:

A. ANT: Ants are social insects that live together in colonies or large family groups. Within the colony are the queen who lays the eggs, the workers who gather food and care for the young, and the drones. An ant has powerful jaws which can carry an object 50 times its body weight. Ants communicate with one another by tapping their antennae.

B. BEE: There are approximately 20,000 species of bees. Five percent of all bees are social, living in colonies consisting of thousands of bees. The remainder are solitary bees that live alone or in small family groups. Some bees have stingers which they use to protect themselves. Bees usually won't sting unless they are annoyed because a bee will die after it stings. Bees, more than any other insect, benefit man. They help pollinate plants. For information about honeybees refer to HONEY-COMB (see page 158).

C. CRICKET: The cricket has the same general characteristics as the grass-hopper but does have longer feelers. Crickets are generally found under rocks. Only males produce sound. The chirping sound is made when the cricket scrapes one wing across the edge of another. A female is distin-guished from a male by a long spike on the female's tail.

D. GRASSHOPPER: The grasshopper has powerful leg muscles which help it leap into the air to fly. One kind of grasshopper uses its rear legs to "sing." Others rub one wing over another like a bow rubbed over a fiddle to produce their sounds. A grasshopper has narrow, tough, front wings that cover and protect its large, thin, hind wings when resting. Observe sharp claws on each foot. Watch it eat a green leaf with its two pairs of jaws. When handled, grasshoppers "spit" a brown liquid called "tobac-co juice," which helps protect it from attacks by some insects.

E. INCHWORM: Inchworms belong to a family of moths whose larvae are called measuring worms. An inchworm walks by moving its abdominal and back legs, forming its body into a loop. This gives the impression that it is measuring space with its body.

F. KATYDID: A katydid is a large long-horned grasshopper with strong hind legs and four wings that extend beyond the body. Most are pale green, although some are gray, tan, brown, or pink. They eat leaves of trees and shrubs. The male makes a noise that sounds like its name, katydid.

G. LADYBUG: A ladybug is a beetle. Ladybugs are helpful because they eat aphids. They clean themselves by washing their faces with their front legs and then cleaning the legs. Their color keeps birds away. Birds do not eat ladybugs because of their terrible taste.

H. LIGHTNING BUG: This soft-bodied beetle is sometimes called a firefly because its abdomen glows with luminescent light. Lightning bugs rest on plants in the daytime and are active at night when they fly, blinking their "taillights." The wingless females, which are called glowworms, lay eggs on the ground. The eggs hatch and take 1 to 2 years to mature. There are 50 kinds of fireflies in the United States.

I. ROLY-POLY: A roly-poly, also called sow bug or wood louse, resembles an insect but is not one. It is a crustacean. It is a small, black, flattened creature with a jointed pair of feelers or antennae. It is found in moist dirt under rocks, boards, and flowerpots. It can roll itself into a ball. Thus comes the name, roly-poly.

10. ANT FARM: Fill a one-gallon jar partially full of soil. Find an ant hill and with shovel lift surrounding dirt. Place dirt and ants into jar. Be sure to place queen ant in jar. She is larger and has wings. Wrap dark paper around jar to encourage ants to make tunnels. Place bread crumbs and a damp cotton ball on top of soil. Pour a little water on the cotton every few days. Remove dark paper in several days and observe tunnels.

11. CATERPILLAR, COCOON, BUTTERFLY: Find a caterpillar on a milkweed plant. Place caterpillar, milkweed leaves, and twig into jar with holes in lid for air. Set in a cool place. Keep moist by draping a damp cloth over top of jar. Clean jar daily and replace with leaves from milkweed plant. Caterpillar will eventually fasten itself to the twig and twist violently for several hours. Within a day the skin will split, revealing a cocoon. Set jar in a warm area and keep moistened. The cocoon will become transparent and split open. A butterfly with crumpled wings will struggle from the cocoon. It will cling to the cocoon while slowly unfolding its wings. The entire process takes approximately one month.

12. SPIDER WEB: Locate a spider web and carefully put black paper against it. Gently paint with clear acrylic spray. When it dries, the web will be cemented against the paper. Discuss how a spider uses its web. Spiders spin webs for their homes and to catch and preserve food. The web is made of silk which is produced in a spider's abdominal glands and emitted from tubes called spinnerets. It hardens into fibers that are elastic and strong. Insects caught in the web cannot free themselves.

MUSIC

1. THE GARDENER PLANTS THE SEEDS: (Tune--"Farmer in the Dell")
    The gardener plants the seeds.
    The gardener plants the seeds.
    Heigh ho the derry oh,
    The gardener plants the seeds.
Second verse: The rain falls on the ground.
Third verse: The sun shines bright and warm.
Fourth verse: The seeds begin to grow.
Fifth verse: Flowers grow everywhere.

2. OATS, PEAS, BEANS, AND BARLEY GROW: (Traditional)
    Oats, peas, beans, and barley grow. (hold hands and circle clockwise)
    Oats, peas, beans, and barley grow.
    Can you or I or anyone know
    How oats, peas, beans, and barley grow?
    First the farmer sows his seed. (pretend to plant seeds)
    Then he stands and takes his ease. (stand and place hands on hips)
    Stamps his feet and claps his hands (stamp feet and clap hands)
    And turns around to view the land. (turn around)

3. PURPLE LILAC: (Tune--"A-Hunting We Will Go").
    A purple lilac here,
    A yellow tulip there,
    A crocus and daffodil,
    Spring flowers everywhere.

4. MOWING: (Tune--"Row, Row, Row Your Boat")
    Push, push, push the mower.
    (Child's name) will push the mower.
    Mow, mow, mow, mow,
    Down the grass will go.

5. I'M BRINGING HOME A BABY BUMBLEBEE: (Tune--"Arkansas Traveler")
    Buzz! (clap hands)
    I'm bringing home a baby bumblebee.
    Won't my mommy be so proud of me.
    I'm bringing home a baby bumblebee.
    Buzz. OUCH!! It stung me.
                                    Traditional

6. ZUM, ZUM, ZUM: *Songs for the Nursery School* by Laura Pendleton MacCarteney,
   The Willis Music Company, Cincinnati, Ohio
    Zum, zum, zum
    Busy bees must hum.
    Fly away and get some honey
    In the fields so warm and sunny.
    Zum, zum, zum
    Busy bees must hum.

7. HEAR THE LIVELY SONG: (Tune--"Farmer in the Dell")
    Hear the lively song
    Of crickets in a throng.
    Click, click, clickety, click,
    Let's sing their chirping song.
    CHIRUP!

8. A-HUNTING WE WILL GO: (Adapted from traditional verse)
    Oh! A-hunting we will go,
    A-hunting we will go.
    We'll catch a (insect)
    And put him in a box,
    And then we'll let him go.

9. EENSY WEENSY SPIDER: (Traditional)
    Eensy, weensy spider climbed up the water spout.
    Down came the rain and washed the spider out.
    Out came the sun and dried up all the rain.
    So the eensy, weensy spider crawled up the spout again.

10. CREEPING CATERPILLAR: (Tune--"Brownie Smile")
    I see a creeping caterpillar
    Crawling on the ground.
    Creeping, creeping caterpillar
    Creeping all around.

11. SQUIGGLY, WIGGLY WORMS: (Tune--"Farmer in the Dell")
    Oh! Squiggly, wiggly worms
    Make tunnels in the ground.
    Squiggle, wiggle, squiggle worms
    Are squirming all around.

12. GLOW LITTLE GLOWWORM: Turn flashlights on and off to beat of song, "Glow Little Glowworm."

13. RED BIRD SANG A LITTLE SONG: (Tune--"Bingo")
        A red bird sang a little song
        And Tweetie was his name-o.
        Tweet, tweet, tweetie-o,
        Tweet, tweet, tweetie-o,
        Tweet, tweet, tweetie-o,
        And Tweetie was his name-o.

14. THE ROBINS ARE SINGING: (Tune--"Mary Had a Little Lamb")
        The robins are singing, singing, singing.
        The robins are singing the ringing news of spring.
        From the south they're bringing, bringing, bringing,
        From the south they're bringing the ringing news of spring.

15. SWING: (Tune--"Row, Row, Row Your Boat")
        Swing, swing, swing up high.
        Try to touch the sky.
        Think of bugs, birds, and planes:
        All the things that fly.

16. SKIP IN THE SPRING: (Tune--"Skip to My Lou")
        Skip, skip, skip in the spring.
        Skip, skip, skip in the spring.
        Skip, skip, skip in the spring.
        Skip in the spring, my darling.
Variation: Instead of "skip," sing: hop, jump, swing, or plant.

FIELD TRIPS

1. GREENHOUSE
2. SEED STORE
3. SPRING SEARCH: Take walk and observe signs of spring.

SUMMER

SUMMER, the season between spring and fall, begins mid-June and ends mid-September in the Northern Hemisphere. In many places the weather is hot and dry during the summer months. Because the weather is pleasant and most schools are closed, families often vacation during these months. The beach provides a perfect respite from the hot days. Fishing, boating, swimming, camping, sunbathing, and picnicking are popular summer activities. Summer sports include baseball, golf, tennis, and track and field.

CONCEPTS TO BE TAUGHT

1. Summer is the season between spring and fall.
2. The weather is usually hot and dry.
3. People seek comfort from the heat by wearing appropriate clothing, eating chilled foods, enjoying water activities, and using air cooling systems.
4. In the summer families vacation and enjoy many outdoor activities.

ART ACTIVITIES

1. SUMMER COLLAGE: Cut pictures from magazines, travel brochures, and posters. Glue pictures onto paper to make collage. Use the following as topics: vacation, summer sports, picnic, water fun, or camping.

2. SUMMER FUN WATERCOLOR: Using watercolors, paint a picture of a favorite summer activity on light-colored construction paper.
   Variation: Instead of watercolors, paint with liquid tempera that has small amount of sand added to it. Paint will have a granular texture.

3. SUNSHINE PAINTING: Drop blobs of yellow, white, and orange paint onto a piece of construction paper. Paint a picture of the sun by spreading paint with brush, feather duster, cotton-tipped swab, or toothpick.

4. BAREFOOT PAINTING: Place a long strip of butcher paper on sidewalk or floor. Add soap flakes to liquid tempera. Place paint in aluminum trays or cake pans. Set paint beside paper. Remove shoes and socks. Sit on chairs at edge of paper. Place feet in tempera and then "foot paint" on paper.
   Variation: Step barefoot into paint and then onto sand or dirt. Tiptoe or walk across paper. This will add texture and paint will not be slippery.

5. OUTDOOR PAINTING: Tape large piece of paper to fence or outside of building. Fill juice cans with paint. Paint with large easel brushes.

6. SAND-CASTING: Moisten sand in sandbox. To form mold, make impressions in small area by pushing shells, rocks, or twigs into sand. Remove items. If impressions collapse, add more water and repeat process. Pour plaster of Paris into mold. Allow to dry. Remove sand-cast form.
    Variations:
    A. Use indoor sandbox which can be made by lining a sturdy cardboard box with a large trash bag. Fill with sand.
    B. To form mold, make hole by scooping sand from area with hands.

7. SAND PAIL: To form handle, tie rope to opposite sides of gallon, cardboard, ice cream container. Decorate pail using SUMMER COLLAGE (see page 163). Cover finished collage with thin coat of glue.

8. SEASCAPE: Cut fish and seaweed from paper. Provide sand, small rocks, shell macaroni, and styrofoam packing. Create seascape by gluing materials to blue construction paper.

9. UNDERWATER SCENE: Draw underwater scene with crayons. Paint over it with a thin wash of blue tempera.

10. FISH: Cut a strip of paper 1" x 8". Color paper. Draw fish face on center of strip. Cut 1/2" slots at A and B. Place slot A into slot B to form fish.

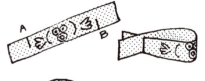

11. PAPER PLATE FISH: Cut a triangular piece from paper plate for mouth of fish. Attach triangular section to plate for tail fin. Draw scales and eye on fish. Variation: Use two small paper plates. Cut first plate according to diagram. For tail, attach half of plate to back of second plate. Attach quarters to sides of plate for fins. Draw scales and eye.

12. STARFISH: Cut starfish from large piece of heavy paper. Cover with glue. Sprinkle sand over entire starfish. Remove excess sand.

13. FISH NET MOBILE: Attach one end of pipe cleaner to open end of green, plastic, net bag. (Many fruits are sold in this type of bag.) To other end of pipe cleaner, hook precut paper fish by mouth which has been made with paper punch. Several fish can be attached. Tie string to closed end of bag. Hang. Variation: Cut fish from nylon netting.

14. TACKLE BOX: Use an egg carton. Make two holes approximately 3" apart in center of lid. To form handle, thread cord through holes and tie. Paint. In box, place paper clips for hooks and S-shaped styrofoam pieces for worms.

15. SAILBOAT: Color styrofoam meat tray. Stick pipe cleaner in center of tray and secure by bending end on underside. Fold diamond-shaped paper in half for sail. Place pipe cleaner in fold of sail. Glue sail together or staple at fold.

16. POPSICLE RAFT: Place two popsicle sticks 3" apart and parallel to each other for raft base. Glue popsicle sticks across base to form top of raft. Allow to dry. Paint raft.
    Note: To prevent base from moving, glue raft base to sheet of paper. Remove paper when raft is completed and glue is dry.

17. TUBE RAFT: Color three cardboard tubes. Glue tubes together at sides for raft base. To make sail, cut a slit in straw from open end and only along one side of straw. Slide triangular-shaped construction paper sail into slit. Poke hole in one cardboard tube. Stand straw in hole.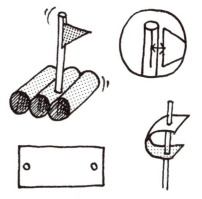
    Variations:
    A. Instead of triangular-shaped sail, cut strip of paper 3" x 8". Punch hole in each end of strip. Place straw through two holes.
    B. Glue raft to blue paper. Raft ahoy!

18. SNAKE GRASS JEWELRY: Make jewelry by interlocking snake grass pieces together at joints until desired length is reached.
    Note: Snake grass grows 1 to 2 feet tall and has sections 1" to 2" long which will fit together.

19. PEBBLE PICTURE: Collect pebbles. Glue pebbles to a piece of cardboard or driftwood to create picture.
    Variation: Glue stones together to form fish, people, or animals. Allow glue to dry. Add facial features with felt-tipped pens.

20. POPSICLE: Add lemon, vanilla, or peppermint extract to paint to give popsicle a scent or "flavor." Paint rectangle cut from piece of construction paper or cardboard. Attach popsicle stick to bottom of rectangle.

21. FAN: Color a rectangular piece of construction paper. Accordion-fold paper. Staple or hold at one end.

22. LITTER BAG: Fold open end of lunch bag several times to make cuff. Staple construction paper to handle opposite sides of cuff. Decorate bag.

23. CAMERA: For lens, poke hole with pencil through opposite sides of small cardboard box. Paint box to decorate camera.
    Variation: Glue smaller boxes or cardboard tube on box to create a more complex camera.

COOKING ACTIVITIES

1. LEMONADE: 1 cup water   3/4 tablespoon sugar
              1 1/2 tablespoons lemon juice   ice
   Cut and squeeze lemons to obtain lemon juice. Combine juice with water and sugar. Add ice.

2. SUMMER SLUSH: Freeze apple juice in ice cube trays. Place cubes in blender. Blend. Add apple juice until desired consistency is obtained.
   Variations:
   A. Use grape, orange, pineapple, or cranberry juice.
   B. Add fresh or canned fruits to slush.

3. BANANA ORANGE SHAKE: 6 ounces frozen orange juice concentrate
                          2 bananas, peeled
                          3 pints vanilla ice cream, softened
                          6 cups cold milk
Liquefy orange juice and bananas in blender. Place ice cream in gallon mixing bowl and add fruit mixture. Beat with mixer until blended. Continue beating and gradually add milk. Beat until smooth and frothy.

4. SUNSHINE SHAKE: 1 cup plain yogurt   1 cup sliced peaches or apricots
                    1 cup vanilla ice cream   4 ice cubes
In a blender combine first three ingredients. Place blended ingredients and ice cubes in tight-sealing container. Shake.
Variation: Instead of ice cream, use orange sherbet.

5. CARBONATED SODA: Add frozen fruit juice concentrate to carbonated mineral water until desired flavor is obtained.

6. GARNISHES FOR DRINKS: Add variety and flavor to cold drinks with the following:
    A. String fruit on straw.
    B. On rim of glass place a strawberry, peach, or orange slice.
    C. Float on top of drink a puff of whipped cream sprinkled with cinnamon, shredded coconut, or grated orange rind.
    D. Float on top of drink a scoop of ice cream or sherbet.
    E. Add colorful ice cubes. Freeze in ice cube trays: punch; milk mixed with orange juice; water with a strawberry, cherry, banana slice, or pineapple chunk in each cube.

7. PICNIC BASKET FRUIT SALAD: To form basket cut two sections from cantaloup or watermelon as shown in diagram. Remove seeds. Form melon balls. Clean remaining fruit from basket. Mix balls with seedless grapes, apples, bananas, oranges, pineapple, or strawberries. Place in basket.
Variation: Place fruit on a toothpick and serve as a kabob.

8. SINK OR FLOAT SALAD: 1 envelope unflavored gelatin
                         1/4 cup apple juice, boiling
                         1 tablespoon grape or blueberry juice
                         1 1/4 cups cold apple juice
                         3 ice cubes
Mix gelatin with boiling apple juice. Stir in remaining ingredients. Pour serving into clear plastic cup. Add any of the following fruits: mandarin oranges, seedless grapes, canned pineapple, cherries, or apricots. Watch them sink! Add coarsely chopped nuts or fresh fruits such as strawberries, oranges, peaches, bananas, or apples. Watch them float! Chill until firm.

9. SHIPS AHOY: 7 hard-cooked eggs   1/4 teaspoon salt
                 1/3 cup cream-style cottage cheese   1/4 teaspoon dry mustard
Cut eggs in half lengthwise. Place yolks in dish. Mash with fork. Add remaining ingredients. Mix lightly with fork. Place the yolk mixture into the white halves. For sail, attach toothpick to triangular slice of cheese. Insert toothpick into each egg white.
Variations:
    A. Use hard-cooked eggs cut into halves. Do not remove yolks.
    B. Instead of eggs, use pear halves with center sides facing upward. Raisins can be used to represent each ship's crew.

166

10. POTATO SALAD: 4 cups diced cooked potatoes   1/2 cup mayonnaise
                    3 diced hard-cooked eggs   1/2 cup sour cream
                    1 cup diced celery

Mix mayonnaise and sour cream in a bowl. Place remaining ingredients in another bowl. Add dressing. Stir. Add salt to taste. Cool. Serve.
Variation: Instead of mayonnaise and sour cream, use 1 cup yogurt.

11. GAZPACHO: 1 cup chopped tomato   2 cups tomato juice
               1/2 cup green pepper   2 teaspoons parsley
               1/2 cup celery   1/2 tablespoon olive oil
               1/2 cup cucumber   1 teaspoon salt
               1/4 cup green onion   1/2 teaspoon Worcestershire sauce

Chop all vegetables. Combine all ingredients. Chill. Serve as cold soup.

12. SANDWICH SPREAD:
    A. Spread peanut butter on one bread slice and applesauce on second. Form sandwich.
    B. Spread peanut butter on one bread slice. Sprinkle with grated carrots. Place mashed or sliced banana on second slice. Form sandwich.
    C. Combine 1 mashed banana, 1 grated apple, and 1 teaspoon lemon juice.
    D. Combine 1/4 cup cottage cheese and 1/4 cup raisins.
    Variation: Instead of bread use crackers.

13. CHEESE SPREAD: 3/4 pound American cheese, cubed   1 beaten egg yolk
                     1 1/2 tablespoons margarine   1 tablespoon flour
                     5 1/2 ounces evaporated milk

Melt margarine and cheese over low heat. Combine remaining ingredients. Add to cheese and margarine. Stir until blended. Cool. Spread on crackers.

14. CRISPY CHEESE BALLS: 1 cup grated Cheddar cheese   1 cup enriched flour
                          4 ounces margarine   1 cup crispy rice cereal

Set cheese and margarine at room temperature until soft. Mix well. Add remaining ingredients. Combine. Make into marble-sized balls. Place on ungreased pan. Bake at 350° for 10 to 15 minutes.

15. CORN CHIPS: 1 cup boiling water   1/2 teaspoon salt
                 1/4 cup margarine   1 cup cornmeal

Combine first three ingredients. Add cornmeal. Make into 1" balls. Place on lightly greased cookie sheet. Spread with spoon or pat with fingers until very thin. Bake at 350° for 20 minutes or until crisp and golden brown.

16. CONE SANDWICH: Fill ice cream cone with tuna salad or chicken salad.

17. FROZEN FOODS: Serve frozen fruits or vegetables in a paper cup. Examples are peas, beans, carrots, strawberries, green grapes, and peach slices.

18. FROZEN BANANAS: Cut a firm ripe banana in thirds. Insert a popsicle stick lengthwise through the center of each section. Cover with plastic wrap. Freeze. Remove wrap. Frost with peanut butter diluted to spreading consistency with orange juice. Roll in toasted wheat germ or chopped nuts.

19. STRAWBERRY ICE CREAM: 10 ounces frozen strawberries   2 eggs
                           2 cups evaporated milk   1/4 cup sugar
                           1/2 tablespoon cornstarch   dash salt

Allow frozen strawberries to partially thaw. Beat all ingredients. Place in ice cream freezer, following directions of freezer.

167

20. CEREAL PARFAIT: In a clear, plastic, drinking cup, layer each of the following: cornflakes, softened ice cream, and sliced strawberries. Repeat layers.

21. SICLES: Freeze sicles in any of the following: purchased popsicle molds, ice cube trays, or paper cups. To hold stick in center of paper cup, cut a circle from paper that is slightly larger than rim of cup. Cut a slit in center of circle. Slide stick through slit. Place circle on top of cup filled with sicle mixture. Push stick to bottom of cup.

    A. YOGURT SICLES: 8 ounces plain yogurt
                          6 ounces frozen concentrated grape juice
                          1 teaspoon vanilla

    Combine ingredients. Pour into containers and freeze.

    B. JUICE SICLES: Freeze any of the following juices: apple, grape, orange, cranberry, or any combination of these juices.

FINGERPLAYS

1. These are my sun glasses. (circle eyes with fingers)
   This is my great sun hat. (hands over head)
   This is the way I fold my hands (fold hands)
   And rest them, just like that. (place hands in lap)
          Adapted from traditional verse

2. The summer sun in the sky
   Shining, shining up so high (form circle with hands above head)
   Makes it warm for outside fun.
   To play at the park and run, (move fingers as if running)
   To swim and hike and fish, (pretend to do each)
   And go on a picnic if you wish. (rub stomach)

3. Two little houses across the street, (two fists)
   Open the doors and then friends meet. (open fists)
   How do you do? How do you do? (move one finger on one hand and then index finger on other hand)
   Such nice, sunny weather (form circle in air)
   Off they hurried to the park
   Two little friends together. (make fingers on two hands walk)
          Author Unknown

4. Pack the paper plates and napkins. (pretend to pack)
   Don't forget the food and drink: (shake head sideways)
   Hot dogs, potato salad, cake,
   And lemonade pink.
   It's fun to go on a picnic.
   I simply cannot wait
   To eat and play, have fun all day, (rub stomach)
   And get home very late. (yawn)

5. Teeter, totter, teeter, totter, (down, up, down, up)
   Teeter down with a bump. (down)
   Totter up with a jump. (jump)
   Up and down, up and down,
   Now sit quietly on the ground. (sit)

6. One of my favorite wishes (one finger)
   Is to play in mud that squishes.
   To make a mud pie and mud cake (pretend to make pie and cake)
   And place them in the sun to bake. (form circle in air)
   Will it feel good, do you suppose, (point to friend)
   To squish the mud between my toes? (wiggle toes)

7. In the sand, I shovel and dig.
   (pretend to dig)
   I make two holes very big. (two
   fingers)
   I make a tunnel between the two
   (make arch with arms)
   For my cars and trucks to travel
   through.
   Varoom!!! (move hand quickly)

8. Summer brings us nice warm sun
   (make circle in air)
   For swimming, fishing, and lots of
   fun; (pretend to swim and fish)
   For finding seashells in the sand;
   (cup hands to form shell)
   For sunbathing to get a tan;
   (stretch arms and legs)
   To do all these things and more
   At the beach and seashore.

9. I'm glad we have water.
   I jump and splash and swish!
   (jump, pretend to splash)
   I dive down in the water (dive)
   And play that I'm a fish. (wiggle)
                   Adapted from Thea Cannon

10. Swimming in the water cool and
    bright, (pretend to swim)
    I kick my feet with all my might.
    (kick feet)
    And when I'm tired, I float, (pre-
    tend to float)
    Pretending that I'm a boat.
    I like to hold my breath and dive.
    (pretend to dive)
    I swim beneath the water and count
    to five. (hold breath and count
    with five fingers silently)
    Wow! What a dive!

11. See the little fish
    Swimming in the sea. (wiggle hand)
    Wiggle, wiggle goes his tail
    As he swims by me. (point to self)
    My face goes in the water.
    And what do you suppose?
    That squiggly little fish (wiggle
    hand)
    And I are nose to nose! (point to
    nose)

12. Here is a starfish. (open hand)
    He's quite alive. (wiggle fingers)
    Let's count his arms:
    1-2-3-4-5. (point to each finger)

13. 1-2-3-4-5 Once I caught a fish
    alive. (clasp hands)
    6-7-8-9-10 Then I let it go again.
    (open hands)
    Why did I let it go?
    Because it bit my finger so. (open
    and close hand)
    Which finger did it bite?
    The little finger on the right.
    (point to little finger on right
    hand)

                   Traditional

14. Pick up a wiggly worm, place it on
    the hook.
    Drop the line so gently into the
    bubbling brook. (pretend to
    fish)
    Sh--I see a little fish nibbling at
    the bait. (finger over mouth)
    He tugged upon the line, and the
    worm he ate! (pretend to tug and
    then open and close hand)

15. Little fishie in a brook, (place
    palms together, wiggle hands)
    Daddy caught him with a hook.
    (pretend to fish)
    Mommy fried him in a pan, (pretend
    to fry fish in pan)
    And (Ted) ate him like a man. (use
    different names, point to person)
                   Traditional

16. Motor boat, motor boat, goes so
    slow. (stamp feet slowly)
    Motor boat, motor boat, goes so
    fast. (stamp feet faster)
    Motor boat, motor boat, step on the
    gas! (stamp feet as fast as
    possible)
                   Traditional

17. Here is the sailor. (two fingers)
    Here is his boat. (other hand)
    It is made of (wood) (substitute
    things that will float)
    So it will float. (walk fingers
    onto opened hand, rock hand)

18. In the summer when the days are
    hot, (wipe forehead)
    I like to find a shady spot, (sit)
    And hardly move a single bit (do
    not move a muscle)
    And sit, and sit, and sit, and sit.
                          Author Unknown

19. A little ball, (form little circle
    with fingers)
    A larger ball, (form ball with
    hands)
    A great big ball I see. (form
    large circle with arms)
    Now let's count the balls we've
    made. 1-2-3. (three fingers)
                          Traditional

20. The baseball player is up to bat.
    (pretend to hold bat)
    The pitch is straight and fast.
    (pretend to throw ball)
    He swings the bat. "Whack," goes
    the ball. (pretend to swing)
    It whizzes swiftly past.
    The outfielder has his glove out-
    stretched. (hold out hand)
    His eyes look to the sun.
    He watches the ball go sailing by.
    (move head horizontally)
    It is a long home run!

21. My popsicle is cold and good to
    eat. (form circle with arms
    above head)
    But I must lick quickly
    Or it will melt from the heat.
    (drop hands as if melting)

LANGUAGE DEVELOPMENT

1. SUMMER SUN: Summer is the season when the sun shines most directly on a
   region. This causes the temperature to be hot most of the time. Discuss:
   A. The sun is a star located many miles (93 million) from earth. It is made
      of very hot gases. All life on earth depends on energy from sunlight.
   B. People seek comfort from summer heat by wearing appropriate clothing,
      eating chilled foods, enjoying water activities, and using fans and air
      conditioners.
   C. Many vegetables and fruits ripen in the summer due to hot weather.
   D. Some animals shed their heavy fur coats.

2. SUMMER SAFETY: Discuss the following:
   A. Swim in safe areas and only with adult supervision.
   B. Always wear a life jacket when in a boat.
   C. Protect skin from the hot sun by sunbathing for short periods of time,
      using suntan lotion, and covering body where exposure is not desired.
   D. Wear sunglasses to protect eyes.
   E. When picnicking, chill foods that will spoil from heat. Examples are
      meats, fish, and foods made with eggs or mayonnaise.

3. VACATIONS: Summer is an opportune time for vacationing because the weather is
   pleasant, and many schools are closed during the hot months. Discuss where and
   why people go on vacations. The following can be included:
   A. Many people like to go sightseeing on their vacations.
   B. Vacationers often visit relatives or friends.
   C. People often seek a change in the environment. For example, a person
      living in the mountains might vacation at the seashore.
   D. Vacation spots are often determined by type of recreation people enjoy.
   E. Some people relax at home with family and friends during vacations.
   F. Share personal experiences about vacations. Where each child would like
      to go for a vacation can be discussed.

4. VACATION SHOW AND TELL: On the wall place a large map that includes places children have journeyed or vacationed. Examples of maps are USA, state, or community. Place a table below the map. Have pins and ribbons available. Ask each child to bring a "treasure" from his vacation. Pinpoint on the map the location where the object was found. Extend ribbon from pinpointed area to "treasure" on the table. Encourage children to tell about their "treasures."
Variation: Bring "treasure" from weekend outing or activity.

5. PACK THE BAG: Adult arranges articles of clothing so they are easily viewed by children. A suitcase is placed on the floor. Adult gives instructions to children concerning packing the bag to go on vacation. For example: "(Child's name), pretend you are going on a vacation to a friend's house who has a swimming pool. Pick something to pack in the suitcase to wear in the pool."
Adult varies instructions depending on clothes that are displayed.
Variations:
    A. Instead of a suitcase, use a large box.
    B. Instead of a suitcase and clothes, use a shoe box and pictures of clothing cut from a catalog.

6. SUMMER SPORTS AND PASTIMES: Fishing, boating, swimming, track and field, baseball, tennis, camping, sunbathing, and picnicking are popular summer activities. Display pictures depicting each activity. Discuss:
    A. What is happening in each picture?
    B. What equipment is needed for each activity?
    C. Who has participated in each sport or pastime?
Variation: Display actual equipment and discuss how each is used.

7. FOOTPRINTS IN THE SAND: Go barefoot in wet sand and discuss the following:
    A. Feel the sand on bare feet and between toes. How does the sand feel? Does it feel different from bare feet on grass or cement? What are the differences?
    B. Make footprints, toe prints, and heel prints. What size are the prints?
    C. Make a left footprint and a right footprint. Is there a difference between the left and the right? What is it?
    D. Jump in the sand. How deep are the prints? How far is it between footprints?

8. LAND OR SEA: Name items related to land or sea. If item relates to land, players pretend to hike. If item relates to sea, players pretend to swim.

9. THE BIG FISH: Tell following story. At (A) in story draw diagram A. Add additional features to initial sketch at points indicated in story.

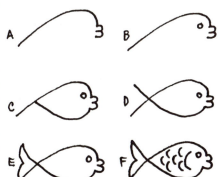

One hot summer day Mark and Heather decided to go fishing. They walked over a big hill and sat on some rocks (A). They started fishing in the lake (B), but didn't catch one fish. They decided to fish along the stream (C). After they had fished awhile, Mark felt a fish tug on his line. He tried to reel it to shore, but it was very strong. Finally it jumped out of the water (D) and went over the waterfall (E). That caused Mark's line to break, and it swam away. But Mark and Heather said it was the biggest fish they'd ever seen (F).

171

10. FISHING: (Tune--"Mary Had a Little Lamb")
   (Child's name) is going fishing, going fishing, going fishing.
   (Child's name) is going fishing. What will he catch?
   I caught a (color) fish, (color) fish, (color) fish.
   I caught a (color) fish. That's what I did catch.
   (Child's name) caught a (color) fish, (color) fish, (color) fish.
   (Child's name) caught a (color) fish. That's what he did catch.

For fishing pole, use string attached to dowel. On other end of string, attach a small magnet. Cut fish from various colors of construction paper. Attach paper clip to each fish for mouth. Place fish in a plastic swimming pool. One player is chosen to be fisherman. While first two lines are sung, he catches fish by attaching magnet to paper clip on one fish. Fisherman then sings next two lines identifying color of his catch. Everyone sings last verse. Repeat with new player as fisherman.
Variations:
   A. For fish, use washers that have been painted different colors.
   B. Place any of the following on fish: letter, number, or a shape. Fisherman identifies fish by letter, number, or shape.
   C. Write different instructions on each fish. Adult reads instructions and fisherman completes command. For example, jump three times.

11. BOOKS:
   The Witch's Vacation--Bridwell
   Summer Noisy Book--Brown
   Seashore Noisy Book--Brown
   Henry--Fisherman--Brown
   Norman Plays Second Base--Gault
   One Fish, Two Fish, Red Fish, Blue Fish--Geisel
   On a Summer Day--Lenski
   City in the Summer--Schick
   Fishes--Wildsmith

GAMES AND SOCIAL ACTIVITIES

1. SWIM ROUND THE LAKE: (Tune--"Sally Go Round the Sun")
   (Child's name) swam round the lake.
   (Child's name) swam round the bay.
   (Child's name) swam round the swimming pool.
   On a summer day. Hey!

Three players are chosen to represent lake, bay, and pool. These children stand and form a circle. Remaining players form a line. First player moves around lake, bay, and pool while everyone sings. When "Hey" is sung, player should touch next person in line. Repeat until all players in line have had a turn.

2. ONE LITTLE FRIEND: (Tune--"Twinkle, Twinkle Little Star")
   (One) little friend went out to play,
   Out to the park on a summer day.
   He had such enormous fun,
   He called for another little friend to come.

Sit in circle. One player walks around circle while verse is sung. At end of verse, he chooses second player to join him. Verse is repeated with, "Two little friends ..." At end of verse, second player chooses friend. Repeat, increasing number of friends.

3. MARY TAKES A TRIP: (Tune--"Farmer in the Dell")
      (Child's name) takes a trip.
      (Child's name) takes a trip.
      She packs her bags and calls a cab.
      (Child's name) takes a trip.
Sit in a circle. One player walks around inside of circle while everyone sings verse. At end of verse, player chooses partner to go on trip. They decide how they will get there. Examples are plane, bus, train, car. Both players walk around inside circle pantomiming method of transportation while everyone sings:
      They travel there by (type of transportation).
      They travel there by (type of transportation).
      Up and down, and all around,
      They travel there by (type of transportation).
First player returns to circle, and game is repeated with second player.

4. YONDER SHE COMES: (Traditional)
      Yonder she comes and it's howdy, howdy do.
      Oh, where have you been since the last time I met you?
Two players raise arms and hold hands to form bridge. Other players pass in a line under bridge. At end of song, two players drop hands and catch one player. The captured player sings, "I've been to (place)." Other players echo, "(Child) has been to (place named)." Two players lift arms, and game is repeated. Encourage players to name location where they have gone or would like to go for a vacation.

5. OFF TO TIMBUCTOO: (Traditional)
      We are off to Timbuctoo.
      Would you like to go there, too?
      All the way and back again,
      You must follow our leader then.
Stand in circle and hold hands. As verse is recited, circle moves clockwise. One player walks outside moving circle, going opposite direction. At end of verse, player asks closest person in circle, "Would you like to go to Timbuctoo?" Person responds, "Yes, I would." First player asks, "Would you like to take a friend?" Second player responds, "Yes." and turns to next player in circle asking, "Would you like to go to Timbuctoo?" Player responds, "Yes, I would." Two players join hands with first player. Game is continued with last person in line asking closest person in circle if he would like to go to Timbuctoo. Repeat until all players are in line.
Variation: Last person in line names a place where he would like to vacation. Instead of Timbuctoo, sing place named when game is repeated.

6. FISHERMEN FISHED IN THE WATER: (Tune--"My Bonnie Lies Over the Ocean")
      Fishermen fished in the water.
      Fishermen fished in the sea.
      Fishermen caught a big fish.
      But this fisherman can't catch me.
Sit in circle. One player is selected to be Fish. Other players are Fishermen. Fish walks around outside of circle while verse is sung. When last line is sung, Fish touches player closest to him. Player chases Fish around circle. Fish attempts to reach player's place in circle without being caught. Player then becomes Fish. Game is repeated until all players have had a turn to be Fish.

7. SIDEWALK MURAL: (Group project) Make a mural on the sidewalk with colored chalk.
   Variations:
   A. Wet the sidewalk so it is damp before drawing.
   B. Instead of chalk, create mural using mud.

8. SAND PLAY: Provide water and tools for digging, molding, sifting, pouring, and filling. Encourage experimentation with water and sand in following ways:
   A. Play with wet, dry, damp, or very wet sand.
   B. Dig rivers, streams, and lakes which can be filled with water from hose or bucket. Use these for sailing boats.
   C. Make things to "eat," such as mud pies. To make "cakes" fill container with moistened sand. Press sand. To unmold, carefully overturn container.
   D. Build sand castles, houses, cities, and other structures.
   E. Make roads and tunnels for cars and trucks. Ramps from ground to sandbox can also facilitate this play.

9. SPLASH PARTY: If pool facilities are not available, use several small wading pools. Place pools outside on grassy area and fill with several inches of water. Allow water to warm in sun. Dress in swimsuits. Each participant should have a towel. Allow time for play. Any of the following can be added for interest:
   A. INNER TUBE: Place tube in pool. Hold onto tube with hands, raise feet, and float. Jump into tube. Lie or sit on tube.
   B. BOBBER: Use container with tight-sealing lid for bobber. For example, use small, plastic, pill bottle. Place end of 12" string in container and glue container together. Allow glue to dry. Place bobber in water. Pull bobber under water with string. Release string and watch bobber BOB!
      Variation: Purchase bobber or use plastic toy container from coin machine.
   C. PADDLE BOAT: Remove rim from styrofoam meat tray. Tray can be decorated with crayons. For paddle, cut small rectangle from one end of tray. Trim 1/8" from edges of paddle. Cut small notches on boat and paddle as shown in diagram. Stretch rubber band around boat so it fits into notches. Place paddle between rubber band. Wind paddle. Place in water. While holding paddle, place boat in water. Release boat.
   D. SAILBOAT: Cut a milk carton in half lengthwise. Tape pouring spout together to form bow of boat. Sail boat in pool.
      Variation: For boat, use cork with toothpick sail.
   E. ADDITIONAL ACCESSORIES: Use sponges, corks, funnels, measuring spoons, muffin tins, sieves, plastic bottles, or squeeze bottles.
   F. GARDEN HOSE WITH SPRINKLER: In addition to, or instead of, pools, use garden hose with sprinkler attached. Children can run through sprayed water.
      Variation: Remove sprinkler. Allow a small trickle of water to come through hose.

10. ICE CREAM SOCIAL: Make STRAWBERRY ICE CREAM (see page 167). Make or buy vanilla and chocolate ice cream. Provide a variety of toppings. Examples are whipped cream, chopped nuts, strawberries, and banana slices. Scoop ice cream into paper cup and spoon on desired topping.
    Note: Social can be held out-of-doors if weather permits.

174

11. LEMONADE STAND: (Group project) Discuss what jobs need to be completed to have a lemonade stand. Examples are collecting supplies, making lemonade, making sign, and serving the lemonade. Divide into groups to complete jobs. Serve lemonade to members of group. Play money can be used for payment.

12. GROUP PICNIC: Prepare the following: (Recipes are found in COOKING ACTIVITIES on pages 165 to 167.)   CHEESE SPREAD SANDWICHES
POTATO SALAD
PICNIC BASKET FRUIT SALAD
CARBONATED SODA
Go to park and have picnic lunch.

13. INDIVIDUAL PICNIC: Prepare the following picnic. Individual lunches can be wrapped in a bandana and tied to a pole. Each child carries lunch over shoulder. (Recipes are found in COOKING ACTIVITIES on pages 165 to 167.)
SANDWICHES FILLED WITH CRACKER OR BREAD SPREAD
CARROT AND CELERY STRIPS
CRISPIE CHEESE BALLS OR CORN CHIPS
WATERMELON
LEMONADE
Note: Adult will need to carry watermelon and lemonade separately.

CREATIVE DRAMATICS

1. SUN AND FUN BOX: Prepare a box with items often used at the beach or when sunbathing. Examples are sun hat, sunglasses, sun visors, beach towels, beach ball, fins, goggles, and camera. Allow time for creative play. The following can be made and added to box:
   A. SUNGLASSES: For frames use two connected plastic rings from six-pack holder of pop cans. Wrap a pipe cleaner around each side of glasses. Bend pipe cleaners to fit around ears. Use colored cellophane for lens.
   Note: Yellow cellophane will make a gloomy day look sunny.
   B. PLASTIC FAN: Cut fan from gallon, plastic, bleach bottle as indicated in diagram. To flatten, cover fan with a towel and press with a warm iron. While plastic is warm, place it under a book to cool.

2. FAN FUN: Use PLASTIC FAN (listed above) or FAN (see page 165). Move fan to different tempos of music.

3. SUNBATHING: Pretend to be lying on a beach towel and sunbathing. Lie flat on back. Close eyes and relax. Feel the hot rays of the sun touching your toes. Wiggle toes. Tightly curl toes and then relax. Feel sun touch your legs. Raise legs and tighten leg muscles. Relax. The sun is touching your tummy. Shake tummy, moving it up and down. Breathe in and then relax. Feel sun on your arms. Raise arms and clench fists. Drop arms. Relax. Your face is hot. Turn head from side to side. Touch your chin to your neck. Relax. Now your entire body is HOT from head to toe. Relax. For relief from the heat, go for a swim in the cool water.

4. BAREFOOT WALK: Pretend to be barefoot and walk on cool grass that tickles your toes, mud that squishes, grainy sand on the beach, and a sidewalk that is smooth and hot. Then pretend to wade in cool water and splash.

5. VACATION TRAVEL: Adult prepares "surprise box." Box contains sacks with one of the following activities in each sack: plastic bottles with lids to screw and unscrew, playing cards, rubber bands wrapped around a plastic glass, key and padlock, sewing card and string, pipe cleaners, crayons and paper, magnet with metal and nonmetal items, magic slate, puppet, viewmaster, old photos, old Christmas cards, storybook, and lap-sized flannel board with felt pieces. Dramatize the following:

> Let's pretend to take a vacation. Where shall we go? (Players respond with places.) We will travel on the bus. Let's arrange the chairs to form the bus. Now find a seat on the bus. Is everybody ready to go? It is going to be a long drive. I have a surprise box of things to do. Each of you reach into the box. Take one sack. Open it. Discover what you can do with the objects inside the bag. When finished, return items to sack. Return sack to box and take another sack.

Variation: Place tape on floor to designate bus. Sit on floor inside tape.
Note: This can be used when actually taking a trip to occupy little hands.

6. CURIOUS TRAVELERS: Dramatize responses to the following questions:
   A. Pretend you are going to take a trip. Where would you like to go?
   B. What method of transportation will you use to travel there?
   C. What will you do when you arrive at your destination?
   D. How will you travel home? What do you do when you return home?

7. A-CAMPING WE WILL GO: Use outside play area as a camping site. The following can be enjoyed while pretending to camp:
   A. TENT: Set up tent. This can be used for creative play or as a quiet area by placing a quiet activity in each of the four corners. Examples are felt board with felt shapes, suitcase to pack and unpack, clothespins to snap on can, and puzzles.
       Note: Be careful of tent stakes and ropes.
       Variation: For tent, place sheet over card table or climber.
   B. SLEEPING BAGS: Place bags inside or outside tent. Crawl into bags, zip bags, and pretend to sleep.
   C. CAMPFIRE: Place sticks in a stack on ground or in a barbecue grill. Sing songs or pretend to prepare food around imaginary campfire.
   D. BACKPACK: Provide backpack filled with camping items. Examples are canteen and cooking utensils. Use around CAMPFIRE and for hiking.
   F. FISHING: Make fishing pole by tying string to end of long dowel or stick. For hook, tie paper clip to end of string. Hook S-shaped styrofoam on paper clip for worms. Provide additional equipment. For example, use TACKLE BOX (see page 164). Pretend to fish.

8. SWIMMING FISH: Pretend to be a fish swimming in the water. What type of fish do you want to be? Lie on your stomach with your arms close to your side. Wiggle your body and try to move. How would you rest when you are tired? How would you eat? Where would you hide if there was danger? Describe what you see in your underwater world. Dramatize the following verse:

> There is so much activity beneath the sea.
> The crab crawls. The eel wiggles.
> The octopus swims. The jellyfish jiggles.
> Dramatize the creature you want to be.

9. LEMONADE: One player is chosen as leader. Players and leader exchange lines:
    Players: "What's your trade?"
    Leader: "Lemonade."
    Players: "Show us a summer sport if you're not afraid."
Leader then pantomimes a summer sport, and remaining players guess which sport
he is pantomiming. New leader is chosen, and activity is repeated.

10. MOVING BALL:
    I move the ball everywhere.
    I move the ball high in the air.
    Now I'm moving with the ball.
    I drop the ball, then down I fall.
Each participant holds ball between hands or legs and does actions to verse.
Variation: Two players hold one ball between each other's feet or hands.

11. ICE CREAM CONE: Pretend to be an ice cream cone on a sunny day. What flavor
of ice cream do you want to be? (Players respond with flavor of ice cream.)
Now stand tall and place arms over head in a circle to form an ice cream cone.
The ice cream is cold, round, and firm. Soon the sun shines. The temperature
becomes hotter and hotter. You begin to melt. It is hotter. You slowly melt.
(Players slowly fall to ground.) Now you are a puddle on the ground.

PHYSICAL DEVELOPMENT

1. INNER TUBE PLAY: Players stand in line. Inner tube is placed on floor in
front of line. First child steps in the center of the tube. He pulls tube up
and over head. He then drops tube by next player in line. Repeat until all
have had a turn.
    Variations:
    A. Use several inner tubes.
    B. Instead of inner tube, use bicycle tire.

2. BALLOON CATCH: During SPLASH PARTY (see page 174), play catch with water-
filled balloons.

3. PING-PONG BOAT: Use margarine tubs for boats. Float in swimming pool. Toss
ping-pong balls into boats. Repeat poem while tossing balls:
    Ping-pong boat, ping-pong boat,
    Ping-pong in the boat, watch it float.

4. OUTDOOR OBSTACLE COURSE: Arrange the following obstacle course outdoors:
    A. TUNNEL: Crawl through a tunnel made from a large box.
    B. STEPPING STONES: Place inner tubes or bicycle tires in a row. Jump or
        step from the center of one tube to the center of the next tube.
    C. CROSS THE MISSISSIPPI: Place a ladder flat on the ground. Step on each
        rung of the ladder to cross the river.
    D. SWING ACROSS RAVINE: Tie a strong rope to a tree branch. Hold rope and
        swing across rug placed on path.
    E. WINDING PATH: Place garden hose or one foot high garden fence in a
        spiral. Walk into center and then out again.
    F. CLIMB ROCKY MOUNTAINS: Climb over several sawhorses.
    G. WATERFALLS: Drape a garden hose with a fine mist sprinkler over tree.
        Go under falls.

5. BAREFOOT PICK UP: On the floor, drop a facial tissue or piece of cloth. Pick up the tissue or cloth with toes.
    Note: Place tissue near a wall or table so child has something for support.

6. TRACK AND FIELD MEET: Set up a track and field meet with each activity in a different area of the playground so participants can go from one activity to another.
    A. DISCUS THROW: Use Frisbee™ for discus. Throw discus for distance or at a target for accuracy.
    B. SHOT PUT: Throw a softball.
    C. BROAD JUMP: Stand on a marker at the edge of the sandbox. Jump toward center of box.
    D. HIGH JUMP: Place broomstick or yardstick about 3" from ground between two blocks. Jump over stick.
    E. 440 INCH DASH, 880 INCH DASH: Mark a distance 440" and 880". Use a stopwatch or second hand on a watch to record the time it takes each participant to run or hop each distance.
    F. HURDLES: Tie a ribbon between two blocks. Make several hurdles. Hurdlers hop over hurdles and run a designated distance.
    G. LONG DISTANCE RUN: Run from one spot to designated place and return.
    Each participant receives a blue ribbon or medal for participating in meet. To make medal, cover cardboard circle with aluminum foil. Punch hole in circle. Thread with 24" piece of yarn and tie.

7. CALL BALL: Use beach ball or other large ball. Players form line facing the leader. The leader calls the name of a player and tosses, rolls, or bounces the ball to named person. The player catches the ball and then returns it to the leader in the same manner.

8. SOFTBALL: Use sponge balls or socks rolled into balls. Players are paired. Each pair tosses ball to one another with overhand or underhand throw.

9. BATTING PRACTICE: In the middle of a large piece of styrofoam, cut a hole slightly smaller than diameter of plastic protective tube used to encase golf club. Stand tube in hole. Top of tube should be level with batter's waist. Place ball on top of tube. Examples of balls are sponge ball, rubber ball, or hollow plastic softball with holes. Practice hitting ball with plastic bat.
    Variation: Suspend hollow plastic softball with holes from tree branch.

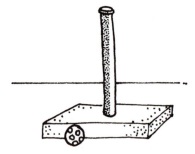

10. TENNIS: Inflate round balloon and tie end. Attach string to balloon. Tie other end of string to cord that is strung horizontally at player's eye level. Balloon should not touch ground. Players hit balloon back and forth over cord using large wooden spoons as rackets.
    Variations:
    A. Tie rope between two chairs. Suspend balloon from rope.
    B. Use hands to hit balloon instead of wooden spoons.
    C. Instead of spoon, use racket made from wire coat hanger. Elongate hanger to form diamond shape. Stretch nylon hose over diamond and secure at hook. Squeeze hook together to form handle.

11. GOLF: Dig a hole in the ground. Use hollow plastic ball with holes. Hit ball into hole with a yardstick, plastic baseball bat, or golf club.
Variations:
A. Make several holes.
B. Instead of hole in ground, hit ball into can that is lying on its side. Various sized cans can be used.

12. GOLDFISH GOLF: Remove rim from gallon ice cream container to make body of fish. Invert and cut large mouth from edge. Cut tail from piece of cardboard and attach to body. Spray gold. Glue two large eyes on fish. Use hollow plastic ball with holes. Hit ball into fish's mouth with yardsitck or plastic bat.
Variation: Hit marbles into mouth with dowel stick.

MATH

1. SUN CLOCK: Glue a spool to center of heavy cardboard bowl or plate. Place a pencil or dowel in the spool. Take the sun clock outdoors. Place it in a location which will remain in the sunlight most of the day. At every hour mark spot on rim where shadow falls. Under the mark write the number which indicates the hour of the day. If possible, leave the sun clock in the same location. Cover it with a bucket to protect it from rain and wind. The following day check the sun clock every hour to see if it's accurate.

2. SAND NUMBERS AND SHAPES: Smooth sand in sandbox. Write number or make shape in sand. Participants identify number or shape. Smooth sand and repeat with different shape or number.
Variation: Do activity indoors by spreading thin layer of sand, salt, or cornmeal in rectangular-shaped, shallow, plastic container.

3. FISHING CARD GAME: Make a set of cards by writing a number on each card. Make a matching set. Each player is dealt five cards. The remaining cards are placed face down in a pile at the center of the table. The object of the game is to accumulate the most pairs of cards. As soon as a player has a pair, it is placed on the table. The first fisherman asks any player if he has a certain card. If he has it, the player must give it to the fisherman. If he does not have the card, the fisherman must "Fish." and draw a card from the pile in the center of the table. The next fisherman is the player on the left. Continue clockwise around circle. When all sets are matched, each player counts the number of pairs he has.
Variation: Instead of numbers, use colors, animals, or letters.

4. GEOMETRIC FISH: From paper cut a large circle, small circle, large triangle, and small triangle. Adult instructs child on placement of shapes. Shapes are placed on blue piece of paper. Instructions are: "Object is to form fish. Glue large circle to center of paper. To form tail fin, glue one point of large triangle to edge of circle. Glue side of small triangle to opposite side of circle to form mouth. Attach small circle for the eye."

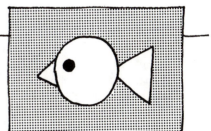

5. GOLF TEE NUMBER GAME: Fold rectangular piece of cardboard in half so it will stand. Print a number on one half of the card. Punch corresponding number of holes in same half of card. Make several cards using a different number on each card. Fit golf tees into holes. Count tees used in each card.

6. POPSICLE MATCHING: Attach circles to popsicle sticks. Write number on each popsicle. Recite verse and identify number.

   I'm a little popsicle for you today
   If you can tell me what number I display.

   When player identifies correct number, he receives popsicle.

   Variation: Make another set of popsicles using pictures to depict each number. Match correct pair of popsicles. For example, match two apples on picture set with 2 from the number set.

SCIENCE

1. SUN'S WARMTH: Explain that the sun is the source of the earth's heat. Experiment with the following to discover that the sun makes objects feel warm.
   A. Place one metal roller skate in the sun and one in the shade. After several moments touch each. How do they feel? Which is warmer? Why?
   B. Place a wooden baseball bat and metal baseball bat in the sun for a short period of time. Which is warmer? Why? This happens because the objects are made of different materials. Each material absorbs or holds a different amount of the sun's heat.

2. BALANCE BOARD: Make balance board that is similar to teeter totter by using small board and block for fulcrum. Experiment with the following:
   A. Place two objects on balance board and maintain a balance.
   B. Place many objects on board and maintain balance.
   C. Balance with three objects on each side of the fulcrum. Try moving one object and still maintaining balance.
   D. Balance two pieces of wood. Keep wood in same place but change position of one piece. For example, place wood that is lying horizontally in vertical position. What happens? Experiment with different positions.
   E. Go outside and balance two children on seesaw. Have one child lift one foot. What happens? Have one child place one foot in front of the other. What happens?
   Variation: Make balance board on floor using large wood block and large board.

3. WET AND DRY: Contrast objects that are wet and dry. Experiment with a leaf, cloth, paper, and soil. Are wet things darker than dry things? Does the shape change? Is the texture different? Feel the difference. Wet objects are usually heavier. Sometimes wet objects, like wool cloth, smell differently. Some things absorb liquid more quickly than others. Experiment with paper towel, waxed paper, newspaper, magazine page, and aluminum foil. Which would work best to wipe up spills? In certain instances it is not desirable for things to dry. Examples are jar of paint and watermelon. How can something be kept from drying?

4. SINK OR FLOAT: Provide a variety of objects that sink or float and a container of water. Experiment with the following:
   A. Which objects sink? Which objects float?
   B. Can you make something that sinks, float? This can be accomplished by placing a sinking object on one that floats. For example, place a marble on a sponge.
   C. What object can hold the most things and still float?
   D. Make different shapes with plasticine or SNOW CLAY (see page 83). Which ones float? For example, a long string will float.
   E. Place 1/4 cup salt in two cups water. Place two cups water in an equal container. Submerge a plastic spoon in each container. Do they float?
   Note: If the spoons are not submerged, they will float in both containers due to surface tension and water displacement.

5. SHELLS: Display and examine shells. Shells are the hard, protective, outer covering for some soft-bodied animals. Many shells are found at the seashore. However, some animals with shells live in fresh water or on land. Many shells are beautifully colored and marked. These shells are used for jewelry, buttons, knife handles, cameos, or inlays on musical instruments. Many people collect shells as a hobby or to decorate their homes.
   Variation: Display picture book of shells.

6. BODY WATER: Human bodies are 3/5 water. To demonstrate this, measure and weigh a child. If he is 40 inches and 40 pounds, approximately 25 inches and 25 pounds will be water. People lose water every day from their bodies. A person should drink at least six glasses of liquid a day. This is important during the summer because a person perspires more, and more liquid is lost from the body.

7. ICED TEA: Fill a clear glass with ice cubes. Boil a cup of water. Add a tea bag to the hot water. Pour hot tea over ice cubes. What happens to the ice cubes? Is the hot tea still hot? Why?

8. CAMERA ART: Purchase studio proof paper and a box of fixer at a photo supply store. Mix the fixer in a shallow pan which is large enough to hold a sheet of studio proof paper. Fill another shallow pan with water. Place a piece of studio proof paper on a piece of cardboard. On the paper, away from sunlight, arrange collected plants. Examples are leaves, flowers, seeds, and seaweeds. Place arrangement in direct sunlight until paper turns dark purple. Remove plants and place paper in the fixer for approximately five minutes. Then place paper in water for ten minutes. Lay on newspaper to dry. If paper curls while drying, press in a book.
   Variation: To receive different shades on the paper, move the plants around paper or remove part of the arrangement during the exposure.

MUSIC

1. A-CAMPING WE WILL GO: (Tune--"A-Hunting We Will Go")
           A-camping we will go. A-camping we will go.
      We'll pack our bags and take a trip.
      A-camping we will go.
   Variations: Instead of "We'll pack our bags and take a trip," use:
   A. We'll find a site and pitch our tent.
   B. We'll build a fire and cook our food.

2. ROW, ROW, ROW YOUR BOAT: (Traditional)
          Row, row, row your boat gently down the stream,
          Merrily, merrily, merrily, merrily life is but a dream.

3. DOWN BY THE SEASHORE: (Tune--"Down by the Station Early in the Morning")
          Down by the seashore
          In their swimming suits galore
          See the children swimming and in the water run.
          Then they lie on the beach tanning in the hot sun.
          Ah, ah, whew, whew, (pretend to wipe perspiration from forehead)
          Summer has begun.

4. OVER IN THE MEADOW: (Traditional)
          Over in the meadow in the sand in the sun,
          Lived an old mother toad and her little toadie one.
          "Wink," said the mother. "I wink," said the one.
          So they winked and they blinked in the sand in the sun.
     Second verse:
          Over in the meadow where the stream runs so blue,
          Lived an old mother fish and her little fishes two.
          "Swim," said the mother. "We swim," said the two.
          So they swam and they leaped where the stream runs so blue.
     Third verse:
          Over in the meadow in a hole in the tree,
          Lived an old mother bluebird and her little birdies three.
          "Sing," said the mother. "We sing," said the three.
          So they sang and were glad in the hole in the tree.

5. FRIENDLY FONZ: (Tune--"Brownie Smile")
          I have a little fish. His name is Friendly Fonz.
          I put him in the bathtub to teach me how to float.
          He drank up all the water. (slurp)
          He ate up all the soap, (chomp, chomp)
          And now he's sick in bed
            (pat hands over lips while singing following words)
          With bubbles in his throat.

6. BAREFOOT MARCH: March barefoot to music. March on toes, heels, and sides of
   feet. Stamp feet. March using heel-toe, heel-toe.

7. RECORD:
          "Fishing Trip" from *Creative Movement and Rhythmic Exploration* by Hap Palmer,
          Educational Activities Inc., Box 392, Freeport, New York 11520.

                          FIELD TRIPS

1. PARK
2. TROUT FARM
3. TRACK AND FIELD MEET
4. BEACH
5. HIKING: Go hiking and explore environment. Observe and collect grass, rocks,
   insects, and leaves.
6. HUG-A-HIKE: Hike to a grassy area. Lie on the grass on stomach. Extend arms
   above head in a circle or a "hug." Identify the items discovered in the area
   encompassed inside arms.

OTHER NATIONAL HOLIDAYS

This chapter includes national holidays that are observed by most people in the United States. Some of these are legal holidays set aside by the United States Congress for observance. Dates for these holidays are occasionally changed or new holidays are added. The President can also proclaim a certain day to be celebrated as a national holiday.

The holidays will be listed in chronological order beginning with January. Holidays included are New Year's Day, Ground Hog Day, Lincoln's Birthday, Washington's Birthday, St. Patrick's Day, April Fools' Day, Pan American Day, Arbor Day, Law Day, May Day, Mother's Day, Memorial Day, Flag Day, Father's Day, Independence Day, Labor Day, Columbus Day, United Nations Day, Veterans Day, and Election Day.

NEW YEAR'S DAY

The date chosen to begin the new year has varied from one time and people to another. In the United States NEW YEAR'S DAY is a legal holiday celebrated on January 1. The history of New Year's in America probably originated with the ancient Romans, who honored Janus, god of beginnings and discovery. The month of January is named for this god. The New Year's celebration says farewell to the old year, and the new year begins with hope of a brighter future. It is customary to stay awake until midnight on New Year's Eve to "see the old year out and ring the new year in." Traditionally, the New Year is a holiday of merriment. It is celebrated with noisemakers, parties, fireworks, parades, family gatherings, and football games.

CONCEPTS TO BE TAUGHT

1. New Year's Day is celebrated on January 1 in the United States.
2. Many people await the new year's arrival on New Year's Eve with celebrations.
3. At this time, promises are often made to be a better person in the year to come.

EXTENDED ACTIVITIES

1. HAT: Decorate cone-shaped paper cups with felt-tipped pens, crayons, gummed stickers, or scraps of paper. With a paper punch. make holes in opposite sides close to rim. Tie elastic thread in holes forming a loop for chin strap.

2. EGGNOG: 4 eggs   4 cups milk   4 ice cubes
             1/4 cup sugar   1 teaspoon vanilla
   Blend all ingredients in blender. Lightly sprinkle with nutmeg. Serve cold.
   Note: Use clean eggs, with no cracks in shells.

3. FINGERPLAY #1: (Alfred Lord Tennyson)
          Ring out the old, ring in the new. (pretend to ring bell)
          Ring happy bells across the snow. (smile)
          The year is going--let him go. (wave)
          Ring out the false, ring in the true. (pretend to ring bell)

4. FINGERPLAY #2:
          January one has come. (raise one finger)
          The new year has begun.
          In 19__ I'll try to do (hand on heart)
          Things that are good and true.

5. NEW YEAR'S ACTIVITIES: Have children share personal experiences about things
   they do with their families on New Year's. The following can be discussed:
       A. Celebrating New Year's Eve with parties, noisemakers, and fireworks
       B. Watching football games and parades

6. NEW YEAR'S RESOLUTION: Discuss that a resolution is a decision or determination to do something better or different in the future. Ideas for discussion
   are:
       A. What would you like to do in the new year?
       B. How could you be helpful to your parents?
       C. What would you like to learn this year?
       D. Whom would you like to visit?
   Adult can write each child's resolution on paper with child's name. The paper
   can be taped to the wall.
   Note: Years ago children wrote their promises on a piece of paper and placed
   the paper on the wall above their bed.
   Variation: To give insight into expectations, have each child make a resolution for a family member. For example, "This year I want my mother to . . ."

7. GONG SONG:
          This is the gong song.
          Listen to all the gongs.
          If twelve gongs should sound,
          Stand up and walk around
          Until a new chair is found.
   Arrange chairs in a circle. Each player sits in a chair. Adult recites poem
   and then hits a metal lid with a wooden spoon to produce gongs. If twelve
   gongs sound, players say, "Happy New Year" and change seats. If less than
   twelve gongs sound, players remain seated. Repeat with different number of
   gongs.

8. ALARM CLOCK HIDE AND SEEK: Adult hides an alarm clock that is set to ring in
   several minutes. Discuss with players that people who celebrate on New Year's
   Eve wait for midnight and then say, "Happy New Year!" When the alarm rings,
   say, "Happy New Year!" and try to find the clock. If the alarm stops before
   the clock has been found, listen for the ticking sound. Repeat game.

9. AULD LANG SYNE: (OLD LONG SINCE)
          Should auld acquaintance be forgot and never brought to mind?
          Should auld acquaintance be forgot and days of auld lang syne?
                              Robert Burns

184

GROUND HOG DAY

GROUND HOG DAY is celebrated on February 2. According to popular legend, a ground hog awakens from hibernation and emerges on this day to see if winter is over. If it sees its shadow, the ground hog is frightened and returns to its home in the ground, indicating six more weeks of winter weather. If the day is cloudy, the ground hog will not see its shadow and will stay above ground. This signifies the arrival of spring.

CONCEPTS TO BE TAUGHT

1. Ground Hog Day is celebrated on February 2.
2. According to legend, the ground hog emerges on Ground Hog Day to see if winter is over.
3. Ground hogs are true hibernators and do reappear when the weather warms.

EXTENDED ACTIVITIES

1. FINGERPLAY:
>   The ground hog emerges on February two (two fingers)
>   To see if the sky is sunny and blue. (point to sky)
>   It seems rather funny (look puzzled)
>   That if it is sunny, (form circle in air)
>   The ground hog goes back in his hole (make hole with fingers on one hand,
>   fingers of other hand jump in hole)
>   For six weeks of winter. (six fingers) Bless my soul!

2. GROUND HOG INFORMATION: A ground hog is a ground squirrel that is also known as a woodchuck. The woodchuck is a burrowing animal that lives in an underground tunnel with two or three entrances and several chambers. It usually has coarse, reddish-brown fur. The woodchuck eats grass and other vegetation. The story of Ground Hog Day is a legend. However, a ground hog does hibernate in his home during the cold winter months and then reappears when the weather warms. Observe pictures of a ground hog.

3. GROUND HOG DAY LEGEND: Dramatize the legend of Ground Hog Day. Pretend to be a ground hog curled in a ball under the ground in a winter home. It is February 2. Awaken and stretch. Crawl from your home. Look! There's a black shadow on the ground. Ooooo! Crawl back into your home and sleep for six weeks. Does this actually happen? Dramatize what a ground hog actually does. Sleep in a ball in your home under the ground. The weather warms. Slowly awaken. You are very hungry because you have not eaten throughout the winter. Crawl from your home and look for grass or clover to eat.

4. STRETCHING GROUND HOG: Trace and cut outline of ground hog. Fold along dotted lines. With folded parts facing upward, float ground hog on water. Soon the ground hog will "awaken from his winter nap" and slowly stretch his arms and legs. Happy Ground Hog Day!
   Note: As the paper absorbs the water, it unfolds.

5. SHADOWS: On Ground Hog Day, go outside and observe shadows. Discuss that the sun shines on an object, and the shadow appears on the opposite side. It is the dark area on the ground. The object blocks sunlight from shining on the ground in that area. Predict whether or not the ground hog will see its shadow.
   Note: Refer to WHAT IS A SHADOW (see page 24) and SHADOWS (see page 31).

LINCOLN'S BIRTHDAY

ABRAHAM LINCOLN was born on February 12, 1809, in a small backwoods cabin south of Hodgenville, Kentucky. He walked nine miles to school. Although he spent only one year in school, he learned to read and write. He would read until late at night. His father, who thought he was foolish, once asked Abe how he would use the knowledge he gained from reading. Abe replied, "I'm going to be President."

Lincoln became the sixteenth President of the United States in 1861. During his term, the nation faced its most difficult years because the Civil War was fought. After four years of fighting, the only war that ever divided the country ended. Five days later, Lincoln was shot to death by John Wilkes Booth at Ford's Theatre in Washington, D.C. Lincoln was a peace-loving man who disliked slavery and felt all men should have equal rights. He is admired for rising to the highest office in the United States through determination, skill, and hard work. Many historians consider Lincoln to have been one of America's greatest men. He is remembered every February 12 (in most states) when his birthday is celebrated.

CONCEPTS TO BE TAUGHT

1. Every February 12, we honor Abraham Lincoln because it is the birthday of this great man.
2. Lincoln was noted for his determination, hard work, and skill.
3. As President of the United States, Lincoln freed the slaves.

EXTENDED ACTIVITIES

1. LOG CABIN: Frost square cracker with peanut butter. Place several frosted crackers on top of one another to form cabin.

2. FINGERPLAY:
   Through hard work, skill, and determination. (wipe forehead)
   Lincoln became one of America's greatest men. (one finger)
   He was a peace-loving man who was just. (hand to heart)
   Equal rights for all was a must! (spread arms)

3. LINCOLN PUPPET: Trace and cut outline of Abraham Lincoln from heavy piece of paper. Glue popsicle stick to back of picture. Dramatize Abe Lincoln. Have Abe chat with George Washington. Glue outline of Washington (see page 188) to popsicle stick.

4. PENNY PLAY: Place a sheet or blanket on the floor to designate an area for penny play. Use Lincoln pennies and an assortment of containers. Examples are:
   A. Make banks by cutting slits in lids of various containers.
   B. Experiment with shakers. Shakers can be made from plastic, cardboard, or metal containers with lids. Discuss sound pennies make in each container.

5. LINCOLN IN HAT: Cover an oatmeal container with black paper. Cut a large black circle for brim. Place oatmeal container in center and trace around bottom of container. Draw tabs inside circle and cut out inner circle, leaving tabs. Tape tabs to inside of container. Stand hat with open side upward. Toss Lincoln pennies into hat.
   Note: This hat can also be used for dramatic play.

6. LINCOLN LOTTO: For each lotto card, outline ten pennies on a piece of cardboard. Cut a 2" circle from cardboard to make lotto coin. On one side of the coin, glue or tape one penny with Lincoln's face showing. On the other side, attach three Lincoln pennies. Each player receives a lotto card. Players take turns flipping the lotto coin. Player flipping coin draws corresponding number of pennies from container and places them on his lotto card. When a player's card is filled with ten pennies, he says, "Lincoln lotto."

7. PENNY COUNTING: Players sit in a circle. Each player is given five pennies. Adult instructs players to:
   A. Stack pennies on top of each other.
   B. Place pennies in a line. Place pennies in a circle.
   C. Give one penny to the neighbor on your right side. How many do you have?
   D. Place one penny in the center of children. How many do you have? (Adult places one penny per child in center of children.) Take two pennies from the center. How many pennies do you have now?
   E. Pass container to each participant. Place all pennies in container. Count total number of pennies.

8. HAPPY BIRTHDAY, ABE: Sing "Happy Birthday" to Abe.

WASHINGTON'S BIRTHDAY

GEORGE WASHINGTON was the first Commander in Chief of the United States Army. He led the Continental Army, who defeated the British forces in the Revolutionary War. Thus, America became a completely independent nation. Washington served for eight years as the first President of the United States. He helped establish the Constitution and provided the foundation for the new government so the United States could grow into a great nation. For these services, he is referred to as the "Father of His Country."

Washington was born February 11, 1732. The Julian calendar was changed to the Gregorian calendar 20 years later, and his birthday became February 22. Washington was raised in Virginia on his family's plantation where he enjoyed planting crops and caring for animals. At 16, he moved to Mount Vernon on the Potomac River in Alexandria, Virginia, which was his home for the remainder of his life. Today Mount Vernon is a famous landmark in the United States. Many other things like Washington Monument, Washington state, and Washington, D.C. are named after this great man. Today we commemorate his birthday as a legal holiday celebrated on the third Monday in February.

CONCEPTS TO BE TAUGHT

1. George Washington was the first President of the United States.
2. He is called the "Father of His Country."
3. Washington was a brave and honest man.

EXTENDED ACTIVITIES

1. HAT: Cut 8 1/2" x 11" piece of construction paper crosswise to form three equal rectangles. Staple narrow ends of strips together to form triangular-shaped hat. Attach bow or cherry sprig.

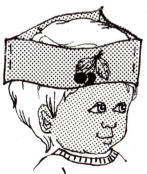

2. WASHINGTON SILHOUETTE: Trace outline of George Washington on a piece of poster board. Form template by cutting silhouette from center of paper leaving edges intact. Place template over piece of construction paper. Paint over entire silhouette. Remove template.

3. CHERRY PARFAIT: In a clear plastic glass, layer yogurt and cherry pie filling. Repeat layers.

4. CHERRY POPOVER: Place one tablespoon of cherry pie filling in center of a flattened crescent dinner roll. Place another crescent roll over the top. Pinch edges together. Bake according to directions on package of rolls.

5. FINGERPLAY #1: (Traditional)
        My hat, it has three corners. (form triangle above head)
        Three corners has my hat.
        If it did not have three corners, (raise three fingers)
        It would not be my hat. (shake head sideways)

6. FINGERPLAY #2:
        A very old legend tells me (point to self)
        George Washington cut down a cherry tree. (pretend to chop)
        Because he would not tell a lie, (shake head sideways)
        When asked who did this terrible deed, (deep voice, place hands on hips)
        He said, "Dear Father, it was I." (point to self)
        Although this story is only a legend, (shake head sideways)
        It reminds me that George Washington
        Was a brave and honest man!

7. THE CHERRY TREE: Read the story *George and the Cherry Tree* by Brandenburg. Discuss that Washington did not cut down the cherry tree and confess the misdeed to his father. This story was created years after his death to show that this great man was brave and honest.

8. WASHINGTON CROSSES DELAWARE: Place two ropes parallel to each other for the Delaware River. On one side of the river, place a cake pan to represent the German campsite. Players stand on the opposite side and toss George Washington quarters across the Delaware into the cake pan campsite.
Note: George Washington led his army across the Delaware River in a blinding snowstorm on Christmas night, 1776, to surprise and capture a British force of German Hessians at the campsite near Trenton, New Jersey.

9. CHOPPING DOWN THE CHERRY TREE: Sit in circle. One player is the Cherry Tree, who stands in center of circle with eyes covered. Adult chooses one player to touch Cherry Tree and say, "Chop, chop." Cherry Tree squats and player returns to place in circle. All players then say with deep voices, "Who chopped down the cherry tree?" Cherry Tree opens eyes and guesses who it was. That player then becomes Cherry Tree, and game is repeated.

10. WASHINGTON PUPPET: Glue a George Washington quarter on the end of a popsicle stick. Dramatize George Washington. Have George chat with Abraham Lincoln (made by gluing Lincoln penny to a popsicle stick).
Variation: Tape quarter to finger instead of gluing it to a popsicle stick.

11. HAPPY BIRTHDAY: Display picture of George Washington found in an encyclopedia or library book. Sing "Happy Birthday" to George.

SAINT PATRICK'S DAY

St. Patrick, the patron saint of Ireland and the Irish, was born about 385 A.D. in Northern Wales. He studied religion in Europe to become a priest and bishop. He then brought Christianity to the Irish by teaching in Ireland for 29 years. According to early Irish tradition, he died on March 17, 461 A.D. The anniversary of his death is celebrated as SAINT PATRICK'S DAY.

The first official celebration of St. Patrick's Day in the United States occured in Morristown, New Jersey, in 1780. It was authorized by George Washington. Today St. Patrick's Day is celebrated by the Irish as well as many Americans with parades, parties, wearing of green, Irish songs and jigs.

CONCEPTS TO BE TAUGHT

1. St. Patrick's Day is celebrated on March 17.
2. People wear green on this day in memory of Ireland.
3. One symbol of St. Patrick's Day is the shamrock which is used as the floral emblem by the Irish.

EXTENDED ACTIVITIES

1. SHAMROCK: Cut a shamrock from construction paper. Glue pieces of green variegated tissue paper or scraps of green paper on shamrock.
   Variations:
   A. Decorate with crayons, felt-tipped pens, or paint.
   B. Cover shamrock with glue. Sprinkle with green glitter. Remove excess.

2. HEARTY SHAMROCK: Cut three hearts from green construction paper. Form shamrock by gluing points of hearts together on a piece of paper. Draw stem.

3. GROWING SHAMROCK: Cut shamrock from terry cloth. Moisten shamrock. Sprinkle with alfalfa seed. Keep moist. Set in dark place. Allow several days for shamrock to grow. Set in sunlight for shamrock to turn green.

4. GREEN VEGETABLE SNACK: Prepare a snack using slices of fresh green vegetables. Examples are cabbage, cucumber, avocado, zucchini squash, and lettuce. This can be served with SHAMROCK SHAKE (listed below).

5. SHAMROCK SHAKE: Blend 1 banana, 2 cups lime sherbet, and 2 cups milk.

6. FINGERPLAY:
   > On St. Patrick's Day a shamrock we often see. (point to eyes)
   > Let's count the leaflets--1-2-3. (raise three fingers)

7. MAP OF IRELAND: Display a map of Ireland and discuss:
   A. Ireland is an island.
   B. People who come from Ireland or whose ancestors came from Ireland are called Irish.
   C. An emerald is a precious stone which is green. Ireland is often called the "Emerald Isle" because it is so green with vegetation.
   D. The color green symbolizes Ireland and the Irish.
   E. Many Irish immigrated or came to the United States which is why this holiday is celebrated here.

8. ST. PATRICK'S DAY FESTIVITIES: Discuss:
    A. In Ireland, St. Patrick's Day is celebrated by wearing a sprig of shamrock and attending religious services. Afterward it becomes a festive celebration.
    B. In America, St. Patrick's Day is celebrated with parades, parties, wearing of green, Irish songs and jigs.
    C. Greet children with traditional Irish greeting, "Top of the morning."

9. LEPRECHAUNS: Observe picture of a leprechaun or use a puppet for this discussion. The Irish love folktales about imaginary fairies. The most famous of these "wee folk" are leprechauns, who are shoemakers for all other fairies. A leprechaun looks like a tiny old man. He is tricky and mischievous. If you catch one, he is forced to reveal the location of his pot of gold if you look him steadily in the eye. Once you relax your gaze, the leprechaun will escape! Pretend to be this imaginary fairy.

10. WEARING OF THE GREEN:
    As we look around the room, what can be seen?
    Someone has a (article of clothing) on: it's the wearing of the green!
    Adult recites verse and players guess who is wearing the green article of clothing named. Repeat, changing the green article of clothing.
    Variation: Instead of clothing, use green objects found in the room by changing the last sentence to: There's an (object) in the room and it's green!

11. SHAMROCK: Display a real shamrock or a picture of a shamrock. Discuss color, number and shape of leaves, and any distinguishing characteristics. For example, shamrocks close their leaves in the evening. The shamrock is considered by many people to bring good luck. A legend tells that St. Patrick used the shamrock as a symbol of the Trinity. The shamrock has become a national symbol of Ireland.

12. SHAM-ROCK: Three children hold hands and rock to an Irish jig. "McNamara's Band" can be used. For a slower tempo, play "When Irish Eyes are Smiling."
    Variation: Individual children can dance an Irish jig to Irish music.

APRIL FOOLS' DAY

April 1 has long been known as APRIL FOOLS' DAY, or All Fools' Day. It is a day for playing practical jokes, with the victim being called an April fool. This custom has obscure beginnings but may be related to the spring (vernal) equinox when nature fools people with unpredictable weather. It might also have begun with ancient Hindus, who celebrated the Feast of *Holi* (see page 203), a spring festival held between March 25 and April 1 in which pranks and tricks played a large part. Some scholars believe it started in 1856 when the king of France adopted a new calendar which made the year begin January 1 instead of April 1. Anyone forgetting or resisting the change was fooled by pranksters and called an "April fish."

EXTENDED ACTIVITIES

1. CLOWN PARTY: Have each child dress in silly clothes or a clown outfit. Children can make-up each others' faces. Apply a small amount of cold cream to face before applying make-up. Provide rouge, powder, eyebrow pencil, eye shadow, lipstick, and cold cream for removal of make-up. Cotton-tipped swabs can be used to apply make-up.

2. TRICKS: Teach children to use their imaginations by displaying yours. Examples are serving a glass of cotton balls for milk, writing names on paper using mirror writing, providing only a table knife for eating a meal, and serving snack with applesauce in a glass and juice in a bowl.

PAN AMERICAN DAY

PAN AMERICAN DAY is observed on April 14 by Presidential proclamation to commemorate the friendship of 24 American republics. The First International Conference of American States met at Washington, D.C., in 1889 and adopted a resolution which resulted in an organization now known as the Pan American Union. It consists of nations from South, Central, and North America. Pan American Day is the anniversary of this union, formed on April 14, 1890. The United States has celebrated this day since 1931. Schools and interested groups have programs presenting ways in which the Pan American countries work together. Ceremonies are also held in the Pan American Building in Washington, D.C., which displays the flags of all the Pan American nations.

ARBOR DAY

The first ARBOR DAY was observed April 10, 1872, in Nebraska. The idea of setting aside one day a year for planting trees was promoted by Julius Sterling Morton, a Nebraska conservationist who later became United States Secretary of Agriculture from 1893 to 1897. On the first celebration, more than a million trees were planted because prizes were offered to those who planted the greatest number of trees. Nebraska, known as the Tree Planter's State, now celebrates Arbor Day on April 22, which is the anniversary of Morton's birth. Morton is called the Father of Arbor Day.

Now Arbor Day is observed in every state (except Alaska) either by legislation or proclamation by state officials. The date in each state varies depending upon the climate, but most often it is held in April. In most Northern states, Arbor Day is observed in April, May, or sometimes March. In the Southern states, it is held during the winter months.

The purpose of Arbor Day is to assist in planting trees in scantily wooded areas and to beautify yards, neighborhoods, public parks, and towns. It is generally held in cooperation with schools to emphasize to children the importance of tree preservation and conservation.

LAW DAY

In 1958 President Dwight D. Eisenhower proclaimed May 1 as Law Day. In 1961 Congress established Law Day as an official holiday. The day is designed to help us recognize the importance of laws in the United States. The observance of Law Day is marked annually by the American Bar Association, local bar associations, and law schools throughout the United States. Programs are presented concerning legislation, law enforcement, operation of courts, and administration of justice.

MAY DAY

MAY DAY, celebrated May 1, is a spring festival that marks the revival of life in early spring. It probably originated with ancient Romans who honored Flora, goddess of fruits and flowers, by gathering spring flowers. In medieval times it became a favorite holiday of English villagers who celebrated the anniversary of the traditional date for Robin Hood's death. They elected a queen, gathered flowers to decorate homes and churches, danced around a Maypole, and enjoyed games and festivities.

Today children in the United States make baskets, fill them with spring flowers or candy, and hang the baskets on doorknobs of friends and neighbors. They ring the doorbell and run away or hide until the basket is discovered. Traditional May Day festivities include singing songs while dancing around a Maypole and selecting a May queen.

CONCEPTS TO BE TAUGHT

1. May Day celebrates the coming of spring.
2. Often baskets filled with flowers or candy are given to friends on this day.
3. Customs include selecting a May queen and dancing around a Maypole.

EXTENDED ACTIVITIES

1. DOILY BASKET: Glue crumpled pieces of brightly colored tissue paper to center of doily for flowers. Attach pipe cleaner, yarn, or ribbon to opposite sides of doily to form handle.
   Note: Doily will curve at sides when suspended and form basket.

2. MAY BASKET: For base use any of the following: small box, bottom of milk carton, margarine tub, berry basket, or paper rolled into cone shape and stapled. Decorate base with scraps of tissue paper, ribbon, yarn, or gummed stickers. To opposite sides of base, attach handle made from pipe cleaner, strip of paper, ribbon, or yarn. Fill basket with FLOWERS (listed below).

3. FLOWERS: Create flowers in the following ways:
   A. Paint individual cups of an egg carton and attach pipe cleaners for stems.
   B. Cut flowers from magazines and attach pipe cleaners with glue for stems.
   C. Cut or tear flowers from colorful paper. Glue to pipe cleaners.
   D. Roll cotton balls in dry tempera. Attach pipe cleaners for stems.
   E. Wrap pipe cleaner around center of facial tissue.

4. FINGERPLAY #1:
   When you give a May basket, (point to friend)
   That's a time for fun. (smile)
   Set it on the step; (pretend to set basket down)
   Knock on the door, (pretend to knock)
   And run, run, run! (make fingers run)

5. FINGERPLAY #2:
   I made a basket on May Day (form circle with hands)
   And left it at your front door. (point to friend)
   It means I hope you have a happy day
   And many, many more! (open and close hands)

6. FLOWERS FOR MAY BASKET: Each player receives one picture of a flower. Adult has May basket and explains that flowers are needed to fill it. Adult then describes and names a flower. Player holding flower places picture in basket.

7. MAYPOLE DANCE: For this game, players are divided into two groups. One group forms circle, leaving space between each player. Second group weaves through first group to music while holding streamers or scarfs. After music stops, groups reverse roles.
   Variation: Attach long streamers to tetherball pole. Players dance around pole holding opposite ends of streamers.

MOTHER'S DAY

MOTHER'S DAY, a day devoted to honoring mothers, is celebrated on the second Sunday in May. Anna M. Jarvis is recognized as the founder of Mother's Day in the United States. In 1908, Miss Jarvis suggested that a special service be held for mothers in a Philadelphia church. She began a nationwide campaign for the observance of Mother's Day by writing letters and persuading influential people. Through her enthusiastic campaigning, the idea was accepted by other churches and then by the general public. She chose the second Sunday in May and began the custom of wearing a carnation.

In 1914, President Wilson issued a proclamation ordering all United States' flags on public buildings be flown on this day. Official observance began the following year. Many people follow the tradition of wearing a carnation. The wearing of a colored carnation on Mother' Day indicates that one's mother is living. A white carnation indicates that she is not.

CONCEPTS TO BE TAUGHT

1. Mother's Day is celebrated to pay tribute to mothers.
2. Cards and gifts are given to mothers to show love and appreciation.

EXTENDED ACTIVITIES--GIFTS

1. PAPER PLATE LETTER HOLDER: With crayons or felt-tipped pens, decorate a paper plate and half of another paper plate. Place plates together with rounded edges matching. Punch holes in bottom edge. Lace two plates together with yarn. Punch hole in top of whole paper plate. Thread another piece of yarn through hole and tie to form loop for hanging holder.
   Variation: Staple two plates together, instead of lacing with yarn.

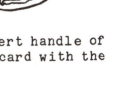

2. RECIPE HOLDER: Place plaster of Paris in spray can lid. Insert handle of plastic fork into center of plaster. Weave through prongs, a card with the following message:
   When you prepare those yummy cakes,
   You can easily see what it takes
   By using this holder until you're through.
   Happy Mother's Day. I love you!

3. BUDDING BLOSSOM: Cut 2" circle from colored paper. Poke hole in center of circle. Insert 1/2" of green pipe cleaner into hole and bend. Glue snapshot of child over pipe cleaner in center of circle. From green construction paper, cut two leaves. Write on leaves: "Happy Mother's Day! From your budding blossom, (child's name)." Poke hole in one end of each leaf. Thread leaves onto pipe cleaner. Insert pipe cleaner into pot that contains petunia or marigold. Use clay pot decorated with acrylic paint or a styrofoam cup painted with felt-tipped pens.

4. DECORATIVE SPOON: Stain a wooden spoon. Glue tiny straw flowers in the bowl of the spoon. Tie a ribbon above the bowl. To hang, attach hook to end of handle.

5. PORTRAIT OF MOM: Draw a portrait of Mom in center of a paper. Make frame by folding in half another piece of paper that is the same size as the paper with the portrait. Cut a rectangle from the folded edge leaving a frame 1 1/2" in width. Open. Glue frame over portrait.
Variation: Instead of a frame, draw portrait on front of folded piece of construction paper to make a card. As child dictates, adult can write message inside the card.

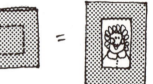

6. WALL HANGING: Use a large blunt-ended needle and yarn to embroider a design on burlap. Glue back of burlap to cardboard. Punch a hole in each upper corner. Thread a piece of yarn through holes. Tie ends of yarn. Hang.
Variation: Instead of burlap, use loosely woven fabric.

7. HAND PRINT: Place hand with fingers spread into paint. Press hand onto piece of construction paper. Attach either of the following poems:
   My dirty little fingerprints I've left on every wall,
   And on the drawers and table tops. I've really marked them all.
   But here is one that won't rub off. I'm giving it to you.
   Because I'm thankful for a mother just like you!
                    Author Unknown
Variation: Instead of above poem use:
   This is to remind you
   When I have grown so tall
   That once I was quite little.
   And my hands were very small.
                    Author Unknown
Variation: Instead of paint, use baby powder. Cover hand print with hair spray so it will not smudge.

8. MOTHER'S DAY CARNATION: Curl strips of tissue paper by wrapping around a pencil. Glue end of each curled strip to center of doily. Attach pin to back of doily.

9. PLACEMAT: Cut 12" x 18" rectangle from decorative vinyl which has solid color on the reverse side. Decorate reverse side of vinyl with permanent felt-tipped pens.

MEMORIAL DAY

MEMORIAL DAY, or Decoration Day, is a special day for remembering those Americans who have been killed in war defending our country. The date for this federal legal holiday held in most states is the last Monday in May. However, in the past it was observed on May 30. Today people honor their dead by decorating graves with flags and flowers.

FLAG DAY

The colonists wanted a flag as a national symbol of the country after they declared their independence from Great Britain. FLAG DAY commemorates June 14, 1777, when the Continental Congress adopted the United States flag. The original flag was made by Betsy Ross. It had 13 alternate stripes of red and white, and 13 white stars arranged in a circle on a field of blue. As each state joined the union, an additional star was added. Our present flag has fifty stars, representing the fifty states. Flag Day was first observed on June 14, 1877, which marked the 100th anniversary of the adoption of the flag. On August 3, 1949, President Truman permanently designated June 14 as Flag Day.

CONCEPTS TO BE TAUGHT

1. The flag is a national symbol of our country and should be respected.
2. The 13 red and white stripes represent the original 13 states.
3. Each white star represents one state in the union.

EXTENDED ACTIVITIES

1. ORIGINAL FLAG: Cut seven 7/8" x 18" strips of red paper. Cut six white strips of equal size to the red strips. Cut a 7" square from blue construction paper. Starting with red, glue alternate strips of red and white on a large piece of construction paper. Glue blue square in upper, left-hand corner over strips. Attach 13 gummed stars in a circle on the blue square.

2. FINGERPLAY:
   My flag has stars and stripes
   Of red, white, and blue. (point to colors)
   To my flag, I'll always be true. (hand on heart)

3. RESPECT FOR FLAG: Discuss that the American flag is displayed on many homes, schools, and government buildings. Because the flag is a symbol of our country, it must be respected and properly displayed. Examples are when carrying the flag, it should not touch the floor; when a flag passes, you should stand. Adults and older children often recite the Pledge of Allegiance to the flag at school and before certain meetings and ceremonies.

4. COMPARING FLAGS: Display a picture of the original flag and the flag as it has appeared at different times in our history. Compare these flags to our present flag. Count the stars in some pictures. Count the stripes. What has changed in each flag? Why?

FATHER'S DAY

On FATHER'S DAY people express love, gratitude, and appreciation to fathers by giving them cards and gifts. The occasion is often celebrated with family gatherings. The official flower for Father's Day is the rose. A red rose signifies a living father. A white rose is worn if he is dead.

Father's Day originated with Mrs. John Bruce Dodd, who wanted to honor her own father. She persuaded the Ministerial Society of Spokane, Washington, to salute fathers in special church services held on the third Sunday of June in 1910. The custom spread throughout the United States. The idea was officially approved by President Woodrow Wilson in 1916. In 1924 President Calvin Coolidge recommended national observance of the occasion. Today Father's Day is not an officially established holiday, but it is celebrated nationally on the third Sunday in June.

CONCEPTS TO BE TAUGHT

1. Father's Day is celebrated to honor fathers.
2. Cards and presents are given to fathers to show love and appreciation.

EXTENDED ACTIVITIES--GIFTS

1. CHIP OFF THE OLD BLOCK: Print words, "Chip Off the Old Block," on a piece of paper. Glue paper and small photo of child to small block of wood. Spray with clear varnish, if desired.
   Variation: Before gluing picture and paper, stain wood.

2. LEATHER-LOOK ACCESSORIES: Entirely cover any of the objects listed below with small pieces of masking tape. Rub brown paste shoe polish over tape. Wipe off excess polish.

   A. VASE: Use a small jar or soft drink bottle.
   B. PENCIL HOLDER: Use a juice can.
   C. DESK BLOTTER: Decorate four right triangles with tape. Staple or tape edges of triangles to corners of 12" x 18" cardboard. Insert 12" x 18" piece of construction paper under triangles.

3. BOOKMARKS: Arrange paper shapes on a piece of clear self-adhesive plastic. Place another piece of clear self-adhesive plastic over shapes. Cut into strips or free-form shapes to make several bookmarks.
   Variation: Place crayon chips between two pieces of waxed paper. Adult covers waxed paper with fabric or paper and presses with a warm iron. Cut into strips.

4. DAD'S RECIPE BOOK: Adult writes as each child recites own recipe for his favorite food. Make as many copies of each recipe as there are children. Form booklet containing one copy of each recipe. Place construction paper on front and back of copies. Punch two holes on left side. Thread with ribbon or yarn and tie. Decorate construction paper covers.

5. SAND CANDLE: Candles can be made in the sandbox. Make hole in sand for mold. Tie candle wick to nail head. Push nail into center of mold. Tie other end of wick around center of pencil. Lay pencil across opening of mold. Adult pours melted wax into mold. When wax is congealed, remove candle from sand.

6. WASTEPAPER BASKET: Cover sides of gallon, cardboard, ice cream container with pictures cut from magazines. When finished, cover with a thin coat of glue. Variation: Instead of making collage, paint sides of the container.

7. MEMO PAD: Cut piece of felt that is as wide and twice as long as small memo pad. Fold felt in half lengthwise. Glue fold to top of pad. Felt will cover front and back of pad. Decorate by gluing small pieces of felt to covers.

8. TIE HOLDER: Bend wire coat hanger according to diagram. Cut 2" circle from construction paper. Draw facial features on circle. Cut bow tie from a different color of paper. Glue head and bow tie to hanger just below the hook.

INDEPENDENCE DAY

INDEPENDENCE DAY, held on July 4, is the legal holiday when the United States celebrates its birth as a nation. It is celebrated throughout the country with picnics, parades, and firework displays after dark.

This holiday commemorates the adoption on July 4, 1776, of the final draft of the Declaration of Independence by the Continental Congress to proclaim America's freedom from British rule. On that day John Hancock, President of the Congress, signed the document. The document was then rewritten on parchment (animal skin). The signing of the document began on August 2, 1776, with 56 men supplying their signatures. Today the parchment, displayed in the National Archives Building, is sealed in a helium-filled, bronze-bound glass case for protection.

CONCEPTS TO BE TAUGHT

1. Independence Day, held on July 4, celebrates the United States' birth as a nation.
2. It commemorates the adoption of the Declaration of Independence by the Congress.
3. Symbols of our country's independence include our flag, the Liberty Bell, and the Statue of Liberty.

EXTENDED ACTIVITIES

1. FIRE CRACKER: Cover a small cardboard tube with red paper. Glue a short piece of string or yarn to one end for the fuse. Variation: Color or paint the cardboard tube, instead of using paper.

2. ROCKET: Decorate a cone-shaped cup with felt-tipped pens. Cut a narrow wedge that is 2" long from rim on opposite sides of cup. Insert an 18" string through the triangles. With cup pointing upward, pull sharply on ends of relaxed string. Cup will fly into the air. Variation: Regular paper cup can be used instead of cone-shaped cup.

3. ROMAN CANDLE: With crayons, decorate two long cardboard tubes. One tube should be slightly smaller in diameter so it will fit inside second tube. Place cotton balls inside larger tube. Push smaller tube through larger tube, and cotton balls will fly in the air.

4. CRACKER SNAPPER: Glue together two 6" squares cut from construction paper. Cut in half another 6" square of typing paper, to form two triangles. Match one triangle to corner of square. Tape along sides. Fold snapper in half through the center of triangle. With snapper folded, place corner opposite triangle between thumb and forefinger keeping the opened edge down. Snap the wrist quickly and triangle will pop out making a cracking sound.

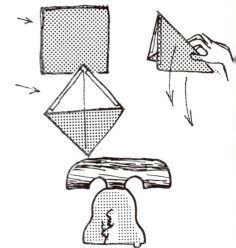

5. LIBERTY BELL: Cut a bell shape from a large piece of paper. Draw a jagged line to represent crack. Attach bell to a piece of brown paper that has been cut as shown in diagram.

6. FIRE CRACKER DESSERT: Stand half of banana on pineapple slice. Place stick pretzel in top of banana to make a "fuse."

7. FINGERPLAY:
   I'm a little fire cracker on the Fourth of July. (squat)
   Light my fuse and see me fly! (jump up)

8. LIBERTY BELL: Display a picture of the Liberty Bell and discuss:
   A. Written on the bell is the Biblical quotation, "Proclaim liberty throughout the land unto all inhabitants thereof."
   B. The Liberty Bell first cracked when it was tested on its arrival from England in 1752. It was recast in 1753.
   C. It was rung for every important occasion including July 8, 1776, when the Declaration of Independence was read to the public.
   D. It cracked again and was finally silenced on Washington's birthday in 1846.

9. STATUE OF LIBERTY: Display a picture of the Statue of Liberty and discuss:
   A. The Statue of Liberty is a symbol of our country's freedom.
   B. It was made by French sculptor Frederic Bartholdi and was given to the United States by the French government in 1884.
   C. It stands on Liberty Island in New York harbor.
   D. The statue is 150 feet high.

LABOR DAY

LABOR DAY, held the first Monday in September, is a legal holiday to honor all wage earners. The celebration was first proposed by Peter J. McQuire, President of the United Brotherhood of Carpenters and Joiners of America. Consequently, a parade was held in New York City by the Knights of Labor on the first Monday of September in 1882. Oregon was the first state to recognize Labor Day as a legal holiday in 1887. The idea spread to other states, and seven years later on June 28, 1894, the United States Congress made it a national holiday.

COLUMBUS DAY

COLUMBUS DAY, or Discovery Day, honors the discovery of America by Christopher Columbus in 1492. It was first celebrated in the United States in 1792 when President Benjamin Harrison declared October 12 for this holiday. Today it is a federal legal holiday held on the second Monday in October.

Christopher Columbus, an Italian explorer, left Spain on August 3, 1492, to reach India by sailing west. He had three ships: the Pinta, Nina, and Santa Maria. They sailed for 72 days and touched land at San Salvador on October 12, 1492. Columbus thought he had reached the East Indies, but he had really discovered two entirely new continents. It is generally believed that the Vikings landed in America 500 years earlier. Columbus's discovery, however, awakened interest in the Western Hemisphere.

CONCEPTS TO BE TAUGHT

1. Columbus Day celebrates the discovery of America by Christopher Columbus.
2. Columbus was a courageous explorer with vision, imagination, and determination.

EXTENDED ACTIVITIES

1. SHIP: Use half of a walnut shell for the ship. Place play dough in the bottom of the ship. Glue a triangular-shaped sail to a toothpick. Stick the toothpick into the play dough. Sail the ship in a pan of water. Try to navigate the ship by blowing on the sail.

2. COLUMBUS'S VOYAGE: Trace Columbus's journey from Spain to San Salvador on a globe. Discuss the voyage. It was a long tiresome journey for the 100 sailors of the Pinta, Nina, and Santa Maria. Weeks passed with no sight of land. The food, water, and supplies were almost gone. Most of the sailors were restless and wanted to turn back. Columbus cheered them by talking about the riches they would find in the Indies. Finally signs of land appeared. Branches with green leaves and red berries floated past the ships. They then saw in the distance LAND! Sailing closer, sandy beaches and green forests appeared. Columbus and the sailors thought they had arrived in India, but actually they had discovered America! Dramatize the voyage.

3. WATCH FOR SOMETHING NEW: Sit in circle. Discuss that sailors were on a ship for many days with nothing to see but water and sky. They were constantly watching for something different. Observe everyone in the circle: what they are wearing, how they are sitting, and where they are sitting. Place head in lap and close eyes. Adult changes something in the circle. Open eyes. What is different?
   Variation: Every day for a week take a walk or look out the same window. Discuss observations that were not noticed the previous day.

4. PINTA, NINA, AND SANTA MARIA: (Tune--"Here We Go Round the Mulberry Bush")
   I saw three ships come sailing by, come sailing by, come sailing by.
   The Pinta, Nina, and Santa Maria to find Japan, China, or India.
   Who's in the three ships sailing by, sailing by, sailing by?
   Some hundred sailors making a fuss and their fearless leader, Columbus.
   I saw three ships sight the land, sight the land, sight the land.
   Birds and branches gave them a clue on October twelfth, fourteen ninety-two.
   Sway to music as song is sung.

UNITED NATIONS DAY

UNITED NATIONS DAY, held October 24, is the anniversary of the United Nations being formed in 1945. It has been celebrated since 1948. The United Nations is an international organization of nations established to maintain world peace and security. It attempts to solve disputes between nations by peaceful means. The United Nations also deals with social and economic problems such as acquiring adequate food, clothing, shelter, child care, and education for those in need.

VETERANS DAY

VETERANS DAY is a legal holiday, that was observed on November 11 until 1971, when it was changed to the fourth Monday in October. It originated as Armistice Day in 1926 to commemorate the signing of the armistice on November 11, 1918, that ended World War I. It was renamed Veterans Day on June 1, 1954, by President Eisenhower to honor veterans of all wars.

GENERAL ELECTION DAY

GENERAL ELECTION DAY for national congressional elections occurs on the first Tuesday after the first Monday in November on every even-numbered year. Every four years on Election Day, people vote for the President and Vice-President of the United States, who are chosen by the electoral college. Many states, cities, and counties also elect officials on this date. Every United States citizen who is 18 years of age or over has the opportunity and responsibility to vote.

RELIGIOUS AND ETHNIC HOLIDAYS

This chapter includes RELIGIOUS AND ETHNIC HOLIDAYS that may be celebrated by certain groups of people in America. There are many customs and traditions associated with each holiday or festival. Therefore, the same feast may be celebrated in a variety of ways. This chapter is intended only as an overview of these holidays.

Holidays are arranged in chronological order within each religious or ethnic section. The religious holidays will be discussed in the following order: Buddhist, Christian, Hindu, Jewish, and Moslem. Many of the ethnic holidays are adapted from these religious beliefs. Other ethnic festivals are derived from nature and national or historical events and people. Some ethnic groups are more active in preserving the heritage of the land from which they or their ancestors came. However, every American, with the exception of the American Indian, has descended from a foreign ancestor and is a part of some ethnic group or groups. The ethnic groups included are American Indian, Black American, Canadian, Chinese, Dutch, English, French, German, Greek, Irish, Italian, Japanese, Mexican, Polish, Puerto Rican, Scandinavian, and Vietnamese.

BUDDHIST HOLIDAYS:

BUDDHISM was founded by Siddhartha Guatama, who is the "Buddha," or "Enlightened One." The main ideas of Buddhism are contained in statements known as the Four Noble Truths and the Eightfold Path. The Four Noble Truths are:
  A. There are sufferings in life.
  B. Suffering is caused by craving or grasping.
  C. Suffering ceases when one ceases to crave or to grasp. When a person reaches this condition, he is said to be enlightened, or to have attained Nirvana.
  D. The way or path to overcome the causes of suffering is the Eightfold Path.
      The Eightfold Path consists of right understanding, right thoughts, right speech, right conduct, right occupation, right effort, right mindfulness, and right meditation.
Approximately one-fifth of the world's population is Buddhist; however, many of these people also practice Confucianism or Taoism. Buddhism also consists of many sects with some so different that they appear to be separate religions. Therefore, there are no holidays that are generally celebrated by all Buddhists. Holidays depend on the ethnic background and particular sect. Examples of BUDDHIST HOLIDAYS can be located in JAPANESE FESTIVALS (see pages 222 to 223).

CHRISTIAN HOLIDAYS:

CHRISTIANITY is divided into three main groups: Protestant (consisting of many denominations), Roman Catholic, and Greek Orthodox. The religion, based on the teaching of Jesus Christ, focuses on three important events in His life: His birth, the Crucifixion, and the Resurrection. All Christians celebrate Christmas, which commemorates the birth of Jesus Christ in Bethlehem almost 2000 years ago, and Easter, which commemorates the death and Resurrection of Jesus. (Refer to previous CHRISTMAS and EASTER chapters for additional information.)

Some Christians also celebrate the following:
A.   THE FEAST OF CHRIST THE KING is celebrated on January 1.
B.   EPIPHANY, celebrated on January 6, is a remembrance of the Adoration of the Magi, Christ's baptism, and the Miracle of Cana, when Jesus turned water into wine.
C.   CANDLEMAS, celebrated on February 2, commemorates Jesus' presentation in the Temple of Jerusalem.
D.   LENT is a fasting period of forty days prior to Easter Sunday that begins with Ash Wednesday. Holy Week, the final week of Lent, is the most solemn week of the period. It begins with Palm Sunday, commemorating Jesus' triumphant arrival into Jerusalem for the celebration of the Jewish Passover. Thursday of Holy Week commemorates the celebration of the Last Supper of Jesus with His Apostles. Good Friday recalls the crucifixion and death of Jesus.
E.   ASCENSION, celebrated forty days after Easter, commemorates Jesus' ascension into heaven.
F.   PENTECOST, celebrated on the seventh Sunday after Easter, commemorates the descent of the Holy Spirit upon the Apostles.
G.   ADVENT is the four-week period of preparation before Christmas.
H.   OCTAVE OF CHRISTMAS is the eight days immediately following Christmas.

HINDU HOLIDAYS:

HINDUISM, which consists of many sects, is the religion of the majority of people in India. There are so many holidays and festivals associated with Hinduism that often two, three, and sometimes five holidays fall on the same day. All holidays are not celebrated by all sects, and the same holiday may be celebrated differently in different parts of India and in other countries. There are three kinds of Hindu holidays: holidays that honor the sun, moon, or stars; holidays that honor the gods; and holidays that honor spirits, plants, and animals. In all of India the cow, monkey, and snake are considered sacred.

The Hindu religion is based on three keys. These are:
A.   KARMA is the eternal law of life which says, "From good must come good, and from evil must come evil."
B.   AVATAR is the incarnation of a god in human form or the new form that the soul of a living thing may take after leaving its old form.
C.   TRIMURTI is the three-in-one god which rules the universe. The three gods are Brahma, the Creator; Vishnu, the Preserver; and Siva, the Destroyer. These gods have married and multiplied until there are now millions of gods, each ruling a special domain in the world.

HOLI

HOLI, or the Fire Festival, is a joyous spring festival that occurs in March. A week before *Holi*, children go from door to door collecting fuel for bonfires. On the evening of *Holi*, when the moon is high, bonfires are lit throughout India while people shout for joy, blow horns, and beat drums. Folk dances are performed around the fires. At sunrise water is poured on the embers to extinguish the fires. Everyone marks his head with ashes to bring luck for the coming year. The custom of lighting bonfires may be related to the destruction by fire of the wicked ogress Holika.

Also during this holiday, *Holi* players shower friends and passersby with liquid or powdered colors. Bamboo blowpipes or squirt guns are used. This appears to be related to the god Krishna, who was an incarnation of Vishnu. As a boy Krishna loved to play pranks on the milkmaids. They retaliated by squirting colored water at him.
Note: For extended activity, squirt paint outline of child. Fill dishwashing liquid bottle with water that is mixed with small amount of tempera. Prepare several colors. Adult draws outline of child who lies on large piece of butcher paper. Squirt outline with paint. After paint dries, cut outline of child from paper.

DURGA PUJA

DURGA PUJA, or the Festival of the Divine Mother, is a ten-day holiday which occurs in September and is celebrated chiefly in Bengal. The festival honors Durga, who is the wife of Siva and the goddess of war, power, and destruction. For many weeks before the holiday, modelers create life-size images of Durga from clay. These are placed in the shrines. Village women model smaller clay figures for household worship. *Puja* means worship, and for nine days the image of Durga is worshipped. On the tenth day all the images are carried through the streets in a serious procession and then set afloat in the rivers and streams which are also sacred to the Hindus. Eventually the images sink. During the festival a pageant called *Ram Lila* is presented every day. It is concerned with the events in the wars between Rama and Ravana, a cruel demon. Rama is an incarnation of Vishnu, who with Durga's assistance, destroyed Ravana and saved the world from destruction.
Note: For extended activity, create PLAY DOUGH (see page 84) figure of Durga.

DIVALI

DIVALI, also called the Festival of Lights, is an exciting Hindu holiday which occurs in October or November. It lasts for five days with each day celebrating a new and different holiday. During this festival houses are cleaned, and the walls are whitewashed. Good luck symbols are drawn on the doors and walls with colored powders. Business accounts are settled. New clothes are purchased and worn. Friends are entertained and daughters return home to visit their families.

Houses and buildings are decorated with lighted *diyas* in one of the most memorable customs of *Divali*. A *diya* is a little clay pot filled with oil that has a small wick inserted in the center. *Diyas* are placed so they outline roofs, doors, windows, and roads leading to houses. People who live along the river fasten lamps to little rafts and set them afloat. All of this is done to attract into the Hindu homes Lakshmi, who is the wife of Vishnu and the goddess of wealth and fortune. It is hoped she will leave her blessings when she visits.

EXTENDED ACTIVITIES

1. GOOD LUCK SYMBOL: With colored chalk, draw picture or symbol of good luck on piece of construction paper. Attach picture to door or wall.

2. CLAY *DIYA*: Make one or several *diyas* or pots from uncolored baking clay. Stand small birthday candle in center of each *diya*.
   Variation: Remove candle, place *diya* on shallow baking pan, and bake at 300° for 20 to 30 minutes or until dry. Paint. Replace candle in center of *diya*.

JEWISH HOLIDAYS:

JUDAISM is a monotheistic religion based on the Old Testament and the Talmud. Judaism is one of the oldest great world religions and is the mother religion of both Christianity and Islam. Jewish people trace their ancestry to the ancient Hebrews of the Bible. In the U.S., Judaism is divided into three groups: Orthodox, Conservative, and Reform. These groups may celebrate the same feast in a variety of ways. Dates for these holidays also vary, since they are determined by the Jewish lunar calendar. However, all Jewish holidays begin at sundown and end at sundown. With the exception of Hanukkah and Purim, no work is done on these holidays.

PURIM

PURIM is celebrated in February or March on the fifteenth day of Adar according to the Jewish lunar calendar. This feast commemorates the good Queen Esther and her cousin Mordecai, who saved the Jewish people from being destroyed by a wicked man named Haman. During Purim people gather in the synagogue to listen to the story of Purim, which is recorded in the Book of Esther. Whenever Haman's name is mentioned, the children stamp their feet and shake wooden rattles called *greggers*. Many legends which have been added are also related. Some parts are enacted in pageants and plays. Purim is also a time for giving gifts, holding carnivals and masquerades, and serving special cakes and sweets. *Hamantaschen*, a three-cornered tart usually stuffed with poppy seed filling, is traditionally served.

EXTENDED ACTIVITIES

1. *GREGGER*: Use white drinking cup that has plastic lid. Decorate cup with crayons or felt-tipped pens. Place several beans in bottom of cup and attach lid. If desired, a popsicle stick can be taped to side of cup for handle.
   Variation: Instead of cup, place beans in plastic egg container. Seal halves with glue and decorate with colored tissue paper dipped in liquid starch.

2. *HAMANTASCHEN*: 2 1/2 cups flour   1 egg
                    3 teaspoons baking powder   3/4 cup milk or water
                    1 teaspoon salt   1/3 cup butter, melted, cooled
                    1/4 cup sugar   purchased poppy seed filling
   Mix dry ingredients. Add liquid to egg. Pour egg mixture and butter into center of flour. Stir. Knead. Roll 1/4" thickness. Cut 3" circles. Place filling on each. Pinch edges of circle together leaving approximately 1/3 open to form cornucopia. Fold over flap and pinch these edges together. Place on greased cookie sheet, brush with egg yolk, and bake at 350° for 15 to 20 minutes.
   Variation: Place filling in center of biscuits. Fold and pinch edges.

3. PIN THE HAT ON HAMAN: For Haman, place picture of a man on wall. Each player with eyes closed or blindfolded attempts to pin a three-cornered hat on Haman.

4. PARADE: Participants parade as Queen Esther, wearing ROYAL CROWN (see page 216), Haman, wearing HAT (see page 187), or as soldiers.

PASSOVER

One of the major Jewish religious festivals is PASSOVER, or PASCH, which commemorates God's deliverance of the Hebrew people from slavery in Egypt as told in the Bible's Book of Exodus. It is celebrated for eight days in March or April on the fifteenth to twenty-second of Nisan according to the Jewish calendar. In the modern observance of this feast, the home must be thoroughly cleaned and rid of all leaven and leavened foods before Passover begins. The father of the family is responsible for this ceremony called *Bedikat Hametz*, The Search for Leaven. The father, accompanied by one of his children, makes an inspection of the house and gathers scraps of leavened bread that have been previously hidden.

The outstanding feature of Passover is a ceremony called the Seder, which means "an order of service." During the Seder the story of the first Passover is recalled. The story is read from the Haggadah and includes speaking parts, action parts, and songs for adults and children. The service also includes the Seder plate of roasted lamb shank, roasted egg, parsley, *charoses*, bitter herbs called *moror*, and unleavened bread called *matzoh*. Two of the *matzoh* are used in the ceremony and a third is hidden. Whoever finds it is given a reward which is then divided among everyone for good luck. The third *matzoh* is called *afikomon*.

CONCEPTS TO BE TAUGHT

1. Passover commemorates Moses leading the Hebrews to the Promised Land to begin a new life of freedom.
2. A special service called the Seder is held during Passover.

EXTENDED ACTIVITIES

1. PASSOVER SYMBOLS: Discuss the following symbols of Passover:
    A. LAMB SHANK recalls paschal lamb that was sacrificed and eaten by the Israelites on the eve of their flight from Egypt.
    B. ROASTED EGG is the symbol of life.
    C. *MATZOH* is unleavened bread. It represents bread that was made in haste and eaten at the first Passover meal.
    D. *MOROR*, bitter herbs, symbolize life of hardship undergone by Jewish people in bondage of Egypt. Horseradish is commonly used.
    E. PARSLEY symbolizes spring and growth. It is dipped in salt water to symbolize tears of the captive people.
    F. *CHAROSES* is a mixture of apples, nuts, and wine which represents mortar used to build cities for Pharoahs.
    During the Seder the above are served on the Seder plate and their symbolism is explained. A Seder plate can be prepared and served using the following: broiled lamb chops from which small pieces can be served, hard-cooked eggs, *matzoh* which can be purchased, horseradish, parsley, and *CHAROSES* (see page 3). Variation: Instead of actually serving the Seder plate, children can cut pictures of these foods from magazines and paste them on a paper plate.

2. LEAVENED OR UNLEAVENED: Discuss that leaven is a fermenting agent used to make batter or dough rise before or during baking. An example of leaven is yeast. Discuss the effect yeast has on bread. Compare *matzoh* to bread that has been made with yeast. Discuss the difference in color, texture, and taste.

3. SEARCHING GAMES:
   A. *BEDIKAT HAMETZ (THE SEARCH FOR LEAVEN)*: Hide pieces of bread in the room. Players search for bread and place it in a lunch sack.
   B. *AFIKOMON*: Hide a *matzoh* called *afikomon* and search for it.

SHAVOUT

SHAVOUT, The Holiday of Weeks, is celebrated on the sixth and seventh of Sivan, which occurs in May or June. The holiday celebrates the weeks that elapsed from the time the Hebrews left Egypt to the time Moses received the tablet of the law on Mount Sinai. *Shavout*, which literally means "weeks," is celebrated on the fiftieth day after the second day of Passover (the fiftieth day is the day after the completion of a week of weeks or 49 days). In a sense, this holiday completes Passover, when the Hebrews were freed from slavery in Egypt because on *Shavout* they were made into free men by the Ten Commandments. *Shavout* was first celebrated in biblical days at the conclusion of the grain harvest. Today in the synagogue, it is customary to read the Book of Ruth, which tells in part how the Hebrew farmer was instructed by God to leave a corner of his field and the gleanings for the poor. One custom associated with *Shavout* is the decorating of houses with plants and flowers. The greens recall the mountains of Sinai, where the commandments were given as well as fruits from the ancient harvest festival.

ROSH HASHANAH

The Jewish New Year is called ROSH HASHANAH, which is held the first of Tishri and occurs in September or October. It is regarded as the birthday of creation. It is the first day of a holiday period which lasts for ten days called the TEN DAYS OF REPENTANCE, which ends with Yom Kippur. Jewish people believe that each year on Rosh Hashanah God examines the Book of Life, in which every deed, word, and thought of each living person is recorded. On the basis of this record, the fate of each individual for the coming year is inscribed. For this reason people greet one another with the words, "May you be inscribed for a good year." The Jewish people also believe if a person repents during the days of repentance, his fate may be changed for the coming year. On this day services are held in the synagogue which begin with a blast of a trumpet made from a ram's horn. It is called the shofar and recalls God's providence. In many homes special prayers are announced over apples dipped in honey.
Note: For snack, serve apple sections dipped in honey.

YOM KIPPUR

YOM KIPPUR, the Day of Atonement, ends the Ten Days of Repentance and is the most solemn day of the Jewish year. It is held on the tenth of Tishri in September or October. It is a very serious day which includes fasting for adults, praying in the synagogue, and holding memorial services for the dead. At the conclusion the shofar is blown to signal the closing of the Book of Life. As they leave the synagogue, people greet one another saying, "May your fate be sealed for a good year."
206

SUCCOTH

SUCCOTH, also called the Feast of Booths, is celebrated in September or October and begins five days after Yom Kippur on the fifteenth of Tishri. It lasts for seven or eight days. It is a festival of thanksgiving for the harvest. A custom associated with this holiday is the building of a booth called a *succah* to commemorate the building of booths in the fields of Palestine so farmers would not have to return to their homes in the villages during the harvest. The *succah* is made of green branches which are decorated with flowers and fruit. It is built in a garden, or a porch, or on a roof. During the festival the family eats all meals in the *succah*.

The day after Succoth is called Simchath Torah. It is a happy day dedicated to the Five Books of Moses called the Torah. Simchath Torah means "rejoicing in the law." On this day the annual cycle of reading of the Torah is completed and begun. In the synagogue there is a procession in which scrolls are carried around the pews. The children carry flags, kiss Torah scrolls, and are given fruits and sweets.

EXTENDED ACTIVITIES

1. *SUCCAH* CENTERPIECE: Cut top and one side from milk carton. Cover remaining portion of carton with popsicle sticks. Decorate *succah* with small strips of tissue paper and flowers cut from magazines.

2. TORAH SCROLL: Color picture on 3 1/2" wide strip of paper. Glue a popsicle stick to each narrow edge of paper. Roll two sticks toward center to form scroll.

3. *SUCCAH*: Decorate corner of room with paper streamers that are covered with paper flowers and fruit. Use corner for creative play in a *succah*. Variation: Decorate and use large appliance box for *succah*.

HANUKKAH

HANUKKAH, also called the Festival of Lights, is celebrated for eight days beginning the twenty-fifth of the Hebrew month Kislev. This occurs in late November or December. It is a joyous festival commemorating a great victory won by the Jewish people more than 2000 years ago. At this time the Syrians, led by King Antiochus IV, had captured the country of Judea, forcing the Hebrews to worship the Syrian gods. The Syrians also seized the Jewish Temple of Jerusalem. A man called Judas Maccabaeus took command of a small army of Hebrews. In 165 B.C., after three years of fighting, the Jewish army--called the Maccabees--defeated the Syrians and recaptured the Temple, thereby winning religious freedom for the Jewish people. Once the Temple was regained, the Jewish people believed that it had to be purified before they could worship there. A legend states when it was time to light the Temple lamps for the rededication, there was enough sacred oil to burn only for one day. Miraculously, it burned for eight days.

Today Jewish families celebrate the miracle in the Temple by lighting one candle for each of the eight days of Hanukkah. A special candlestick called the *menorah* is used. During the modern celebration of Hanukkah, a characteristic food called *latkes*, or potato pancakes, is served. Houses are decorated with the traditional Star of David. Gifts are usually exchanged among family members on each of the eight days with the intent to spread light and joy. Many children receive a cubical top called a *driedel* as a Hanukkah gift.

CONCEPTS TO BE TAUGHT

1. Hanukkah commemorates the recapturing of the Temple of Jerusalem.
2. Hanukkah symbolizes religious freedom for the Jewish people.
3. One candle in the *menorah* is lit for each day of Hanukkah.
4. A nonreligious symbol of Hanukkah is the *driedel*.

EXTENDED ACTIVITIES

1. *MENORAH*: Glue nine straws in a row onto a piece of construction paper. The middle straw can be placed higher than the rest for the *shamash*. For flames, glue a small piece of orange pipe cleaner above each straw. Draw base of *menorah* with crayons or felt-tipped pens.

2. *DRIEDEL*: On a 4" cardboard square, draw a line from one corner diagonally to opposite corner. Draw another line from other corners to form an X. Adult writes each of the following letters on each triangle of square: N, G, H, S. Place pencil through intersection of X. When *driedel* spins, it will land on one of the four sides. (Refer to *DRIEDEL* INFORMATION for significance of letters. For use of *driedel* refer to *DRIEDEL* GAME on page 209.)

   Variation: Instead of cardboard square, use a half-pint milk carton whose spout has been folded to form a box. Cover box with tissue paper. Poke a pencil or dowel through center of carton. Adult writes one of the following letters on each side of the carton: N, G, H, S.

3. STAR OF DAVID: From blue paper cut two identical triangles. Glue to white paper inverting one over the other.
   Note: Blue and white are the colors of the Jewish flag.

4. EDIBLE *MENORAH*: Spread softened cream cheese on a slice of bread. For candles, arrange eight pretzel sticks in a row on bread leaving a space in the center. Place carrot stick in center for *shamash*. Use a raisin for each flame.

5. *LATKES*:   1 onion, grated   6 medium-sized potatoes, washed, pared, grated
                 1 teaspoon salt   3 tablespoons flour, *matzoh* meal, or bread crumbs
                 1 egg   1/2 teaspoon baking powder
   Add first three ingredients to potatoes and beat well. Mix remaining ingredients and beat into potato mixture. Drop by spoonfuls into hot oil. Brown on both sides. Drain. Serve with applesauce or sour cream.

6. *DRIEDEL* INFORMATION: The *driedel* is a four-sided top stamped with a Hebrew letter on each side. The letters are N or "nun," G or "gimel," H or "heh," and S or "shin." These letters represent the Hebrew words which mean, "A great miracle happened there." This is a reference to the miracle of the sacred oil which burned for eight days in the Temple of Jerusalem.

7. *MENORAH* INFORMATION: The *menorah* is a nine-branched candlestick made of wood, brass, silver, or gold. The first *menorahs* burned little pots of oil, but today candles are used. On the *menorah*, usually in the center and slightly higher than the other candles, is a place for the *shamash*. It symbolizes the man who is responsible to keep the candles lit in the synagogue. The *shamash* is lit first, and then it is used to light the other candles. Each night the candles are placed in the *menorah* from right to left using the required number of candles. One is used on the first evening with an additional one added on each of the succeeding seven days of the festival. The candles are lit from left to right beginning with the newly placed candle. New candles are used each night. Therefore, 44 candles are needed for Hanukkah.

8. *MENORAH*: (Group project) Glue eight wood or styrofoam spools of equal size to a piece of wood or cardboard strip leaving a space in the middle. Glue a larger spool in the middle. Spray with gold or silver paint. *Menorah* can be lit during eight days of Hanukkah. Place candle in center hole of each spool. (Refer to *MENORAH* INFORMATION for use.)

9. PIN THE FLAME ON THE *SHAMASH*: Draw on a large piece of construction paper a *menorah* and *shamash* with candles. Mount on wall. Cut several flames from orange construction paper. Each player with eyes closed or blindfolded attempts to pin or tape the flame above the *shamash*.

10. *DRIEDEL* GAME:

    See the *driedel* spin and spin: nun, gimel, heh, shin.
    Round and round watch it go. Where it lands no one can know.

    Each player starts with 10 to 15 pennies, nuts, or raisins. Each player places one object in the Pot. *DRIEDEL* (see page 208) is spun by one player while verse is recited. Whether spinning player wins or loses depends on which side of *driedel* lands upward when it falls. Use the following as a guide:

    N means *nisht* or nothing: player receives nothing from pot.
    G means *gantz* or all: player receives all objects in pot. Each player must then add two objects to pot.
    H means *halb* or half: player takes half of what is in the pot.
    S means *shtel* or put in: player adds two objects to pot.

    When one player has won all the objects, the game is over.

11. RECORD: "Hanukkah" from *Holiday Songs and Rhythms* by Hap Palmer, Educational Activities, Inc., Box 392, Freeport, New York 11520.

MOSLEM HOLIDAYS:

ISLAM is the religion of the Moslems. Mohammed is their Prophet. The Koran is the sacred book. Mecca is the most holy city. The Islam religion is based on the Five Pillars of Faith, which are:
  A. The duty to recite the creed: There is no god but Allah, and Mohammed is his Prophet.
  B. The duty to worship the One God in prayer five times a day.
  C. The duty to distribute alms and to help the needy.
  D. The duty to keep the Fast of Ramaden.
  E. The duty to make the pilgrimage to Mecca at least once in a lifetime.
The Moslems follow the lunar calendar strictly; therefore, holidays shift by eleven days per year. Any holiday can come in any season. Every 33 years a holiday will be celebrated on the same date according to the Gregorian calendar.

MUHARRAM

The first month of the Moslem lunar year is called MUHARRAM. It is also the name of a ten-day holiday which is the New Year. The Moslems believe that on the first day of Muharram, an angel shakes a lotus tree which grows on the boundary of Paradise. The tree has a leaf for every person in the world. The names on the leaves that fall off the tree are those who will die in the coming year. Therefore, the year begins with prayers for mercy and prayers for the dead. The people prepare for the New Year by pitching black tents and decorating them with flowers, swords, draperies, and lamps. Mourning clothes are worn. Everyone goes to the mosque for evening prayers and for reading from the Koran about death and life hereafter. Coins are often exchanged for good luck. Muharram also observes the death of Hussein, an early leader of Islam. Pageants and plays are held depicting the battle in which Hussein died.

ASHURA

ASHURA is held on the tenth day of the first month. It is the day that Moslems remember with great joy the landing of Noah's ark safely on dry land. According to legend, Noah asked his wife to prepare a pudding in celebration of their safe landing. She gathered nuts, dates, grapes, figs, currants, and prepared the best and largest pudding ever made. The pudding was called *ashura*. On this holiday a similar pudding is prepared and eaten by Moslems to express their thanksgiving for the sparing of the human race.
Note: Prepare and serve instant pudding.

THE PROPHET'S BIRTHDAY (MAULID AN-NABI)

MAULID AN-NABI commemorates the birthday of the Prophet Mohammed. Since the exact date of his birth is not certain, the date of Mohammed's death has been adopted as his birthday. It occurs on the eleventh day of the third month, *Rabi'u l-aw' wal*. It is a joyous holiday observed by all Moslems. However, it is celebrated differently in different countries. During the holiday the circumstances of his birth in Mecca and stories of the miracles which took place on that night are related. One legend tells that the mountains danced when Mohammed was born singing, "There is no God but Allah." The trees answered, "And Mohammed is his Prophet." Then 7000 angels brought a golden vase filled with heavenly dew to his mother, who bathed the baby in it. Many thousands of legends are retold about Mohammed.

RAMADAN

RAMADAN is the name of the ninth month of the Moslem calendar. During the entire month the Fast of Ramadan is observed as directed in the Koran. Eating and drinking are done either before sunrise or after sunset. The fasting commemorates the receiving of the Koran by Mohammed. The keeping of this fast is one of the Five Pillars of the Moslem faith. Ramadan is observed differently from one country to the next, but all Moslems take Ramadan very seriously. Much time is spent in the mosque in prayer and in reading the Koran. The end of the fast is celebrated for three days in a joyous holiday called *ID-AL-FITR*. New clothes are worn, parties are held, and gifts are exchanged by families and friends. In many cities fairs and games are held to mark the end of the Fast of Ramadan.

AMERICAN INDIAN CELEBRATIONS:

There are hundreds of AMERICAN INDIAN CELEBRATIONS, most of which have been performed in the same ways for many years. These ceremonials vary depending upon where the Indians live, the weather, and their own customs. The ceremonies are performed carefully according to rituals believed to have been handed down from the spirits. The dance or movement in the rituals is important to express a thought to the spirits. Among the Indian ceremonies are those for planting, growing, harvesting, thanksgiving, making rain, granting good health, and deliverance from evil. (Refer to THANKSGIVING chapter for additional information.)

AMERICAN INDIAN DAY

Today most states celebrate AMERICAN INDIAN DAY on the fourth Friday of September. To initiate this celebration, a Blackfoot Indian named Red Fox James rode horseback across the U.S. asking governors to adopt a special day to honor all American Indians. When he arrived in Washington, D.C., in 1914, he presented his idea to President Woodrow Wilson. New York State observed the first American Indian Day in 1914.

BLACK AMERICAN HOLIDAYS:

MARTIN LUTHER KING, JR.

January 15 is the birthday-anniversary of MARTIN LUTHER KING, JR. He is honored on this day for his nonviolent efforts to obtain equal social, political, and economical rights for all minority groups.
Note: Display picture of Martin Luther King, Jr. found in an encyclopedia or library book. Sing "Happy Birthday" to Martin.

KWANZA

KWANZA, which is observed by some black American families, begins on Christmas Day and lasts for a week. *Kwanza*, which means "fresh fruits," commemorates traditional African harvest festivals. Traditional celebrations included following symbols of togetherness: lighting candles called *mishumaas* and drinking from a unity cup called the *kikombe* at the final feast. Today the celebration includes daily parties with gifts given each day. The gifts are usually homegrown or homemade. The festivities conclude on New Year's Day with a community harvest feast or party. This holiday emphasizes the unity of the black family.

EXTENDED ACTIVITIES

1. SWEET POTATO DESSERT: 2 cups cooked sweet potatoes   4 eggs
                            2 cups cottage cheese   1/3 cup honey
                            1 teaspoon cinnamon
   Blend all ingredients until smooth. Pour into 8" x 8" baking dish. Set dish in pan of boiling water and bake at 325° for one hour. Serve chilled with whipped topping.

CANADIAN HOLIDAYS:

Many CANADIAN HOLIDAYS, such as Christmas and Halloween, are similar to United States' customs. Unique holidays celebrated in Canada include:
- A. APPLE BLOSSOM FESTIVAL is held for a week during late May or early June in the Annapolis Valley of Nova Scotia. It occurs when the delicately scented apple blossoms are in bloom. Festivities include a parade, a barbecue, dances, and crowning a queen. This traditional holiday originated in 1933.
Note: For extended activity cut large apple blossom from white construction paper. Color blossom with red and pink crayons.
- B. ST. JOHN'S DAY is celebrated by French Canadians in June to honor St. John the Baptist's birthday. During this holiday a parade is held. The most important feature is a float carrying a boy dressed as a shepherd who represents St. John. With the child is a lamb that has a ribbon and bow tied around its neck. The celebration is also accompanied with races and games.
Note: For extended activity draw float with boy figure. Glue piece of cloth to back of figure for cloak. Make lamb beside boy by gluing pieces of cotton to paper. Add legs with crayon.
- C. DOMINION DAY, held July 1, commemorates the day in 1867 when Canada became a nation and a member of the British Commonwealth. It is similar to the United States' Fourth of July with picnics, speeches, and colorful parades.
Note: For extended activity make Canadian flag. Glue 5" x 8 1/2" piece of white paper in center of 8 1/2" x 11" piece of red construction paper. In center of white strip, glue a maple leaf cut from red paper.
- D. BOXING DAY is celebrated on December 26. On this day wealthy people prepare boxes of gifts which are given to poor and needy people.
Note: Fill a box with fruits, old toys, and baked goods made by children. Decorate outside of box. Give box to a needy family.

CHINESE HOLIDAYS:

CHINESE NEW YEAR (YUAN TAN)

CHINESE NEW YEAR, the most important and merriest Chinese festival, is celebrated by Chinese all over the world. Its date, which falls between January 21 and February 19, is fixed according to the Chinese lunar calendar as the second new moon after the winter solstice. Traditionally the Chinese New Year is also considered everyone's birthday. It is especially exciting for the children because they receive presents of money in red envelopes. Red, the symbol of happiness, is used in decorations and presents for the New Year festivities.

No one knows when New Year celebrations originated in Chinese history. Tradition does involve removing bad luck from the old year and obtaining good luck for the next. Therefore, houses are thoroughly cleaned, all debts are paid, and businesses are closed. Also, new clothes are worn--especially new shoes--because it is bad luck to step on the ground wearing old shoes on New Year's Day. Window seals and door frames are decorated with red pieces of paper that have inscriptions to bring good luck. The old paper image of the Kitchen God is ceremoniously replaced with the new Kitchen God. On New Year's Eve a special feast is held. Special sweets and desserts are also prepared for the celebration. Traditionally the festivities lasted fifteen days until the Lantern Festival. The Lantern Festival is highlighted by a parade of elaborate paper lanterns led by a paper-covered dragon.

212

CONCEPTS TO BE TAUGHT

1. The Chinese New Year is the most important and happiest Chinese holiday.
2. It is a time to start anew with good luck.
3. Red is the Chinese symbol of happiness.

EXTENDED ACTIVITIES

1. NEW YEAR PRESENT: Draw picture denoting happiness. Place picture in red envelope or piece of red construction paper that is folded and stapled.

2. EGG DROP SOUP: 1/2 teaspoon salt   2 eggs, beaten
                   3 cups chicken broth   1/2 cup peas
   Pour chicken broth into saucepan and heat to boiling. Add beaten eggs and salt while stirring rapidly. Add peas and bring to boil. Serve hot.

3. PUFFED RICE BARS: 2/3 cup sugar   1 teaspoon vanilla
                      2/3 cup light corn syrup   2 tablespoons water
                      2 cups peanut butter   6 cups crispy rice cereal
   Combine sugar and syrup in saucepan and heat until mixture comes to a full boil. Remove immediately. Add peanut butter, water, and vanilla. Stir. Coat cereal with mixture. Pat into a 9" x 13" buttered pan. Cool.
   Note: Sweets denote joy, peace, and long life to the Chinese. These bars are actually an American version of a Chinese recipe which is made with rice syrup and puffed rice.

4. NEW YEAR'S GREETINGS: Teach children the following New Year's greetings:
   A. *Kung-Hi* (pronounced Kaw-ng Hee): I wish you joy.
   B. *Kung-hsi Fa-ts'ai* (pronounced Kaw-ng-hsee Fah-tsai): Happy greetings and may you gather wealth.

5. CHINESE NEW YEAR CELEBRATION: To remove bad luck, give room a thorough cleaning. Decorate doors and windows with red pieces of paper or ribbon. Place red tablecloth on table. Serve EGG DROP SOUP or PUFFED RICE BARS for New Year's Eve feast. Participants can exchange NEW YEAR PRESENTS and NEW YEAR'S GREETINGS.
   Variation: Instead of EGG DROP SOUP or PUFFED RICE BARS, purchased Chinese cookies or crackers can be served.

FESTIVAL OF LANTERNS (TENG CHIEH)

Traditionally the Chinese New Year ends with the FESTIVAL OF LANTERNS or *TENG CHIEH*. It is also called the Feast of the Full Moon. On the evening of *Teng Chieh*, people have a big parade of lanterns headed by a huge cloth or paper dragon that is carried on the shoulders of many men and boys. Included with the parade are fireworks and music made with gongs, cymbals, and drums. This gay celebration is also accompanied with religious ceremonies and dancing. It is mostly a festival for the amusement of the young.

The dragon is a Chinese symbol of strength and goodness. It is an imaginary animal that is considered one of four divine creatures which dispel evil spirits and therefore represents good fortune. At one time the dragon symbolized the Chinese emperor. Today it is used in art forms and for other celebrations.

CONCEPTS TO BE TAUGHT

1. The Festival of Lanterns ends the Chinese New Year celebration.
2. It is celebrated with a parade of lanterns led by a huge cloth or paper dragon.
3. The dragon is a Chinese symbol of strength and goodness.

EXTENDED ACTIVITIES

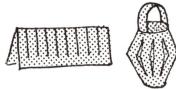

1. LANTERN: Fold piece of paper in half lengthwise.
    At inch intervals cut into fold to within 1" of
    opposite side. Open paper and tape or staple ends
    together. Attach paper handle to top of lantern.

2. DRAGON: Discuss that the dragon is a Chinese symbol of strength and goodness.
    Its appearance according to Chinese legend combines the head of a camel, the
    horns of a deer, neck of a snake, claws of a hawk, belly of a frog, and scales
    of a fish. Make a dragon as a group project. Draw dragon face on a large
    paper sack. Cut out eyes. Glue colored papers and streamers over entire head.
    For body, decorate a sheet with felt-tipped pens. Place paper sack over head
    and drape sheet over shoulders.

3. PARADE: A small group of children wears the DRAGON (listed above) and leads
    the parade by weaving back and forth through room or rooms. The remaining
    children hold LANTERNS (listed above) or beat home-made drums and follow the
    dragon.

CLEAR AND BRIGHT FESTIVAL (CH'ING MING)

In late March or early April the Chinese celebrate a spring festival called *CH'ING
MING*, or the CLEAR AND BRIGHT FESTIVAL. The three days before *Ch'ing Ming* are known
as *Han Shih* or "cold food" because no fires are lit and only cold food is eaten. On
the holiday Chinese people visit family burial grounds where graves are repaired and
decorated. A picnic is then held. People return home and start new fires in their
stoves. Although this is equivalent to Memorial Day, it is a joyous celebration.
On this day it is also customary for government officials to plant trees in public
ceremonies. Therefore, this holiday, which celebrates the coming of spring, is also
known as the First Feast of the Dead and as the Tree Planting Festival.

DRAGON BOAT FESTIVAL (TUAN WU)

During the summer the DRAGON BOAT FESTIVAL, or *TUAN WU*, is celebrated on the fifth
day of the fifth lunar month of the Chinese calendar. On this day the Chinese honor
the dragon by racing long narrow boats which look like dragons. The dragon, which
is a Chinese symbol of goodness and strength, is the giver of rain. He also rules
the rivers, lakes, and seas. Therefore, the Chinese seek favor from the dragon for
summer rains so their crops will not fail. A special food eaten during this festival is rice dumplings wrapped in dry grape leaves. These dumplings are also dropped
into the water to honor and feed the spirit of Ch'u Yuan of Ying, who protested for
better social conditions and less corruption during the third century until he
drowned himself as a martyr to the cause.
Note: For extended activity, have dragon boat races. Use a long piece of styrofoam
for base of boat. From paper cut head and tail of dragon. Decorate. Tape a
toothpick to head and tail. Stick into base. Race boats in container of water.

214

DUTCH HOLIDAYS:

TULIP FESTIVAL

In the middle of May, Dutch communities hold a TULIP FESTIVAL. One of the largest celebrations in the United States is in Holland, Michigan. This holiday centers around the tulips for which Holland is famous. During the celebration tulips are judged in tulip contests. Traditional Dutch costumes are worn. Folk dances are also performed which are called *Klompen* Dances because the dancers wear wooden boat-shaped shoes called *klompen*. Other activities include parades and street cleaning, which is done by women carrying willow brooms and water buckets hung from wooden yokes on their shoulders.

EXTENDED ACTIVITIES

1. TULIP: Hold fingers together on one hand. Place hand in bright-colored paint. Place hand onto paper. Dip side of hand into green paint and press onto paper to make stem. Repeat to make leaves. Display tulips on wall.

2. *KLOMPEN*: Cut boat-shaped shoes from paper. Decorate with chalk or crayons.

3. STREET CLEANING: Give participants brooms to sweep sidewalks. Participants can also "wash" sidewalk using brushes and containers filled with water.

DUTCH CHRISTMAS CUSTOMS

Saint Nicholas is the patron saint of Amsterdam. On December 5 someone portraying Saint Nicholas arrives by ship at the wharf amid the crowds of cheering people and the ringing church bells. At the port he mounts his white horse and is escorted through the streets by the mayor. The children believe Saint Nicholas rides over the roof tops on his horse and leaves presents to be opened on Saint Nicholas' Day, celebrated on December 6.

Christmas is a two-day holiday celebrated on December 25 and 26. It is a quiet family gathering. A fancy wreath-shaped pastry with almond paste inside and frosted with white icing and candied fruits is often enjoyed. Small presents are wrapped in many layers to disguise the contents and are given to family members. Christmas trees are usually decorated with a star and red apples which are tied to the branches.
Note: For extended activity wrap yarn or crepe paper around a trinket. Continue to wrap until a large ball is formed. Fasten end with a gummed star. This is a good gift for a child to give a friend or for an adult to give a child.

ENGLISH HOLIDAYS:

CORONATION OF KING OR QUEEN

In England the greatest celebration is the CORONATION OF A NEW KING OR QUEEN. The ceremonies are attended by people and dignitaries from all over the world who often wear native costumes. Parties, balls, and parades are held throughout England to honor the new royal leader.
Note: Make and wear ROYAL CROWN (see page 216).

GUY FAWKES DAY

GUY FAWKES DAY, also called Bonfire Day, is celebrated throughout England on November 5 to commemorate the failure of a plot against King James I. In 1605 Guy Fawkes and a group of conspirators attempted to blow up the House of Parliament with gunpowder to protest for religious freedom. Fortunately, Fawkes was caught as he was about to light the fuse. Today, Guy Fawkes Day is mainly a holiday for children and is similar to Halloween. Funny costumes are worn, parades are held, fireworks are lit, and bonfires are set ablaze. In many places straw dummies of Guy Fawkes are made which are sometimes burned. Traditionally, sweet potato pudding is served. Note: For extended activity, make sweet potato pudding. Combine the following: 2 cups boiled and mashed sweet potatoes, 2 cups grated raw sweet potatoes, 1 mashed banana, 1 tablespoon butter, 1 egg beaten, salt, brown sugar to sweeten, 1/2 teaspoon allspice, 1/2 teaspoon orange or lemon peel, flour to bind. Place in greased 8" x 8" pan. Bake 30 minutes at 350°.

FRENCH HOLIDAYS:

MARDI GRAS

MARDI GRAS is a carnival celebration which occurs in many Christian countries. The Mardi Gras in New Orleans originated when French Roman Catholics settled in Louisiana. In the southeastern United States the carnival season opens January 6, called the Twelfth Night. It climaxes during the final festivities on Shrove Tuesday, or Fat Tuesday, which is the French meaning of Mardi Gras. It is called Fat Tuesday because all meats and fats must be used before Lent begins. The Mardi Gras celebration is a time for feasting and fun before Lent, which is a solemn period of fasting and self-denial for many Christians.

The celebration includes parades and balls which are organized by social clubs whose sole purpose is to plan these events for the Mardi Gras. Each parade has bands, floats, and a king and queen. The parades usually follow a 15 mile course, with favors being thrown from the floats to watching crowds. As the carnival season progresses, more parades and balls are held each day. On the final day masks and costumes are worn by the general public until sundown, with the climax being the parade of the Comus Club in the early evening. Mardi Gras festivities also include games, races, folk dances, songs, and theatrical productions.

CONCEPTS TO BE TAUGHT

1. Mardi Gras is a carnival celebration which occurs in the southeastern United States.
2. It is a festive and fun-filled celebration which occurs before Lent.

EXTENDED ACTIVITIES

1. ROYAL CROWN: Use a strip of construction paper. Cut points along one side of strip. Decorate strip with gummed stars, felt-tipped pens, crayons, or glitter. Adjust to fit head and staple ends.

2. NEW ORANGE PANCAKES: 4 eggs   4 cups flour   1/2 teaspoon salt
                           1/2 cup oil   1/2 teaspoon soda   3 cups orange juice
    Beat eggs and oil. Add dry ingredients to mixture. Gradually add orange juice
    while mixing. Cook pancakes in an oiled, medium-hot, frying pan. Serve with
    syrup, honey, yogurt, or sour cream.
    Note: Long ago in England pancakes were made and eaten on Shrove Tuesday, so
    it became known as Pancake Day.

3. RASPBERRY LEMONADE: Place 6 ounces frozen lemonade concentrate, 5 ounces
    frozen raspberries, and 4 cups water in blender. Blend and serve cold.
    Note: Often before the children's parade, which is held on the Saturday before
    Mardi Gras, raspberry lemonade is served if the weather is warm. If it is
    cool, hot chocolate is served.

4. FINGERPLAY #1:
        The Mardi Gras is fun.
        We eat, dance, and in the races run. (pretend to eat, dance, run)
        There's a big parade with a band.
        When the queen and king pass, we all stand. (stand)

5. FINGERPLAY #2:
        There is a parade today.
        Here comes the band: make way. (spread arms wide)
        A whistle the leader blows; (pretend to blow)
        A baton twirls--into the air it goes. (look upward)
        The flutes go toot, toot. (pretend to play flute)
        The cymbals go crash, crash. (clap hands)
        The tuba goes omph, omph! Toot! Crash! Omph!
        The people are cheering and clapping. (clap hands)
        I can't stop my feet from tapping. (tap feet)

6. PARADE: Decorate tricycles and wagons with crepe paper. The queen and king
    can wear ROYAL CROWNS (see page 216) and can be pulled in wagons. A band using
    home-made instruments can be added. Parade through rooms or outdoors.
    Variation: Instead of decorating tricycles and wagons, walk with streamers.

7. COSTUME BALL GAME: Players can dress in ROYAL CROWNS (see page 216), tie
    scarves around shoulders, or use costumes. Half of group sits on chairs facing
    center of circle. Remaining players march around outside of circle to music.
    When music stops, sitting players stand, turn around, and curtsy as other
    players bow. Music begins and game is repeated.

BASTILLE DAY

BASTILLE DAY, observed on July 14, commemorates the capturing by the French people
on July 14, 1789, of the infamous French prison, the Bastille, which held many
political prisoners during the French Revolution. The prisoners were freed, and the
prison was destroyed. This success led to French democracy and independence from
absolute monarchies in France. Today it is a joyous celebration which includes huge
parades, firework displays, carnivals, and dances.
Note: For extended activity, make French flag. Use
8 1/2" x 11" piece of white construction paper, 3 5/8" x
8 1/2" piece of blue paper, and 3 3/8" x 8 1/2" piece of
red paper. Glue blue strip to right side of white paper.
Glue red strip to left side of white paper.

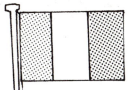

GERMAN HOLIDAYS:

NEW YEAR CUSTOMS

The Germans feel the first day of the NEW YEAR should be lived as every day of the year. The homemakers clean their homes, and the family members wear their best clothes. Traditionally a family meal is held during which roast suckling pig or pork roast is served. It is followed by visiting family and friends and wishing them good luck in the new year.

MAY DAY

On MAY DAY every town has a May pole which is made of a pine tree with all its branches removed. A wagon wheel is hoisted to the top of the tree, and strips of paper are suspended from the wheel. Children then dance around the May pole. The pole remains standing throughout the entire month of May. On this day May baskets are made and presented to mothers.

EASTER

Prior to EASTER the German people hold a celebration called *Fasching*, which is similar to Mardi Gras. It lasts from January 6 to Ash Wednesday. Lent is then observed until Easter. The Thursday evening before Easter, fires are extinguished in German homes. On Saturday a fire is started by the priest, and a flame is carried to each house to relight the fire. In preparation for Easter, children build a nest hoping the Easter bunny will fill it. The nest is filled with eggs, some of which are hand-painted with traditional patterns and others with verses written on them. On Easter Sunday some of the eggs are taken to church to be blessed.
Note: For extended activity, use a symbol for the group or each child. For example, symbol can be child's initial. Write symbol on hard-cooked egg with white or yellow crayon. Dye egg. Refer to DYED EASTER EGG (see page 107).

OKTOBERFEST

OKTOBERFEST originated with King Ludwig's wedding in 1810. It is an autumn festival that is held in Munich. It occurs in October and lasts for 16 days. During this carnival celebration, tents are built in the center of the city. People dress in colorful, historical German costumes. Horsedrawn wagons carry food and drink. The festivities include feasting, singing, and dancing to the tunes of the Bavarian Brass Band. People also enjoy games, plays, and athletic events.

ST. MARTIN DAY

On November 11 the German people celebrate ST. MARTIN DAY in honor of St. Martin, who was a friend of children and the poor during the fourth century. On this day children parade through the streets carrying lights or pumpkin lanterns. After the parade a doughman gives each child pretzel dough which is formed into a man that represents St. Martin.
Note: For extended activity, create pretzel man. Spread peanut butter on graham cracker. On peanut butter create stick man with thin pretzels.
218

GERMAN CHRISTMAS CUSTOMS

The Christmas season is the happiest holiday for the German people. On the evening of December 5, children set their shoes in a special place. When they awake the next morning on Saint Nicholas Day, the shoes are filled with cookies, candy, nuts, and one special toy. The advent wreath originated with the German Lutherans. On each of the four Sundays before Christmas, one candle is lit in the wreath as the family joins in saying a prayer, reading a scripture, and singing carols. Traditional holiday foods include *pfefferkuchen*, or gingerbread, and *Weihnachtsstollen*, also called *stollen*.

EXTENDED ACTIVITIES

1. CHRISTMAS SHOES: Draw shoes on a piece of paper. Fill shoes with pictures cut from catalogs or magazines. Pictures can include food and one special toy.

2. GINGERBREAD: Make gingerbread following directions on packaged mix. Serve with whipped cream for snack.

3. *STOLLEN*: Use loaf of frozen raisin bread which is thawed. Roll dough into an oval that is 1/2" thick. Spread half of oval with soft butter. Mix 1/4 cup sugar and 2 teaspoons cinnamon. Sprinkle mixture over butter. Fold unspread half over sugar and cinnamon half. Place on greased baking sheet. Curve ends to form a crescent shape. Press down on the folded edge. Cover and allow to rise for 2 to 6 hours. Bake at 375° for 20 minutes or until lightly browned. Frost with 3/4 cup powdered sugar and 1 tablespoon milk mixed together. To decorate add cherries and nuts to top of frosting.

SAINT SYLVESTER DAY

On SAINT SYLVESTER DAY, celebrated December 31, Germans sing songs of thanksgiving. Punch is served with jelly-filled doughnuts. For fun some doughnuts are filled with mustard. Later in the evening, family members have a ceremony which consists of holding a lump of lead in a spoon over a lamp. When the lead melts, it is dropped into cold water. An adult is selected to be the fortune teller who predicts the future from the shape of the cooled lead. Today many families use wax instead of lead.

EXTENDED ACTIVITIES

1. JELLY-FILLED DOUGHNUTS: Thaw frozen sweet roll dough. Place individual balls of dough on a cookie sheet. Flatten each ball into a rectangle that is 1/4" thick. Place jelly on center of rectangle. Fold rectangle in half. Pinch open sides of dough together. Doughnuts can be deep-fat fried or baked on greased cookie sheet for 10 to 15 minutes at 375°.

2. FORTUNE TELLING: Adult drops a spoonful of melted wax into cold water. One child describes what the shape of the wax looks like. Glue wax to a piece of paper with child's interpretation written on the paper. Repeat for each child in the group.

GREEK HOLIDAYS:

There is a GREEK HOLIDAY celebrated almost every day, except during Lent. These celebrations are usually accompanied with folk dancing. Most people in Greece are Greek Orthodox. Therefore, feast days of the church as well as various saints' days are often celebrated. Every town has a patron saint who is honored with a festival called *Panegyri*. On the night of a village's festival, people dress in their finest clothes to attend church services which are followed by dancing and singing. Traditionally, Greek people are named after saints. A Greek person might celebrate his saint's day as well as his birthday.

ST. BASIL'S DAY

ST. BASIL'S DAY, celebrated January 1, honors St. Basil, who is one of the four founders of the Greek Orthodox Church. He is also considered Greece's Santa Claus. Therefore, gifts are given on this day. Traditionally served on this holiday is St. Basil's bread, which is called *vasilopitta*. A coin is hidden in the bread, and the family member who finds it in his slice is assured good luck for the coming year.

EPIPHANY

On EPIPHANY, celebrated January 6, an official of the Greek Orthodox Church blesses the fishing fleet and the waters. In some seaports a cross is thrown into the water by the priest. Men and boys dive for the cross, and the one who retrieves it receives a special blessing from the priest. The fleet is then ready to sail. After the ships sail, the priest blesses those gathered and their homes with water. This festival occurs on the southeastern seaboard of the United States where shrimp boats are blessed.
Note: For extended activity, place popsicle crosses in water. To make cross, glue two popsicle sticks together. Color cross with crayons. Place several different colored crosses in water. Child removes designated color of cross from water.

EASTER

EASTER is the most widely celebrated Greek holiday. Before Easter is Lent, which is preceded with a four-week celebration of feasting, masquerade parties, and parades. The first day of Lent is called Clean Monday. After this day Greeks fast until Easter. On Easter Eve, at the conclusion of the candlelight church service, the priest announces, "Christ is risen." The congregation responds, "Yes, He has truly risen." Everyone attending the service then carries a lighted candle home. To arrive home with a candle that is burning means good luck. On Easter Sunday there is much celebration with roasted lamb, wine, red Easter eggs, and *magaritsa*, which is an Easter soup. Red symbolizes the blood of Christ. Families crack the eggs to allow blessings to come forth. Traditionally, a bread is made which has a hard-cooked red egg baked on top of the dough.

EXTENDED ACTIVITIES

1. EASTER EGG CUSTOM: Use red-dyed Easter Eggs. One child holds egg on table and says, "Christ is risen." Another child cracks egg saying, "Yes, He has truly risen." Egg is then shelled and eaten.

2. EASTER BREAD: Thaw frozen sweet bread dough. Form into three balls. Place
    balls on greased baking sheet forming a three-leaf clover. Place red Easter
    egg in center. Cover and allow to rise for 2 to 6 hours. Bake 20 minutes at
    375°. Remove from baking sheet and cool on rack. When cool, frost with 3/4
    cup of powdered sugar and 1 tablespoon milk. Add almonds and cherries to top
    of frosting.
    Note: The three small loaves baked as one larger loaf represents the Trinity.
    When the bread is served, each person receives a slice from each small loaf.

GREEK CHRISTMAS CUSTOMS

The Greek people consider Christmas to be basically a religious holiday and a family
feast. There are no Christmas trees or exchanging of presents, but children do
receive cookies, sweets, almonds, walnuts, figs, and sometimes money. On Christmas
Eve it is believed that the *Kallikantzari*, or goblins, come to play tricks on
people. The *Kallikantzari's* fun ends on January 6, when a priest tosses a cross
into the water. The goblins run back to their huts. To insure none are hiding, the
priest goes from door to door sprinkling water to bless the people's homes.

IRISH HOLIDAYS:

The most widely celebrated IRISH HOLIDAY is ST. PATRICK'S DAY, held on March 17.
(For additional information refer to page 189.)

ITALIAN CELEBRATIONS:

Many ITALIAN CELEBRATIONS center around religious holidays and saints' days. On
these festive occasions there is much visiting, eating of traditional Italian foods,
and street dancing. Italians also celebrate:
  A. VERRAZANO DAY, on April 17, commemorates the birthday of Giovanni da Ver-
      razano, an Italian navigator who recorded his explorations of the eastern
      seacoast of the United States in 1524.
  B. FEAST OF CORPUS CHRISTI, which occurs 60 days after Easter, is highlighted by
      beautiful processions where young girls spread flowers in the path of the Holy
      Eucharist, which is carried through the streets.
  C. REPUBLIC, OR CONSTITUTION DAY, on June 2, recalls the Italian vote that abol-
      ished monarchy and established democracy on June 2, 1946.
      Note: For extended activity, make an Italian flag.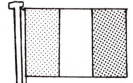
      Use a 8 1/2" x 11" piece of white construction
      paper. Attach 8 1/2" x 3 1/2" piece of green paper
      to left side of white paper. Attach 8 1/2" x 3
      1/2" piece of red paper to right side of white
      paper.
  D. COLUMBUS DAY, on the second Monday of October, is celebrated with particular
      pride because Columbus was an explorer from Genoa, Italy. (For additional
      information refer to page 199.)
  E. *PALIO* is a horse race with riders that are dressed in medieval costumes. It
      occurs twice yearly in the Italian city of Siena. It also includes banquets
      and parades with people dressed in traditional costumes.

JAPANESE FESTIVALS:

JAPANESE NEW YEAR (OSHOOGATSU)

OSHOOGATSU, or JAPANESE NEW YEAR, which begins on January 1 and lasts for three days, is the greatest Japanese holiday. It is also considered everyone's birthday. Preparations include a thorough housecleaning that must be concluded before New Year's Eve so good spirits will not be swept away. Doors and gateways are decorated with traditional symbols: *kado-matsu* (pine and bamboo boughs that represent long life and happiness) and *shime-nawa* (rice-straw rope for protection from harm and evil). Businesses are closed and all debts are paid. On New Year's Eve adults stay awake to hear a special gong ring 108 times symbolizing the cleansing of 108 human weaknesses described in the teachings of Buddha. On New Year's Day new clothes are worn, and children receive gifts which are usually coins in special envelopes. Families have a New Year's feast that includes traditional festive rice cakes called *omochi*. In the afternoon children fly kites and play battledore which is similar to badminton. January 2 is called *kakizome*, which means "first writing." On this day every member of the family writes a poem or proverb. On January 4, stores are reopened and food deliveries are made in trucks with banners.
Note: For extended activity, have New Year celebration. Give room a thorough cleaning. Decorate doors with *kado-matsu*. Place a pine bough on both sides of the door. Place a rope along top of door for the *shime-nawa*. Sing "Happy Birthday" to everyone in group. Give each person a coin in an envelope. Have each child create a poem or saying as adult writes it on piece of paper.

GIRLS' DOLL FESTIVAL (HINA MATSURI)

On March 3, the Japanese celebrate *HINA MATSURI*, or GIRLS' DOLL FESTIVAL. It is also called the PEACH BLOSSOM FESTIVAL because peach blossoms often bloom during this time. On this day doll collections used only for this festival are displayed on a rack of shelves covered with red cloth. Many of the dolls are family heirlooms that often include the emperor, his empress, and their attendants. Furniture, trees, and a branch of a flowering peach are also displayed. The peach blossom symbolizes happiness in marriage, as well as mildness, softness, and peacefulness, which are qualities many girls strive to acquire. Young girls and their mothers dress in party kimonos and go visiting during this festival to admire doll collections and have refreshments which often include tea and rice cakes. It is believed that this is a lucky day to marry.
Note: For extended activity, display dolls and have refreshments. Cover shelves with red cloth or paper. Every boy and girl brings a doll, small piece of furniture, or branch from a tree to display on shelves. Invite other children to view collections. For refreshments serve rice cakes or rice crackers which are available at Japanese food stores.

FLOWER FESTIVAL (HANA MATSURI)

HANA MATSURI, or FLOWER FESTIVAL, celebrated on April 8, is the birthday-anniversary of Gautama Buddha, founder of Buddhism. On this day people visit the shrines dedicated to Buddha and decorate them with fresh flowers. The feature of the day is the ceremony of bathing Buddha with *amacha*, a sweet tea prepared from hydrangea leaves. Children wear white face powder to appear clean and fresh to Buddha.
Note: For extended activity, powder face with white powder. Discuss Japanese custom. Look in mirror to observe appearance.

BOYS' FESTIVAL (TANGO-NO-SEKKU)

BOY'S FESTIVAL, or *TANGO-NO-SEKKU*, is observed by Japanese on May 5, which is the fifth day of the fifth month on the lunar calendar. It is also known as the FEAST OF THE FLAGS and the KITE FESTIVAL. For this occasion a paper or cloth carp kite or banner is purchased for each son, with the largest for the oldest and progressively smaller ones for each younger son. The carp are hung on bamboo poles outside the home with the largest at the top followed by progressively smaller kites. The carp symbolizes perserverance, strength, and bravery which are qualities young men strive to achieve.

Boys' Festival is held on the same date as CHILDREN'S DAY. It was established by the Japanese government to encourage boys and girls to respect and love each other. On the morning of these festivals, the family traditionally takes a special bath called *shobu-yu* to wash away bad spirits and bad luck. Many young children are then taken to a Shinto shrine where a priest asks for their health and happiness. Afterward a special meal is prepared including the children's favorite sweets.

EXTENDED ACTIVITIES

1. CARP KITE: Fold large piece of butcher paper in half lengthwise. Draw fish as shown in diagram. Cut and unfold fish. Color. Fold mouth twice and staple. Fold fish in half lengthwise. Staple cut edges together leaving mouth open. Leave cut edge unstapled about 4" from mouth until stuffing is completed. Stuff fish with newspaper. Staple. Tie string to mouth of fish. Attach string to pole.
Variation: Instead of butcher paper, use colored comic pages.

2. *SHOBU-YU*: Discuss that *shobu-yu* is special bath with water containing cut iris leaves. Place iris leaves and water into large container. Bathe dolls.

FESTIVAL OF LANTERNS (BON MATSURI)

On *BON MATSURI*, or FESTIVAL OF LANTERNS, which occurs in mid-July, Buddhists honor family members who have died. On the first day lanterns are taken to cemeteries to guide spirits back to earth for the festival. Food offerings are made to the spirits. On the third and final day, farewells are said to the spirits as tiny lantern-boats are set afloat on lakes and in the sea. *Bon Matsuri* is a joyous celebration with dancing and singing.
Note: For extended activity, make LANTERN (see page 214).

JAPANESE NATIONAL HOLIDAYS

JAPANESE NATIONAL HOLIDAYS include the following:
   A. CONSTITUTION DAY, on May 3, commemorates the day Japan became a democracy.
   Note: For extended activity, make Japanese flag. Glue 5" red circle to center of 8 1/2" x 11" piece of white construction paper.
   B. LABOR-THANKSGIVING DAY, celebrated on November 23, honors all workers. Also people give thanks for what they have.
   C. PEACE FESTIVAL is a solemn ceremony which honors those killed at Hiroshima in 1945. On this day prayers are said for world peace.

MEXICAN FIESTAS:

CINCO DE MAYO

CINCO DE MAYO, meaning May 5, celebrates the day the Mexican army, led by General Ignacio Zaragoza, defeated an invasion of French forces in Puebla, Mexico. The festivities include a parade of people dressed as Mexican and French soldiers. Later in the day a mock battle occurs between the soldiers. The battle climaxes when the two commanding generals meet in face-to-face combat with swords, and the Mexican wins. The celebration ends with a giant display of fireworks. This day is also celebrated by Mexican Americans with *mariachi* bands, dancing, feasting, crowning a queen, and piñatas for the children.
Note: For extended activity, make PIÑATA (see page 225).

MEXICAN INDEPENDENCE DAY

MEXICAN INDEPENDENCE DAY commemorates September 16, 1810, when a priest named Miguel Hidalgo issued the first call for Mexican independence in a small town of Dolores, Mexico. Hidalgo shouted from the pulpit, *"Viva la Independecia! Viva Mexico!"* and the struggle for freedom from Spain began. Although Mexico did not win independence until 1821, which was eleven years after Hidalgo's call, he became a national hero. He is remembered as the Father of the Mexican Revolution. The town of Dolores was renamed Dolores Hidalgo in his honor.

To begin this celebration, the president of Mexico appears on the balcony of the National Palace at 11:00 p.m. on September 15. After the ringing of an historic church bell, he shouts Hidalgo's words, *"Viva la Independecia! Viva Mexico!"* People in the square respond with *"Viva!"* Confetti and paper streamers are thrown in the air, and there is an elaborate fireworks display. After the night of celebrating, September 16 is considered a day of rest.
Note: For extended activity, ring bell and have one child say, *"Viva la Independecia! Viva Mexico!"* Remaining children respond, *"Viva!"* Wave crepe paper streamers. Explain that the saying means "Long live the Independence."

OUR LADY OF GUADALUPE DAY

OUR LADY OF GUADALUPE DAY, held December 12, honors the Virgin of Guadalupe, which is the patron saint of all Mexico. It commemorates the Holy Virgin's appearance to Juan Diego in 1531. She told Diego that she wished a church to be built on Tepeyac Hill, which had previously been a holy place to the Aztecs. It symbolized that the hill could still be considered holy to the Indians as Christians and that Christianity was replacing the Aztec religion. To make the bishop believe Juan, the Virgin Mother instructed him to pick roses on the hill where they normally would not grow. When Juan opened his cloak to show the bishop the roses, a picture of the Holy Virgin appeared on the rough cloth of the cloak. This miracle convinced the bishop, and on the hill a church was built in which Juan's cloak was placed.

Today this is the greatest religious fiesta in Mexico. Thousands of people make a pilgrimage to a cathedral at Tepeyac Hill called the Bascilica of Our Lady of Guadalupe. They crowd into the church and square, buy curios and holy objects, make vows, leave offerings, light fireworks, play music, and dance. Many of the dances relate to ancient Aztec dances. For those who cannot make the pilgrimage, special masses on the Day of Our Lady of Guadalupe are held in churches throughout Mexico.

MEXICAN CHRISTMAS CUSTOMS

Many Mexican and Mexican-American families celebrate Christmas from December 16 to January 6. The period of nine days before Christmas is the celebration of the POSADA, which commemorates Joseph and Mary's journey and search for lodging in Bethlehem. On each of these nights, a group of people carrying candles parades through the streets led by two children holding statues of Mary and Joseph. The procession goes from house to house seeking shelter that cannot be found until the group enters the home of the family appointed to host the posada. They place the statues in a manger scene. The hosts then provide refreshments and a piñata. On the ninth night which is Christmas Eve, known as *Noche Buena*, or the Good Night, a statue of the Baby Jesus is added to the manger scene. After this last posada, midnight mass is attended.

Christmas Day itself is quiet with no exchanging of gifts or special activities except for church services. However, on January 5, children leave their shoes usually stuffed with straw near an open window or outside the door. On the morning of January 6, known as the DAY OF THE THREE KINGS, the straw has been replaced with presents in and around the shoes. On this day, also known as EPIPHANY, or TWELFTH NIGHT, a piñata is broken and a special ring cake called *La Rosca de Reyes*, or The Circle of Kings, is often served. One child finds a small doll in his piece of cake which was mixed with batter. The child keeps the doll but in return has a party on February 2, which is the Day of the Candlemas. The Feast of the Three Kings is the climax of the Christmas season for the children. It recalls the visit of the Wise Men to Bethlehem to bring gifts to the baby Jesus.

CONCEPTS TO BE TAUGHT

1. Many Mexican and Mexican-American families celebrate Christmas from December 16 to January 6.
2. Most of the Christmas celebrations are accompanied with a piñata for the children.

EXTENDED ACTIVITIES

1. PIÑATA: Stuff a large brown sack with newspapers, candies, and peanuts. Tie a string around the open end of the bag, leaving enough sack for a tail. Glue eyes to bottom of sack. Decorate with streamers and colored scraps of paper to make fish piñata. Variations:
   A. Individual piñatas can be made with lunch sacks.
   B. Refer to PAPIER MÂCHÉ JACK-O'-LANTERN (see page 26).

2. BREAKING THE PIÑATA: Discuss that a piñata is usually made of clay or papier mâché that has various forms and shapes. It is filled with candy and treats. The piñata is then hung from the ceiling. Children sit a safe distance away from the piñata. One player is handed a plastic bat or broomstick, turned around three times, and given three attempts to break the piñata. Repeat until the piñata is broken and everyone receives a treat. If desired, blindfold older children.

3. *BURRITOS*: 1 pound ground beef   16 ounces refried beans   flour tortillas
   Fry ground beef. Drain. Add beans. Heat mixture. Place three tablespoons of mixture on tortilla. Roll tortilla. Serve.
   Variation: Shredded lettuce, grated cheese, and chopped tomatoes can be added.

POLISH HOLIDAYS:

POLISH HOLIDAYS include:
A. EASTER includes Polish customs of church services and egg decorating which are similar to customs in America. However, children do celebrate Easter Monday by throwing water on one another which is a game called *smigus*.
B. WARSAW UPRISING DAY, celebrated on August 1, commemorates that day in 1944 when Polish people liberated Warsaw from Nazi occupation.
C. PULASKI DAY is celebrated on October 11 with parades and memorial dinners. It commemorates Count Casimer Pulaski, a Polish officer, who fought with the forces of George Washington and was killed.
D. CHRISTMAS is celebrated on Christmas Eve with the traditional *Wilia* supper, in which no meat but many courses are served. It begins as soon as the first star is seen in the sky with a ceremony that symbolizes love and peace. When the meal is over, the candles on the Christmas tree are lit and presents are exchanged. Christmas is a special time for family togetherness.
Note: For extended activity, hide paper stars in room. Prior to snack, hunt for stars. When first star is found, snack is served.

PUERTO RICAN HOLIDAYS:

PUERTO RICAN HOLIDAYS include the main United States holidays plus some traditional fiestas and saints' days. Every city and village has its own saint's celebration. Examples are:
A. In San Juan people celebrate the festival of the patron saint John the Baptist, by dancing in the streets. On St. John's Day Eve, June 23, they go for a midnight swim. The swim is supposed to bring good luck for the year.
B. The festival of Loiza Aldea honors Saint James of Santiago on July 25 to 28. Religious processions are mixed with masquerades, parades, street music, and dancing.

PUERTO RICAN CHRISTMAS CUSTOMS

The week before CHRISTMAS, young people go caroling in the morning to announce the news of the Magi. For musical instruments they use rhythm sticks, maracas, and *guiros*. A *guiro* is a dried, hollow gourd about 15" long with horizontal lines scratched on it. To produce music the *guiro* is scraped with a three-pronged wire fork. On January 5th, Three Kings Day Eve, children place shoe boxes filled with grass under their beds. When they awake on January 6, the grass is gone and there are presents left by the three kings. A traditional food served during the Christmas holidays is *arroz con gandures*, or Spanish rice, which includes rice, pork, and beans.

EXTENDED ACTIVITIES

1. *ARROZ CON GANDURES*: Prepare box of Spanish rice according to package directions. Add cooked pinto beans and small pieces of sauteed link sausage.

2. CAROLING: Go caroling using musical instruments which include rhythm sticks, maracas, and *guiro*. Maracas can be made by placing beans inside plastic container. For handle, tape stick to side. Use cheese grater and fork for *guiro*.

SCANDINAVIAN HOLIDAYS:

SCANDINAVIAN HOLIDAYS include:
A. NORWAY'S CONSTITUTION DAY, on May 17, marks the establishment in 1848 of the constitutional monarchy which still exists today. On this day children hold-ing flags march to the royal palace where they are greeted by the king.
Note: For extended activity, march around room carrying Norway's flag. Make Norway's flag like Swedish flag listed below except use red paper for back-ground and white cross. Place narrower blue cross over white cross.
B. SWEDISH FLAG DAY, on June 6, honors the Swedish flag and the adoption of Sweden's constitution in 1809.
Note: For extended activity, make Swedish flag. 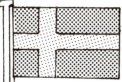 Glue yellow strip of paper that is 2" x 11" to center of 8 1/2" x 11" piece of blue construction paper. Form cross by gluing 2" x 8 1/2" piece of yellow paper perpendicular to first strip and 3" from left side of blue paper.
C. MIDSUMMER FESTIVAL, held the third week in June, marks the night when the sun never sets in northern Scandinavia. It is celebrated with bonfires, games, folk dances, and refreshments.
D. DANISH FESTIVAL is celebrated during the summer with feasting, bands, and sports.
E. LEAF ERICSSON DAY, on October 9, commemorates the Norse sailor who is believed to be the first European to discover North America.

VIETNAMESE HOLIDAYS:

TET

TET is the Vietnamese New Year, which usually falls in February. It is a holiday celebrated by feasting, wearing new clothes, and exchanging gifts among family members and friends. A long bamboo pole is erected in many courtyards. It is decorated with pieces of cacti, gold and silver paper, leaves, feathers, tiny bells, and a lantern which is lit at night. A whitewash drawing of a bow and arrow is placed beside the pole to ward off evil spirits. At midnight on New Year's Eve, each family offers thanks for the good things received during the past year and prepares to welcome the new year.
Note: For extended activity, adult draws a bow and arrow on white paper with white crayon. Child paints paper with diluted black tempera. Bow and arrow will appear.

TET TRUNG-THU

TET TRUNG-THU, or Mid-Autumn Festival, is the biggest holiday for the children of Vietnam. It is celebrated in September or October on the fifteenth day of the eighth month on the lunar calendar. It is believed this festival originated in the eighth century when Emperor Ming-Hoang composed a poem for his Empress, Duong-Quy-Pho, and read it to her at a lake by the light of the moon. Today the festival is celebrated with traditional moon cakes which are made of rice and filled with raisins, sugar, peanuts, and other good things. For this celebration elaborate lanterns are made which are lit on the night of *Tet Trung-Thu*. The children then parade through the streets with the lanterns.
Note: For extended activity, parade around room carrying LANTERNS (see page 214).